The Ancient Spartans

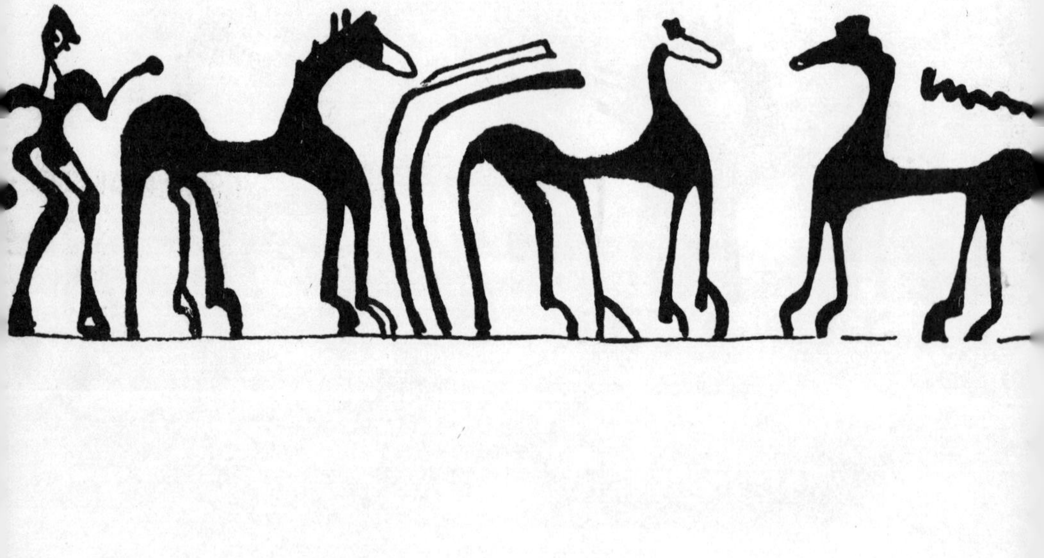

The Ancient Spartans

J T Hooker

J M Dent & Sons Ltd
London Toronto Melbourne

First published 1980
© Text, J. T. Hooker, 1980

All rights reserved. No part of this publication
may be reproduced, stored in a retrieval system,
or transmitted, in any form or by any means,
electronic, mechanical, photocopying, recording or
otherwise, without the prior permission of
J. M. Dent & Sons Ltd.

Photoset by Northampton Phototypesetters Ltd and
printed in Great Britain by
Billing & Sons Ltd, London, Guildford, Oxford and Worcester
for J. M. Dent & Sons Ltd
Aldine House, Welbeck Street, London

This book is set in 11 on 13 pt VIP Plantin

British Library Cataloguing in Publication Data

Hooker, J T
   The ancient Spartans.
   1. Sparta – Civilization
   I. Title
   938'.9   DF261.S8

ISBN 0–460–04352–8

Contents

Index to figures 6
Index to plates 7
List of abbreviations 9
Preface 11
1 The discovery of Sparta 13
2 From Bronze Age to Iron Age 25
3 Cults and cult-places 47
4 Music and poetry 71
5 Art 82
6 The era of Spartan expansion (800–540 B.C.) 99
7 The Spartan state 115
8 Life in the Spartan state 132
9 The era of Spartan intervention (540–491 B.C.) 145
10 The Persian Wars and their aftermath (490–432 B.C.) 158
11 The war against Athens (432–404 B.C.) 185
12 The era of Spartan supremacy (404–370 B.C.) 211
13 The idea of Sparta 230
Chronological table 241
Index 245

Index to figures

1 Map of Greece and the Aegean 18–19

2 Plan of the Vaphio *tholos* 34

3 Extended drawings of the gold cups from Vaphio (*Athens: National Museum*) 36

4 Gold ring from Vaphio. Cult-scene in the open air (*Athens: National Museum*) 37

5 Lentoid from Vaphio. Priest leading griffin (*Athens: National Museum*) 37

6 Amygdaloid from Vaphio. Priest carrying axe (*Athens: National Museum*) 37

7 Lentoid from Vaphio. Lion looking back (*Athens: National Museum*) 37

8 Lentoid from Vaphio. Cult-scene with daemons (*Athens: National Museum*) 37

9 Plan of ancient Sparta 50

10 Plan of the sanctuary of Artemis Orthia 52

11 Plan of the Amyklaion hill 64

12 The Throne of Apollo at the Amyklaion 66

13 Figured scenes on Geometric pottery from the Amyklaion and the Orthia sanctuary 83

14 Sketch of the Vix Crater (*Chatillon-sur-Seine Museum*) 91

Index to plates

Between pages 64 and 65
1 The Taygetus range seen from the Spartan acropolis
2 The Parnon range seen from the Amyklaion
3 The valley of the Eurotas seen from the Menelaion hill
4 The harbour of Gytheum (modern *Gytheion*); Taygetus in background
5 Mycenaean jug from Melathria. Warrior *(Sparta Museum)*
6 Mycenaean house on the Menelaion hill
7 The Menelaion; Taygetus in background
8 The Amyklaion: retaining-wall
9 The Amyklaion: conjectural restoration of the Throne of Apollo
10 Laconian cup from Taranto. Tunny-fish and dolphins *(Taranto Museum)*
11 Laconian cup from Etruria (Naucratis Painter). Zeus *Lykaios* *(Paris: Louvre)*
12 Laconian cup from Etruria (Naucratis Painter). Symposium *(Paris: Louvre)*
13 Laconian cup from Etruria (Arcesilas Painter). Arcesilas *(Paris: Bibliothèque nationale)*
14 Laconian cup from Etruria (Arcesilas Painter). Atlas and Prometheus *(Vatican Museum)*
15 Laconian cup from Boeotia (Chimaera Painter). Chimaera *(Heidelberg: Archäologisches Institut)*

Between pages 128 and 129
16 Laconian cup of unknown provenience (Rider Painter). Rider *(London: British Museum)*
17 Laconian cup from Sicyon (Rider Painter). Comasts *(London: British Museum)*
18 Laconian *hydria* from Rhodes (Hunt Painter). Battle-scene *(Rhodes Museum)*
19 The same. Comasts

20　Relief-amphora from a Spartan grave. Hunting-scene, battle-scene *(Sparta Museum)*
21　Laconian (?) bronze crater from Vix. Gorgon-handle, part of procession of warriors and horses. *(Chatillon-sur-Seine Museum)*
22　The same. Part of statuette on lid
23　Bronze statuette from Orthia sanctuary *(Sparta Museum)*
24　Bronze statuette from Menelaion *(Sparta Museum)*
25　Clay head from Spartan acropolis *(Sparta Museum)*
26　Clay ('Dedalic') head from Orthia sanctuary *(Oxford: Ashmolean Museum)*
27　Bronze mirror and statuette from Taygetus *(Sparta Museum)*
28　Bronze statuette from Olympia. Zeus? *(Olympia Museum)*
29　Bronze bull from Spartan acropolis *(Sparta Museum)*
30　Bronze statuette from Spartan acropolis *(Sparta Museum)*
31　Bronze statuette from Amyklaion *(Athens: National Museum)*

Between pages 192 and 193
32　Terracotta mask from Orthia sanctuary *(Sparta Museum)*
33　Terracotta mask from Orthia sanctuary *(Sparta Museum)*
34　Terracotta roof-tile from the modern town *(Sparta Museum)*
35　Clay head from Orthia sanctuary *(Sparta Museum)*
36/37　Selection of lead figurines from Orthia sanctuary *(Sparta Museum)*
38　Limestone relief from Orthia sanctuary. Horse *(Sparta Museum)*
39　Marble relief from Chrysapha. Heroized dead *(East Berlin: National Museum)*
40　Marble relief from the modern town. Dioscuri *(Sparta Museum)*
41　Ivory plaque from Orthia sanctuary. Goddess with animals *(Athens: National Museum)*
42　Ivory comb from Orthia sanctuary. Judgment of Paris *(Athens: National Museum)*
43　Ivory plaque from Orthia sanctuary. Lapith and Centaur *(Athens: National Museum)*
44　Ivory group from Orthia sanctuary. Lioness, calf, man *(Athens: National Museum)*
45　Ivory plaque from Orthia sanctuary. Warship *(Athens: National Museum)*
46　Remains of the marble statue of a warrior. Leonidas? *(Sparta Museum)*

List of abbreviations

AA	Archäologischer Anzeiger (Berlin)
ABSA	The annual of the British School at Athens (London)
AC	Acta classica (Cape Town)
Acme	Acme: Annali della Facoltà di filosofia e lettere dell'Università Statale di Milano (Milan)
AE	Archaiologike ephemeris (earlier, EA) (Athens)
Aegyptus	Aegyptus: Rivista italiana di egittologia e di papirologia (Milan)
AeR	Atene e Roma (Florence)
AfR	Archiv für Religionswissenschaft (Leipzig/Berlin)
AJA	American journal of archaeology (Princeton)
AJP	American journal of philology (Baltimore)
AM	Mitteilungen des Deutschen Archäologischen Instituts: Athenische Abteilung (Athens)
Ant	Die Antike: Zeitschrift für Kunst und Kultur des klassischen Altertums (Berlin)
AO	The sanctuary of Artemis Orthia at Sparta (ed. R.M. Dawkins) (Hellenic Society suppl. paper no. 5) (London, 1929)
AR	Archaeological reports (circulated with JHS) (London)
Archaeologia	Archaeologia, or: Miscellaneous tracts relating to antiquity (London)
AS	Ancient society (Louvain)
ASAA	Annuario della Scuola archeologica di Atene (Rome)
ASI	Ancient society and institutions: studies presented to V. Ehrenberg on his 75th birthday (ed. E. Badian) (Oxford, 1966)
Athenaeum	Athenaeum: Studi periodici di letteratura e storia dell' antichità (Pavia)
AuA	Antike und Abendland (Hamburg)
AZ	Archäologische Zeitung (Berlin)
BAGB	Bulletin de l'Association Guillaume Budé (Paris)
BCH	Bulletin de correspondance hellénique (Paris)
BJ	Bonner Jahrbücher des Rheinischen Landesmuseums (Bonn)
BJRL	Bulletin of the John Rylands Library (Manchester)
CAH	The Cambridge ancient history (Cambridge, 1923–1975)
CFC	Cuadernos de filología clásica (Madrid)
CM	Classica et mediaevalia (Copenhagen)
CP	Classical philology (Chicago)
CQ	The classical quarterly (Oxford)
CR	The classical review (Oxford)
CSCA	California studies in classical antiquity (Berkeley/Los Angeles)
EA	Ephemeris archaiologike (later, AE) (Athens)
EE	Epistemonike epeteris (Salonika)
Emerita	Emerita: Revista de linguistica y filología clásica (Madrid)
Eos	Eos: Commentarii Societatis Philologae Polonorum (Lwow)
Gnomon	Gnomon: Kritische Zeitschrift für die gesamte klassische Wissenschaft (Munich)

GRBS	Greek Roman and Byzantine studies (Durham, N.C.)
Gymnasium	Gymnasium: Zeitschrift für Kultur der Antike und humanistische Bildung (Heidelberg)
Helikon	Helikon: Rivista di tradizione e cultura classica (Messina)
Hermes	Hermes: Zeitschrift für klassische Philologie (Wiesbaden)
Historia	Historia: Zeitschrift für alte Geschichte (Wiesbaden)
HZ	Historische Zeitschrift (Munich/Berlin)
JDAI	Jahrbuch des Deutschen Archäologischen Instituts (Berlin)
JHS	The journal of Hellenic studies (London)
JOAI	Jahreshefte des Österreichischen Archäologischen Institutes (Vienna)
JP	Journal of philology (Cambridge/London)
JWG	Jahrbuch für Wirtschaftsgeschichte (Berlin)
Kadmos	Kadmos: Zeitschrift für vor- und frühgriechische Epigraphik (Berlin)
Klio	Klio: Beiträge zur alten Geschichte (Berlin)
LCM	Liverpool classical monthly (Liverpool)
LEC	Les études classiques (Paris)
LS	W. den Boer Laconian studies (Amsterdam, 1954)
Maia	Maia: Rivista di letterature classiche (Genoa)
MDOG	Mitteilungen der Deutschen Orient-Gesellschaft (Berlin)
Meander	Meander: Revue de civilisation du monde antique (Warsaw)
MH	Museum Helveticum (Basel)
Mnemosyne	Mnemosyne: Bibliotheca classica batava (Leiden)
PAAH	Praktika tes en Athenais Archaiologikes Hetaireias (Athens)
Paideuma	Paideuma: Mitteilungen zur Kulturkunde (Frankfurt)
PBA	Proceedings of the British Academy (London)
PCPS	Proceedings of the Cambridge Philological Society (Cambridge)
Pel	Peloponnesiaka (Athens)
Philologus	Philologus: Zeitschrift für das klassische Altertum (Berlin)
Phoenix	The phoenix: the journal of the Classical Association of Canada (Toronto)
PP	La parola del passato (Naples)
PW	Philologische Wochenschrift (Leipzig)
QU	Quaderni Urbinati di cultura classica (Urbino)
RA	Revue archéologique (Paris)
RAL	Rendiconti dell'Accademia dei Lincei (Rome)
REA	Revue des études anciennes (Paris)
REG	Revue des études grecques (Paris)
REH	Revue des études historiques (Paris)
RFC	Rivista di filologia classica (Turin)
RhM	Rheinisches Museum für Philologie (Frankfurt)
RIL	Rendiconti dell'Istituto Lombardo (Milan)
RM	Mitteilungen des Deutschen Archäologischen Instituts: Römische Abteilung (Rome)
RP	Revue de philologie de littérature et d'histoire anciennes (Paris)
RSA	Rivista storica dell'antichità (Bologna)
SA	Skandinavisches Archiv: Zeitschrift für Arbeiten skandinavischer Gelehrten (Lund)
SBAW	Sitzungsberichte der Bayerischen Akademie der Wissenschaften (Munich)
SIFC	Studi italiani di filologia classica (Florence)
SMEA	Studi micenei ed egeo-anatolici (Rome)
SOAW	Sitzungsberichte der Österreichischen Akademie der Wissenschaften (Vienna)
TAPA	Transactions and proceedings of the American Philological Association (Philadelphia)
VDI	Vestnik drevney istorii (Moscow)
ZA	Živa antika (Skopje)

Preface

I have tried in this book to give an introduction to the most important aspects of Spartan life and history down to 371 B.C. A bibliography at the end of each chapter suggests further reading. I mention here, in addition, W.G. Forrest's well-known and excellent book *A history of Sparta 950–192 BC* (London 1968), of which a second edition is imminent. I am sorry that Paul Cartledge's book *Sparta and Lakonia: a regional history c. 1300–362* B.C. (London 1979) appeared too late for me to make any use of it.

I record my best thanks to my wife and also to Mr J.H. Betts, Dr H.W. Catling, Dr R.A. Higgins, Dr I. Kollias, and Dr G. Steinhauer. I am indebted to University College for giving me a travel grant in 1978. I thank the Committee of the Egypt Exploration Society for permission to refer to an unpublished papyrus.

Mrs Jean Bees, Mrs Brenda Timmins, and Mr Kenneth Wass made the drawings for me, and I am very grateful to them.

I am pleased to acknowledge receipt of photographs and permission to publish from the following persons and institutions: Archaeological Institute, Heidelberg (pl. 15); Bibliothèque nationale, Paris (pl. 13); Dr R.A. Higgins (pl. 26); the Managing Committee of the British School at Athens (pll. 41–5); Musée du Louvre (M. Chuzeville) (pll. 11 and 12); Presses Universitaires de France (pll. 21 and 22); Rhodes Museum (pll. 18 and 19); Taranto Museum (pl. 10); the Trustees of the British Museum (pll. 16 and 17); Vatican Museum (pl. 14); Walter de Gruyter and Co., and German Archaeological Institute, Athens (pl. 28).

University College, London   September 1979

1

The discovery of Sparta

The great peninsula of southern Greece was called in antiquity, and is again called today, the 'Island of Pelops', or Peloponnese. But throughout the Middle Ages and up to quite recent times it was often known as the Morea. It thrusts three narrow and rocky promontories deep into the Mediterranean. The two easterly promontories, known as Taenarum and Malea, embrace the large expanse of sheltered water called the Laconic Gulf. The region on the landward side of the Gulf comprises the modern province of Laconia. The heart-land of the province is formed by the basin of the river Eurotas, which has its source some fifty miles to the north-west and, after flowing through a wide and fertile plain, empties into the Laconic Gulf near the small town of Helos. The boundaries of Laconia are purely natural ones. To the south are the waters of the Gulf. The northern frontier is sealed by a series of steep crags, which to this day make entry difficult except by way of a few narrow and winding roads. Eastwards, the Parnon range stretches for more than thirty miles on a north-west/south-east axis. To the west is an even more formidable range, the Taygetus, running almost exactly north/south and reaching a peak of nearly 7,900 feet – the highest point in the Peloponnese.

Laconia is thus locked in by natural obstacles which external enemies would find, and in the event did find, almost impossible to surmount, so long as the morale of the inhabitants remained unimpaired. From this fortress, as we might call it, the Laconians of old time went out to the conquest of the Messenians, who lived beyond Taygetus to the west, and the Arcadians, a people occupying the region beyond Parnon to the north and east. Later still, the rest of the Peloponnese was to a large extent subject or allied to Laconia.

The capital of modern Laconia is Sparte, a town of about 11,000 inhabitants, situated close to the Eurotas at a distance of some twenty-five miles from its principal harbour of Gytheion (Roman Gytheum), on the west side of the Laconic Gulf. No Greek city occupies a more impressive or more favoured site than Sparte. The town is low-lying and is overshadowed by the Taygetus mountains, which rear up only six miles away: in front of the sharp ridge formed by the Taygetus range proper there stands a line of lower, rounded hills. Looking south to the horizon, one sees a wooded plain, well watered by the numerous tributaries of the Eurotas which flow into it from Taygetus. The fertility of the plain was famous in antiquity; and it comes as no surprise that its populace played such a large part in the affairs of the Greeks, endowed as they were with such tenacity and singleness of purpose and living in a self-sufficient and virtually impenetrable region.

Laconia was not a name in use among the ancient Greeks: it is a Latin coinage, appearing first in the works of the elder Pliny. Greek terminology, indeed, varied in a confusing way. The whole state was sometimes called *Lakonike*, or more often *Lakedaimon;* but in official usage the latter term was reserved for the capital and its immediate neighbourhood. The familiar name of the city, however, was Sparte or, in the local dialect, Sparta. It will make for ease of understanding if we adhere to one set of terms throughout, whatever the loss in formal correctness; so the state will be called Laconia, the city Sparta, and its inhabitants Spartans, except when it is necessary to refer to Spartans with full political rights: then we may follow the ancient example and call them Spartiates.

After the sixth century B.C. the Spartans practised reticence almost as part of their faith. Since they do not speak to us directly, the student of Spartan history is driven to make use of other kinds of evidence: principally statements about the Spartans by their fellow-Greeks and observations and excavations made in Laconia in comparatively modern times. It is obvious that both classes of evidence are unsatisfactory and partial. The Greeks who were eye-witnesses of the Spartan achievement can hardly have attained complete objectivity even if they wished to do so. The development of their own cities, and particularly Athens, was so intimately bound up with that of Sparta that they could not sit back and regard her affairs with academic detachment. But it is an interesting circumstance that the three ancient writers who concern themselves most with Sparta (Herodotus, Thucydides, and Xenophon) are by no means biased against her; rather the contrary. Herodotus balances her political achievements against those of Athens; but then he was an Asiatic Greek, from Ionia, and so could regard the evolution of mainland Greece with an impartial eye. And Thucydides, though an Athenian, failed his city in a crucial engagement of the great war between her and Sparta. In consequence of his mishandling of military affairs he went into exile for twenty years. Where he spent them is unknown; but, by his own account, his banishment enabled him to gain an insight into the attitudes and policies of both sides, especially the Spartan. It seems likely, then, that he passed at least some of the time at Sparta itself. Xenophon too was an Athenian citizen, and he also was banished. He lived in Sparta and

The discovery of Sparta

wrote books in overt admiration of the Spartan way of life and the Spartan political system: witness his *Constitution of the Spartans* and his life of the Spartan king Agesilaus. His *Hellenica* complete the account of the Peloponnesian War begun by Thucydides and bring the history of Greece down to 362 B.C. (An anonymous papyrus-fragment, known as the *Hellenica Oxyrhynchia*, relates some events of the year 396.) The fourth-century writer Ephorus was credited with a universal history in thirty books, extending from the Return of the Heraclids to the year 340: it seems to have had little independent value, but it was drawn upon by later authors, especially Diodorus of Sicily.

In the works of the Athenians Plato and Isocrates we see further progress towards the idealization of Sparta, for which Xenophon had prepared the way; but that subject is best postponed for discussion in the final chapter. In Aristotle's *Politics*, however, we have a magisterial survey of the Greek states; and this book offers the best ancient investigation into the working of the Spartan constitution. Aristotle's position is not that of an idealist, eager to seize upon the political mechanism which has produced such legendary greatness, but that of the scientist, who reports what he actually finds and fits his observation into a general treatment of the Greek city-states in general.

Aristotle lived at a time when the cities of classical Greece were about to become submerged in much larger political groups. The extinction of their independence in the Macedonian and Roman empires is a theme which will not be pursued in the pages which follow; but the name of Polybius, at least, must not go unmentioned. The subject of his history, written in the second century B.C., is the rise of Rome to pre-eminence in the Mediterranean. Like subsequent writers, Polybius detects many points of resemblance between the Spartan and the Roman constitution. (Cicero draws the same comparison in his *De re publica*, only he naturally considers the Roman to be of superior excellence.) Political theorizing apart, Polybius includes some useful indications of Laconian topography. Of some use topographically, although not much, is the eighth book of Strabo's *Geographica*, written at about the beginning of our era. Strabo displays little direct acquaintance with the terrain of Laconia, but he preserves much curious antiquarian lore from earlier authors.

There will be occasion to refer to some of the voluminous works of Plutarch, who flourished in the first century A.D. He was a writer of no originality, and claimed none. Like Strabo, he made extensive use of valuable sources in pursuing his many lines of research; and, but for him, those sources would have been lost completely. Plutarch's *Moralia* comprise essays on philosophy, cult, morals, education, and so forth. The treatise 'On music', which gives precious information about the early history of music in Greece, is contained in the medieval manuscripts of the *Moralia*, but it was not written by Plutarch himself. Some collections included in the *Moralia*, however, are obviously Plutarchan: these include 'Sayings of the Spartans', 'Sayings of Spartan women', and 'Customs of the Spartans'. Their historical worth varies greatly, but they all exemplify Plutarch's love of pointed anecdote and his deftness in sketching a character in well-chosen words. Both attributes appear to advantage in his biographies, most of which are arranged in pairs: a famous Greek being compared with a famous Roman. The life of Lycurgus is an indispensable source for the student of Sparta, although in parts it is difficult to interpret: the half-legendary Spartan lawgiver is paired with the half-legendary Roman lawgiver Numa. The vast work by Athenaeus in fifteen books, *Deipnosophistae* ('Banquet of learned men'), may be mentioned here. Its value lies in the profuse quotations which each diner adduces to support his point of view. As we shall see, our knowledge of Laconian cult and the poetry of Alcman would be even more defective than it is if the work of Athenaeus had not survived; and these topics are only two out of the multitude which are discussed.

With the second century A.D. we come to the earliest, and by far the most important, of all travellers to Laconia who have left an account of their journeys: Pausanias, the author of the *Description of Greece*. His importance arises from his personal observation of the places he describes and from an honest attempt to fit his observations into the framework of history and legend; and, if he does not always dissociate history from legend, that is a methodological fault sometimes committed by the greatest Greek writers, Thucydides included. Pausanias describes Laconia in the third book. The city of Sparta had prospered greatly under Roman rule, and she still exhibited to the curious traveller many of the works of art with which she had been embellished in her prime. The shrines of Sparta and her suburbs were famous; of even greater fame was the Amyklaion, which lay only a few miles from the city. The Amyklaion is the subject of a long description by Pausanias, which allows us to go far towards a reconstruction of the principal monuments at that important site.

Laconia, like the other Greek components of the Roman empire, fell to barbarian invaders at the end of the fourth century A.D. Alaric swept into the Peloponnese in the course of his victorious career westwards, which was to culminate in the conquest of Rome. According to Claudian, the last poet of old Rome, Alaric burnt the acropolis at Sparta and enslaved her women; but Claudian's account may not be as accurate as it is colourful. Nevertheless, the days of Sparta as a place of any importance were now clearly at an end. It was later re-established in a modest way as

The discovery of Sparta

a small Byzantine town, and portions of its Byzantine walls are still standing. Never of any consequence in the Middle Ages, it was completely overshadowed when the Norman conquerors of the Morea built a great castle at Mistra (or Misitra or Mizethra) in the foot-hills of Taygetus, a few miles west of Sparta. The castle, in time, formed the nucleus of the most impressive city in the whole of the Peloponnese. After two centuries of brilliant history, during which the imperial government in Constantinople regained control of the Morea, Mistra was taken by the Turks in 1460. Apart from an interval of Venetian rule, the Morea remained in Turkish hands until the declaration of Greek independence in 1830. With the coming of independence Mistra in its turn was abandoned and the new Sparte was founded upon level ground to the south of the ancient city.

Although the 'idea of Sparta' has proved endlessly fascinating to western man, not many Europeans seem actually to have travelled in the Eurotas valley before the era of excavation, which began in the second half of the nineteenth century. Or, if they did, very few described their experiences. Bernard Randolph did visit Mistra late in the seventeenth century, but he writes of his visit in rather leaden fashion in the pamphlet he published on his return:

> The Town is large, and is esteemed the second for bigness in all the *Morea*, yet *Patrass* hath more houses. The Ruines about it are very great, and towards the South they reach above four Miles, having in some places the Foundation of a thick Wall, which they say was the Walls of *Sparta* . . . The Plain is very pleasant, full of small Villages, Olive, and Mulberry Trees . . .

Towards the end of the long night of Turkish rule, two Englishmen of parts made interesting observations on Mistra and also on the ruins of Sparta, which were an easy ride from Mistra. These were William Martin Leake, an officer in the British army, and Sir William Gell. They are the first travellers of modern times who are known to have explored the site of ancient Sparta in a systematic manner and envisaged the possibility of excavation. Gell was struck by the great size of the Hellenistic theatre and the meagreness of the other remains:

> While Athens remains the treasury of architecture and the arts, Sparta boasts scarcely any thing that can be cited with certainty, as a remnant of the real city of Lycurgus. The theatre, which we first visited, is partly scooped out of a little hill, which may in aftertimes have formed a sort of citadel, . . . it must have been intended for the amusement of a very great population . . . Stretching to the southward from the

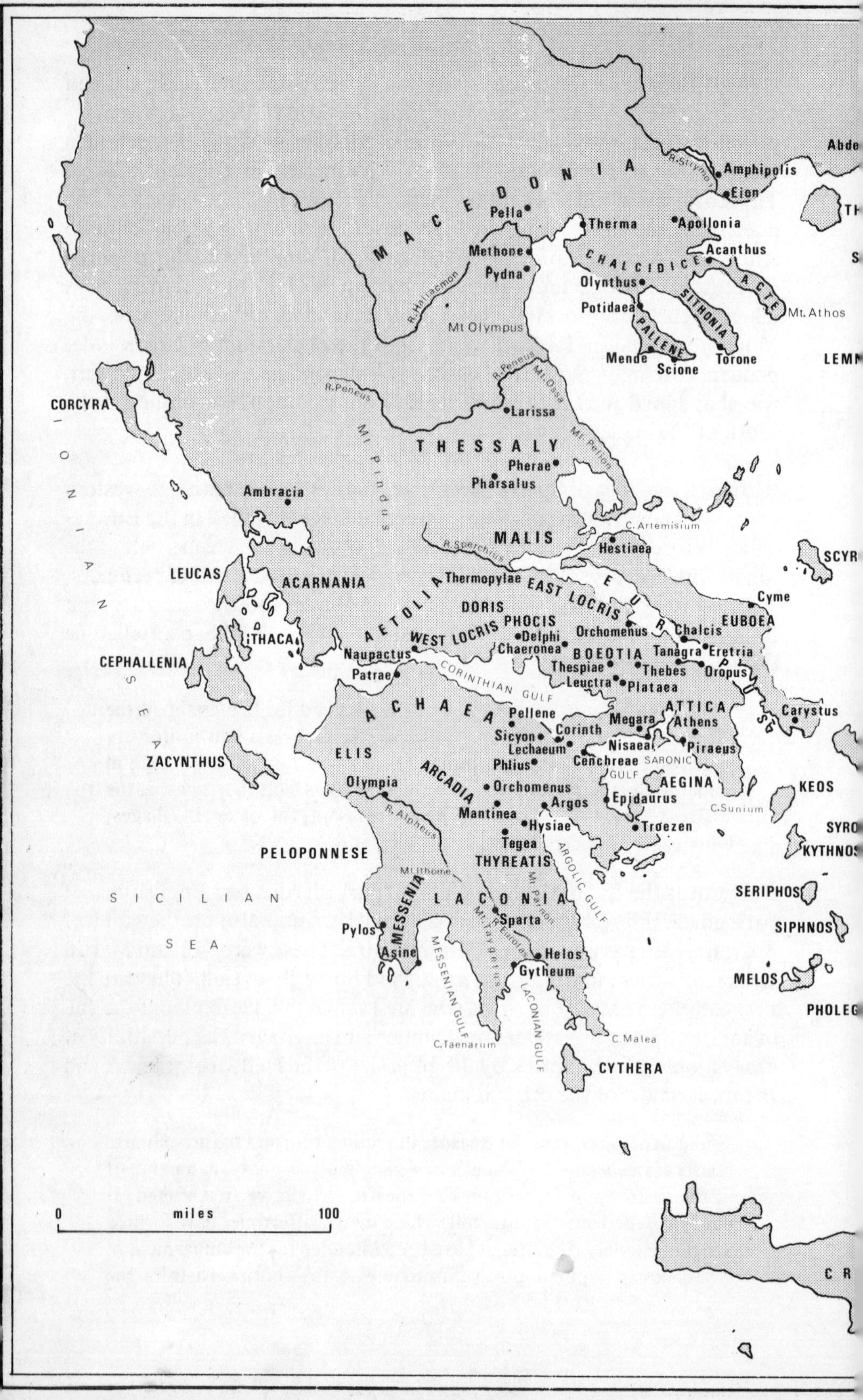
MACEDONIA
R.Strymon
Amphipolis
Eion
Pella
Therma
Apollonia
Methone
Pydna
R.Haliacmon
Acanthus
CHALCIDICE
ACTE
Olynthus
SITHONIA
Potidaea
PALLENE
Mt.Athos
Mt Olympus
Mende
Scione
Torone
CORCYRA
R.Peneus
R.Peneus
Mt.Ossa
Larissa
IONIAN SEA
THESSALY
Mt Pelion
Mt Pindus
Pherae
Pharsalus
Ambracia
C.Artemisium
MALIS
R.Spercheus
Hestiaea
LEUCAS
ACARNANIA
Thermopylae
EAST LOCRIS
EURIPUS
Cyme
AETOLIA
DORIS
PHOCIS
Orchomenus
Chalcis
EUBOEA
ITHACA
WEST LOCRIS
Delphi
Chaeronea
BOEOTIA
Tanagra
Eretria
CEPHALLENIA
Naupactus
Thespiae
Thebes
Oropus
Patrae
CORINTHIAN GULF
Leuctra
Plataea
ACHAEA
Pellene
ATTICA
Carystus
Megara
Athens
Corinth
Sicyon
Lechaeum
Nisaea
Piraeus
ELIS
ZACYNTHUS
Phlius
Cenchreae
SARONIC GULF
AEGINA
KEOS
Olympia
ARCADIA
Orchomenus
Epidaurus
Argos
C.Sunium
Mantinea
R.Alpheus
Hysiae
Troezen
Tegea
PELOPONNESE
THYREATIS
ARGOLIC GULF
Mt.Ithome
Mt Parnon
SERIPHOS
SICILIAN SEA
MESSENIA
LACONIA
Sparta
SIPHNOS
Pylos
Mt Taygetus
R.Eurotas
Asine
Helos
MELOS
Gytheum
MESSENIAN GULF
LACONIAN GULF
C.Malea
C.Taenarum
CYTHERA
0 miles 100

1 *Map of Greece and the Aegean.*

theatre is a long wall, not exhibiting the appearance of very remote antiquity, and has at some period served as a defence to that part of Lacedaemon which might be called the citadel, and is connected with the theatre . . . There is scarcely any thing else at all curious on this elevation, except some remains of what I have no doubt was a small temple, or other very ancient edifice, the plan of which might yet be ascertained . . . This is almost the only relic of ancient Sparta, and it appears that it would afford a variety of curious information, and possibly inscriptions or sculptures, to any one who would undertake the excavation of it, when such a work shall become again feasible. The hill of the theatre, being the highest, has been esteemed the citadel of Sparta; the still higher elevation on the north does not seem certainly to have been included in the city.

This is really a very accurate appraisal of the appearance which Sparta and her acropolis must have presented early in the nineteenth century. In only one of his assumptions is Gell seriously at fault, for in fact the use of the modest hill as the acropolis ante-dated by many centuries the construction of the theatre on its southern side. Leake too picks out the theatre and one or two remains on the acropolis as 'the only considerable relics of Hellenic workmanship'. He has some remarks of great interest on the identification of the site of the Amyklaion, which Pausanias had located on a hill to the south-east of Sparta. In Leake's time its location was still in dispute, and in fact it was still being debated eighty years later; but Leake was able to mention a piece of epigraphical evidence in support of the site he favoured:

> I here [at Ayia Kyriaki] perceive that the heights, at the north-east extremity of the plain upon which Sparta stood, are a part of the chain of low hills following the course of the Eurotas through the whole length of the plain of Mistrá, and separating the latter from the lower level of the vale of the Eurotas, leaving openings only for the streams which descend from Mount Taygetus into the Eurotas. Ayia Kyriaki and another summit farther south are the only eminences of any considerable height in this little chain, which is not readily distinguishable from the opposite side of the plain. Nothing is to be seen at Ayia Kyriaki but two imperfect inscriptions, in one of which are the letters AMY following the name DEXIMACHOU and leaving little doubt that the incomplete word was AMYKLAIOU. As far as this evidence goes, therefore, St. Kyriaki has as good pretensions to be considered the site of Amyclae as Sklavokhóri.

Considerable geographical precision was attained in two French surveys of the Morea, published in the 1830s. To consult these magnificent books is a delight; but it cannot be pretended that they do a great deal to

The discovery of Sparta

elicit the ancient state of the country from the observable remains. Still, they are what they claim to be, careful surveys, and they may well have formed the basis for two searching works in German which appeared within the next few years: *Journeys through Greece* by Ludwig Ross and *Peloponnese: a historical-geographical description of the peninsula* by E. Curtius. These books are truly scientific works dedicated to the solution of specific problems. Ross makes strenuous attempts to relate the descriptions of ancient authors to what he can see on the ground. He is, for that early time, a considerable scholar in the Laconian dialect of ancient Greek. His linguistic knowledge, combined with the excellence of his methods in general, enables him to make an identification of first-rate importance. He publishes an inscription containing a dedication to ORTHIAI ARTEMIDI, rightly claiming that this must belong to the sanctuary of Artemis Orthia, which Pausanias saw in the quarter of Sparta called Limnae. When the precinct was eventually excavated, in the early years of this century, it was found to contain artefacts of a number and quality unequalled at any other Spartan site. Ross was in no position to proceed to the excavation of the Orthia sanctuary; but it should be noted that he did make significant surface discoveries on the hill to the east of Sparta which the old authors call Menelaion or Therapne. Curtius, for his part, considered the topographical relationship between old and new Sparta, and gave it as his opinion that excavation would yield valuable results, since Sparta had never been destroyed: obviously, therefore, he gave no credence to Claudian's turgid account of its sack by Alaric. But in so far as Curtius surmised that the sanctuaries still contained their ancient treasures, his hopes have not been realized, with the single great exception of the site of Artemis Orthia.

A gentleman of ancient Scotch family, William Mure of Caldwell, travelled extensively in Greece, beginning his tour in 1838. The two-volume book he wrote as a result is rather sententious and patronizing, but it does contain some very acute observations. Of particular interest is the description of the Mycenaean tholos-tomb at Vaphio, which was excavated by Tsountas more than forty years after Mure visited it:

> The name Baphió was marked on my map, so that I had no great difficulty in finding the site of the 'Treasury', about a mile to the south of the tower. It is, like that of Mycenae, a tumulus, with an interior vault, entered by a door on one side, the access to which was pierced horizontally through the slope of the hill. Its situation, on the summit of a knoll, itself of rather conical form, while it increases the apparent size of the tumulus adds much to its general loftiness and grandeur of effect. The roof of the vault, with the greater part of its material, is now

gone, its shape being represented by a round cavity or crater on the summit of the tumulus. Count Capo d'Istria enjoys the credit of its destruction. The doorway is still entire. It is six feet wide at its upper and narrower part. The stone lintel is fifteen feet in length. The vault itself was probably between thirty and forty feet in diameter. Menelaus is said to have been buried at Amyclae. This, therefore, may have been the royal vault of the Spartan branch, as the Mycenaean monument was of the Argive branch of the Atridan family.

We are now able to rectify Mure's chronology; but, as the next chapter will show, he was by no means wholly astray in his speculation.

Last in the series of Victorian travellers to Laconia may be mentioned William George Clark. He deserves credit for a coherent exposition of medieval Mistra (a subject of which Leake seems to have had no knowledge) and of the foundation of modern Sparte. He makes a further observation on the remarkable ruin to be found within the northern part of the modern town:

> In the valley near the centre of the old city is an Hellenic building called 'The Tomb of Leonidas', though it is too far from the theatre to have the slightest claim to the name. It is, in fact, a small temple, or heroum, about thirty feet in length, and of great antiquity, to judge from the enormous size of the stones comprising it.

About the so-called Tomb of Leonidas we know no more than Clark did, except that we would agree with him that it cannot be Leonidas' tomb. The immense blocks of stone, which he rightly noted, seem of disproportionate size for a temple; and the whole structure may simply be a massive altar, like the one later excavated in the bed of the Eurotas (p. 51). Its date still eludes us as it did Clark; we cannot tell exactly what he meant by his phrase 'of great antiquity'.

Whatever acumen was brought to the study of Sparta by the nineteenth-century travellers (and the acumen of a Leake or a Ross was very great), no serious advance could be made until likely spots were inspected minutely, trenches dug, and the top-soil cleared away. We are on the very threshold of the era of excavation. Before crossing it, we may notice the curious episode of the excavation that did *not* take place. After his epoch-making campaigns at Troy, Mycenae, and Tiryns, Heinrich Schliemann made constant visits to Greece. On 9 December 1888 he wrote from Athens to his friend Rudolf Virchow about a recent journey in Messenia and Laconia; and we are astonished to read his words (in translation):

> I came to Sparta with great hopes: the more so since the hills to the north-east of the Eurotas were known as the Menelaion, where

The discovery of Sparta

Menelaus and Helen were worshipped in a temple. But, apart from a small circular building of the classical period, I found no trace of antiquity in these hills. It is true that the site of ancient Sparta is strewn with classical and later sherds; but, by an irony of fate, the whole of the rising ground upon which we could have expected to find a prehistoric royal palace contains not even a rubbish-dump, and there is nowhere the slightest trace of prehistoric sherds or building-blocks.

Schliemann's faith in the old sources, which had carried him to such envied triumphs in Argolis and in Asia, completely failed him here; for in fact the Menelaion *was* there to be found and, although neither Sparta nor any other site in Laconia has yet disclosed the remains of 'a prehistoric royal palace', the spade has uncovered all the principal holy places which Pausanias saw at Sparta and in its vicinity.

Christos Tsountas was the first systematic excavator of Laconian sites, in the eighties and nineties of the last century. His reputation rests chiefly on the work he did at various Bronze Age sites in Greece, and especially at Mycenae: he is the author of a valuable book on Mycenaean Greece, published in English under the title *The Mycenaean age* (London 1891). To his great credit stands the excavation of the Mycenaean tholos at Vaphio, which had been described by Mure. Furthermore, he made a determined beginning on the investigation of the hill which Ross and others had taken to be the site of Apollo's great shrine, the Amyklaion. Tsountas demonstrated beyond question that the hill had been correctly identified, but in the event he failed to complete the task, and he never uncovered the base of Apollo's statue. That work was brought to a successful conclusion by the great German archaeologist Adolf Furtwängler, whose methods (at least as exemplified by his excavation of the Amyklaion) betray more than a hint of ruthlessness. The three other most notable sites of the Spartan plain – the acropolis of Sparta, the sanctuary of Artemis Orthia, and the Menelaion – have been for many years the preserve of the British School at Athens. A very talented group worked before the first world war at Athena's temple on the acropolis, at shrines and tombs in the city, at the Mycenaean and later levels on the Menelaion hill, and above all at the Orthia sanctuary. The principal members of this group were Bosanquet, Dawkins, Dickins, and Wace. All of them, except Dickins, went on to do invaluable work elsewhere: he was killed in the war, having spent most of his short life in digging at Sparta and in elucidating her early history. A few years ago members of the British School returned to the Menelaion; H. W. Catling directed further work at this site, in particular the excavation of the Mycenaean house, which had been begun by Dawkins. Since the days of Tsountas, the main Greek effort had been concentrated on the Amyklaion and its neighbourhood (Skias and, more recently, Christos). Christos has also excavated in the region of the ancient city.

Such are the main phases of the discovery of Sparta in modern times. It is almost certain that the tale of discoveries has not yet come to an end. Quite apart from unlooked-for finds, we might reasonably hope that renewed excavation will uncover more material in Sparta dating from the archaic age as well as Mycenaean remains on the Menelaion and other hills.

Bibliography

The geology of Laconia: A. Philippson, *Der Peloponnes: Versuch einer Landeskunde auf geologischer Grundlage* I (Berlin, 1891). The geography of Laconia: A. Philippson, *Die griechischen Landschaften* III/2 (Frankfurt, 1959).

Various names of the Spartans and their country: A.J. Toynbee, *Some problems in Greek history* (Oxford, 1969), 168–71.

Commentaries on Herodotus: R.W. Macan (books 4–9 only) (London, 1895–1908); H. Stein (Berlin 1906[6]); W.W. How and J. Wells (Oxford, 1912); see also B. Niese *Hermes* 42 (1907), 419–68. Commentaries on Thucydides: W.H. Forbes (book 1 only) (Oxford, 1895); A.W. Gomme, A. Andrewes, K.J. Dover (Oxford, 1945–). Commentary on the *Hellenica Oxyrhynchia*: I.A.F. Bruce (Cambridge, 1967). On Xenophon: J.K. Anderson, *Xenophon* (London, 1974). On Ephorus: R. Laqueur, *Hermes* 46 (1911), 161–206, 321–54; G.L. Barber, *The historian Ephorus* (Cambridge, 1935); R. Drews *AJP* 84 (1963), 244–55. Commentary on Aristotle's *Politics*: W.L. Newman (Oxford 1887–1902); see also P. Cloché, *LEC* 11 (1942), 289–313. Commentary on Polybius: F.W. Walbank (Oxford, 1957–1979). Commentary on Pausanias: J.G. Frazer (London, 1913[2]). On Plutarch's *Life of Lycurgus*: E. Kessler, *Plutarchs Leben des Lykurgos* (Berlin, 1910); K. Ziegler, *RhM* 76 (1927), 20–53.

Travellers in Laconia. B. Randolph, *The present state of the Morea called anciently Peloponnesus* (London, 1689[3]) (quotation from p. 8). W. Gell, *Narrative of a journey in the Morea* (London, 1823) (quotation from pp. 327–30). W.M. Leake, *Travels in the Morea* I (London, 1830) (quotation from pp. 135–6). E. Puillon Boblaye, *Recherches géographiques sur les ruines de la Morée* (Paris, 1835). Bory de Saint-Vincent, *Expédition scientifique de Morée: section des sciences géographiques* (Paris, 1836). L. Ross, *Reisen und Reiserouten durch Griechenland* I (Berlin, 1841). E. Curtius, *Peloponnesos: Eine historisch-geographische Beschreibung der Halbinsel* I (Gotha, 1852). W. Mure, *Journal of a tour in Greece and the Ionian Islands* II (Edinburgh, 1842) (quotation from pp. 246–7). W.G. Clark, *Peloponnesus: notes of study and travel* (London, 1858) (quotation from pp. 164–5). E. Meyer (ed.), *Heinrich Schliemann: Briefwechsel* I (Berlin, 1958) (quotation from pp. 295–6).

Topographical investigations at Sparta before the full era of excavation: H.K. Stein, *Topographie des alten Sparta* (Glatz, 1890); K. Nestorides, *Topographia tes archaias Spartes* (Athens, 1892); N.E. Crosby, *AJA* 8 (1893), 335–73.

2

From Bronze Age to Iron Age

Every reader of Thucydides is struck by the contrast he draws between the two principal antagonists in the Peloponnesian War: 'If the city of the Spartans were to be made desolate, and nothing remained but her temples and the foundations of her buildings, I believe that in times to come her power would hardly seem commensurate with her fame; ... whereas, if Athens suffered the same fate, men would judge from her appearance that her power was double what it had actually been.' (1.10.2) Now that the classical city of Sparta has indeed been desolated we can perceive the essential truth of Thucydides' remark. Anyone who looks to-day at the Athenian acropolis does not need to exercise his imagination very powerfully in order to realize that this was once the crown of a mighty state. The acropolis at Sparta forms, by comparison, only a hillock in a petty township. And yet excavations, especially those conducted at the sanctuary of Artemis Orthia, reveal that in the archaic age (eighth and seventh centuries B.C.) Sparta had disposed of great wealth, had been in direct and fruitful contact with the major innovating centres of Greek art, and had retained the services of highly skilled artificers. To this splendid period belongs also the poetical activity of Terpander and Alcman. Neither the achievement nor even the reputation of archaic Sparta is reflected in the pages of Thucydides; and it is true that by his time Sparta appeared almost the direct opposite of what she had previously been.

But, if Thucydides knows nothing (or, at least, says nothing) of the archaic period, he does incorporate into his History a number of references to a much more remote epoch. To this epoch he never gives a name: in his eyes it comprises the times of the great thalassocrats Minos and Agamemnon, the Trojan War, and the generations immediately subsequent to that war. The epoch as a whole, extending from about 1550 to about 1150, is nowadays called the Late Bronze Age. The designation Bronze Age arises, of course, from the predominant use of bronze for weapons and utensils; iron was not completely absent, but it was far scarcer and, we may suppose, more precious than it later became. The use of bronze as a distinctive feature of the whole epoch was not, in general, recognized by the ancients; but it is interesting to note Pausanias' comment that some weapons he has found dedicated in temples are made of bronze and that this is consistent with Homer's description of heroic spears and swords (3.3.8). And Homer is crucially important, since the systematic excavation of Bronze Age sites in Greece took its impetus directly from Homeric references to Greece, and other parts of the Mediterranean, in the heroic age. As is well known, the Homeric poems contain also a great amount of colouring derived from post-Bronze Age sources; nevertheless the general configuration of the Greek (or 'Achaean') kingdoms envisaged by Homer is confirmed, from a positive point of view, by the evidence of excavations – while, from a negative view-point, a completely different picture is presented by the states of Iron Age Greece.

When Homer describes the siege of Troy by the Achaeans and Odysseus' return to Ithaca after Troy has been sacked, he speaks of these events as having happened in the remote past: an age of heroes, when men were stronger and nobler than they have since become. But the *Iliad* and *Odyssey* are no mere literary confections. Alongside mythical elements and motifs belonging to folk-lore, these epics present descriptions of places and material objects which modern excavators have shown to be more or less accurate. But, although the Homeric poems purport to relate matters belonging to what we now call the Late Bronze Age, not all of the Homeric descriptions fit the Bronze Age as it can be reconstructed on the evidence of archaeology. Some items, such as the tower-shield carried by the greater Ajax, can have arisen only from a genuine reminiscence of Bronze Age Greece; whereas others, including the description of heavy-armed troops, or hoplites, cannot have entered the epic tradition until a long time after the beginning of the Iron Age. Putting these facts together, we might reconstruct the probable course of events along the following lines. The Greeks of the Bronze Age possessed heroic narrative of their own: narrative which may well have been expressed in poetic form. This narrative was carried by Greek migrants, after the end of the Bronze Age, to the colonies in Asia Minor, where it underwent a process of growth, modification, addition of later episodes, and, we should probably add, falsification to some extent. This process lasted for several centuries and resulted in the composition in Ionia of the two epics, perhaps roughly in the form in which they have been transmitted to us. The most likely approximate date for the final composition of the epics is 700 B.C.

Sparta is of peculiar interest to Homer, since it was the abduction from Sparta of Menelaus' wife Helen that led to the conflict between Achaeans and Trojans. The *Iliad* tells us that ambassadors were first sent to Troy to demand satisfaction; when the demand was refused, ships from many Achaean kingdoms joined forces under the command of Menelaus' brother Agamemnon and set sail for Troy. The so-called Catalogue of Ships in *Iliad* 2 gives a brief description of each of the Achaean contingents, mentioning the name of its leader, the principal places in his kingdom, and the number of ships he is taking to Troy. The kingdom of Menelaus is called 'hollow Lacedaemon' (*Iliad* 2.581); and the epithet is well chosen as a description of the Eurotas valley, set between the mountain ranges of Taygetus to the west and Parnon to the east. Familiar names applied to towns in Menelaus' kingdom are Sparta, Amyclae, and Helos (all in the valley of the Eurotas), together with Laas and Oetylus in the south. The composer of the Catalogue seems to visualize only quite a narrow region as acknowledging the overlordship of Menelaus, namely the Eurotas valley as far north as Sparta, with an extension southwards in the direction of Cape Taenarum. It should not be thought objectionable that Menelaus, one of the principal Achaean heroes, is given such a diminutive realm. The difficulties of interpreting the Catalogue, and in particular its relationship to the rest of the *Iliad*, are well known; and it seems certain that for a number of the Achaean kingdoms only a sort of topographical sketch appears, by no means a full account of all the important towns.

Imperfect though the Catalogue is, some at least of the information it imparts must have descended from the Bronze Age, since the picture conveyed by it is compatible with Greece in the Bronze Age but not with Greece as it was at any later period. The same guarantee of authenticity does not necessarily extend to all the prominent persons of Homeric saga. Some of these could, in theory, have actually existed in the Bronze Age, while others might owe their place in the epic to the free invention of the poets. When we ask the question specifically about Menelaus and Helen we are faced with an interesting, but difficult, problem. It is true that in the Homeric epic both Menelaus and Helen, and especially Helen, have about them something of the mystery, or even magic, with which they were to be invested in later ages. When Helen steps upon the battlements of Troy in *Iliad* 3, her beauty appears to the old men sitting by the gate to be no human attribute but the very quality possessed by immortal goddesses. And when, in the *Odyssey*, Telemachus comes to the palace at Sparta, Helen alludes to the uncanny powers she once displayed in recognizing Odysseus on his entry into Troy (4.250); nor is it without significance that in this passage her descent from Zeus is dwelt on. The connexion with Zeus becomes important later in the same book of the *Odyssey*. Menelaus recounts, for the pleasure and interest of his young guest, the adventures he met with on his way home from Troy, so foreshadowing the narrative unfolded by Odysseus at the court of Alcinous. Menelaus says that he received a prophecy from Proteus to the effect that he is not destined to die as mortal men usually do, going down to the house of shades: because of his privileged status as the son-in-law of Zeus, he is to be sent to the Elysian plain, which Proteus' description reveals as a sort of paradise. We are thus accorded powerful hints, in both the *Iliad* and the *Odyssey*, that Helen and Menelaus are beings beyond the normal run, for whom a special future is in store. The shrines and cults of Menelaus and Helen, which in the Iron Age were cherished in the neighbourhood of Sparta, will be mentioned in the next chapter. Here it may be noted that Greek writers emphasize the fact that the couple were worshipped not as heroes but as gods. While we may well credit the Homeric poems with sufficient influence and prestige to bring about the institution of hero-cults in the places where the heroes had lived or had been buried, it is going very much farther to suppose that Homeric heroes could ever have been elevated into gods in the ordinary cult-usage, unless perhaps some powerful political motive were present. And, in the case of Menelaus and Helen, it does not seem necessary to suppose that such a drastic step was taken. On the one hand it can be shown that Helen and her brothers the Dioscuri have close analogies elsewhere in Indo-European mythology; on the other, Helen's cult at Sparta (as described in Greek writers) contains elements which are not derived from Homer but which have the appearance of being local survivals. Helen at least, then, had long been the object of worship in Laconian cult: perhaps from the Bronze Age, but of that there is as yet no positive proof. It was the mortal counterpart of this Helen – mortal, yet still having much of the goddess about her – who found her way into the epic tradition.

In the *Iliad* Menelaus is regarded as one of the great Achaean heroes who took part in the siege of Troy; while in the *Odyssey* he is the king of a wealthy and fertile domain, lavish in hospitality and conspicuous for his courtesy. We now have to ask to what extent the Homeric picture of Menelaus and his kingdom is verified by the results of modern excavation: whether, in fact, Homer here reflects some historical reality, as he undoubtedly does when he describes the seat of Agamemnon at Mycenae or that of Nestor at Pylos.

What we now call the Mycenaean civilization constitutes the sum of many external features which recur at sites in Greece in the Late Bronze Age. This civilization arose from a fusion of the old 'Helladic' culture of the Greek mainland with the 'Minoan' culture of Crete. Although Crete had long been in contact with the mainland, it was not until the sixteenth century that the Minoans made a decisive impact upon Greece, particularly in the manufacture and decoration of artefacts. The two circles of Shaft Graves at Mycenae contain offerings of great splendour, many of which betray the hand of Minoan craftsmen or of mainlanders trained by Minoans. The appearance of lavish wealth at Mycenae and the introduction of Minoan styles are due to unknown causes; but, whatever the reasons for its enrichment and its new-found awareness of material resources beyond Greece, Mycenae now became (*c.* 1550), and remained for more than three centuries, the most important site in Argolis, and probably in the whole of continental Greece. It was believed for a long time that the spread of Mycenaean culture over the south of Greece could be explained as a simple process of diffusion from the centre at Mycenae. But excavations in Messenia have revealed rich grave-offerings and also the appearance of Minoan influence at a time roughly contemporary with that of the later grave circle at Mycenae. With this new evidence at our disposal, it seems best to think that the impetus towards developing the typical culture of Bronze Age Greece came both from the east and from the west of the Peloponnese. We accordingly feel little surprise that Laconia, which lies between Messenia and Argolis, became an early beneficiary (or perhaps we should say an early victim) of the young civilization.

The Mycenaean culture is essentially different from both the Helladic and the Minoan out of which it sprang; but we sometimes find, especially in the early phases of the Late Bronze Age, that Mycenaean objects occur side by side with Minoan imports and Helladic survivals. An excellent example of this cultural co-existence is provided by the Vaphio tomb in central Laconia, which will be examined below. A characteristic 'Mycenaean' style manifests itself in a wide range of products which have been found in some profusion at a number of sites: above all at sites in Argolis, Messenia, Corinthia, Attica, and Boeotia. These products include pottery, terracotta figurines, gold rings, seal-stones, carved ivory figures, frescoes, statuettes, weapons, and clay tablets incised with writing in the 'Linear B' script.

Among Mycenaean artefacts, the clay pottery is of great diagnostic value. The large number of excavations conducted in mainland Greece, and also at Mycenaean sites abroad, has enabled a chronological series of vessel-shapes and decorative motifs to be worked out. The earliest phase of Mycenaean pottery witnesses a diffident attempt by mainlanders to adapt Minoan decoration to Helladic shapes; later, during the fifteenth century, the attempt is much more successful, resulting in the development of a pottery-style in its own right. By the fourteenth century Mycenaean pottery, though still often of fine quality, was a mass-produced ware. At the same time the decoration became standardized: marine and vegetable motifs lost contact with their originals and degenerated into wavy lines, scrolls, and spirals. A decisive break with Minoan tradition is seen in the introduction of bulls, men, and chariots as decorative motifs. During the final two centuries of the Mycenaean era, the pottery is notably homogeneous over a wide area; and its break-up into local styles in the twelfth century is one of the surest signs of the fragmentation of Mycenaean culture. No less typical of the culture are the small terracottas in the shape of women and animals which have been discovered in immense quantities at Mycenaean sites. Gold rings and seals were buried as offerings in the Shaft Graves; and, thereafter, their presence in Mycenaean tombs is a further mark of the culture. These examples of miniature art show strong Minoan influence, especially in the depiction of cult-scenes; but a native strain continues as well, with plant and animal motifs disposed in quasi-heraldic postures. A formal style is displayed also by the ivory-carver's art, which can rise on occasion to the creation of splendid masterpieces. The swords known from the beginning of the Mycenaean period are derived from Crete: they are long and somewhat cumbersome. Shorter and lighter types are later developed on the mainland and, to suit the new kind of fighting for which these short swords are intended, a light, round shield is used in preference to the tall body-shield which was in vogue earlier in the Mycenaean age.

In the period following that of the Shaft Graves, important personages at Mycenae were buried in built tombs known as tholoi: there, but not always at other sites, tholoi were driven into the side of a hill. The round burial-chamber, or 'tholos' proper, was constructed by making each course of stone overhang the one below, until a slightly pointed dome was produced. The tholos was approached by a long entrance-passage, and its mouth closed by doors. Although at Mycenae the tholos seems to have been the successor of the shaft grave for the most important burials, tholoi of smaller size were in use much earlier in Messenia. At about the same time as the first appearance of tholoi at Mycenae, the earliest chamber-tombs are found there. Subsequently, down to and later than the era of destruction in 1200, they became the chief mode of sepulture in Mycenaean Greece, often being used over and over again. Whole cemeteries of chamber-tombs are known at a number of sites. The chamber-tomb consists of a simple vault roughly cut out of the hill-side and closed with stones; like the tholos, it commonly possesses a sloping entrance-passage.

The Mycenaean house is built round a nucleus which follows the Helladic model without any clear break. That nucleus usually comprises a rectangular room with an ante-room. A third room is sometimes added at the back – for instance in the Mycenaean house near the Menelaion. This arrangement of rooms is the forerunner of the 'megaron' in the later Mycenaean palaces at Mycenae and Tiryns (Argolis) and at Pylos (Messenia). The megaron lies at the centre of a complex of rooms. Vestibule and ante-room lead to a large, almost square chamber with a round hearth fixed in the centre of its floor; the roof of the megaron is supported upon four pillars. The three palaces already mentioned, and others in central Greece, consisted of large aggregates of buildings, including ceremonial rooms, shrines, living-quarters, magazines for storage, and administrative areas. Large numbers of frescoes, derived from a Minoan tradition of wall-painting, decorated the interior of the Mycenaean palaces. A steep hill or at least an elevated position was usually chosen as the site for the palaces and larger settlements. During the Mycenaean period these sites were further strengthened by the addition of massive circuit-walls: of the major palatial settlements, only Pylos seems to have been left unfortified.

The archives of Linear B tablets found in some of the later palaces give some hint of the complexity of the economic and social structure, but they say very little about the motives underlying the varied and far-flung activities of the Mycenaeans. For, like the Minoans before them, they had a marked tendency to expand, both to the west and more especially to the east of the Mediterranean. Important Mycenaean settlements were established in Rhodes and on the coast of Asia Minor, while the presence of rich deposits of Mycenaean artefacts in Cyprus and the Levant shows that these regions maintained a lively trade with mainland Greece.

The unified Mycenaean culture, which had spread over the Peloponnese and had reached eastwards into Attica and northwards as far as Thessaly, suffered a severe disruption during the restless century which lasted from about 1250 to about 1150. The destruction of the chief Mycenaean palaces was accompanied by the disintegration of the characteristic Mycenaean style as manifested in a whole range of artefacts. Evidence of this disintegration is seen in the pottery-decoration, which often affords a good index to the speed and nature of decisive cultural changes, and by the abandonment of many habits which had marked the Mycenaean civilization at the time of its ascendancy. The tholos-tomb, for example, went completely out of use. The practice of combining fortress and palace in a well-defended citadel was lost; in fact there was now little building in stone, compared with the Mycenaean heyday. The houses that were erected often had a different orientation from that of their Mycenaean predecessors. The Linear B script, which had been employed for the keeping of accounts in the palatial centres, disappeared at the time of the great disturbances; and the mainland of Greece remained virtually illiterate until the introduction of alphabetic writing from the east in the eighth century. Finally, two crucial changes affected the way of life of the Greeks; but these did not come about suddenly and did not have a uniform impact over the whole of Greece. Gradually in some areas, and more rapidly in others, the Mycenaean practice of burying the dead in built tombs gave way to cremation. The reason for this change is quite unknown; and it is likely that there was no single cause. Nor is any obvious explanation available for the second major change, the replacement of bronze by iron as the predominant useful metal.

The devastation of so many Mycenaean centres naturally led to extensive movements of population. The inhabitants of Greece suffered a decline in numbers, and they tended to live in more widely scattered settlements. A further result of the disasters was the migration of Greeks eastwards to found colonies along the west coast of Asia Minor. The migrations may have begun as early as the eleventh century, and they continued for an incalculable time. When the Asiatic colonists emerge into the light of history in the seventh century, they are seen to be grouped in two great areas: Aeolis in the north, comprising the island of Lesbos and the neighbouring shores of the Asiatic mainland, and Ionia in the south. These groups of colonies, and in particular the Ionian, were in time responsible for momentous achievements in the intellectual and creative life of the world.

We now have to ask how the Mycenaean culture manifested itself in Laconia, and especially in that part of it close to Sparta. We can say at once that no Mycenaean palace has yet been discovered in Laconia. There is so far lacking a great princely centre to which we might point and say: this, at however great a remove, is the model of the palace in which Menelaus and Helen dispense their hospitality in the *Odyssey*. In the absence of a convincing model we are driven to embrace one of two explanations. Either there never was a Mycenaean palace in Laconia, and the modest Mycenaean house near the Menelaion was grossly exaggerated in scale as the Greek epic tradition developed. That explanation is possible, but it is not very satisfactory; for we wonder, in that case, what motive there could ever have been for thinking that in the heroic age Laconia owed allegiance to a powerful king, the brother of the greatest king and the husband of the daughter of Zeus. An alternative explanation is that there was indeed a Mycenaean palace in Laconia, but that this has never been discovered. Reluctant though we might be to accept this explanation, it is better than the other. For the time being we have to reckon with a serious lacuna in the material evidence; and we would not even realize there was any lacuna if it were not for the Homeric allusions to Menelaus and his kingdom.

The site of archaic and classical Sparta itself has yielded very little Mycenaean material. No Mycenaean buildings have been found there; and it seems clear that the important Bronze Age settlements were situated elsewhere, upon hill-tops which lent themselves more readily to defence. To the south of Sparta three hills rise out of the plain, and each has made its contribution to our knowledge of this part of Greece in the Bronze Age. Amyclae, Palaiopyrgos, and Ayios Vasilios were all inhabited in Mycenaean times, and they all conform to the usual Mycenaean custom of choosing a defensible hill-top for their settlements. It is possible that all three sites were walled, but actual evidence of a Mycenaean wall is found only at Ayios Vasilios. Little else is known about that site. No remains of Bronze Age buildings have been discovered, but large quantities of Mycenaean pottery yielded by surface exploration on the hill-side suggest that it was a place of considerable importance, especially in the later Mycenaean age.

Amyclae is chiefly famous for the great shrine of Apollo (the Amyklaion) which was built there in the Iron Age. Attention has been concentrated on this shrine by the excavators of the nineteenth and twentieth centuries; but the three major campaigns undertaken at the site have uncovered, incidentally, some interesting Mycenaean objects. A quantity of pre-Mycenaean pottery indicates that a settlement existed here in the Early Bronze Age, but the most significant deposit dates from the Mycenaean period. The deposit was remarkable for the terracotta figurines, which included a few animal-shapes and seventy-five in the shape of women. The excavators concluded from the presence of the figurines that a shrine or sanctuary had been established on the hill of the Amyklaion in the Mycenaean age; but they based this conclusion on grounds which are not entirely satisfactory. It is an unfortunate fact that the purpose of Mycenaean figurines remains unknown. It used to be widely believed that they were votive-offerings which persons (presumably women) had placed in tombs; but, now that figurines have come to light in settlements as well, such a belief is less easily tenable. It is possible that the existence of a later shrine at this site also weighed with the excavators; but, as will be seen later, it is impossible at the Amyklaion to establish the certain continuity of cult from the Mycenaean age into later times. There is, however, no indication that the Mycenaeans who lived there suffered the devastation which afflicted many Bronze Age sites in Greece.

The hill situated to the south of Amyclae has two summits, the northerly one being known in modern times as Vaphio and the southerly as Palaiopyrgos. The slopes of Palaiopyrgos have never been subjected to systematic excavation, but surface inspection reveals the presence of fragmentary Mycenaean pottery, especially late Mycenaean pottery, in great profusion, while the remains of what were possibly Mycenaean houses and walls can be seen here and there. Associated with this settlement was the renowned tholos of Vaphio. While it was still standing, the tomb must have formed a prominent feature of the landscape, because it had been built on the very top of the hill. At any rate, it is mentioned by more than one of the travellers who explored this part of Laconia in the nineteenth century. During that century its condition deteriorated, until it was excavated by Tsountas in 1888. The long passage-way, measuring more than thirty yards from one end to the other, led to a circular vault, the upper part of which had collapsed. One or two traces of carbonized material were found in the passage: these appear to be the remains of burnt offerings made at, or after, the time of the burials. Such sacrifices are well attested in Mycenaean tholoi and chamber-tombs; the most impressive so far discovered are those of two horses, whose skeletons were excavated in the Marathon tholos, a tomb not far distant in date from the tholos at Vaphio. A few pieces of gold leaf, a lump of amber, and sherds of Mycenaean pottery had been deposited in the passage when the sacrifices were made: they were perhaps intended as offerings to the dead or to some divinity. Tsountas found no post-Mycenaean pottery in the passage and inferred that the tomb had not been opened and re-used. No wall or door was present at the entrance to the circular vault, but a large number of stones had fallen to the floor, and Tsountas considered that these had originally been built up to block the approach. The diameter of the tholos was considerable, about eleven yards. Its floor was uneven: a circumstance Tsountas attributed to the practice (now known to be common in Mycenaean tombs) of using a grave for repeated burials and sweeping away previous remains which impeded the space required for the new interment. The surface of the floor was covered with a mixture of black soil and carbonized bones; but

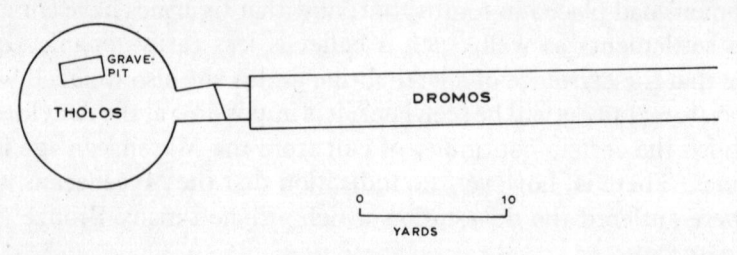

2 *Plan of the Vaphio tholos.*

it was not possible to determine whether the latter were the remains of human beings or of animals.

Very few Mycenaean tholoi have escaped the attentions of tomb-robbers, and the Vaphio tholos is no exception. But at Vaphio the robbers did their work less thoroughly than at many other sites. They overlooked, or could not be bothered to remove, a number of small objects which the excavator found scattered about the floor. These comprised twelve engraved seal-stones, two gold rings, some ornaments of gold and silver, fragments of stone vessels, and bronze nails. The remains, meagre though they are, suffice to show that the early Mycenaean custom of burying grave-goods with the dead was observed at Vaphio. The grave-goods include on the one hand objects of personal adornment, such as jewellery, and on the other utensils of purely domestic employment. It may be legitimate to infer from this circumstance that the dead person in a Mycenaean tomb had to be equipped both with possessions peculiar to himself and with everyday objects, to be at his disposal at least during the time that elapsed before the decay of the flesh. But the whole question of Mycenaean beliefs about the afterlife is much disputed, and the last-named is only one among several possibilities.

The finds on the floor would never, by themselves, have conferred on the Vaphio tholos the unique distinction it has enjoyed ever since its excavation. But a little to one side of the circular vault Tsountas found that a rectangular pit had been sunk into the floor, to the depth of about a yard. One male skeleton was present in this tomb, and there were no signs of burning. It is obvious that the robbers missed this pit-grave completely: there was no sign of intrusion, and the various heaps of offerings were still roughly in the places where they had been deposited. The first heap lay about the head of the corpse. It included utensils and vessels made of bronze, silver, alabaster, and clay, together with weapons: two spear-heads and a sword some three feet long fitted with three large gold nails, of a kind familiar in the Shaft Graves. In the region of the throat and chest, about eighty stones of amethyst had once formed a double necklace. By the left side of the corpse there were two dagger-blades plated with gold. Here also were gold ornaments, gold nails, and a delicately worked silver dish with a gold rim. In the region of the man's hands Tsountas found engraved seal-stones, a gold ring, a bronze ring, an iron ring, and two gold cups. These cups are among the finest artefacts to have come down to us from the Greek Bronze Age, and they are prominent even among the masterpieces on display in the Mycenaean Room of the National Museum in Athens (fig. 3). They present a somewhat heavy and massive appearance; but the scenes they bear, designed and executed by an unerring hand, remove any sense of intolerable weight. The technique used is now known as repoussé, whereby the desired parts are raised in relief by hammering on the reverse side. Each cup bears a triple composition depicting the capture of bulls. The choice of this theme immediately suggests that the cups were made in Crete, where bull-grappling had long been practised and represented. The impetus towards this type of representation must have come from Crete; but it does not necessarily follow that the cups were actually made there, since it is beyond our powers to distinguish artefacts manufactured in Crete from those produced on the mainland under strong Cretan influence.

3 *Extended drawings of the gold cups from Vaphio.*

A similar ambiguity attends many of the seals and rings which are abundant in the grave-pit and in the tholos itself. In the art of seal-engraving, as in most of the other fine arts, the Mycenaeans were the pupils of Crete; but it would be strange if some mainlanders were not by this time engraving seals on their own account, and so once again we can make no final statement about the origin of the Vaphio seals and rings, or any one of them. The gold ring illustrated in fig. 4 shows an outdoor cult-scene of Minoan type. Each of the elements in this composition has close parallels in Cretan art: a figure reaching out as if to touch the tree; the ecstatic dance by a bare-breasted, full-skirted woman; religious symbols, in particular the double axe (upper right) and 'sacral knot' (lower right). Fig. 5 depicts a superbly worked lentoid, upon which a

4 Gold ring from Vaphio.
Cult-scene in the open air.
C. 4/5 × 1/2 in.

5 Lentoid from Vaphio.
Priest leading griffin.
C. 1 × 4/5 in.

6 Amygdaloid from Vaphio.
Priest carrying axe.
C. 3/4 × 1/3 in.

7 Lentoid from Vaphio.
Lion looking back.
C. 1 × 9/10 in.

8 Lentoid from Vaphio.
Cult-scene with daemons.
C. 3/4 × 3/4 in.

figure of hieratic appearance leads a griffin: the motif is originally Syrian, and has come to Greece by way of Minoan Crete. Closely allied to this is the subject of fig. 6: again a priest is involved, this time carrying an axe of Syrian appearance. An interesting seal shows two 'daemons' in an antithetic pose (fig. 8). The 'daemon' is a creature which walks upright, having on its back a kind of carapace, and takes part in ritual activities. Here the daemons hold jugs of a shape often found in sacral contexts; between them at the bottom is one of the commonest and most potent objects of Minoan religion, the 'horns of consecration'. A further lentoid is without sacral significance: it has a fine example of a Minoan animal-motif, in this case the familiar one of a lion looking back (fig. 7).

Many of the contents of the Vaphio tholos thus display unmistakable signs of contact with Crete. If we make the plausible assumption that the whole tomb was erected for the burial of the man in the rectangular pit, the tholos subsequently being used for members of his family, we can hardly avoid the further conclusion that he was a nobleman of considerable wealth and influence and (we should add) of considerable connoisseurship, who was well able to command and appreciate the highest artistic achievements of which the age was capable. The age was one of internationalism, of close links between Minoan Crete and the Greek mainland, especially the southern part of the mainland. For many years the Vaphio tholos remained an isolated instance of the early efflorescence of Mycenaean culture, with its attendant Cretan connexions, in the central Peloponnese. Modern excavations have revealed other examples of Mycenaean settlement and tomb-building in scattered parts of Laconia. To the north, half-way between Sparta and Tegea, a large tholos at Analipsis has provided good Mycenaean pottery of the period to which the Vaphio tomb belongs. Near the south coast lies the settlement of Ayios Stephanos, which was walled in the latest Mycenaean epoch; but even at a time contemporary with the building of the tholos at Vaphio, it enjoyed a period of considerable prosperity. The present state of the evidence leaves open one outstanding question: do the tholoi at Vaphio and Analipsis and the flourishing circumstances of Ayios Stephanos represent disconnected Mycenaean incursions into Laconia, or are they manifestations of a directed and organized movement which took over the whole region and controlled it from the large centre whose existence was postulated above?

Before discussing the last of the major hill-sites to be mentioned, we must say a word about the small cemetery of chamber-tombs which has been excavated at Melathria near the village of Skoura. The pottery found in these tombs dates the use of the cemetery to the period 1400–1200: it therefore came into being a generation or so later than the construction of the Vaphio tholos. The Melathria tombs contained a few items of interest: an iron ring (only the second known from Laconia, after the Vaphio example), objects of personal adornment, three woman-figurines, and pottery. Among the pottery we may single out a jug of metallic shape which is decorated in a way so far unparalleled at this period and in this region of Greece. The main field of the jug is divided into seven panels by curving vertical bands, and in one of the panels the painter has sketchily represented a warrior who appears to be wearing a corslet and holding a weapon (pl. 5). The excavator remarks that the figure may have been excerpted from a prototype in metal; and it is true that vessels of metal are decorated with battle-scenes at Mycenae at least a century before the time of the Melathria jug.

North of Melathria and still to the east of the Eurotas, a long ridge bears the remains of two important buildings: at the south-west end the archaic structure known as the Menelaion, and to the north-east a Mycenaean house (pl. 6). This house has been excavated in two campaigns by the British School, separated from each other by some sixty years. Helladic and early Mycenaean pottery has been found in the general area of the house, but there is no surviving trace of a building there until late in the fifteenth century (a date close to that of the construction of the Vaphio tholos). It is reasonable to suppose that this epoch, which marks the culmination of Cretan influence on the mainland, was also a time of decided prosperity in the Spartan plain.

Three clearly-marked phases can be discerned in the Mycenaean building on the north-east of the Menelaion ridge. The first house, which presumably belongs to the period 1450–1400, is quite a substantial one for its time. Only the foundations are preserved, but it seems likely that the house had originally two storeys. The nucleus, as usual, consists of a rectangular hall with entrance-room at the front and a further room at the back. This nucleus is joined by corridors to rows of smaller rooms on both the longer sides. Not long after its construction this house was destroyed and re-built according to a somewhat different plan. The orientation of the 'nucleus' was changed and it was raised to higher ground, the sets of smaller rooms being lower and communicating with the nucleus by means of steep steps. This house too was occupied for only a short period. It was not destroyed, but was left unused for about a century. Eventually, at some undetermined point within the thirteenth century, it was re-occupied. Nothing further was done by way of construction. The 'nucleus' remained in its abandoned state, and the smaller rooms were prepared for habitation. The third house was destroyed by a serious fire, *c.* 1200, and was not subsequently brought back into use during the Bronze Age.

So much, and only so much, is revealed by excavation. But the observed sequence of events is so remarkable as to demand some attempt to explain it in historical terms. The construction of the original house in the fifteenth century is not difficult to account for. It was at this very time that the Mycenaean civilization, still in intimate contact with Minoan Crete, penetrated deeply into many areas of the Peloponnese. There would be nothing extraordinary at such an epoch if some potentate carved out for himself a parcel of territory and erected his dwelling on a steep hill. Less obvious is the reason for the abandonment of the building after such a short period of occupation. But an analogy may be cited from the development of Messenia in the Mycenaean age. In the first two centuries of the Mycenaean period Messenia saw the proliferation of a number of small sites, some of them with tholos-tombs. But in time most of these sites declined, and by the thirteenth century they were overshadowed in importance by the palatial settlement at Pylos, which seems to have exercised control over large parts of Messenia. That may have been the pattern of events in Laconia as well; the difference here is that, if a large centre was in fact built late in the late Mycenaean period and acquired political control of the Spartan plain, that centre cannot yet be identified.

A further problem is raised by the re-use of the house in the thirteenth century. The circumstances of this re-use point to the habitation of the house by 'squatters' – if it is legitimate to apply here Sir Arthur Evans's description of the denizens of the palace of Knossos after its devastation by fire. These would have been people unwilling, or unable, to re-build the house on the comparatively ample scale of its first and second phases and content to make use only of the smaller rooms. This limited and humble re-occupation is susceptible of the following explanation. It is well known that, after the destruction of the great sites in Argolis and elsewhere, Mycenaean tombs are found in parts of Greece where they had not formerly been known to a significant extent. Such areas are Achaea, in northern Peloponnese, the island of Cephallenia in the west, and Perati in Attica. These sites are usually, and rightly, considered to have been places of refuge for people displaced by the upheavals in southern Greece. But it should be remembered that the era of destructions was a long one, and the possibility entertained that some populations had been uprooted long before the end of the thirteenth century. If small numbers of such refugees made their way westwards into Laconia, they would have found the abandoned house on the Menelaion ridge an answer to their modest needs.

Neither in Laconia nor in the rest of Greece does the Mycenaean age come to an abrupt end. Some sites, for instance that at the Amyklaion, show no signs of destruction; and we may suppose that in such places there was continuity of habitation, with the Mycenaean culture gradually giving way to 'sub-Mycenaean', as it is now termed. Others, like Mycenae and Tiryns, were visited with fearful devastation; but there too life went on, although at a greatly reduced level, and while the Mycenaean culture of the inhabitants lost much of its refinement and all of its exuberance, it remained distinctively Mycenaean and only by slow stages was it transformed into something else. Yet other settlements, which may be represented by Pylos and by the house on the Menelaion ridge, were burnt and never re-occupied; and in those cases we have undoubtedly to reckon with a dispersal of population, but still a population who would have taken with them to their new homes memories of the Mycenaean epoch and some of the skills they had previously known. The causes and effects of this great series of destructions and migrations must now be examined a little more closely.

The writers of classical Greece, beginning with Herodotus and Thucydides, show some knowledge of the upheavals which left abundant traces in the archaeological record of late Mycenaean times. Thucydides, in particular, feels able to express the course of events in a definite chronological order. In his account the Trojan War is followed by a long period of unrest in the Greek states. The most portentous event recorded by Thucydides is the occupation of the Peloponnese by the Dorians, together with the sons of Heracles, eighty years after the conclusion of the Trojan War (1.12.2–3). This movement is recounted by several other Greek writers as well, often with a great accumulation of detail. It has become known in modern times simply as the 'Dorian Invasion', although the Greeks themselves spoke of the 'Return of the Heraclids'. This migration is intimately bound up with the history of the Peloponnese in the Iron Age, and above all with that of Sparta; for in historical times Sparta regarded herself, and was regarded by the other Greeks, as the Dorian city *par excellence*.

The Dorians differed from the rest of the Hellenic tribes in three principal ways: in their political arrangements, in their language, and in their lineage. Politics will engage our attention later. So far as language is concerned, Doric dialects were spoken throughout the Peloponnese (except in the central state of Arcadia), in the islands of Crete, Thera, and Rhodes, and in the Dorian colonies of Italy and Sicily. These dialects, which are well attested in inscriptions but less well in literary remains, present a greater number of archaic features than does the speech of the more northerly and easterly parts of Greece. With regard to lineage, the Dorians seem to have been even more self-conscious than the rest of the

Greeks. The Spartan kings, for instance, traced their descent in a direct line from Heracles. Leonidas, the Spartan king who commanded the Greek army at Thermopylae, is provided by Herodotus with a pedigree reaching back through seven centuries to Hyllus the son of Heracles (7.204). Heracles was really a pan-Hellenic champion, the son of Zeus who in his lifetime rescued cities from pests and oppressors and who, after his death, was deified. But the Dorian tribes revered him as their particular ancestor, since it was his sons who regained the Peloponnese, after he himself had been wrongfully expelled from it.

Both Herodotus and Thucydides speak of Doris, a narrow region lying between Locris and Phocis in central Greece, as the motherland of the entire Dorian race (p. 180). The sons of Heracles are supposed to have set out from there on their expedition to the south. The accounts of the actual invasion given by Herodotus and later authors differ greatly in detail, but they have certain points in common. It is agreed that the first attempt to enter the Peloponnese was foiled at the Isthmus of Corinth; a subsequent attempt (variously dated fifty or a hundred years after the first) was successful. This time the invaders are said to have entered the Peloponnese by sea, making land-fall at Rhium in Achaea. After the conquest of the Peloponnese, lots were cast by the leaders of the expedition for possession of the three principal cities: Messene in the west, Sparta in the centre, and Argos in the north-east.

These accounts by the Greek writers have been widely thought, in modern times no less than in antiquity, to provide adequate basis for the observable differences between the Dorians and the other Greeks. For, naturally, the Dorians on their entry into the Peloponnese would have brought with them a new dialect which usurped the manner of speech previously in use there; and the fact that the Arcadians spoke a non-Doric dialect was easy to account for on this hypothesis, since it could be supposed that the invading Dorians, while conquering the coastal regions of the Peloponnese, never reached the interior. In the same way the Dorian political institutions would have been imposed upon the coastal states of the Peloponnese.

Only a few voices have warned against the acceptance of the ancient accounts at their face value. During the last century, in particular, one or two historians took a sceptical attitude towards all stories told by the Greeks about their own past. In England, George Grote pointed to the suspicious circumstances that the later and more detailed descriptions of the Return of the Heraclids were so shaped as to provide an explanation of the major Dorian institutions and of the early alliance between the Dorians and Elis. But above all, continued Grote, the accounts of the Return conferred legitimacy upon the Dorian royal houses in the

Peloponnese and a valid title to their claim to rule Argos, Sparta, and Messene. Grote seems to believe that what really underlies the narrative of the Return is a feeling of uneasiness, amounting to guilt, on the part of the Dorians that their ancestors had seized power in the Peloponnese by force, without having any right on their side; in consequence they found it necessary to go back to the time of their seizure of power and provide respectable motives for it. The German scholar Karl Julius Beloch denied all historicity to the Return, but on more general grounds. Homer knows nothing of the Return, he says, and it should be accorded no greater historical weight than the belief of the Athenians that they had always dwelt in Attica or that of the Romans that they were descended from Aeneas.

But Grote and Beloch were swimmers against the tide. The immense majority of those who have concerned themselves with the problem wholeheartedly accept the narrative of the Return, at least to the extent of believing that the Dorian invasion of the Peloponnese was a historical fact. This belief appears to receive support from the witness of both Mycenaean and post-Mycenaean settlements. As excavation proceeded, it became evident that many Mycenaean sites in the Peloponnese had been violently destroyed, or at least abandoned, during the era of general devastation. Was not this devastation the work of the Dorians? And did not the profound gap between Bronze Age and Iron Age Greece corroborate the ancient teaching that the Dorians had imposed their way of life upon the parts of Greece they had subdued?

So it would seem at first sight. But when the case is examined attentively it is found to be, in reality, a weak one. First it is difficult to imagine what invaders could ever have managed to overwhelm the mighty Mycenaean citadels in Argolis and elsewhere: their walls and towers were more than sufficient to protect them against direct assault, while in the event of siege they had secure access to water within the circuit of walls. Our difficulty is increased when we are told by some writers of the present day that the postulated Dorian conquerors were at a lower level of civilization than the Mycenaeans; whereas, in order to achieve the exploits ascribed to them, they would have had to be more advanced, both in organization and in technical accomplishment. It cannot therefore legitimately be argued that the devastation of Mycenaean sites affords support for the notion of a Dorian invasion. In the second place, no artefacts directly attributable to the Dorians have ever been identified. Nor were the Dorians responsible for either of the two far-reaching cultural changes in the life of the Greeks: the replacement of bronze by iron and the adoption of cremation. The use of iron was introduced, in all likelihood, from the east of the Mediterranean, not from the northern confines of the Greek world; and, in any case, iron makes its appearance among the Mycenaeans before the days of their final decline. The practice of cremation, as noted above, is of unknown origin; but at least it can be dissociated from the Dorians, since the areas in which it asserted itself are not the same as the presumed regions of Dorian domination. Thus cremation took much longer to oust inhumation at Mycenae, a part of Greece alleged to have succumbed completely to the invaders, than it did at Athens, which by common agreement was never conquered by the Dorians. The evidence of language, finally, presents a drawback to the whole theory of a Dorian invasion. The linguistic pattern presented by the Peloponnese in historical times would, admittedly, be compatible with an invasion of the coastal states – an invasion which never extended to the interior of the Peloponnese or to the eastern parts of Greece. But one fact, which has been perhaps too little noticed, stands in the way of accepting this obvious explanation. Distinct though the Doric dialects were from Arcadian on the one hand and from Ionic and Aeolic on the other, the differences were never so great as to preclude communication between one speech-area and another. How could that have come about if the Dorians had lived apart from the other Greeks and had had no contact with them for several hundred years?

These are formidable difficulties, and they might lead one to wonder whether archaeological evidence and the Greek literary tradition, put together, do not call for the construction of a new theory to account for them. For it is poor method to discard legend and tradition altogether, as Beloch tried to do, merely because they contain some objectionable features. The aim of the prehistorian ought rather to be the reconciliation of archaeology and literary tradition, ridding the latter only of those elements which are incompatible with the archaeological evidence. We cannot, at any rate, wish the Dorians away: there they are, at the outset of the historical period, firmly established in the Peloponnese, speaking dialects of their own but communicating freely with other Greeks. That they could not have arrived where they are by the process alleged in the tradition has been demonstrated above; but there is nothing to prevent our making a very different supposition, namely that *they were there all the time*: that, in the time of the Mycenaean ascendancy, they formed a lower class, speaking their Doric in contrast to the 'Achaean' of their masters. What the tradition represents as the Return of the Heraclids would then be seen not as the arrival of a new stock from outside but as the uprising of a depressed part of the populace. The new approach to the evidence, here advocated, would involve a reversal of cause and effect, as these have been generally understood. Whereas up to now the Dorians have been considered the authors of the economic decline of Mycenaean Greece, they might better be regarded as tribesmen who turned to their own advantage internecine conflict which had already arisen in the Mycenaean states.

In some such way as this, remembering Thucydides' allusion to the political strife which afflicted Greece in the period following the Trojan War, we might attempt to bring the literary accounts of the Return into harmony with the archaeological record (which leaves no room at all for destructive invaders who subsequently settled in the areas they had subjugated). There can be little doubt that the literary accounts have been manipulated and re-fashioned for precisely the purpose indicated by Grote: that of conferring legitimacy upon a wrongful act. But that act is much more likely to have been usurpation from within than conquest from outside. After considering the real character of what has become almost canonized as the Dorian invasion, we may turn to examine Dorian Sparta herself.

Bibliography

Homer. Menelaus' kingdom in the Catalogue: R. Hope Simpson and J.F. Lazenby, *The Catalogue of the Ships in Homer's Iliad* (Oxford, 1970), 74–81. The Homeric Menelaus: W. Kullmann, *Die Quellen der Ilias* (Wiesbaden, 1960), 93–5. The Homeric Helen: F. Focke, *Gymnasium* 65 (1958), 383–401; J.Th. Kakridis, *Homer revisited* (Lund, 1971), 25–53; M.L. West, *Immortal Helen* (London, 1975); L.L. Clader, *Helen: the evolution from divine to human in Greek epic tradition* (Leiden, 1976); H. Homeyer, *Die spartanische Helena* (Wiesbaden, 1977). Homer and the Mycenaean age: H.L. Lorimer, *Homer and the monuments* (London, 1950); T.B.L. Webster, *From Mycenae to Homer* (London, 1958); *Archaeologia Homerica* (various authors) (Göttingen, 1967—); J. Bouzek, *Homerisches Griechenland* (Prague, 1969); L.A. Stella, *Tradizione micenea e poesia dell' Iliade* (Rome, 1978).

The Mycenaean civilization. General surveys: W.D. Taylour, *The Mycenaeans* (London, 1964); G.E. Mylonas, *Mycenae and the Mycenaean age* (Princeton, 1966); E.T. Vermeule, *Greece in the Bronze Age* (Chicago, 1972^2); F. Schachermeyr, *Die ägäische Frühzeit* II (Vienna, 1976). Figurines: E. French *ABSA* 66 (1971), 101–87. Seals: A. Sakellariou, *Mykenaïke sphragidoglyphia* (Athens, 1966). Tholoi: A.J.B. Wace, *ABSA* 25 (1921–1923), 283–402; O. Pelon, *Tholoi, tumuli et cercles funéraires* (Paris, 1977). Chamber-tombs: A.J.B. Wace, *Archaeologia* 82 (1932). Houses and palaces: A.W. Lawrence *Greek architecture* (Harmondsworth, 1973^3), 65–82. Devastation and migration: P. Ålin, *Das Ende der mykenischen Fundstätten auf dem griechischen Festland* (Lund, 1962); V.R.d'A. Desborough *CAH* II/2 (1975^3), 658–71.

Sparta in the Mycenaean age. Summary: H. Waterhouse, *ABSA* 51 (1956) 168–71. Survey: H. Waterhouse and R. Hope Simpson, *ABSA* 55 (1960),

67–107. Amyklaion: Chr. Tsountas, *EA* (1892), 1–18; E. Fiechter, *JDAI* 33 (1918), 126–7; E. Buschor and W. von Massow, *AM* 52 (1927), 10–12, 38–9, 46. Palaiopyrgos: P. Friedländer, *AM* 34 (1909), 71–2. Vaphio: Chr. Tsountas, *EA* (1889), 136–72 (excavation-report); A.J. Evans, *The Palace of Minos* III (London, 1930), 127–9 (dagger-blade); K. Müller, *JDAI* 30 (1915), 325–36 (gold cups); J.G. Younger, *AJA* 77 (1973), 338–40 (seals). Analipsis: K.A. Romaios, *PAAH* (1954), 270–86. Ayios Stephanos: W.D. Taylour and others, *ABSA* 67 (1972), 205–70. Melathria: K. Demacopoulou-Papantoniou, *ABSA* 66 (1971), 95–100 (Mycenaean jug), *AE* (1977), 29–60 (excavation-report). Mycenaean house on the Menelaion hill: Chr. Tsountas, *EA* (1889), 130–1; R.M. Dawkins, *ABSA* 16 (1909–1910), 4–11; H.W. Catling, *AR* 20 (1973–1974), 14–16, 21 (1974–1975), 12–15, 22 (1975–1976), 13–15, 23 (1976–1977), 24–35.

The Dorian settlements. Digest of the Greek literary authorities: G. Busolt, *Griechische Geschichte* I (Gotha 1893²), 201–62. Objections to the historicity of a Dorian invasion: G. Grote *A history of Greece* II (new ed. London, 1883), 1–7; K.J. Beloch, *RhM* 45 (1890), 555–98. The Dorians seen as destroyers of the Mycenaean world: V. Milojčić, *AA* (1948–1949), 12–36; P.A.L. Greenhalgh, *AC* 21 (1978), 1–38. The Dorians seen as invaders of the Mycenaean world about a century after the era of destructions: V.R.d'A. Desborough, *The last Mycenaeans and their successors* (Oxford, 1964), 251–2. The Dorians seen as a submerged element in the population of Mycenaean Greece: J. Chadwick, *PP* 31 (1976), 103–117; C.G. Thomas, *SMEA* 19 (1978), 77–87.

3

Cults and cult-places

A Dark Age of more than three centuries separates the final collapse of Mycenaean civilization (*c.* 1100) from the beginning of the archaic period. The term 'Dark Age' reflects our own ignorance as much as anything else; but it is true that in Greece generally, with the exception of Athens, this was really a dark age, in which (by strong contrast with the Mycenaean period and with the later epochs of archaic and classical Greece) settlements were small, poor, and backward, having little communication with one another.

Outside Athens, the Greeks preserved little from the Mycenaean period; but they preserved something – and that something we can only call an ineradicable sense of national and racial identity. However much the Greeks differed among themselves, the Greeks as a whole differed (at least in their own estimation) in a still more fundamental way from the 'barbarians', or non-Greeks. When in Herodotus the Athenians assure the Spartan envoys that they will make no accommodation with the king of Persia, they cite the powerful ties which unite all the Hellenes, saying that 'the Greeks share the same blood and the same language, they possess shrines of the gods and sacrifices in common, and their way of life is the same' (8.144.2). Although Herodotus is speaking of a time several centuries later than the re-emergence of cities in Greece after the Dark Age, his words hold true for every epoch of Greek history whose beliefs and practices are known to us. Leaving aside the question of 'common blood' (although for the Greeks this expression carried none of the offensive overtones it has now acquired), we can see that two indispensable marks of 'Greekness' were thought to distinguish a Hellenic from a barbarian city: its inhabitants had to speak the Greek language, and they had to worship the Greek gods in the accustomed manner. But the Greeks by no means excluded the veneration of foreign gods or even the identification of some Hellenic deities with those of other peoples, and still less did they try to impose upon any individual the adherence to a specific system of religious beliefs; it is simply that the city as a whole, and official organs of the city such as assemblies and councils at home and armies in the field, sacrificed to the gods, brought offerings to their shrines, and participated in religious duties. The shrines were served by priests and priestesses, but these were concerned solely with the upkeep of the sacred places; they were in no sense teachers, or the guarantors of orthodoxy. Theology and dogma were totally absent, but great weight was attached to the external observances of religion. In this situation, syncretism of cults took place without difficulty, and the worship of some pre-Hellenic deities survived in the Greek cults. There was also, quite understandably, considerable variation in cult-practice between one city and another; and between Dorian and non-Dorian cities the differences were accentuated. Two shrines in particular, the Temple of Zeus at Olympia and Apollo's Temple at Delphi, transcended local allegiances, and were regarded as the common possessions of all Hellenic peoples. Their outstanding importance as cult-centres was confirmed by the establishment of the pan-Hellenic games at Olympia, naturally under the tutelage of Zeus, and that of the oracle at Delphi. With these two exceptions, each city has to be treated separately, since it has a number of cults and institutions peculiar to itself. A deity, even one belonging to the Olympian pantheon, was often invested with cult-titles of purely local validity, because of his especial association with the place or because he was worshipped there under one of his aspects. Besides the cults of divine persons, there flourished in many places hero-cults, which had arisen around the tomb of an epic hero or of some early king or lawgiver who was rendered divine honours in return for the benefits he had conferred on his city.

Most Greek cities possessed an *acropolis*, a walled citadel occupying an elevated position which gave refuge to the populace in time of war and which enshrined the temple of the presiding deity. The Spartan acropolis did not by any means conform to the usual type. It lay on a low hill running from east to west, a little to the north of the modern town, in a locality now covered by olive-groves. Neither the houses nor the market-place of the ancient city have yet been revealed by excavation. It is a notable fact, in which the Spartans took great pride, that the city remained unwalled in the classical period. Walls were not built there until the third century B.C.: considerable traces of these have been found, particularly on the east side, by the Eurotas. Roman and Byzantine walls stand closer to the acropolis.

On the west side of the acropolis, above the Hellenistic theatre, were found the ruins of a temple. The ruins and the associated objects, scanty as they turned out to be, were enough to identify the place as the chief shrine of metropolitan Sparta, dedicated to Athena as protectress of the city. In Laconia, as in Attica, several cities acknowledged Athena as their tutelary deity; and her well-known role as a warrior-goddess peculiarly fitted her to watch over the Spartan acropolis. Her titles at Sparta are given in Greek literature as *Poliouchos*, 'Guardian of the City', which calls for no comment, and *Chalkioikos*, 'She of the Bronze House'. Both Euripides and Aristophanes refer to the Goddess of the Bronze House, and Euripides uses another epithet as well, *Chalkopylos*, 'She of the Bronze Gates'. Thucydides contributes a vivid account of Pausanias the Spartan regent who, when in peril of his life, rushed into the sacred precinct and obtained sanctuary in 'a small building belonging to the temple' of Chalkioikos (p. 177). Plutarch relates that a Spartan king of a later generation, Agis IV, also sought sanctuary in Athena's temple (*Life of Agis* 16.3). But after the overthrow of Agis in 241 the sanctuary was violated. According to Polybius, 'at a certain ancestral sacrifice the young men had to go in armed procession to the temple of Athena Chalkioikos, while the ephors stayed in the sanctuary and performed the rites of sacrifice' (4.35.2). On the occasion mentioned the soldiers broke into the temple and, disregarding the sanctity of the place and of the occasion, slew the ephors. No other source mentions this 'ancestral sacrifice'; and it seems possible that Polybius has confused the sacred aspect of the temple with its function as a rallying-point for the soldiery in time of emergency (4.22.8). An inscribed tablet of marble, part of which was found in the ruins of the Chalkioikos temple, recounts the victories of a man named Damonon and his son in the Laconian games: some of these were held in honour of *Gaiawochos* ('Earth-holder', a name of Poseidon), some in honour of Athena herself, and it was in Athena's precinct that the family set up the tablet. Pausanias gives a detailed description of the temple. The bronze walls, he says, are decorated in relief with many legendary scenes, including those depicting the labours of Heracles; but he makes it clear that the bronze walls belong only to the last stage of building and that there had been earlier and cruder phases (3.17.2). It is possible that one of the names Pausanias applies to the goddess, *Poliouchos*, belongs to an earlier shrine and that the epithet *Chalkioikos* was applied to her when the later temple, with its bronze reliefs, was erected.

Little of the ancient temple, or temples, was revealed by excavation. An east-west retaining-wall marks one end of the precinct. North of this wall were found sherds of Protogeometric and Geometric pottery, presumably comprising the debris from the first phase of the sanctuary, which began in the eighth century. A later stratum contains material ranging from classical to Roman times. Objects from the later level include stamped tiles, some bearing the words DAMOSIOS ATHANAS, indicating that this cult of the goddess was maintained on

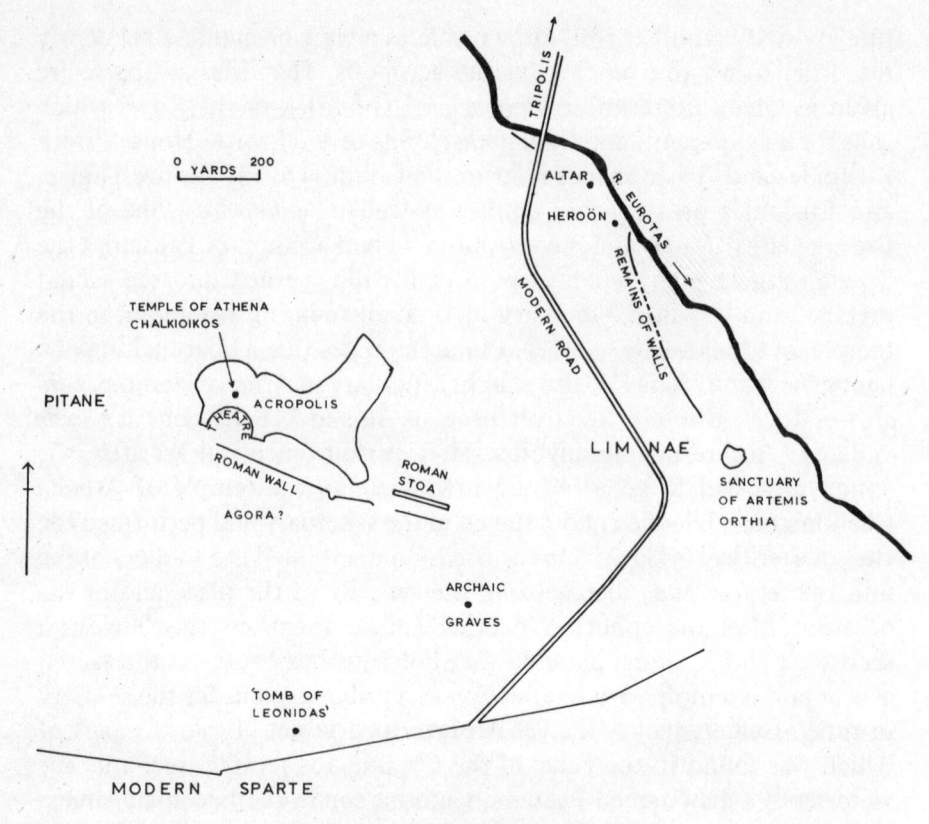

9 Plan of ancient Sparta.

behalf of the public at large (*damos*). The soil inside the retaining-wall contained some excellent miniature bronzes: an Athena and an Aphrodite of archaic type and a man belonging to the classical period who was identified by the excavator as a trumpeter (p. 93). Here also were fragments of more than one of the Panathenaic amphorae which were awarded as prizes to victors in the principal contests at Athens. The victors usually kept their prizes, which were subsequently deposited in tombs; but it seems to have been the Spartan custom for a victor to bring back his prize to his native city and dedicate it in Athena's temple.

Two burial-sites have come to light in the area lying between the acropolis and the modern town. It is well known that the Greeks in general did not permit the burial of corpses within the boundaries of their cities; but to this rule there were two notable exceptions – Sparta and the Spartan colony of Taras (respectively Plutarch in his *Life of Lycurgus* 27.1 and Polybius 8.28.6). Plutarch's testimony is borne out by the discovery of a group of four tombs, arranged in a kind of precinct with a low wall surrounding it. The wall enclosed a mound consisting of ashes and animal-bones, a kiln, many tiles and sherds, and an impressive relief-amphora dating from about 600 (p. 89) (pl. 20). This amphora, like the one in the Heroum (p. 89), was not used for the actual burial, but served as an offering to the dead; perhaps it was placed there by the descendants of the family interred in the tombs. The precinct seems to correspond, in some sense, to our notion of a family-vault. To what extent it was an actual cult-place must remain uncertain; but the building of a wall and the deposition inside it of burnt remains suggest tendance from one generation to another and not merely the offering of sacrifice on the occasion of the burials. Another group of tombs, situated to the north-west of those just described, prove that the custom of burial within the city persisted at Sparta into Hellenistic times, if not later.

Going northwards from the acropolis, we find a small shrine lying to the east of the road to Megalopolis. Several thousand small vases and some figurines were discovered in a walled precinct; and the deposit dates the use of the shrine to a time lasting from the seventh to the third century B.C. No positive identification is possible, but the shrine may be that of Achilles, mentioned by Pausanias, 3.20.8. He says that it stands 'on the road to Arcadia' and that young men sacrifice to Achilles there before taking part in the Laconian contests. Whether or not our shrine is really the one described by Pausanias, it remains true that cults of Achilles are widely attested in Laconia; and this fact is not easy to explain, since Achilles had his home in Thessaly. The presence of his cult in Laconia may arise from a straightforward 'migration' of legendary figures, which can be paralleled over and over again in the history of the Greeks; at any rate, the attempt by some Laconians to annex the great hero to their own region, by asserting that he was one of the suitors of Helen, is dismissed by Pausanias himself as a self-contradictory fabrication (3.24.10–11).

East of the acropolis the remnants of two cult-places have been excavated near the Eurotas but within the walls of the ancient city. The first is the precinct of some hero-cult, yielding good stratification from the Geometric period down to Hellenistic times. This Heroum contained about a hundred hero-reliefs: small pieces of terracotta with a roughly moulded scene showing a seated hero being offered a draught of wine. The upper part of an archaic relief-amphora was the most notable object to come to light in the precinct. Close to the Heroum stands an immense altar, six feet high and measuring seventy-six feet by thirteen. The altar has been identified, very tentatively, as that of Lycurgus; the date of its construction is unknown, and the inscriptions found in the vicinity are too fragmentary to indicate who was the recipient of the offerings.

Farther down-stream is the sanctuary of Artemis Orthia, which was excavated before the first World War (fig. 10). It lies very close to the west bank of the Eurotas in the suburb of Sparta known, with good reason, as Limnae ('Marshes'), and there can be little doubt that the site was subject to flooding when the river was in spate. The high standards to which the excavators worked enable us to distinguish with sufficient clarity three phases in the history of the sanctuary down to the third century B.C., although in fact it continued in use into Roman and even Byzantine times. The visitor today finds the sanctuary untended.

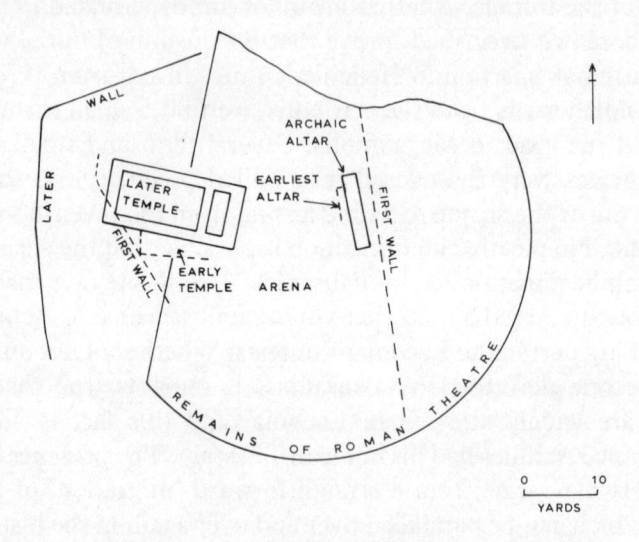

10 *Plan of the sanctuary of Artemis Orthia.*

The first phase does not begin much, if at all, before 800, and it comes to an end in the vicinity of 700. It is marked by the building of the 'Earliest Altar', orientated north-south, in a small unwalled precinct which measured about one hundred feet from east to west and rather more along the opposite side. All that remained of the altar was a layer of unworked stones. Burnt matter, containing animal bones and sherds of Geometric pottery, was found near this altar. No temple corresponding to it came to light, but it is hard to imagine that the sanctuary had no temple, however rudimentary this might have been. The temple, if it existed, may have lain (like its successors) in the western part of the sanctuary and have been obliterated when the later temples were built there. At some point during the first phase the sanctuary was walled and provided with a pavement of pebbles taken from the river-bed.

The second phase of the Orthia sanctuary is marked by the erection of two structures: a well-preserved altar immediately adjoining the 'Earliest

Cults and cult-places

Altar' and a temple, of which only some of the foundations were left. This second altar, known as the 'Archaic Altar', is built of roughly-dressed stones, is long (twenty-nine feet) and narrow (five feet), and stands rather more than a yard off the ground. The soil to the west of the altar was rich in offerings that had been brought to the spot and, from time to time, thrown away. Richer still were the deposits associated with the 'Early Temple', which stood on the west side of the sanctuary. The building itself was largely destroyed in the third phase to make room for its successor, which abuts upon it. The scanty remains, together with analogies drawn from other early temples in Greece, permit a number of features to be inferred with reasonable confidence. The size of the foundations indicates a building forty and a half feet long by seven and a half feet wide: thus its dimensions were quite modest, compared with those of the Archaic Altar. Beams of wood formed the outside walls (where they would have been filled in with bricks) and a row of columns set in the centre of the long axis; these columns supported the roof and divided the interior into two long and narrow naves. In plan and mode of construction the building was a kind of simplified version of the Temple of Hera at Olympia (*c.* 600).

The third phase, beginning at about 570, saw a radical alteration of the entire site. Upon the sanctuary-floor was deposited a layer of sand, which effectively sealed in, and preserved in stratified order, the numerous votives of the archaic age that had been deposited there. A wall was constructed to enclose a larger area than previously, and sections of this wall were preserved to the west and south. The Early Temple was destroyed and replaced by the Later Temple. Little of this was found standing except the foundations, on which yet another temple was erected in Roman times. A painted fragment of stone cut to represent a lion's mane was found in the soil on one side of the temple; and this discovery has suggested that the pediment of the building was decorated with a group of lions. The sand completely covered the Archaic Altar; and, although this altar must have had an immediate successor, it did not emerge in the course of excavation. The next altar known at the site dates from the fifth century, its blocks being used later to form the base of a Roman altar. Further elaborate constructions belong to the Hellenistic period: the third century B.C. sees the building of houses to the east of the altar, a city-wall, and a large drain. In the Roman period the site was converted into a circular theatre, with the arena lying between the seats and the Later Temple (third century A.D.).

The site can be identified positively with the place Limnaion, which according to Pausanias contained the sanctuary of Artemis Orthia. Not only do its altars, temples, and votive-offerings mark it out as a cult-place which was in use for many centuries, but inscriptions found there refer specifically to Artemis Orthia. The earliest of them goes back to the first part of the sixth century B.C. and is scratched on the limestone relief of a horse (the type is illustrated in pl. 38). It records that the horse was dedicated by a man named Epanidas 'to the Virgin Wortheia'. Later inscriptions from the sanctuary regularly mention Artemis Orthia, although the latter word shows a bewildering variety of spellings.

Artemis is one of the most august of the Olympian divinities. Both in poetry and in painting she is celebrated above all as the mistress of wild animals, a virgin huntress armed with bow and arrows who tracks her prey in lonely places. She typifies both the vivifying and the destructive aspects of untamed nature: she presides over child-birth but, like her brother Apollo, she also slays men and beasts by means of her arrows. Her cults are numerous in many parts of Greece, and in Laconia alone no fewer than thirty-seven cult-titles are given her by the ancient authors. Pausanias remarks that images of Artemis, Apollo, and their mother Leto are set up in the market-place at Sparta; and Artemis is associated with the worship of Apollo at Amyclae. But, while many of the cult-names of Artemis are easy to understand (referring as they do to some well-known trait of the goddess or to the place where she was worshipped), the epithet Orthia makes for some difficulty. As already mentioned, it is used in a number of forms: *Borsea, Borthea, Ortheia, Orthosia, Wortheia, Wrothasia*, and so on. Some, but not all, of these variants can be explained as arising from sound-changes peculiar to the Laconian dialect. A particular problem is posed by the derivation of the word. The Greeks themselves generally connected it with *orthos*, 'straight, upright', and explained it as 'the goddess who sets women upright again after child-birth and brings them through safely'. This explanation seems to be based on mere guesswork, of a kind familiar in ancient attempts at providing an etymology. More plausible is the suggestion that *orthos* is an attribute of the goddess's cult-image; in other words, that the image set up in the Orthia sanctuary depicted a standing, not a seated, divinity. That is likely enough in itself, but it does little to explain the variety of forms. Why do we not find simply an *Artemis Ortha*, corresponding to the *Dionysos Orthos* who had a cult at Athens and the *Asklepios Orthos* who had a cult at Epidaurus? It is possible to meet some of these difficulties by making an assumption about the nature of Artemis Orthia: this is that Orthia is not a genuine, original epithet of Artemis but that (as happened with Apollo at Amyclae) the worship of an earlier deity became merged with that of an Olympian. This view finds support in some of the objects revealed by the excavations. For example the inscriptions found in the sanctuary refer either to Artemis Orthia or

Cults and cult-places

to Orthia but never to Artemis; the plain inference to be made is that at first, and perhaps for long afterwards, Artemis and Orthia were felt to be distinct divinities, no matter how closely their cults were assimilated. It is even possible to adduce an approximate date for this assimilation. One favourite type of votive-offering at this as at other Laconian shrines is a small figurine made of lead (p. 94); and there appeared in the sixth century a new animal-type representing a deer, a creature particularly associated with Artemis. Since other changes took place in the cult at about the same time, this epoch may be that in which the worship of Artemis was superimposed on that of Orthia. The latter goddess presumably had a number of attributes in common with Artemis; and the many different forms of her name may point to a pre-Hellenic divinity, whose name fell variously on Greek ears.

The immense quantities of votives found in the sanctuary of Artemis Orthia are the thank-offerings or gifts made to the goddess. It is easy to believe that the majority of the votives were brought by pregnant or barren women or by those who had safely been delivered of a child. Whether that is so or not, the sanctuary was later put to very different uses. A series of inscribed slabs, extending into the second century A.D., were set up in the sanctuary by victors in boys' contests. The exact nature of the contests is obscure, but they seem to have comprised musical competitions and bouts of wrestling (p. 239). That the winners of these events (which presumably took place in the arena) should have presented stones to the goddess of the place is entirely natural. Less obvious is the reason for dedicating the object attached to some of the stones, for this turns out to be an iron sickle. However unlikely we may think it, this can hardly be anything other than the prize, which the pious victor has dedicated along with the stone.

The building which stands at the south-west end of the Menelaion ridge is a simple and massive structure dating from about 500, or a little later. A rectangular wall of large, carefully worked blocks of stone runs round the hill-top, and this wall itself rests on courses of stones (pl. 7). Pieces of marble found in the vicinity suggest that the wall was originally surmounted by a decorative frieze of fine workmanship. The space between the sides of the wall was filled in so as to make a level area measuring about twenty-six yards by eighteen. A sloping path-way, paved at one time, gave access to this area on the west side. Upon the level area were preserved the foundations of a small building, twenty-eight feet long and eighteen wide; and that was, presumably, the shrine or temple which once formed the centre-piece of the whole site. The walled structure with its rectangular shrine was only the latest building to be erected here. An earlier stage is represented by what is called the 'Old Menelaion', a small temple with pediment built *c*. 600. It is not known where the Old Menelaion stood; only individual blocks and other fragments have been found scattered about the site. But the place had been used as a sanctuary even before the construction of the Old Menelaion. Well-stratified deposits north-east of the walls showed that the site had been in use, more or less continuously, since at least the eighth century. Figurines of lead, terracotta, and bronze were present with the pottery in these deposits. No corresponding building is known, and it is likely that at the beginning sacrifices were offered at a simple altar.

The latest building, then, is an imposing structure, and one which gives evidence of a rich past; but what is there about it which justifies the name 'Menelaion'? None of the figurines could well represent Helen or Menelaus. But the literary sources are more informative. Herodotus is the earliest writer to speak of a shrine of Helen in the neighbourhood of Sparta. He relates how an ugly daughter was born into a noble Spartan family. The child's nurse was dismayed at her unfortunate appearance, and took her every day to Helen's shrine 'in the place called Therapne, above the shrine of Apollo'. On one of the nurse's visits she was accosted by a woman who told her that the girl would grow up to be the most beautiful of all the ladies in Sparta (6.61.3–5). There is no need, on this occasion, to try to disentangle history from the obvious elements of folk-lore; and a notable mistake of Herodotus, or of his immediate source, is too obvious to cause much confusion. It is only natural for a reader of Homer, with little direct knowledge of Spartan cult, to assume that because Helen was worshipped at Sparta she was worshipped as a goddess of beauty; and Herodotus himself has earlier identified Helen as a 'foreign Aphrodite' (2.112.2). But scrutiny of the accounts of other writers leads to the conclusion that Helen was a local nature-divinity of long standing and that in Herodotus' mind this aspect of her personality has been to a large extent overlaid by her association with Aphrodite: an association which goes back to the *Iliad*. But two useful items of information can be culled from the story told by Herodotus: first that Helen's shrine lies above that of Apollo (at Amyclae) and second that it is reasonably easy of access from Sparta. No structure revealed by excavation or recorded in ancient sources meets these conditions, except our Menelaion. Polybius writes that the Menelaion stands upon steep and rocky hills to the south-east of Sparta: hills overlooking the plain between Sparta and the Eurotas, which at this point flows close by their foot (5.22.3–4). Once more we find a reference which makes sense only if the place in question is what we now know as the Menelaion. Recent excavations enable us to clinch the matter. They have uncovered two

Cults and cult-places

archaic objects of bronze inscribed in such terms as to make it certain that they were votive-offerings. The first object, a jug, records that it was offered by a man called DEINIS to WELENAI (and) MENELAWO: the names of the recipients here appear in an early form, before the loss of -w-. The second is a pronged instrument of unknown use, scratched with a dedication to WELENAI.

Now that the site of the Menelaion has been identified with certainty, we have to ask what was the nature of the rites held in honour of Helen and Menelaus and the original reason for the rise of their cult. Little of value for our purpose is found in the *Encomium of Helen* written at Athens by the rhetorician Isocrates (*c*. 370). He does indeed mention that Helen and Menelaus are still honoured as gods by the Spartans, who offer them pure and traditional sacrifices at Therapne; but his previous discussion shows that he has not grasped the real reason for Helen's apotheosis. Like Herodotus, he regards Helen simply as a goddess of beauty who has raised to her own divine status her husband and her brothers (61–63). The clue to the truth is provided, as it often is, by Pausanias. He first presents the belief of the Spartans themselves, to the effect that the actual tomb of Helen and Menelaus is situated at Therapne. But among the people of Rhodes, he says, a different belief is current. They hold that after Menelaus' death Helen was driven out of Sparta by his bastard sons, made her way to the eastern Aegean, and took refuge with the queen of Rhodes. The queen was now a widow, having lost her husband Tlepolemus in the Trojan War. For this loss she blamed Helen, as the instigator of the war, and took vengeance on her in the following way. She had maidservants dressed as avenging goddesses, who seized Helen as she was bathing and hanged her on a tree. 'And for this reason', Pausanias concludes, 'the Rhodians have a shrine of Helen Dendritis (Helen of the Tree)' (3.19.9–10). This may sound like a wild story, which has little to tell the enquirer about Spartan cult. But in fact it reveals a trait which recurs countless times in Greek writers, especially in those of later antiquity, namely their desire to identify and name the originator of a cult, a custom, or a law (cf. p. 128). If apparently disparate elements are found in close association, then the reason for the association has to be found; and if no plausible explanation lies to hand, a story is cobbled together. Here the existence of a cult of Helen in Rhodes is, on the face of it, inexplicable; also incapable of obvious explanation is Dendritis, the epithet borne by Helen in this cult. So an account is concocted, bringing together some of the incidents and persons of the Trojan cycle, as it was generally known among the Greeks, in an attempt to explain both the location of the Rhodian shrine of Helen and the name under which she was worshipped there. But, while the story invented to account for these circumstances may well be dismissed as fiction, there is no reason for thinking that the circumstances themselves are not accurately reported. The existence of a tree-cult of Helen is, in fact, confirmed by an allusion in a poem which Theocritus ostensibly composed for Helen's wedding-night. This is supposed to be sung by a chorus of twelve Spartan maidens, who promise to go out early the next morning and gather flowers for a garland they will hang on a plane-tree, and on the bark of the tree shall be written a message for passers-by to read: 'revere me, I am Helen's tree' (Theocritus 18.48). Once again Helen is closely associated with a tree, this time in Sparta itself; and once again the motive for the existence of a particular cult has been found in an observed ritual.

The literary sources, together with the archaeological evidence, enable some tentative conclusions to be drawn. At some date impossible to determine, but fairly certainly before the end of the Bronze Age, the Spartans recognized and worshipped a goddess of luxuriant growth, whose cult had at its centre a tree. After the advent of the Olympian deities, and the heroes closely associated with them, the cult of this goddess continued along two different channels. One led to her identification with Artemis, the Greek divinity of fertile nature, whence the worship at the shrine of Artemis Orthia, described above. But the other, much less predictably, resulted in the conflation with Helen, half-mortal and half-goddess, whose beauty is matched only by her destructiveness. It is not possible to account satisfactorily for this second development; but a slight hint of the motive for it is perhaps provided by the motif of a jealous and vengeful Helen. Under this aspect she is said to have afflicted Stesichorus with blindness until he should recant the poem in which he held her to blame for all the troubles which befell at Troy. It is conceivable that just such a fickle creature, able to cause great happiness or great misery, was thought an apt counterpart to a nature-goddess.

We should next discuss the cults and cult-centres of Apollo, beginning with Apollo Karneios, who had a cult at Sparta and in several other Dorian cities, going on to the Amyklaian Apollo and finishing with the hero-cults practised in the neighbourhood of Amyclae. The artists of Greece, and also her poets from Homer onwards, present Apollo as the distinctively Hellenic god, the personification of youthful male beauty and the bearer of enlightenment; he is the supreme patron of the arts and of medicine and he reveals the future by means of his oracle at Delphi. In his earliest exploit Apollo slays a serpent, so asserting the power of the lords of upper air against the creatures of earth. But we shall find with Apollo, as we found with Artemis, that his cults reveal many aspects

Cults and cult-places

which are additional to, or actually incompatible with, his literary representation.

The cult of Apollo Karneios was expressed above all in the festival known as the *Karneia* or *Karnea*. Pausanias describes the cult, and states that the god was worshipped under the name Karneios by the Dorians in general (3.13.3–4); and his statement is confirmed by evidence from Dorian settlements at Cyrene and also in Thera and Cos. Pausanias is well aware that the name Apollo Karneios arises from a conflation of two deities, or rather from the superimposition of Apollo upon Karnos. His fantastic account of the process of assimilation need not detain us, but involved in it is the equation of *karnos* with *krios*, the Greek word for 'ram'; and even modern etymologists have not been able to do better than see in *karnos* a word allied to the stem of the noun *keras* ('horn'), so that *karnos* would indeed be a 'horned creature' or 'ram'. There is little doubt, in any event, that the Greeks interpreted the word in that sense. Theocritus makes his shepherd Lacon say (trying to go one better than his rival the goatherd): 'Yes, and Apollo loves *me* dearly, and I am fattening a fine ram for him, for the Karnea are approaching' (5.82–83). Now the identification of Olympian gods with animals is securely attested. Hera is sometimes associated with a heifer, Athena with an owl, and Apollo himself with a wolf (if that is really the meaning of his epithet *Lykeios*). But it is Hermes who is shown with the typical attribute of the ram, a pair of horns. These observations tend to indicate that the cult-title Karneios conceals even greater complexity than is usual in such matters. If Karnos was in fact a ram-like divinity, then of course Apollo embodies a much more advanced concept, which has become fused with the primitive one and, at the same time, has usurped a characteristic elsewhere associated with Apollo's half-brother Hermes. There is nothing untoward in this development, since in some sources Apollo shares with Hermes the epithet *Nomios*, 'God of the flocks'; and the pastoral aspect of Apollo is in keeping with his championship of civilization and order. But now a strange fact emerges, which it is difficult to reconcile with what has been said already; for, on reading the descriptions of the Karneia which have been preserved, we find no mention of rams or of the sacrifice of rams. The Karneia marked the vintage, which took place in August. Young men called *staphylodromoi* ('grape-cluster-runners') pursued a man wearing garlands; if they caught him it was considered a good omen for the city, but a bad one if they did not. This conjunction of events recalls an early time, in which the well-being of the city was inescapably bound up with the success or failure of the harvest. But the Karneia had another aspect as well: an aspect which may strike us as typically Spartan. During the time of their participation in the festival the young men lived like warriors on campaign, eating in messes and performing the rite to words of command. The cult of Apollo Karneios and the festival of the Karneia perhaps resulted from two stages of development: first the identification of an old pastoral god with the great 'civilizing' member of the Olympian pantheon, second the incorporation into the cult of a ritual in which the health of the state went hand in hand with productive harvests. For the military colouring of the rite, which seems incongruous, we may suggest an explanation, or at least a parallel. We learn from a hymn, written at Rome in 218 B.C., but incorporating formulae from a remote epoch, that the war-god Mars was invoked on occasion as a divinity of the crops. Apollo, like Mars, was expected to help his people: on the one hand by promoting the harvest, on the other by fighting against the public enemies.

Connected with Apollo, though perhaps only incidentally, were the *Gymnopaidiai* ('Festival of naked youths'). The *Gymnopaidiai* did not amount to a religious festival in the strict sense of the term, but were rather a number of competitions lasting for several days. Three separate teams (one of boys, one of young men, one of older men) competed in singing, dancing, and gymnastic displays. The principal aim of the *Gymnopaidiai* was the habituation of the Spartiate manhood to arduous activity. The competitions were held in the heat of summer, at the end of July. They were perhaps instituted under the impact of the Spartan defeat at Hysiae (p. 105): subsequently they were associated with a solemn thank-offering to Apollo for the success of Spartan arms.

The Hyakinthia, kept at Amyclae in late May and early June, eclipsed in importance the other festivals of Apollo. The chief annual observance of the Dorian tribes was bound up with the Hyakinthia, which were to the Spartans what the Isthmian games were to the people of Cornith or the Pythian to those of Delphi. When a solemn treaty was concluded between Athens and Sparta in 421, the Spartans undertook to set up at Amyclae a column recording the provisions of the treaty and to ratify it each year at the Hyakinthia (p. 198). It seems to have been incumbent upon the citizens to be present at the festival; at any rate, the historians mention occasions on which the Spartan contingents had to be detached from active duty so as to allow their participation. It will not prove easy to account for the high place occupied by the Hyakinthia in the life of the Spartans; but an attempt can be made after discussing Hyakinthos himself, his connexion with Apollo, and the character of the Hyakinthia.

Looking merely at the pan-Hellenic account of the myth, we find a pretty tale of no great depth, and one which conforms to a pattern of

Cults and cult-places

relationships between the high gods and lesser beings. Hyakinthos was a beautiful boy to whom Apollo was irresistibly attracted. Unlucky in love as he usually was, Apollo killed him accidentally with a throw of the discus, and in grief at his loss appointed a day of sacrifice for the land of Laconia. Such is the bare tale, told first in the *Helen* of Euripides (produced in 412); but it was later embellished.

The complex ritual of the Hyakinthia, and its wide diffusion throughout the Dorian states, could hardly have arisen upon such a slight motivation. When we read the account of the festival, we shall acquire a few clues about the real nature of Apollo's connexion with Hyakinthos. It is fortunate that Athenaeus, who had much of interest to say with respect to the Karneia, speaks at length about the Hyakinthia as well. It will be worth while to quote his remarks in full:

> Polycrates relates in his *Laconica* that the Laconians keep the festival of the Hyakinthia for three days running. Because of their mourning for Hyakinthos they wear no garlands at dinner, nor do they bring in bread nor distribute cakes and luxurious food of that sort. They neither sing the paean to Apollo nor behave in the way customary at other festivals. They dine in a very orderly manner, and then take their leave. But in the middle of the three-day period a varied show is put on, and there is a large and remarkable gathering. Boys with their tunics tucked up play the lyre or sing to the pipe; running over all the the strings with plectrum they hymn the god in anapaestic rhythm and high pitch. Others make a procession through the theatre, mounted on gaily bedecked horses. Full choirs of young men come in and sing some of their native songs, and dancers mingled with them move in the old style to an accompaniment of pipe and song. As for the girls, some ride on richly decorated carriages made of wicker-work, while others yoke chariots and drive them in procession for racing. The city as a whole is given over to the bustle and gaiety of the festival. Many victims are sacrificed on this day, and the citizens entertain all their acquaintance to dinner, and their own slaves as well. No one is missing from the festivities; in fact, the city of Sparta is emptied for the spectacle. (4.139d–f.)

Some confusion mars Athenaeus' account, which does not make it plain whether the joyous part of the festival lasts for the second and third day or is merely an interlude in the mourning; furthermore it is inconsistent with the references made elsewhere to a ten-day festival. Nevertheless the narrative quoted from Polycrates helps considerably towards an elucidation of the rite. This consisted of two essential parts: mourning for the dead Hyakinthos and praise for Apollo. The same order of events is indicated by Pausanias, for he states that at the Hyakinthia the ministrants make offering to Hyakinthos before sacrificing to Apollo; and it is noteworthy that Pausanias' word for 'make offering' (*enagizo*) is confined to cults of the dead (3.19.3). What then was the real nature of Hyakinthos before it was misunderstood and debased by later fancy? His very name is significant. It is that of a flower, and it is shown by its ending *-nthos* to be a pre-Greek word. So there is some ground for the assumption that a very ancient vegetation-god was at some point brought into connexion with Apollo, who also (as we have seen) had his vegetative aspects. Such a process might have provided the basis for the story of Hyakinthos slain by Apollo. But it cannot be the whole truth. If it were, we would lack an explanation of the large part still played by Hyakinthos in the cult and of the fact that the festival was named after the older god, not after the younger.

Hyakinthos has not been obliterated by Apollo, but he is still honoured in a cult complementary to that of the great Olympian. He represents death and mourning for the dead. These things are utterly repugnant to Apollo, and can have no part in any rite held in his honour; and yet they have great potency in the world of men, and may not be ignored. The Dorians have achieved a kind of compromise: both the living and the dead are given their due of honour. The two parts of the festival are absolutely irreconcilable, and so they are allowed to remain as opposites. The situation reminds one of the course of events said to have taken place at Delphi. There Apollo killed Python, a creature of the earth, and in this way usurped what was already a venerable centre of cult. Although, of course, Apollo predominated in the Delphic cult thenceforward, Dionysus was worshipped at Delphi along with him. (The entire history is expounded at the beginning of Aeschylus' *Eumenides*.) The opposition between the Apolline and the Dionysiac principles is all but complete; and the anomaly of bringing them together in a cult was explained away by associating Dionysus with the winter months and Apollo with the warmer part of the year. But there is no necessity, in fact, to look for any such explanation. Because of their diverse origins, the functions of many Greek gods overlapped sufficiently for there to be no incongruity if any two of them were brought together in a loose kind of association. In Amyclae, too, Dionysus was worshipped as well as Apollo (Pausanias 3.19.6). Both gods, to some extent, have to do with vegetation; and, if it is correctly surmised that Hyakinthos also had once been a vegetation-deity, the circle is complete, allowing us to see how they could participate in the same cult, while giving expression to very different aspects of it.

'The place called Amyclae,' says Polybius, 'is the best wooded and the most fertile of any in Laconia, and it is twenty furlongs distant from

Sparta. The precinct of Apollo, which is to be found there, is just about the most famous of the shrines of Laconia' (5.19.2–3). The description given later by Pausanias is full of detail, but is in places distressingly vague, because the reader is assumed to have much knowledge of the place already. After mentioning the votive-tripods and statues one would expect to find at such an important shrine, Pausanias devotes a long passage to the show-piece of the sanctuary, the Throne of Apollo. This was a massive structure, more like a raised platform with back and sides than what we should regard as a 'throne'. It was designed by Bathycles, an artist from Magnesia in Ionia, and set up about the middle of the sixth century. Statues of more than life-size supported it in front, while the rear was decorated with a large number of legendary scenes, in relief; according to Pausanias these had not been chosen at random but bore a certain organic relationship to one another. Upon the platform stood a lofty statue of Apollo: 'not the work of Bathycles, for it is in an antiquated style and not made by a skilled hand; it has face, feet, and arms, but the rest resembles a pillar of bronze. On the head is a helmet, and in the hands a spear and a bow. The base of the statue takes the form of an altar, and it is said that Hyakinthos is buried in it' (Pausanias 3.19.1–2). The altar, like the throne itself, carried scenes in relief, one of which showed the apotheosis of Hyakinthos. In a perceptive comment Pausanias observes that Hyakinthos is here represented as a bearded man, whereas a later artist, Nicias, who flourished in the fourth century, portrayed him in the prime of youthful beauty, so giving a hint of the love which Apollo was later said to have had for him. In saying this, Pausanias has put his finger on an important truth about the cult, namely that Hyakinthos and Apollo were in origin quite distinct divinities, whose eventual association was explained by making Apollo the lover of Hyakinthos, even though this explanation involved a drastic change in the role of the two principals.

The ancient town of Amyclae has not yet been found; but the hill known as the Amyklaion, the site of Apollo's shrine and of the throne, was positively identified by Tsountas in the last decade of the nineteenth century. On top of the hill he found roof-tiles dedicated to 'Apollon (or Apellon) in the Amyklaion'. He further uncovered a wall which had been built on the northern and eastern sides of the hill where the slope is steepest (pl. 8). The remains of a circular structure in the western part of the hill-top were taken by Tsountas to be part of Bathycles' throne. Furtwängler re-examined the site in 1904. Many years earlier he had observed that the small church of Ayia Kyriaki, which occupied the highest part of the hill, was built on ancient foundations and that frieze-fragments had been incorporated into its walls. His proposal to

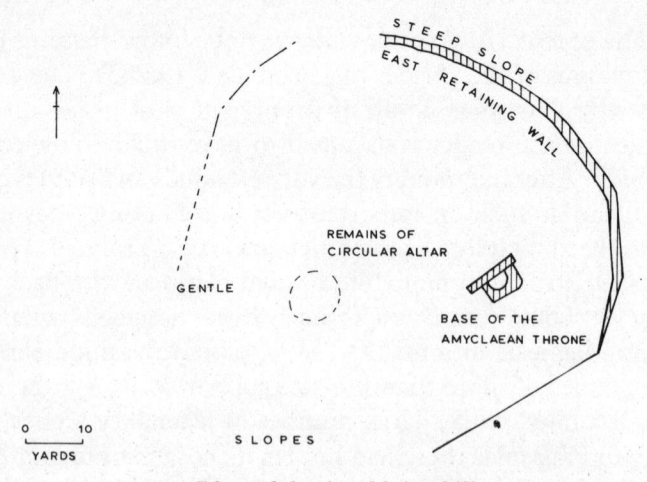

11 *Plan of the Amyklaion hill.*

remove the church and expose its foundations was carried out after his death. No room was left for doubt that the foundations of the church had once underlain Bathycles' throne, and fragments of the throne itself were found in sufficient numbers to corroborate the identification. Later German excavations were conducted in the general area of the hill, and brought to light votive objects from an immensely long period, lasting from the Early Bronze Age into Byzantine times. The results of the different stages of excavation, together with Pausanias' account, form the basis for a history of the site.

The objects from the Mycenaean sanctuary at the Amyklaion were discussed in the last chapter. These objects may have been connected with the worship of Hyakinthos, whose cult was probably established there in the Mycenaean period, if not even earlier; but no Mycenaean shrine or altar has survived at the Amyklaion. The site did not experience the devastation which overtook many places in Greece late in the Mycenaean age, and the sequence of finds continues without a break into the twelfth century. Between that point and the first appearance of Protogeometric pottery there comes a long gap of three centuries or so, reminding us of the extreme paucity of evidence for the Dark Age. As well as Protogeometric sherds and one whole pot, some metal objects of simple type were discovered: rings, wheels, spirals, tripods, nails, pins, and weapons of bronze and iron. None of this material, except perhaps the bronze spear-heads, can much ante-date the end of the tenth century. It has sometimes been thought that the deposition of votives in the Protogeometric epoch marks the establishment of the cult of Apollo, which afterwards coalesced with the Hyakinthine. That is a possible but not a certain inference from the data, since nothing is known which

1   The Taygetus range seen from the Spartan acropolis

2   The Parnon range seen from the Amyklaion

3 The valley of the Eurotas seen from the Menelaion hill

4 The harbour of Gytheum (modern Gytheion); Taygetus in background

5 Mycenaean jug from Melathria. Warrior. Ht. 14 in.

6 Mycenaean house on the Menelaion hill

7 *The Menelaion; Taygetus in background*

8 *The Amyklaion: retaining-wall*

9 *The Amyklaion: conjectural restoration of the Throne of Apollo*

10 Laconian cup from Taranto. Tunny-fish and dolphins. Diam. 8 in.

11 Laconian cup from Etruria (Naucratis Painter). Zeus Lykaios. Diam. 6 in.

12 Laconian cup from Etruria (Naucratis Painter). Symposium. Diam. 8½ in.

13 Laconian cup from Etruria (Arcesilas Painter). Arcesilas. Diam. 11½ in.

14 *Laconian cup from Etruria (Arcesilas Painter). Atlas and Prometheus. Diam. 8½ in.*

15 *Laconian cup from Boeotia (Chimaera Painter). Chimaera. Diam. 6½ in.*

Cults and cult-places

would rule out the worship of Apollo in the Dark Age, or even in the Mycenaean period. The offerings of the Geometric age follow directly upon their predecessors, without any discernible break: again they consist of pottery and objects of metal, such as rings and tripods, but they are now joined by terracotta figurines. The Amyklaion must have witnessed considerable activity at this period, to which probably belong the earliest parts of the circular altar found by Tsountas (fig. 11). What shape the 'Tomb of Hyakinthos' took we can only conjecture: perhaps it was a primitive barrow or tumulus. In the archaic period the sacred precinct was enlarged, a massive wall built to the north and east, and the colossal bronze statue of Apollo erected. Later in archaic times Bathycles was given the task of rearranging the whole precinct and of designing a shrine worthy to house the image of the god and the votive objects dedicated to him. At virtually any other Greek site the answer would have been found by planning a temple along the lines already successfully followed at Olympia and Delphi. But it was not open to Bathycles to adopt that solution at the Amyklaion, since the hill-top was too small to accommodate both the great statue of Apollo and a temple of commensurate size. The compromise he found led him to incorporate the statue in a 'throne' of the kind already described. The resulting structure was unique in Greek lands, so far as we know. The vivid impression conveyed by Pausanias, and given greater precision by excavation, enables us to picture the throne as it must have appeared to worshippers approaching from Sparta along the Hyakinthine Way (pl. 9). The lofty statue, raised still higher by the platform upon which Bathycles had set it, would have faced the setting sun. Its metallic sheen and aniconic shape, belonging to a different world from that of the classical sculptures which accentuate the human attributes of gods, made it an awe-inspiring sight: one conveying nothing of compassion and little even of beauty, such as we find in later representations of Apollo, but threatening harm with grim look and offensive weapons. To what extent the throne succeeded in achieving unity of design can hardly be assessed. Bathycles seems to have aimed, in some of his reliefs, at presenting a legendary cycle rather than disconnected legends, and his inclusion of Hyakinthos' apotheosis was a felicitous means of associating the decoration with the underlying cult. From an architectural view-point the throne stands out as a remarkable compromise by an Ionian artist working in a Dorian milieu. Some fragments remain of supporting-brackets from the entrance: these 'consoles' incorporate a unique fusion of a Doric capital and an Ionic volute. The workmanship of the console-capitals, of the lotus-and-palmette friezes, and of the delicately fluted columns (fig. 12) did full justice to Bathycles' daring conception.

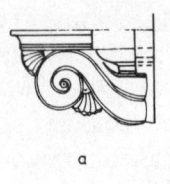

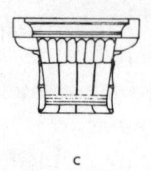

12 The Throne of Apollo at the Amyklaion: (a) capital, (b) lotus-and-palmette frieze, (c) part of column.

The Amyklaion remained into Roman times the principal cult-centre of Laconia, just as the Hyakinthia remained its greatest religious festival, but the era of creative activity at the site virtually ceased with the construction of the throne. With the exception of one or two fine bronzes of the fifth century, the artistic level of the votives is not high: they consist, for the most part, of clay figurines in the shape of women and of miniature clay vases.

Nearly half a mile south of the Amyklaion stands a church called Ayia Paraskevi. A stone slab found in its vicinity a hundred years ago is inscribed with a most interesting dedication, stating that it was set up 'at the shrine of Alexandra'; and above the inscription Alexandra is depicted in relief, as a goddess playing the lyre. It cannot be coincidental that Pausanias refers to a shrine and image of Alexandra at Amyclae (3.19.6). He goes on to mention two facts: first that Alexandra is the name given by the people of Amyclae to Cassandra the doomed prophetess, a daughter of Priam whom Agamemnon took home from Troy as his prize of war; and second that the site contains a statue of Clytemnestra and 'what is thought to be the tomb of Agamemnon'. Pausanias' reluctance to commit himself on the latter point is understandable, for earlier he has described a tomb of Agamemnon at Mycenae (2.16.6). There were, indeed, several conflicting accounts of the murder of Agamemnon and the subsequent death of Clytemnestra. But we are no longer surprised at finding examples of the 'migration' of heroes. The Amyclaeans' reason for giving to Cassandra the name Alexandra is unknown: perhaps it was simply modelled on Alexander, an alternative name of Cassandra's brother Paris. Whatever the reason, the name was adopted by Lycophron, who wrote a poem entitled *Alexandra* soon after 300 B.C. Most of the poem is taken up with a prophecy uttered by Alexandra/ Cassandra, foretelling (among much else) her own death and that of Agamemnon. She prophesies that Agamemnon will be called 'Zeus' by the people of Sparta and will receive divine honours, and she too will be worshipped by the

Cults and cult-places

Spartans. Literary sources thus give us some ground for thinking that a cult-complex arose at Amyclae, involving the worship of Alexandra/Cassandra and that of Zeus Agamemnon. The two matters calling for comment are the association of Alexandra with Agamemnon and the expression 'Zeus Agememnon'.

We have seen that an inscribed stone refers to the shrine of Alexandra, though without associating her with Agamemnon. Excavations in the neighbourhood of Ayia Paraskevi have confirmed the existence of the Alexandra-Agamemnon cult, but they have not yet succeeded in uncovering the shrine itself. The votives, which were found here in their thousands, range from Geometric to Hellenistic times, with the heaviest concentration coming in the archaic age. The usual clay figurines, clay pots (especially miniatures), and objects of lead made up the bulk of the votive-deposit; in some cases these were accompanied by the typical Laconian plaques with hero-reliefs, like those from the Heroum (p. 51). Some of the pottery-fragments bore inscriptions, which both confirm the existence of a cult and identify it. First we have ANETHEKE; '(he) dedicated'. Then a series of remnants which name the persons to whom the dedications were made: AG, AGAM, NO, NONI, from which we unhesitatingly restore AGAMEMNONI: 'to Agamemnon'. Lastly we find ALEX, which has to be completed as ALEXANDRAI, 'to Alexandra'.

We cannot yet confirm the use of the cult-name Zeus-Agamemnon by the evidence of inscriptions, but we may add the testimony of two Christian apologists of the first century, both of whom speak with scorn of the excesses and irrationality of pagan beliefs. Athenagoras, in the very first paragraph of his *Legatio*, gives a list of the Greek states which worship heroes as gods: 'the Spartan', he says, 'reveres Zeus Agamemnon . . . the Athenian sacrifices to Erechtheus Poseidon'. And Clement of Alexandria in the *Protrepticus* cites the historian Staphylus as authority for his statement that 'an Agamemnon Zeus is honoured at Sparta'. Given that this is a genuine cult-title in use at Sparta (or Amyclae), how are we to explain it? This title seemed at one time to lend powerful support to the theory that Greek heroes were, in origin, only etiolated gods. But this theory has long since been abandoned, because there are so many cases which it will not explain. The problem has been approached from the opposite direction, and Agamemnon seen as a primitive local god who was in time closely associated with a new arrival, Zeus. But there are serious difficulties in the way of accepting that explanation. It postulates a process similar to the one whereby Hyakinthos coalesced in the cult with an Olympian god. There is, however, no reason to suppose that Agamemnon was, like Hyakinthos, an early divinity: his name is transparently Greek, and he has left no trace of an old rite, corresponding to the doleful part of the Hyakinthia. A more satisfactory explanation can be reached if the coalescence of Zeus and Agamemnon is seen not as an early but as a late phenomenon, which came about only when the full impact of Homeric poetry was felt in mainland Greece. For in Homer the heroes' attributes are strikingly similar to those of the gods; and, in addition, individual divinities attach themselves to their favourite heroes and further their cause. For example, Apollo is closely identified with Hector in the *Iliad* and Athena with Odysseus in the *Odyssey*. With such analogies in mind, it would have required no great imaginative leap to bring into connexion the chief of the gods and the chief of men, since that is the part played by Agamemnon in the *Iliad*.

Mention of the cult of Zeus Agamemnon throws into relief the lack of good evidence for the Spartan worship of Zeus. It is true that a number of different epithets are attached to the name of Zeus, but they are all of a banal kind, and reflect no very early stage of his worship in Laconia. Some of them simply refer to his majesty and grandeur: such are *Hypatos* 'Highest', *Olympios* 'Olympian', and *Ouranios* 'Sky-dweller'. Two might be called propitiatory epithets: *Euanemos* 'Bestower of fair winds' and *Plousios* 'Bestower of riches'. Others again bring Zeus into social and domestic relationships: *Herkeios* 'God of the courtyard' and *Xenios* 'God who watches over strangers and guests'. A larger number, not surprisingly, emphasize the political role Zeus is expected to play in the Spartan state: *Agetor* 'Leader', *Agoraios* 'Guardian of assemblies', *Amboulios* 'Guardian of councils', *Kosmetas* 'Orderer', *Patroös* 'The ancestral god', and *Tropaios* 'Giver of victory'. The two kings of Sparta were priests of Zeus: one was dedicated to Zeus *Lakedaimon*, the other to Zeus *Ouranios*.

A word should be said, in conclusion, about the problems of cult-continuity. The question is: did Mycenaean cults survive through the Dark Age? A convincing answer is not easy to arrive at. There is no doubt that the worship of individual gods survived; or perhaps it would be more accurate to say that some of the gods worshipped in Greece in archaic and later times bore the same names that had been given to gods in the Mycenaean age. Virtually nothing is known about the Mycenaean conception of Zeus, Hera, and Poseidon; and it may have differed greatly from the view later taken of them. Some sites contained cult-places in Mycenaean times, and contained them again when knowledge of them is regained after the end of the Dark Age; but at very few, if any, sites (except possibly Delphi) is the actual practice of a cult attested throughout the Dark Age, and so we may have to do with the revival of cults, not their survival. It would not be hard to imagine that some measure of sanctity was retained by a place long after the cult had fallen into disuse.

Cults and cult-places

So far as Laconia is concerned, the only known site which could perhaps have witnessed continuity of cult through the Dark Age is the Amyklaion. But even there the sequence of offerings is interrupted for a long period, and so there is no material evidence for survival. Yet, in this case, we have recourse to evidence of a different kind. If it is right to think of Hyakinthos as a divinity whose worship goes back to the Mycenaean age, then the rites performed in his honour in the Hyakinthia must likewise enshrine a reminiscence of Mycenaean cult. Although, in theory, this cult could have been carried on elsewhere and subsequently brought back to the Amyklaion, it is much more likely that it was associated with the same place throughout. At the Amyklaion, if only there, the balance of probability comes down heavily in favour of cult-continuity.

Bibliography

The Dark Age: A.M. Snodgrass, *The Dark Age of Greece* (Edinburgh, 1971).

Greek cults in general: L.R. Farnell, *The cults of the Greek states*, I-V (Oxford, 1896–1909); U. von Wilamowitz-Möellendorff, *Der Glaube der Hellenen* (Berlin, 1931–1932); M.P. Nilsson, *Greek popular religion* (New York, 1940), *Geschichte der griechischen Religion* (Munich, 1967³). Hero-cults: L.R. Farnell, *Greek hero cults and ideas of immortality* (Oxford, 1921); J.M. Cook, in *Geras A. Keramopoullou* (Athens, 1953), 112–18; J.N. Coldstream, *JHS* 96 (1976), 8–17. Laconian cults: S. Wide, *Lakonische Kulte* (Leipzig, 1893).

The Spartan acropolis: A.M. Woodward, *ABSA* 26 (1923–5), 240–76, 28 (1926–7), 37–48. Temple of Athena *Chalkioikos:* G. Dickins, *ABSA* 13 (1906–1907), 137–54, 14 (1907–1908), 142–6. Theatre: A.M. Woodward, *ABSA* 26 (1923–1925), 119–58, 27 (1925–1926), 175–209, 28 (1926–1927), 3–36, 30 (1928–1930) 151–240; H. Bulle, *SBAW* 5 (1937).

City-walls: A.J.B. Wace, *ABSA* 12 (1905–1906), 284–8, 13 (1906–1907), 5–16.

Tombs: Chr.A. Christou, *AD* 19/A' (1964), 123–63.

Shrine by the Megalopolis Road: G. Dickins, *ABSA* 13 (1906–1907), 169–73. Heroum: A.J.B. Wace, *ABSA* 12 (1905–1906), 288–94. Altar by the Eurotas: G. Dickins, *ABSA* 12 (1905–1906), 295–302.

The sanctuary of Artemis Orthia. Consolidated excavation-reports, artefacts, inscriptions, cult: *AO. Addenda:* R.M. Dawkins, *JHS* 50 (1930), 298–9. Review of *AO:* E. Kunze, *Gnomon* 9 (1933), 1-14. Cult: R.C. Bosanquet, *ABSA* 12 (1905–1906), 331–43; A. Thomsen, *AfR* 9 (1906), 397–416. Boys' contests: M.N. Tod, *AM* 29 (1904), 50–6. The first two phases of the sanctuary: E. Kirsten, *BJ* 158 (1958), 170–6. Chronology: J. Boardman, *ABSA* 58 (1963), 1–7. Significance of the iron 'sickles'; J. Boardman, *JHS* 91 (1971), 136–7. Representations of Artemis Orthia: B. Palma, *ASAA* 52–3 (1974–1975), 301–7. The name 'Orthia' and its variants: D.D. Lipourles, *EE* 10 (1968), 363–99.

Apollo *Karneios:* W. Otto, *Paideuma* 7 (1959–1960), 25–30. *Karneia, Hyakin-*

thia, Gymnopaidiai: M.P. Nilsson, *Griechische Feste von religiöser Bedeutung* (Leipzig, 1906), 118–42. *Hyakinthia:* C.F. Unger, *Philologus* 37 (1877), 13–33; Br. Schröder, *AM* 29 (1904), 24–31; B.C. Dietrich, *Kadmos* 14 (1975), 133–42; C. Gallavotti, *QU* 27 (1978), 183–94. *Gymnopaidiai:* F. Bölte, *RhM* 78 (1929), 124–30; H.T. Wade-Gery, *CQ* 43 (1949), 79–81.

Excavations at the Amyklaion: Chr. Tsountas, *EA* (1892), 1–26; A.N. Skias, *PAAH* (1907), 104–7; E. Fiechter, *JDAI* 33 (1918), 107–245; E. Buschor and W. von Massow, *AM* 52 (1927), 1–85.

The shrine of Agamemnon-Alexandra. Inscribed stele: G. Löschcke, *AM* 3 (1878) 164–71. Excavation-reports: Chr.A. Christou, *PAAH* (1956), 211–12; (1960), 228–31; (1961) 177–8.

The cult of Zeus Agamemnon: I. Harrie, *AfR* 23 (1925), 259–69; U. von Wilamowitz *Kleine Schriften* IV (Berlin 1962), 298–9.

The problem of cult-continuity: R.V. Nicholls, in *Auckland classical essays presented to E.M. Blaiklock* (Auckland, 1970), 1–37; P. Lévêque, *PP* 28 (1973), 23–50; B.C. Dietrich *The origins of Greek religion* (Berlin, 1974), 191–289; W. Burkert *Griechische Religion der archaischen und klassischen Epoche* (Stuttgart, 1977), 88–98.

4

Music and poetry

For the development of the visual arts at Sparta we now have a wealth of evidence, enabling us to trace the Spartan achievement in this field from Protogeometric down to the classical age. This evidence will be assessed in the next chapter. By contrast, the remains of Spartan literature would fill only a very few pages. But these relics have a value out of all proportion to their bulk, both because of their intrinsic worth and because of the light they shed on archaic Sparta. Much indirect evidence tells of a number of poets who lived and wrote at Sparta in the seventh century; but the works of only two, Tyrtaeus and Alcman, have survived in such amount as will enable their worth and interest to be judged.

Tyrtaeus is one of the earliest writers of Greek elegy. The form known as the 'elegiac couplet' (dactylic hexameter followed by pentameter) is especially apt to pointed, epigrammatic verse; and it was so employed, to great effect, in many hundreds of extant examples. But in the seventh century, when Tyrtaeus flourished, it was applied to other uses as well. Tyrtaeus himself, and his elder contemporary Callinus of Ephesus, wrote war-poetry in elegiac verse, inculcating a martial spirit in the citizens and reminding them of the glory to be won on the battlefield: glory in which their posterity also will have a share. The motif is Homeric, only it has now been transferred from the heroic sphere to the real world, in which the young city-states were struggling for primacy, and sometimes even for survival. At about the same time Archilochus of Paros took up a defiantly anti-heroic position, asserting the claims of the here and now, ridiculing martial display, and showing contempt for the qualities admired in aristocratic societies, such as high breeding and unthinking courage in the face of the enemy. To Tyrtaeus this attitude would have seemed incomprehensible and fatal. He was a passionate upholder of the established order, both political and military. Whether he was a native Spartan or, as some traditions have it, he came to Sparta from Athens, in his poetry he associated himself wholeheartedly with the political interests and the territorial ambitions of the Spartan kings.

Tyrtaeus' political concerns come to the fore in two fragments of a poem entitled *Eunomia* ('Law and order'). In one of the fragments (No.

2), the Spartans are enjoined to obey their kings, who are closest in lineage to the gods; and it was Zeus himself who bestowed the city on the Heraclids, with whom the Spartans migrated to the Peloponnese. In this way the poet turns the legend of the Dorian invasion to his own account, using it to instil in the citizens reverence for the established order. Another fragment (No. 4) will involve us later in a complex question of interpretation (p. 129); for the present we may note that the authority of the Spartan kings is attributed to a divine source, for it was Apollo, speaking through his oracle at Delphi, who said that the god-honoured kings, together with the elders, should have the right of initiating counsel.

The rest of the surviving fragments belong to war-poems. Sparta at this time was an embattled city, having for twenty years made relentless war upon her Messenian neighbours to the west, for the sake of acquiring their fertile lands (p. 106). Tyrtaeus tells us that the Messenians have been conquered at last, some fleeing and others remaining, but the latter are compelled to yield to their Spartan masters one-half of their produce (Nos. 5, 6, and 7). In a poem now lost (No. 8), Tyrtaeus is said to have mentioned an uprising by the Messenians and their allies, which the Spartans crushed under his own generalship.

The ethos of the warrior-state is proclaimed with great eloquence by Tyrtaeus. Like the Homeric hero, the hoplite or heavy-armed infantry-man whom Tyrtaeus chiefly addresses is envisaged as a youth of noble lineage, handsome, and desirable to women. The splendour of his manhood is not diminished, but is enhanced, if he falls in battle for his city; disgrace comes if he leaves his elders to be killed on the field or if he is forced to leave the city and take his family into exile and beggary (No. 10). The latter sentiment is one frequently heard in Greek poetry, from the *Iliad* onwards. Poverty and subservience are feared much less than the loss of one's part in the life of the community; for, to the Greeks, the individual could grow to his full stature only by participating fully in the city-state. Two poems preserved in an anthology give a picture of the idealized warrior. In one of these (No. 12), Tyrtaeus places martial valour above all the other qualities a man may possess: athletic prowess, bodily strength, swiftness of foot, beauty, wealth, kingly power, and eloquence. It is by valour that the soldier will turn back the enemy from the city-gates. If he is killed in battle, his name and his grave will be held in perpetual esteem, whereas if he lives he will become a respected counsellor, to whom the other citizens defer. The remaining poem from the anthology (No. 11) calls on the warriors to fight aggressively and to plunge shoulder-to-shoulder into the thick of the fray, 'regarding life as their enemy and black death as dear as the rays of the sun'. It is a question

Music and poetry

whether Tyrtaeus wrote that it is 'painful' (*argaleon*) or 'pleasurable' (*harpaleon*) to smite an enemy as he flees. Our manuscripts give the former, but the word seems pointless in its context, and *harpaleon* should probably be read; if it is right, we have to say that Tyrtaeus adds the thrill of killing to the incentives of patriotism and the winning of personal glory he has already set before the Spartan soldiery.

Exactly how Tyrtaeus' poems were performed we cannot tell; but their vigorous invocation of the martial spirit suggests that they might have been chanted, and not merely spoken. Sparta in the seventh century witnessed the rise of another, and quite different, poetical tradition: that of lyric poetry, meaning quite literally songs sung to the lyre. Spartan poets became pre-eminent in both of the great classes of song, monodic and choral. Lyric monody was a comparatively simple species, in which a solo performer was accompanied (or accompanied himself) on the lyre. The song was arranged in short stanzas and was often the vehicle of an intensely personal kind of poetry. The art of choral lyric was much more complex. It called for skill in poetry, musical composition, and choreography; for dancing and music, no less than words, formed essential parts of the performance. It seems probable that the composer usually trained the choir himself and acted as the 'producer'. The choreography and music of early Greek lyric have perished, and even the words are gravely mutilated.

According to the late treatise *On music,* which has come down to us under Plutarch's name, two impulses were given to the early creation of lyric poetry:

> The first school of lyric poetry was organized at Sparta, and the man responsible for its organization was Terpander. The following are said to have been responsible for the second school: Thaletas of Gortyn, Xenodamus of Cythera, Xenocritus of Locri, Plymnestus of Colophon, and Sacadas of Argos; for it was at the instigation of these men that the festival of the *Gymnopaidiai* was instituted. (Pseudo-Plutarch *Moralia* 1134b–c.)

In this list only Terpander is more than a name to us, and even he is not much more. But the others are worth recording, for the source of pseudo-Plutarch has preserved the interesting fact that they all came to Sparta from elsewhere; and not only from Dorian settlements in Gortyn, Cythera, and Argos but from Colophon in Ionia. Terpander himself came from the Aeolian island of Lesbos, whose poets in the next generation were to leave an indelible mark on Greek literature. Terpander would hardly have made the journey to Sparta, still less have settled there to pursue his creative career, if the city did not already, at that early date, enjoy a reputation for enlightenment and encouragement of the arts. We possess only two or three lines ascribed to Terpander, and these do not suffice to confirm his standing as a major poet. But we need not doubt the truth of the ancient testimony that he was the first musician to win a prize at the *Karneia* (according to tradition founded in 675) and that he made important innovations in the art of music, by inventing the seven-stringed lyre and composing melodies to accompany his own and Homer's verses.

Although we are not given specific information on the point, it seems certain that both choral lyric and monody were composed at Sparta in the time of Terpander; for when we come to Alcman, who lived late in the seventh century, we find that his mastery of both media is complete. Also attributed to Alcman are a number of hexameters, which he presumably sang to the lyre, just as Terpander was said to have done. Alcman was the earliest of the nine lyric poets canonized by the scholars of the Alexandrian age. Nothing is certainly known of the circumstances of his birth or life. It was disputed in ancient times whether he was a native Spartan or had been born at Sardis in Lydia; and some of those who asserted his native origin said further that he was no Spartiate but had been born a slave. These matters cannot be decided now, and, in default of any clinching evidence, speculation about them is worthless. A more important fact is that Alcman lived and worked at Sparta at the time of her artistic greatness and composed many of his songs (perhaps all of them) for purely Spartan occasions. At Sparta too he was buried. Pausanias saw his tomb in the city and described it, mentioning (in a patronizing and quite unwarranted aside) that 'the charm of Alcman's songs is not marred by his use of the Laconian dialect, which is the least harmonious' (3.15.2).

Until about a hundred years ago, when the discovery of the 'Louvre Papyrus' transformed our understanding of Alcman's poetry, there were extant only some short fragments which had survived in the form of quotations. It might be interesting to examine the more important of these and then pass to the poems recovered from papyri in modern times.

The quotations reveal an utterly different personality from that of Tyrtaeus. In Alcman we see nothing of the preoccupation with warfare and politics which pervades Tyrtaeus' poetry. But, in a many-sided society such as Sparta must have been (at least in the seventh and sixth centuries), there is obviously room for the exercise of poetical talent in fields unconnected with the immediate business of survival; or, as Alcman himself expresses it (No. 41), 'expert lyre-playing weighs equally in the balance with steel'. The only point of contact with

Tyrtaeus is seen in No. 64, which personifies Eunomia and gives her one of those pedigrees beloved of Greek poets: '[Fortune], sister of Eunomia and Persuasion, and daughter of Foresight'. Alcman seems to mean that good fortune does not come about as the result of mere chance, but will befall those who have taken up the right attitudes beforehand.

Athenaeus quotes the following (No. 17) from Alcman's third book, to show that the poet was a glutton: 'And one day I shall give you a capacious tripod, (in which to gather food in plenty?). It has not yet been on the fire, but soon it will contain the sort of soup that Alcman, who eats anything and everything, loves to devour warm after the solstice. For he does not eat what is daintily prepared but, like the people, he demands common fare.' Is it right to see in this fragment a political allusion? 'People' is a rendering of the word *damos*, which should probably be understood in its strict sense of the 'citizen-body'. Likely though it is that Alcman here identifies his own simple tastes with those of the majority, in contrast to the habits of the few, it remains hard to surmise on what occasion the lines were sung. We might hesitate to assign them to a choral ode of exalted tone, were it not sometimes the Greek practice to juxtapose the sublime with the homely. (In one of Pindar's odes the poet wonders whether he has escaped the 'ancient reproach of the Boeotian swine'; there too a reputation for gluttony is alluded to by means of a humorous, or half-humorous, expression.) It is conceivable that Alcman is addressing the choir who are to sing the ode he has composed for them, and promises them the tripod as a reward.

A similar context may be suggested for No. 26. This fragment comprises four hexameters in which Alcman addresses 'honey-voiced maidens', and regrets that his limbs will no longer carry him; if only he were like the kingfisher, who flies with the hen-birds over the waves, his plumage the colour of the sea! In making this comparison, Alcman means to say that he is now too old to join in the dance of the maidens. The lines thus form an apologetic prologue to an actual maiden-song.

Another famous fragment, and a more baffling one, is No. 89: 'Asleep are the hill-tops, and the glens and headlands and ravines; the woodland too, and the creatures which the black earth rears, the wild beasts of the mountains and the race of bees and monsters in the depths of the dark sea; asleep are the flocks of long-winged birds.' It would be easy, but probably mistaken, to regard this fragment in a romantic or sentimental light. To the poet whose emotions are deeply involved, the 'sleep of nature' needs a complement or a contrast. Thus Sappho observes that, though it is midnight and the moon and Pleiads have set, she sleeps alone. And in the perfect miniature by Goethe, *Wandrers Nachtlied,* assurance is given that the sleep which nature is now enjoying will soon settle on the weary traveller as well. But more than once in Greek literature the hush that lies over everything forms the eerie prelude to the epiphany of some god: a well-known and vivid example is found in the *Bacchae* of Euripides. It may be, then, that the present fragment comes from a poem in the narrative part of which a god is about to appear to a mortal. Little more can be said about it, even by way of surmise; but it may be legitimate to recall, as a possible parallel, that in Pindar's first Olympian ode Pelops calls upon Poseidon 'alone in the darkness'; and in the darkness the god manifests himself in answer to the prayer. What Pindar expresses in one pregnant phrase is expanded by Alcman into the noble vision quoted in the present fragment.

A second night-scene is depicted in another quotation by Athenaeus, No. 56: 'Often on the mountain-peaks, when the gods take their pleasure in the feast which is thronged with torches, you hold a vessel of gold, a great cup, of the shape that shepherds carry. Pouring into it with your hands the milk from a lioness, you fashion a hard cheese for Argeiphontas.'

The Greek makes it plain that a woman is being addressed. She is probably a bacchant, a votaress of Dionysus: the cult of that god is suggested by a number of features. First we have the night-time revelry in a remote spot, then the milk taken from a lioness, and finally the mention of Argeiphontas, an epithet of Hermes. Although there seems to be no obvious connexion between Dionysus and Hermes, Pausanias says that the latter god was shown on the Throne of Apollo at Amyclae 'carrying the infant Dionysus to heaven' (3.18.11).

The extant quotations contain a few specimens of Alcman's love-poetry: love-poetry, that is to say, which originally formed part of choral lyrics, since it does not necessarily reflect the author's own feelings, in the way that poems by Sappho, Alcaeus, and Archilochus often do. Relying on a very indirect tradition, Athenaeus speaks of Alcman as the actual inventor of love-poetry, and quotes the following snatches in illustration. No. 59a: 'Eros again, by the will of the Cyprian [Aphrodite], sweetly overflows my heart and melts it.' No. 59b: 'This gift of the sweet muses was shown forth by one blest among maidens, the fair-haired Megalostrata.' From another source may be quoted No. 58: 'It is not Aphrodite but wild Eros who plays his childish games as he comes down over the tips of the galingale-flowers; do not touch them, I beg you.' These elegant lines already display a view of the relationship between Aphrodite and her son Eros which survives for centuries in Greek poetry. As late as the Alexandrian age both Moschus and Apollonius of Rhodes portray a wanton Eros who is only intermittently under his mother's control. After these tantalizing fragments we turn with high expectations to

Music and poetry

Alcman's partheneion, or maiden-song, discovered in 1855 (No. 1); and our expectations are not disappointed, for the poem is a marvel of grace, full of light and colour. It offers formidable problems of interpretation, which are still very far from solution: these arise partly from the fragmentary state of the beginning and partly from the wealth of allusions, many of which are obscure to us. First a translation of the whole will be attempted, with the insertion of headings to indicate the contents, and then a discussion of the poem and its important details.

1. *The first legend* (lines 1–14). . . . Polydeuces; [I do not] count Lycaethus among the dead, but Enarsphorus and fleet-footed Sebrus and the violent . . . and the helmeted . . . and . . . and lord Areius and . . . pre-eminent among demi-gods; . . . the huntsman . . . the great and Eurytus . . . throng of . . . the noblest . . . we shall pass over . . . Fate of all . . . the eldest . . .

2. *Moral drawn from the first legend* (lines 15–19). Let [not] the winged daring of men fly to heaven [nor] attempt to violate lady . . . Aphrodite, nor any . . . nor a daughter of Porcus.

3. *The second legend* (lines 20–35). . . . and the Graces, whose eyes dart love, [dwell in?] the house of Zeus . . . divinity . . . to dear ones . . . gifts . . . youth . . . went; one of them [was killed] by an arrow, [another] by a marble mill-stone . . . Hades . . . They compassed wicked deeds and suffered unforgettable [pains].

4. *Moral drawn from the second legend* (lines 36–39). Divine vengeance does exist: prosperous is the man who is well-disposed [to the gods], and weaves the day to its end without weeping.

5. *The choral song proper* (lines 39–101). For myself, I sing of the radiance of Agido; I see her like the sun, which Agido summons to shine for us as a witness. But to praise or blame her I am utterly forbidden by the brilliant leader of our choir, who fancies that she stands out pre-eminent above all, as if there were set among grazing herds a powerful stallion, a prize-winner with ringing hoofs, of the race of winged dreams. Do you not see? She [Agido] is an Enetic courser; while the hair of my cousin Hagesichora blossoms like unalloyed gold, and as for her face, shining like silver, why should I tell you openly? Such is Hagesichora; but she who is second to Agido in beauty shall run as a Colaxaean horse against the Ibenian; for the Pleiads, rising through the ambrosial night like the star of Sirius, compete with us as we carry the plough at dawn. For an abundance of purple does not suffice to protect [us], nor dappled snake of solid gold, nor Lydian head-band, the delight of dark-eyed girls, nor even the tresses of Nanno, nor yet god-like Areta, nor Sylacis nor Cleësisera; nor will you go to the house of Aenesimbrota and say, 'may Astaphis be mine, and may Philylla look [upon me with favour], or Damareta, or lovely

Wianthemis'; but it is Hagesichora who keeps watch [?] over me. For is not Hagesichora of the lovely ankles here in this very place, and does she [not] stay [close to] Agido [?] and commend our festivities? Receive [the prayers] of these women, you gods; for fulfilment and accomplishment are in the hands of the gods. 'Choir-leader', I would say, 'I am only a maiden who screeches to no purpose, an owl from the roof-beam; yet, such as I am, I desire above all to propitiate Aotis: for she has proved the healer of our troubles, while it is through Hagesichora that [we] girls have entered upon the peace we longed for'. For to the trace-horse . . . and on ship-board too obedience must be given to the helmsman above all. She [Hagesichora] is not more melodious than the Sirens, for they are goddesses, whereas we are a choir of ten who sing, instead of eleven maidens, and the music we make is like that of the swan on the streams of the Xanthus; and she, with her lovely fair hair . . . (4 lines lost at the end).

The constant shifts, the sequence of apparently false starts, and the breaking-away along different and unexpected lines: all of these features together constitute a hall-mark of choral lyric in archaic times. And yet, if we penetrate beneath this brilliant but perplexing surface, we can detect the unifying themes of Alcman's maiden-song. At its heart lies the description of a rite in which the maidens are actually participating: the dedication of a plough just before sunrise. To what deity they dedicate the plough is not clear to us. Later in the poem a goddess Aotis ('She of the dawn'), otherwise unknown, is mentioned as the 'healer of our troubles'. Alcman does not make explicit the connexion between goddess and dedication; but it seems a reasonable supposition that the maidens dedicate the plough as a thank-offering, in gratitude to the goddess for healing their troubles. Nothing is said about the nature of these troubles: they might be political or merely personal. Closely connected with the rite is the theme of praise. Two women come in for repeated praise: Agido and Hagesichora. Their status and function have been much disputed. About Hagesichora, at least, an important clue is given in two passages. Reading the comment 'it is through Hagesichora that we girls have entered upon the peace we longed for' and observing that this comment immediately follows mention of the goddess, we might conclude that Hagesichora is a priestess or votary of high standing – at any rate the vehicle through whom the divine benefits have been bestowed. This view of Hagesichora is confirmed by the allusion to her presence and her commendation of the rite. About Agido we cannot feel so certain. She too, however, probably exercises some sacral office, in view of her close connexion with Hagesichora and of the description of her 'radiance' at the beginning of section 5. The word here translated 'radiance' is sometimes used in Greek to mean 'light of deliverance'; and, if Alcman is following this usage, he seems to allude to Agido as one who, like Hagesichora, is the human means whereby Aotis has exercised her healing power.

The great themes which dominate section 5, namely the description of the rite, the expression of gratitude to the goddess, and the compliments to her priestesses, are all essentially religious in character. The religious significance is conveyed in the first four sections. Despite their poor state of preservation, these are seen to recount episodes in which mortals took up arms against the gods and were terribly punished for so doing. In sections 2 and 4 mortal men are adjured to remember their due place and not to encroach upon the preserves of the gods, for they have power to harm. The dark deeds narrated in sections 1-4, and their shocking outcome, form a perfect foil to the light-hearted, and in places almost bantering, tone of the last section. But the inclusion of the first four sections by no means arises from a mere trick of style; on the contrary, these elements emphasize a profound religious truth never lost sight of in Greek archaic poetry, that the gods have great power to harm their enemies, but great power also to help their friends. It is in recognition of this fact that the choir make their dispositions of the rite, offering due praise to the goddess and to her helpers.

Although the claims of the divine are paramount, they do not preclude the celebration of the pleasure to be derived from human companionship and affection. Whether Alcman reflects the actual practice of contemporary Sparta or is following a literary convention, we cannot tell; but there is no mistaking the language of homosexual love used by the maidens of the choir. They give a list of the girls whose favour they desire, and allude to the possibility of resorting to the 'house of Aenesimbrota': in such a context she might be a procuress or, possibly, a purveyor of love-potions.

Fragments of another partheneion by Alcman (No. 3) turned up about a century after the discovery of No. 1. The underlying purpose of No. 3 cannot be grasped with certainty, but it seems to be concerned with a rite in honour of Hera. In the extant parts a girl named Astymeloisa occupies a prominent position. The choir are, or profess to be, deeply in love with her; they speak, with a feeling rarely found elsewhere in Greek poetry (except in Sappho), of the physical effects caused by Astymeloisa's mere presence:

> Olympian [muses] about my heart . . . song . . . to hear . . . of voice . . . singing a lovely ode . . . scatters sweet [sleep] from the

eyes . . . and leads me to go to the contest, [where] above all I shall toss my blond hair . . . soft feet . . .
[gap of 50 lines]
. . . and with desire that loosens the limbs, she looks at me more meltingly than sleep or death; and it is not at all by chance . . . sweet . . . but Astymeloisa makes no answer to me; but, holding a garland, like a star that flies through the glittering sky or a golden shoot or soft feathers, . . . she came with long strides . . . the moist charm of Cinyras which rests on maidens' hair . . . Astymeloisa up and down the host . . . the delight of the populace . . . having taken . . . would that . . . silver cup . . . let me but see . . . if she were to come close and take me by the soft hand, [I] would at once become her suppliant; but as it is . . .
[meagre fragments of the remainder]

Relics such as these bring home to us how much of Alcman is lost; but at least we now know enough of his poetry to comprehend the estimate formed of it by ancient critics. After Alcman no poets of any note practised their art at Sparta; and so it seems that the Spartan schools of elegiac and lyric verse, brilliant as they were, died out within less than a century. Other arts, however, had a much longer life; and these must next be considered.

Bibliography

Poetry in archaic Sparta: K. Hinze, *RhM* 83 (1934), 39–52; F. Stoessl, in *Eumusia, Festgabe für E. Howald* (Zürich, 1947), 92–114.

Tyrtaeus. Text (with the numeration followed here): M.L. West, *Iambi et elegi graeci* II (Oxford, 1972), 149–63. Text and translation: J.M. Edmonds, *Elegy and iambus* I (Loeb Classical Library) (London, 1931), 51-79. Text with Italian commentary: C. Prato, *Tyrtaeus* (Rome, 1968). The political background and the concept of valour: W. Jaeger, *Paideia* I (Berlin, 1959[4]) 125–39. The reading *argaleon* vs. *harpaleon:* C. Prato, *QU* 2 (1966), 115–19.

Terpander. B.A. van Groningen, *Mnemosyne* 18 (1955), 177–91.

Alcman. Text (with the numeration followed here): D.L. Page, *Poetae melici graeci* (Oxford, 1962), 1–91, *Supplementum lyricis graecis* (Oxford, 1974), 1–3. Text and translation: J.M. Edmonds, *Lyra graeca* I (Loeb Classical Library) (London, 1928[2]), 44–135. Text with Italian commentary: A. Garzya, *Alcmane, i frammenti* (Naples, 1954). General studies: C.M. Bowra, *Greek lyric poetry from Alcman to Simonides* (Oxford, 1961[2]), 16–73; H. Fränkel, *Dichtung und Philosophie des frühen Griechentums* (Munich, 1962[2]), 179–91; C. Calame, *Les chœurs de jeunes filles en Grèce archaïque* (Rome, 1977). Alcman's birth-place and social status: J.A. Davison, *From Archilochus to Pindar* (London, 1968), 173–6. The date of Alcman: M.L. West, *CQ* 59 (1965), 188–94; F.D. Harvey, *JHS* 87 (1967), 62–73. No. 41: Scaliger's *rhepei* for *herpei* is read. No. 17: V. Ehrenberg,

Hermes 68 (1933), 288–305. No. 89: R. Pfeiffer, *Hermes* 87 (1959), 1–6 (Pfeiffer's *hyla* for *phyla* is read in line 3). No. 56: F.M. Pontani, *Maia* 3 (1950), 36. Nos. 58 and 59: F.G. Sirna *Aegyptus* 53 (1973), 28–70. No. 1: D.L. Page, *Alcman, the Partheneion* (Oxford, 1951); M. Puelma, *MH* 34 (1977), 1–55. (In No. 1, line 77, *tērei* is read instead of *teirei*). No. 3: W. Peek, *Philologus* 104 (1960), 163–80; F.J. Cuartero, *CFC* 4 (1972), 367–82.

5

Art

The Protogeometric style is the first considerable new art-form to appear in Greece in the Iron Age. Athens was the great centre of this style; it is there that we can discern its beginning and trace its evolution. The transition to Protogeometric from the latest Mycenaean pottery-style is traceable in tomb-groups in the Ceramicus cemetery to the north-west of Athens. The profile of the pots becomes less globular, while the painted decoration becomes even more severe. The field is divided rigidly into horizontal zones. Concentric circles and semi-circles, drawn with a multiple brush, triangles, rectangles, and double or triple wavy lines are the decorative motifs most favoured by the vase-painters of Attic Protogeometric. Only when it has reached an advanced stage does Attic Protogeometric become known in Laconia; and even then Laconian potters produce something which is only a pale reflexion of the originals (*c.* 850–750). Taking Attic Protogeometric as their starting-point, they go their own way and in the end arrive at something different from the Attic exemplars. Much Protogeometric pottery has been discovered in Laconia, but little of it is yet published. The few complete vessels are humble objects of everyday use.

Like Protogeometric, the Geometric style of pottery-decoration arrived in Laconia later than in other parts of the Peloponnese. The new style was in vogue at Sparta from about 750 to about 650. Athenian potters initiated the style and produced most of the finest pieces now known. The pottery from Athenian cemeteries enables the development of the Geometric style to be traced in its homeland: at first, a lustrous black paint was applied to most of the surface, with the prominent parts decorated with continuous bands or isolated 'windows' of simple linear motifs such as meanders, rows of zig-zags, and lozenges. The Geometric artists eventually reached a point at which they covered the whole of the pot with horizontal bands of abstract motifs, sometimes varied by rows of highly-stylized animals or birds. A profound change came with the introduction of figured scenes into the abstract pattern. The scenes are, however, usually limited to a zone which is strictly demarcated from the patterns. The subjects depicted are for the most part of a funerary nature, for example the dead person on his bier, a row of mourning figures, and funeral-games including chariot-rides. The human beings and horses are drawn in silhouette, in a highly schematic manner. It is unknown whether the Geometric style was transplanted directly from Attica to Laconia. The undistinguished pieces of 'Middle Geometric' found in Laconia do not suffice to settle the point; but when figures appear on Laconian Geometric they show signs of influence from Argos and Corinth, and it is probable that those cities had long acted as intermediaries. Quite large quantities of Geometric sherds are known from Laconia, especially from excavations at the Amyklaion, the Spartan acropolis, and the Orthia sanctuary; and a few have been found at Scoglio del Tonno, near Taranto. Two *pyxides* (box-like cups without handles) may be chosen to illustrate the figured style of Laconian Geometric. The best-preserved, but not the best-drawn, *pyxis* from the Amyklaion has a figured zone containing a row of dancers with a bough and a lyre (fig. 13a). It is a likely hypothesis that the dance formed part of a ceremony in honour of one of the gods who had their cult at Amyclae. The lyre would represent the musical accompaniment, while the bough might be the object dedicated. The Geometric canons of drawing human figures are observed, although in no very individual or elegant manner. Below the zone run bands of patterns, perfunctorily rendered. Finer work is seen on the figured zone of a small *pyxis* from the Orthia sanctuary (fig. 13b). The free use of curves has imparted greater naturalism and suppleness to the man and the horses.

By the end of the eighth century, the self-sufficiency of mainland Greece (alike in commercial activity and in artistic inspiration) was coming to an end. Greek trade with the east and Greek expansion to the west mark the beginning of four hundred years of oversea involvement, which reached its climax with the conquests of Alexander the Great. The so-called Orientalizing Movement in Greek art did not, in general, bring

13 *Figured scenes on Geometric pottery: (a) from the Amyklaion, (b) and (c) from the Orthia sanctuary.*

about the direct transference of shapes or motifs to Greece from the Near East; the Greeks, rather, drew on their observation of artefacts in Egypt and the Levant so as to expand the range of their own creative activity. The Orientalizing Movement begins earlier in some places than in others. Corinth is the first city of all to loosen effectively the restraints of the Geometric style (late eighth century) and to adopt an entirely new concept of pottery-decoration: one which started to abandon the Geometric norm of closely-filled horizontal bands and set bold motifs against the surface of the entire pot. At the same time a whole range of new motifs was accepted into the pot-painter's repertory, and very high standards of craftsmanship were reached, especially in the detailed animal and human figures of the small vessels. Laconia was very slow to follow the Corinthian lead, and in fact Orientalizing vases were imported from Corinth into Laconia while local Geometric pottery was still being manufactured.

For much of the seventh century, the work of Laconian potters remained at an experimental stage. It is not until near the end of the century that we see the emergence of a distinctive Laconian style, indebted to but quite different from Corinthian. The techniques of incision before painting, over-all decoration of a vessel, and meticulous drawing of figures have all been mastered – at least in the hands of the more accomplished artists. A fine cup from Tomb 285 at Taranto (which also contained Corinthian ware) gives a good idea of what the best Laconian potters were capable of soon after 600 (pl. 10). The two-handled cup is a favourite shape in Laconian pottery for the next century or so, especially for exported vessels. In the interior of the Taranto cup tunny-fish are arranged about a central rosette, and near the rim glide seven dolphins: both fish and dolphins are rendered in black and red. The exterior of the cup is embellished with a frieze common in Corinthian and Laconian pottery; this may contain animals or, as on the Taranto cup, birds. The details of the birds are shown in the purple paint which is very often used in Laconian pottery-decoration.

The sixth century is the great period of Laconian pottery, as it is of other arts. Modern research has reached the point at which it is possible to identify the products of individual painters, or at least of their workshops. It was many years before credence was given to the existence of any school of pottery-painting in Laconia. Until the excavation of the Orthia sanctuary provided an unbroken sequence of native wares extending from the Geometric age into the fifth century, it was widely believed that what we now call Laconian pottery was made at Cyrene in North Africa. This belief seemed to receive support first from the depiction of a Cyrenaean scene on the Arcesilas Cup (p. 86), second from the unlikeli-

Art

hood that such a backward, militaristic, and philistine city as Sparta had given rise to a creditable ceramic style of her own. This picture of Sparta is not inaccurate, but it is anachronistic: it shows what Sparta became by the fifth century, but it gives a completely false impression of Sparta as she had been in the two previous centuries. As for the painting on the Arcesilas Cup, that certainly provides a valuable historical document, but one which must be read otherwise than it used to be. Like the rest of the 'Laconian' ceramic wares, it was fabricated in Laconia; and presumably at Sparta, since it has not yet been possible to identify any other Laconian city which might plausibly have been the centre of a flourishing ceramic industry. Yet the Cyrenaean scene does of course point to an association, of a close kind, between Cyrene and Laconia. West of Cyrene stands the coastal site of Tocra, where modern excavation has revealed the presence of significant amounts of Laconian pottery, together with vases from Corinth and elsewhere. Naucratis, on the Nile delta, has long been known as a find-place of Laconian pottery; and in fact one of the recognized Laconian artists of the sixth century has been given the name of the 'Naucratis Painter'. The discovery of Laconian pottery in southern Italy, and particularly in the neighbourhood of Taranto, causes no great surprise, in view of the Spartan colony at Taras. But the considerable number of good Laconian vases from tombs in Etruria is, at first sight, hard to account for. So is the heavy deposit of Laconian fragments (well over a hundred) on the island of Samos, which has yielded more Laconian pottery than any other area of the Mediterranean; a little comes also from Rhodes and from Smyrna in Ionia.

The subject-matter of the figured scenes may be judged from the samples examined below. There are representations of gods and heroes (especially Heracles); but the artists seem to have been fascinated above all by the possibilities offered by birds and animals, including creatures of fancy. Birds incongruously invade banqueting-scenes, comast-scenes, and rider-scenes. We shall observe one battle-scene, but that is something of a rarity; when the painters depicted real life, they preferred to portray conviviality or the chase.

We may look first at the Naucratis Painter, whose forte lay in drawing animal-friezes, comprising lions, horned goats, cocks, and also sphinxes. Corinthian influence is strong in these depictions. A two-handled amphora from Vulci, in Etruria, comes from his hand: the major decorative band, running round the shoulder, contains eight antithetically disposed animals: animal and bird motifs occupy the other decorative bands. On his shallow cups the Naucratis Painter usually expresses his predilection for animals on the exterior. On one example from the Louvre a sphinx has taken over the interior, which it fills completely except for the usual accessorial decoration (fish and curvilinear pattern). This method of decorating the inside of a cup is the hall-mark of Laconian painted pottery in the sixth century. It is seen on another cup by the Naucratis Painter (pl. 11). The seated figure is that of Zeus *Lykaios* (an Arcadian cult-name) with his attendant eagle. The extensive, perhaps excessive, use of incision is noticeable here; also the stiff, rather lifeless, pose of the god, whose arms and hands are not represented. A defective sense of proportion has made the eagle too large for the scene, so that one of its wings is actually touching the god's knees. In this case, expertise at depicting individual animals and birds and combining them into a frieze has not proved equal to the task of integrating bird and god into a convincing whole. Unlike many other Laconian artists, the Naucratis Painter does not illustrate episodes from heroic legend; he depicts either gods or, occasionally, human beings engaged in some contemporary activity. A cup from Etruria illustrates a stylized symposium, with the drinkers reclining round a central motif (pl. 12). A large crater, in which the wine was mixed with water, stands in their midst; a boy moves among the banqueters, carrying a wine-jug and also a chaplet with which to crown one of them. Other chaplets are brought by fantastic winged creatures with elegantly drawn bodies, arms and hands. The scene has sometimes been interpreted as a funeral-banquet; but there are insufficient grounds for that hypothesis, and it is better to think that we have here the depiction of a drinking-party as it might actually have occurred in sixth-century Sparta, only with the addition of purely imaginary creatures, which come from the painter's own stock of motifs.

From the idealized symposium of the Naucratis Painter it is no long step to the depiction of an actual scene by the Arcesilas Painter. The latter is so called from his best-known work, the Arcesilas Cup, which was first published in 1833 (pl. 13). This is the most famous, although not the most skilfully executed, example of Laconian pottery, and it is rich in historical implications. The scene painted on its interior is, by the standard of Laconian potters, unusually crowded with human figures who are taking part in a specific activity at a specific place. At the left sits a man who is identified by the appended inscription as Arcesilas; and this can only be Arcesilas II, who ruled at Cyrene from about 565 to 560. The scene must therefore be Cyrene. The king presides over the weighing of some substance into containers. On the same level as the king stands an overseer directing the work, while his assistants perform the actual weighing or carry full bags to join those already stacked at the bottom. The scene is effectively divided into three horizontal zones, first by the bar of the scales and second by the ground-level upon which the king's chair rests. The serene composure of the king is set in contrast to the bustle about him: the overseer shouting his orders and the workmen weighed down by their burdens. Two of the king's domestic pets are close by: his monkey squatting on a pole at the top and his cat stretched out beneath his chair. The artist has done his best to add authenticity to the scene by inscribing a word by each of the figures. The name ARKESILAS immediately identifies the protagonist, but the other words are of obscure significance; at least one of them, MAEN, cannot be Greek and, unless the writer has made some error, it might be an Egyptian name. It has been suggested that the words convey the respective personal names of the participants, just as ARKESILAS conveys the king's name; but it is inconceivable that the artist was acquainted with the names of such humble individuals or thought that they would be of the smallest interest to the eventual owner of the cup. According to another hypothesis, the words name not the individuals but their occupations; but that is hardly more credible, since men engaged in the simple activity of weighing out bags would not have been differentiated by special occupation-terms. The nature of the substance weighed is likewise a matter of dispute: it is sometimes identified as wool, sometimes as silphium, a medicinal plant for which Cyrene was famous. The very place where the weighing is done remains in doubt. Does it take place on board ship or in the market-place of Cyrene? Over and above these questions there is a more serious one, to which no convincing answer has ever been given: why should a Laconian artist go to such trouble to paint a detailed scene of life at Cyrene – especially if his work was destined for an Etruscan recipient?

No such difficulty attends the interpretation of a mythological scene by the Arcesilas Painter. The two Titans Atlas and Prometheus confront each other; the first holds up the sky with his head and arms, the second is tied to a post and has his liver torn out by an eagle (pl. 14). The scene is reminiscent of a description in Hesiod, which reads (in slightly condensed form): 'And, through harsh compulsion, Atlas bears with unwearied head and arms the broad heaven, standing at the ends of the earth; for this is the fate that Zeus the Counsellor allotted to him. And he tied the quick-witted Prometheus with cruel bonds, driving a pillar through his middle, and set upon him an eagle; this kept feeding on his immortal liver . . .' (*Theogony* 517–523). Hesiod does not state in so many words that Prometheus and Atlas endured their punishment in the same place, but the artist quite naturally assumes that they did: he brings out with reasonable success the agony of the one and the straining limbs of the other.

A striking realization of a mythical beast, and one perfectly adapted to the round field of a cup, is seen in the masterpiece of the Chimaera

Painter (pl. 15). The chimaera is envisaged by this artist as a winged lion, breathing fire; and the shape of the cup is actually turned to advantage in showing one of the powerful fore-paws raised, as if about to strike. The formidable muscles are well suggested by curved lines, boldly incised, and the strength of the whole monstrous creature is emphasized by the presence of the delicate bird between the fore-paws.

Two artists who excelled in the depiction of human figures are the Rider Painter and the Hunt Painter. The work of the former may be illustrated by two cups. The first (pl. 16) shows a stately horseman with birds and a winged figure carrying chaplets. We may recall the winged chaplet-bearers in the banquet-scene by the Naucratis Painter (pl. 12), and thus doubt the interpretation of the scene as the crowning of a successful athlete by a winged Victory. Winged attendants are obviously part of the stock-in-trade of Laconian vase-painters. On another cup by the Rider Painter two naked revellers, or comasts, are depicted standing on either side of a large crater (pl. 17); one is preparing to draw wine from it, while the other plays on the pipes; there are, of course, birds in attendance.

An important work of the Hunt Painter is a large hydria, or pitcher, from Rhodes. The whole body is segmented horizontally, many of the bands containing abstract motifs. The two principal zones between the side-handles are devoted to scenes with figures. On the front a combat is in progress between two warriors each equipped with thrusting-spear, round shield, helmet, and greaves (pl. 18). That this forms part of a larger battle is indicated by the warrior who lies fallen and by the two riders on horse-back who give their support on either side. The riders provide an element of rest in the composition (analogous to the part of the king on the Arcesilas Cup), in contrast to the vigorous activity displayed in the centre. The names of the two horsemen and the two hoplites are inscribed alongside the respective figures. On the back of the hydria we have a depiction of padded dancers (pl. 19), performing lascivious antics as they had done for long past on Corinthian pottery; and it is from that source that the convention became known in Laconian art. The hydria as a whole is a distinguished product of the Hunt Painter's workshop. His mastery is evident in the satisfying proportions of the vessel, in the delicate incision, and in the tasteful distribution of colour: black for most of the figures but red for some details, such as the equipment of the warriors, the horses' manes, and stripes on the birds' wings. Unlike the types of Laconian pottery considered so far, the Rhodian hydria is modelled on metallic prototypes. The palmettes attached to the horizontal handles and the lion-heads are taken straight from a well-known class of bronze vessels, which will be discussed presently.

Art

Standing apart from the painted ware, and also from plain undecorated pots intended for domestic use, are a small number of impressive clay amphorae. These were not painted, but had applied to their exterior scenes in relief made from moulds. Relief-amphorae have long been known from Boeotia and the Cycladic islands. A large fragment of a good Laconian example was revealed by the excavation of the heroum near the Eurotas (p. 51). The relief on the neck depicts the press of battle, with a helmeted warrior throwing his spear. On the shoulder, a warrior accompanied by his dog drives a two-horse chariot. A rather less fine amphora, though preserved entire, comes from the theatre by the Spartan acropolis. Its relief shows a repeated chariot-scene. The best of the type was found in the tomb-complex already described (p. 50). Two distinct scenes are represented, one on the neck and one on the shoulder. The neck-scene portrays the successful conclusion of a hunting-expedition: two huntsmen, with their hounds, carry off their dead prey – a lion, a boar, a long-horned goat, and a deer (pl. 20). The subject-matter recalls the motifs of some Laconian painted pots, especially the work of the Hunt Painter; but here the artist has added a heroic touch by introducing a lion. No doubt, as the excavator remarked, the hunting-scene is meant to recall the exploits of the man buried in one of the graves. The frieze below contains two repeated panels. A grandee in a finely-ornamented tunic drives a two-horse chariot, while by his side strides a warrior armed with helmet, shield, and spears. So the amphora shows two aspects of the life of the warrior-caste. Our examination of Spartan cults, of Spartan poetry (especially that of Alcman), and of the painted pottery precludes us from supposing that hunting and warfare were the sole interests of the Spartiates; nevertheless, when an artist made an amphora specifically for a Spartiate tomb he singled out these two activities to be the subjects of his friezes. The chariot-driver on this amphora (*c.* 600) displays none of the austerity later associated with the Spartan way of life; in fact, the artist has done his best to bring out the magnificence of his dress and his equipage.

As we saw just now, the Hunt Painter modelled his splendid clay hydria on prototypes in metal. A number of bronze hydrias of Greek workmanship come from sites in Italy and the northern Peloponnese during the first three quarters of the sixth century. One well-marked type will be of special interest to us. Upon this, the two small horizontal handles at the side have palmettes attached. A much higher degree of elaboration is reached in the treatment of the large vertical handle. Its lower part takes the form of a woman's head, while from the top of the handle lions stretch out along the rim. Further detail is often added in the shape of a palmette below the woman's head, of a ram on either side of her head, or of snakes wriggling up the handle. On a few hydrias the woman's head is replaced by that of a gorgon. The archaic gorgon is the most terrifying manifestation of Greek art; her protruding tongue and snakes instead of hair witness the belief in her petrifying power, described by Pindar and later poets. The principal centres of the development of the gorgon in art during the sixth century seem to have been Corinth and Sparta. Where the hydrias with women and gorgons were themselves manufactured we cannot say with certainty; but a Laconian workshop was probably responsible for at least some of them, and it is possible that Spartan influence extended to workshops at Corinth and in Italy.

In contrast to the closed shape of the hydria is the open crater: in effect a large mixing-bowl. Three bronze craters, and fragments of others, are dated to a late phase of the sixth century. Two were excavated in tombs at Trebenischte, in Yugoslavia; the third, which came from Campania, is now in Munich. Each of these craters is equipped with two elaborate volute-handles; and, as with the vertical handles of the hydrias, the lower part is formed by the head and bust of a gorgon from which, instead of legs, two snakes branch out. The two Trebenischte craters show on their neck an animated relief-scene of horses being ridden at the gallop.

Despite the difference in shape, some decorative details of the craters are closely similar to those of the hydrias; and this fact has prompted the suggestion that hydrias and craters come from the same workshop, or from a connected group of workshops. We must now relate to the three craters already mentioned a fourth, which is much larger and more imposing than any of them. This has become known as the Vix Crater, from its discovery in 1953 in a tumulus-burial at Vix near Chatillon-sur-Seine. The offerings in the tomb fall into two groups; objects of local manufacture and imports from Etruria and Greece (including the Vix Crater). In both groups are found artefacts of precious metals and of exquisite workmanship.

The Vix Crater weighs some 458 pounds and stands nearly sixty-seven inches high. In the treatment of the handles it comes closest to the Munich Crater, although it is far more elaborate. The gorgon has snakes for legs, and a pair of snakes writhe upwards from behind her arms. On either side of each handle a console carries a regardant lion, fashioned to the same high standards which distinguish the whole work (fig. 14, pl. 21). Riveted to the neck are twenty-three groups in relief, each comprising a helmeted and greaved warrior with shield who marches in front of a light four-horse chariot driven by another warrior. The groups are not simply repeated without variation; for instance, the treatment of the horse nearest the viewer differs from group to group. When the groups were detached from the crater after excavation, it was found that each of them bore a mark on its reverse side corresponding to a mark on the neck of the crater itself. This discovery not only indicates the matchless care lavished on the construction and decoration of the crater but provides a valuable clue to its place of manufacture. Some of the marks are in fact letters of the Greek alphabet, and specifically the Laconian alphabet. Leaving aside the presence of Laconian letters, we might have thought that Chalcis or Corinth was no less likely as a place of origin than Sparta; but this piece of evidence must be allowed to tilt the balance of

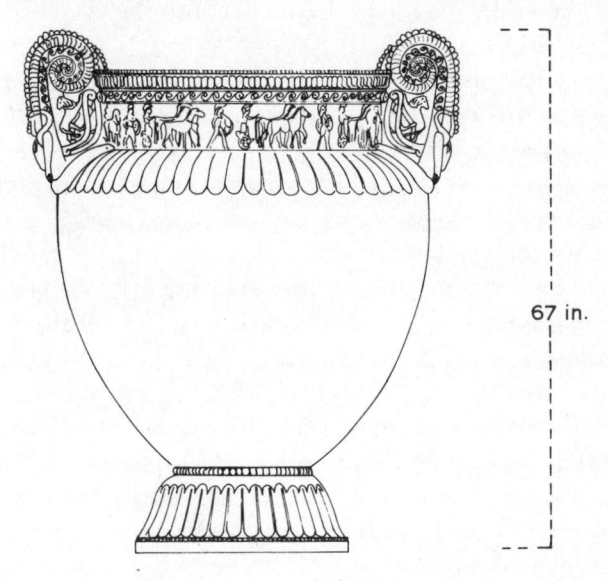

14 *Sketch of the Vix Crater.*

probability irresistibly towards the conclusion that the Vix Crater was made in Sparta, or perhaps at a Laconian workshop in southern Italy.

When the Vix Crater was dug out of the soil, it was found to be covered by a bronze lid. Out of a deep depression in the centre of this lid there rises a plinth bearing the bronze statuette of a robed woman (pl. 22). The left arm is extended to the front, while the right is held to the side. The stiffness of the pose and the serenity of the face can be paralleled over and over again in the heads and figurines (both in clay and in bronze) from archaic Sparta. Such wares, in fact, have a long and distinguished history at Sparta; and it may be of interest to trace the principal stages of their development.

We begin with the late Geometric period. Geometric bronze-work is known from many Greek sites: it comprises, as well as articles of everyday use or adornment, statuettes of small animals, mythical creatures, and human beings. The makers of these bronze miniatures did not yet have at their disposal a completely satisfactory technique for casting bronze, and they had to proceed for the most part by cutting and chiselling bars of metal. The shapes they produced, with unnatural bulges and attenuations, bear a close affinity to the human figures drawn by the Geometric vase-painters. This style allowed the manufacture of fine work, as can be seen above all in a small bronze horse from Olympia. Similar horses are known from Laconia as well, but they are now so badly corroded that their quality cannot be assessed. The sanctuary of Artemis Orthia, however, yielded a Geometric bronze, in which the schematization of the human frame is taken to its practicable limits (pl. 23). This bronze is like nothing found elsewhere in Greece, although sketchy representations of human figures are known from Athens. The effect induced in the observer by the Orthia bronze is a powerful one since, in revealing only the essential framework of the human body, the artist has omitted everything irrelevant to his purpose: flesh, bodily organs, and facial features.

Next in time comes the bronze figurine of a woman from the Menelaion, belonging to the seventh century (pl. 24). With this bronze we are in a different world from that of the Geometric example just described. Again, no precise parallel to this bronze is known, so that it is difficult to say whether it arises from an isolated experiment or forms one of a series. But it is clear that certain problems of representing the human figure have not been surmounted: the posture is stiff and awkward, while the head is too large for the body, and the mouth too large for the face.

A woman's head in moulded clay from the Spartan acropolis (pl. 25) shows some advance towards a more naturalistic type than the preceding bronze, despite the closeness in date of the two artefacts. The buff clay has been modelled to give quite faint indications of nose, mouth, chin, and eyes; pupils, ears, hair, and necklace are drawn, crudely but effectively, in dark brown paint. As with the Menelaion bronze, we cannot tell whether this head represents an entire school or the effort of an individual artist; the depiction of human features, at any rate, is still fairly unrestrained and has not yet been brought within the restraints imposed by an artistic formula.

Such a formula was evolved later in the seventh century by artists in the Dorian states of Laconia, Crete, Corinth, and Rhodes. By reacting upon one another, these four schools produced what is now known as 'Dedalic', the classic style of Doric plastic art. A terracotta head may represent Laconian Dedalic (pl. 26). As with the whole series, the head is so fashioned as to appear to look slightly downwards, in contrast to the upward gaze of the two preceding figures. The rather pointed chin, curved and full lips, and summarily rendered eyes are all characteristic of Laconian Dedalic. The hair falls in long tresses on either side, and on the top it is held by a narrow head-dress.

The Dedalic style at its best could produce powerful results, but there was always about it something heavy and unyielding, which inhibited progress towards greater flexibility and naturalism. That movement came in the sixth century, with the assimilation of Dorian weight and Ionian grace. On a huge scale, the two artistic traditions came together in Apollo's Throne at Amyclae (p. 65). In miniature bronzes too the effect is an impressive one. It is well exemplified in a work of the mid-sixth century: a bronze mirror with a stand in the shape of a woman (pl. 27). The mirror was found with other bronzes, presumably forming a votive deposit, on the slopes of the Taygetus mountain. Although the woman is nude, she wears some festive ornaments and carries offerings in her hands. The artist seems to have visualized a young woman taking part in some open-air festival, probably one held in the neighbourhood of Sparta. In artistic quality, the mirror easily survives comparison with similar examples from other parts of Greece: the female figure is statuesque without being stiff or ponderous. A somewhat later, and quite different, expression of the art of Laconian bronze-smiths is seen in the bearded figure found at Olympia in 1955 (pl. 28). The intent expression on the face and the well-rendered muscles of the body need no emphasis. What the hands held has been lost; but the figure is in the familiar pose of Zeus hurling his thunderbolt, and that is the most likely interpretation of our bronze.

In complete contrast to these fine bronzes stands the figure of a bull from the acropolis (pl. 29). Besides the usual incised lines on neck and body, which give a rough indication of hair, the bull bears an inscription in bold characters, ATHANAIAS, certifying its dedication to the principal goddess of the acropolis. Many similar bronzes, representing bulls and other animals, are known from the late sixth century: by this date they were being mass-produced.

Finally two bronzes must be mentioned as showing the skill which some Laconian artists still brought to their work shortly before their activity ceased early in the fifth century. The excavator of the nude male figure (pl. 30) called it a 'trumpeter' because of the arm raised as if holding a trumpet. We cannot now accept this interpretation. The Spartans marched to battle to the sound of pipes, and the use of trumpets among them is never mentioned; furthermore, the bent arm of the bronze does not belong to the original construction of the piece. It is, however, easy to agree with the estimate of this bronze as a 'little masterpiece of Spartan art'. The powerful, muscular body of the young man has been very well caught, and we must remain in ignorance about the activity in which he is engaged. A bronze miniature of a boy (pl. 31) evinces a quality which would not immediately be associated with the Spartans or their art: an irresistible charm. He is a nude from the Amyklaion, wearing a pert smile and a head-dress of extraordinary type. The objects (presumably offerings) which the boy held in his hands have been broken off; so that, while appreciating the quality of the work, we cannot know the exact purpose for which it was made.

An arresting class of votives from the Orthia deposit comprise what are loosely described as terracotta 'masks': loosely, because they were not actually used as masks, and in fact their purpose is mysterious. Most of the best work belongs to the sixth century. The poignant mask of an old person (man or woman?) displays with crude vigour the wrinkles on the face, the hopeless mouth, the few remaining teeth (pl. 32). Nothing resembling such masks is known from other Greek cities, and they may be regarded (if anything may) as authentic products of a purely local art. The smaller gorgon-mask (pl. 33) is well-rendered work of its type, with features less boldly accentuated than on the masks of old persons. The snub-nose, protruding tongue, and snaky hair are all essential elements of the gorgon-head (p. 90): comparison may be made with a sixth century roof-tile(*akroterion*) from Sparta(pl. 34). Different in conception from the masks discussed so far is a life-sized fragment of a head modelled in thick clay (pl. 35). Although this could not actually be 'worn', it was perhaps held in front of the face. But all conjecture about the purpose of these offerings seems pointless; we must accept them as very welcome illustrations of the diversity and skill of Spartan plastic art in its finest period.

Absolutely characteristic of Spartan votive-offerings are the lead figurines. These have been found at each one of the major sanctuaries and above all at the Orthia site, which has yielded tens of thousands of these objects, mainly from the sixth century (pl. 36, pl. 37). Beginning with quite careful work, showing affinities with plaques in ivory, the figurines degenerate into mass-produced types. The range of subjects depicted is enormous: animals (both real and legendary), gods and goddesses, warriors, musicians, ornaments.

Soft limestone was carved in relief to produce votives at the Orthia sanctuary. The most popular subject was the horse. A good example is illustrated in pl. 38: the inscription (running from left to right along the top edge and continuing down the right-hand side) reads 'Thiokormidas dedicated [it] to Wo[r]theia'. Spartan artists used marble for their finer

Art

reliefs. An excellent specimen may fittingly represent a whole series of hero-reliefs (pl. 39). The dead couple are shown seated on a high, straight-backed chair, the man looking directly at the spectator. The snake at the back of the chair is a familiar accompaniment of chthonic scenes. Two much smaller figures approach from the right, bringing offerings to the heroized dead; the man presents a cock and an egg, the woman a pomegranate. Wine too has presumably been brought, since the dead hero holds a large goblet *(kantharos)*. The artist has followed a convention which seeks to bridge the gap between this world and the other. The view of the after-life here exemplified has no room for the concept of the dead as insubstantial shades: they are regarded as delighting in the food and drink offered by their votaries in the hero-cults. Plate 40 illustrates a relief of different type, in which the workmanship is considerably less careful. At the top, in a kind of pediment, the egg and the snakes stand as chthonic symbols. Below, depicted in a very stiff (almost heraldic) pose, are Helen's brothers the Dioscuri. They wear a kind of loose cloak *(chlamys)*, and are carrying long javelins in readiness for hunting. The tall lidded amphorae between the heroes are undoubtedly cult-symbols, but what they signify is not known for certain.

The Orthia sanctuary proved more prolific in carved ivories than any other site in mainland Greece. Out of such a profusion of ivories, dating from the seventh and sixth centuries, one can do little more than choose a few which illustrate the development of style and technique. Very early in the series comes a small plaque attached to a bronze pin (pl. 41). In manner and content this piece closely follows oriental models. The fantastic female figure, winged, crowned, and dressed in a long skirt, fills the whole of the available space: with each hand she grasps a bird. Do we see here the uncritical reproduction of a foreign type, or the adaptation of that type so as to represent the goddess of the sanctuary? The close association with wild creatures is certainly a well-marked feature of later depictions of Artemis (p. 55); and it is possible that this characteristic was common to Artemis and to her predecessor in the Orthia cult.

A somewhat later date should be given to a poorly-preserved ivory comb (pl. 42). It illustrates one of the most famous and most portentous episodes of Greek legend, in which Paris awards the prize of beauty to Aphrodite, by holding out an apple to her. Aphrodite's unsuccessful rivals, Athena and Hera, come behind. The pastoral aspect of Paris is completely lost sight of here: he is regarded as an oriental king, seated on a low throne and dispensing his favours. The statuesque character of the preceding plaque is seen again here, but the carver of the comb shows an advance towards the representation of a narrative scene. The three goddesses are differentiated by their dress, and there is an awareness of the demands of a composition. The bird on the right seems to be brought in as an inadequate counterbalance to Paris; it resembles those inquisitive, but idle, birds already noticed on Laconian vases (p. 86).

Later than the comb comes a plaque, broken at the left, displaying another legendary scene (pl. 43). A Centaur shows the extremity of his agony as his hair is clutched and a dagger driven into his side by a Lapith, during the furious struggle which ensued when the Centaurs attempted to carry off the Lapith women.

Spartan ivory-carving reaches its acme in two pieces of the sixth century. The type of recumbent animal, carved in the round, becomes a common one: it is given the most elaborate expression in a group of three figures (pl. 44). A lioness is intent on devouring a calf, the head of which protrudes from her mouth. A diminutive man (whose head is missing) catches the beast unawares, swiftly goes down on one knee, and plunges his dagger into her neck. To freeze all these stages of the action, express them as one, and render them in an intractable material argues for a mastery paralleled only in a large plaque (pl. 45). A warship is about to set sail (or, less probably, is just approaching land). The round shields of hoplites hang over the side, and the heads of some of the warriors can be seen. One man plays a fish from the prow; underneath his line another member of the crew seems to be inspecting the fabric of the ship. At the stern, the captain (whose head is lost) greets, or says farewell to, a long-skirted woman, who is stepping on the paddle. So far as we know this plaque could equally well represent a scene of real life (like the lioness-group) or a legendary episode (like the Judgment of Paris or the fight between Lapiths and Centaurs). The many-sided activity about the ship is conveyed in a convincing manner; but the individual figures are not carved with great fidelity, while the proportions of the whole are defective. The dedication to the goddess WORTHAIA is incised on the bow of the ship. At some point in the sixth century the supply of ivory seems to have dried up; thereafter some of the artistic motifs previously employed on ivory were transferred to objects of bronze.

Finally must be mentioned the head and trunk of a helmeted warrior (pl. 46). This is part of a marble figure, of more than life-size, from the region to the south of Athena's temple on the acropolis. It is good work of the first quarter of the fifth century, and is the only example of sculpture on such a scale ever to be found at Sparta. The excavator, and many other writers on the subject, have considered it out of the question that a native sculptor was capable of the competent craftsmanship displayed by this statue, and have suggested that it was made in Athens. There is, however, no positive reason for thinking of Athens as the place of fabrication. And whom does the statue represent? If we agree with a frequently-expressed view, we shall say that Spartans at the appropriate period would have considered only one of their warriors worthy to stand on their acropolis; and that man is Leonidas. The probability is strong; but again no single fact can be found to give it support.

Bibliography

Protogeometric pottery: W. von Massow, *AM* 52 (1927), 46–9; V.R.d'A. Desborough, *Protogeometric pottery* (Oxford, 1952), 283–90. Two sherds from Thouria: R. Hope Simpson, *ABSA* 52 (1957), 245.

Geometric pottery: W. von Massow, *op. cit.*, 49–53; J.P. Droop, *AO*, 54–66; E.A. Lane, *ABSA*, 34 (1933–1934), 101–7; J.N. Coldstream, *Greek Geometric pottery* (London, 1968), 214–19.

Pottery of the seventh and sixth centuries. General studies: J.P. Droop, *JHS* 30 (1910), 1–34, *AO*, 70–113; O. Waldhauer, *JDAI* 38–9 (1923–1924), 28–37; E.A. Lane, *op. cit.*, 115–89; E. Homann-Wedeking, *Archaische Vasenornamentik* (Athens, 1938), 56–67; B.B. Shefton, *ABSA* 49 (1954), 299–310; P. Pelagatti in *Enciclopedia dell'arte antica, classica e orientale* IV (Rome, 1961), 445–50; R.M. Cook, *Greek painted pottery* (London, 1972²), 93–101; C.M. Stibbe, *Lakonische Vasenmaler des 6. Jhts. v.Chr.* (Amsterdam, 1972). The Naucratis Painter: G.P. Schaus, *AJA* 83 (1979), 102–6. The Arcesilas Cup: F. Chamoux, *Cyrène sous la monarchie des Battiades* (Paris, 1953), 258–63. The Rider Painter: C. Rolley, *BCH* 83 (1959), 275–84. The Rhodian hydria: L. Laurenzi in *Clara Rhodos* VIII (Rhodes, 1936), 85–95. Laconian pottery from Olympia: W. Gauer *Olympische Forschungen* VIII (Berlin, 1975), 136, 137, 169, 210. Laconian pottery from Perachora: B.B. Shefton in *Perachora* II (ed. T.J. Dunbabin) (Oxford 1962), 378–85. Laconian pottery from Samos: E. Walter-Karydi, *Samos* VI/1 (Bonn, 1973), 28, 32, 42, 43; H.P. Isler, *Samos* IV (Bonn, 1978), 102, 103, 166, 167. Laconian pottery from Tocra: J. Boardman and J. Hayes, *Excavations at Tocra* I (London, 1966), 81–95, II (London, 1973), 39–41. Laconian pottery in the Taranto Museum: P. Pelagatti, *ASAA* 33–4 (1955–1956), 11–44. Connexions between Laconian art and the eastern Aegean: E. Langlotz, *AM* 77 (1962), 115–17.

Relief-pottery. General: A. de Ridder, *BCH* 22 (1898), 439–71, 497–519; F. Courby, *Les vases grecs à reliefs* (Paris, 1922); J. Schäfer, *Studien zu den griechischen Reliefpithoi* (Kallmünz, 1957). Laconian: A.J.B. Wace, *ABSA* 12 (1905–1906), 292; A.M. Woodward, *ABSA* 27 (1925–1926), 199–201; Chr. A. Christou, *AD* 19/A' (1964), 164–265.

Bronze hydrias: K.A. Neugebauer, *RM* 38–9 (1923–1924) 371–83, *AA* (1925), 177–203; L. Polites, *AE* (1936), 147–74; G. Vallet and F. Villard, *BCH* 79 (1955), 70–4; C. Rolley, *BCH* 87 (1963), 459–84.

Gorgons: Th.G. Karagiorga, *AD* 19/A' (1964), 116–22.

Bronze craters: K.A. Neugebauer, *RM* 38–9 (1923–1924), 383–93. The Vix Crater: P. Amandry, *RA* 43 (1954), 125–40; R. Joffroy, *Le trésor de Vix* (Paris, 1954); A. Rumpf in *Charites, Studien zur Altertumswissenschaft* (ed. K. Schauenberg) (Bonn, 1957), 127–35; L.H. Jeffrey, *The local scripts of archaic Greece* (Oxford, 1961), 191–2.

Miniature bronzes and terracottas. The earliest types: E. Kunze, *AM* 55 (1930), 141–62. Laconian miniatures: E. Langlotz, *Frühgriechische Bildhauerschulen* (Nuremberg, 1927), 86–98; R.J.H. Jenkins, *ABSA* 33 (1932–1933), 66–79, *Dedalica* (Cambridge, 1936); E. Homann-Wedeking, *AuA* 7 (1958), 63–72; R.A. Higgins, *Greek terracottas* (London, 1967), 23–4; G. Kaulen, *Daidalika* (Munich, 1967). Bronze mirrors: Th.G. Karagiorga, *AD* 20/A' (1965), 96–109. Bronze boy from the Amyklaion: P. Wolters, *JDAI* 11 (1896), 1–10.

Relief-plaques: H. Dressel and A. Milchhoefer, *AM* 2 (1877), 443–74; A. Furtwängler, *La Collection Sabouroff* I (Berlin, 1883–1887), 25–37; M.N. Tod and A.J.B. Wace *A catalogue of the Sparta Museum* (Oxford, 1906), 102–18; M. Andronikos, *Pel* 1 (1956), 253–314.

Ivories. General study: E.-L.I. Marangou, *Lakonische Elfenbein- und Beinschnitzereien* (Tübingen, 1969). Oriental antecedents: F. Poulsen, *Der Orient und die frühgriechische Kunst* (Leipzig/Berlin 1912), 111–16. Judgment of Paris: R. Hampe in *Neue Beiträge zur klassischen Altertumswissenschaft, Festschrift zum 60. Geburtstag von B. Schweitzer* (Stuttgart, 1954), 77–86.

'Leonidas' statue: A.M. Woodward, *ABSA* 26 (1923–1925), 253–66; G. Karo, *Greek personality in archaic sculpture* (Cambridge, Mass., 1948), 156–8.

6

The era of Spartan expansion (800–540 B.C.)

For the early part of the Iron Age, down to the middle of the eighth century, archaeological evidence provides the sole reliable source for the development of Sparta; and the extreme paucity of that evidence has been emphasized in earlier chapters. Little of value can be deduced about the course of Spartan history in this period. At least one fact seems reasonably certain, namely that the period witnessed the formation of a unified state, embracing Sparta itself, Amyclae, the outlet to the sea at Helos, and probably also Gytheum, with its excellent harbour. It is often assumed that power was concentrated at Sparta from the very outset of the Iron Age and that Sparta subsequently extended her sway over the rest of Laconia, first by the reduction of Amyclae (which is supposed to have been a pre-Dorian settlement and to have put up a determined resistance to the Dorian newcomers), then by the conquest of Helos, and so on. But there is little to inspire belief in this pattern of events. It is based on no facts, but rather on late legends of the Dorian invasion, according to which the city of Sparta was one of the three prizes awarded to the conquering dynasts, whereas Amyclae formed the centre of resistance put up by the indigenous population. None of this can form an adequate basis for an historical reconstruction. The progressive subjugation of Laconia by a Sparta already purposeful and well organized in both a political and a military sense forms an alluring picture, in the light of what is known about the later activities and attributes of the Spartans; but it is likely to be a false one. Nothing indicates that Sparta was from the first the most powerful of the Laconian settlements; it seems probable that she was not, in view of the fact that her natural defences are far less strong than those of many other sites in Laconia. Hence the unified state, whose expansion is witnessed in the eighth century, may just as well have been formed by the coalescence of a number of scattered, hitherto independent, places. That is probably the way in which the towns of Attica came together to form a political unit, and there is nothing against making a similar assumption in respect of Laconia.

At what time the supremacy of Sparta was recognized by the other Laconians cannot be established, but at least a suggestion may be made as to the likely reason for their accepting Spartan overlordship. The legends of the Dorian invasion make it clear how potent the force of propaganda could be in the ancient Greek world, and especially propaganda which aimed at the legitimation of ancestral rights. Just as the Dorian tribes in general imposed on the rest of Greece a sense of their own right to rule the territory in which they found themselves, so may the Dorian Spartans have constructed such an imposing pedigree for their kings as to make themselves the strongest claimants for the Laconian supremacy.

The first recorded exploit of the unitary Spartan state is a war (to all appearance a war of aggression) against Messenia. By the time of Strabo this had become known as the First Messenian War, to distinguish it from its successors. No contemporary account of this war exists, and the only reference to it of any value is that of Tyrtaeus. As already mentioned (p. 72), Tyrtaeus took a considerable part in the Second Messenian War of the seventh century, both as commander and as patriotic poet. Writing after the Spartan victory in that war, he speaks of an earlier conflict with Messenia, which he calls 'Messene'. Unfortunately the first quotation of his lines begins in the middle of a sentence, but the allusion to the First Messenian War is clear enough:

> ... to our king Theopompus, beloved of the gods, through whom we have taken broad Messene: Messene good to plough, and good to sow; the spearmen who were fathers of our fathers fought for it nineteen years unremittingly, keeping always a steadfast heart; and in the twentieth year the (Messenians) left their rich acres and fled from the great hills of Ithome. (No. 5.)

Short as the passage of Tyrtaeus is, it establishes three facts about the First Messenian War: that the main thrust of the Spartan attack was against Ithome, that the aim of Sparta was the acquisition of fertile land in the Messenian plains, and that the Spartans achieved their aim only after overcoming protracted resistance by the Messenians, who had established themselves in a defensible position. Nothing is said about a Spartan expansion farther to the west, and the Spartans do not seem to have been much concerned with the western and southern coasts of Messenia until the time of the Second Messenian War. Whether Tyrtaeus' figure of 'nineteen' should be regarded as factual is less than certain. In the Homeric epics events are sometimes said to occur 'in the twentieth year'; and it is likely that the Greeks had not yet acquired the habit, or conceived the necessity, of precisely delimiting a span of time. All Tyrtaeus may mean is that the war persisted 'for a long time'. Nor can an exact date be extracted from his statement that the war was fought in the time of his contemporaries' grandfathers.

The era of Spartan expansion (800–540 B.C.)

Late authors give varying dates for the outbreak of the war, although they are all agreed that it must have started in the second half of the eighth century. It is possible that greater precision can be attained by consulting the list of Olympic victors, which was reduced to a definitive form by Hippias of Elis (died c. 410). This list reveals that at the seventh, eighth, ninth, tenth, and eleventh Olympiads (752–736) the victory was won by a Messenian; for many years thereafter no Messenian won an Olympic victory. Conversely, no Spartan won a victory until the sixteenth Olympiad (716). So far as this information goes, it encourages the belief that the First Messenian War is to be placed within the twenty years separating the last Messenian victory from the first Spartan. But what reliance is to be placed upon the victor-lists? Their accuracy has sometimes been regarded with scepticism, especially so far as the earlier entries are concerned. And yet, on general grounds of probability, it seems likely that from the very foundation of the Olympic Games the pride of the competing cities kept alive the memory of the victors' names. The names could have been written down by about 700; and there was every advantage to be gained from their being kept impartially by the priesthood at Olympia. At the very least, the victor-lists provide just as truthful a record as do the later chronographers, since they do not rest on the computation of generations, and have not been altered in an attempt to relate one historical event to another.

It goes without saying that Tyrtaeus' bare reference to the First Messenian War was much embellished by later fancy; also, perhaps, by facts which had been transmitted by independent means. Following a frequent practice of Herodotus, Pausanias gives two contradictory accounts of the immediate cause of the war, one derived from the Messenian side, one from the Laconian (4.4.1–3). The Laconians claimed that young women from Sparta had been assaulted by Messenians at a shrine venerated by the two nations in common; when the Spartan king intervened, the Messenians killed him. According to the Messenian version, the same king was responsible for dressing young Spartans as girls and inciting them to make a treacherous attack upon the Messenians. Such stories are not necessarily to be dismissed as pure fiction. Although it seems certain from the words of Tyrtaeus that the First Messenian War arose simply from Spartan desire to acquire fertile areas of Messenia, it is quite probable that the Spartans devised some less discreditable motive for beginning the war. According to Pausanias, they were able to accuse the Messenians of violating a sacred place as well as of committing treachery against themselves: acts which fully entitled them to seek revenge by invading Messenian territory.

The time of the First Messenian War was also the time of the great colonizing movement from Greece to Sicily and southern Italy. It is unfortunate that the Greek word *apoikia* has come to be rendered by the English 'colony'; although it would be more confusing still if a different term were now to be introduced. The motives underlying Greek colonization were, indeed, very similar to those which have led to colonization in modern times: over-population at home and a desire to escape from crowded conditions; sheer adventurism and brigandage; political intolerance. But the Greek 'colony', once founded, did not remain under the control of its mother-city; it was entirely independent and formed a new political entity, although the existence of common commercial interests, common cults, and a common dialect often meant that mother and daughter maintained a close relationship.

One of the earliest Greek colonies in Italy was the settlement at Rhegium, in which Messenians participated. The traditional date for the foundation of this colony is 720; if that is correct, the foundation must be seen as one result of the First Messenian War, which perhaps by this time had reached a critical stage. The Spartans in their turn sent out a colony towards the end of the century: the date of its foundation is given in later sources as 706, and archaeological evidence indicates that such a date cannot be far wrong. The site chosen by the Spartans for their only venture in the great age of Greek colonization was Taras (Roman *Tarentum*, modern *Taranto*), which commands a very fine natural harbour. By their expedition to the Gulf of Taranto, the Spartans were following the example of the Mycenaeans, who had been active in the area and had probably settled at Scoglio del Tonno. It is possible that a trace of these Mycenaeans is preserved in Strabo's allusion to 'Cretans who had previously taken possession of the site' (6.3.2).

Of the possible motives for colonization enumerated just now, the political one seems to have operated in the foundation of Taras. That motive shines clearly through the mass of fantastic detail accumulated in various sources. The earliest and simplest is given by Aristotle in his *Politics* as an instance of the divisions that may arise in a state when the aristocracy arrogates to itself all the political privileges: 'for example the so-called *Partheniai*, whom the Spartans detected in a conspiracy and sent away to be the founders of Taras' (5.6.1). The name *Partheniai* is not adequately explained by Aristotle. In later authors it is constantly associated with the word *parthenos*, 'virgin, unmarried woman', and the most straightforward explanation is that it was a term of contempt used by one political faction of their 'womanish' opponents. According to the account of Ephorus reproduced by Strabo 6.3.3, the *Partheniai* were offspring of Spartan wives and men who had not taken part in the First

The era of Spartan expansion (800–540 B.C.)

Messenian War. Spartan women left at home for the duration of the war were afraid that no man-children would be born at Sparta to keep pace with the birth of Messenian warriors; hence they persuaded their husbands to allow them to bear children by younger men, but when the Spartan soldiers returned home they repudiated the offspring of these unions and denied them the citizenship because of their bastardy. A rising on the part of the *Partheniai* was averted by the proposal that they should go out to found a colony. The story provides an instructive example of the way in which purely fictitious details gather about a historical event: it is difficult to believe that the entire manhood of Sparta was absent continuously on campaign, especially if the war did in fact last for nineteen years; again, since it was the custom at Sparta always to place the public interest above family ties, we would not have expected the returning warriors to show such unanimous disapproval of the children begotten solely to keep the city strong; finally, the soldiers' wives were by definition not *parthenoi*, and so there is no reason for their children to have been called *Partheniai*.

Two final facts are transmitted by Strabo about the beginning of Taras. The name of the founder was Phalanthus, and his title to the colony was confirmed by Apollo's oracle at Delphi in these words: 'I give you Satyrion, both to settle the rich land of Taras and to be a source of grief to the Iapygians'. These Iapygians were a non-Greek people who lived to the north-east of Taras, and there can be no doubt that conflicts did arise between them and the Tarantines. It may be that Phalanthus was a historical personage, but one about whom fanciful tales were later woven: for instance Pausanias mentions that he was shipwrecked on his way from Greece and was carried to the shore of Italy on the back of a dolphin (10.13.10).

The Laconian settlers of Taras chose as the site of their acropolis the tip of a peninsula which was provided with natural defences. In this area have been found the remains of a Doric temple, belonging to the early sixth century. It is not certain that the acropolis was ever walled. The peninsula becomes wider towards the east, and a channel was dug across it in the Middle Ages. Here natural defences are not so strong as at the acropolis, and the Tarantines fortified it with a circuit of walls. The eastern part of the city contained cemeteries which have yielded many thousands of votive terracottas.

For more than two centuries the Tarantines lived under a monarchy. They seem to have had no close political connexions with Sparta; nor would any be expected, in view of the alleged reasons for their departure from Spárta in the first place. On the other hand, there is no record of any overt hostility such as sometimes arose between a Greek colony and its mother-city. Despite her complete autonomy, Taras continued Spartan cults and even fused Apollo and Hyakinthos into one deity. Down to the fifth century Taras remained small and only moderately wealthy; she must have been engaged, for at least some of the time, in struggles with the Iapygians and other Italic peoples and in rivalry with other Greek colonies. Taras, like her Greek neighbours in Italy, was early drawn into the Corinthian trading-area; and it is not until the great period of Laconian art in the sixth century that imports from Laconia appear to any considerable extent. Native works of art too are strongly influenced by Laconian models. But even then Taras vigorously asserted her economic independence by minting her own silver coinage (something that Sparta never found it necessary to do). An early coin, dating from the sixth century, clearly depicts Phalanthus on his dolphin, the name of the city appearing with equal clarity as TARAS.

The bronze-smiths and sculptors continued to produce good work into the Hellenistic age. Their most impressive achievement is the large marble figure of a seated goddess (perhaps Persephone). The piece may be dated to about 470, but its archaic aspect is reminiscent of an earlier generation; considerable skill is apparent in the representation of the drapery. The goddess was fashioned at a time of strife for the Tarantines. Their long-standing quarrels with barbarians came to a head. Against some they were successful, and they marked their victories by dedicating offerings at Delphi. But at the hands of their inveterate enemies the Iapygians they suffered a great defeat; although they summoned to their aid allies from Rhegium, the number of their dead was larger than that known to Herodotus elsewhere among Greek cities (7.130.3). Just after their defeat, and perhaps as a result of it, the Tarantines abandoned the monarchical system and instituted a democracy. Under this new form of government they made a rapid recovery. By planting a colony on the south-west of the Gulf of Taranto in 433, they secured a position of unassailable strength in the area; and they then began their rise to the pre-eminent place among the Greek cities of Italy which they were to enjoy for nearly two hundred years. Taras became in time a byword for extravagance and degenerate luxury (Athenaeus 12.522d–f).

For the greater part of the seventh century there are very few, if any, fixed points in Spartan history. It is beyond doubt that Sparta was engaged in another conflict with Messenia and in a war, or wars, with Argos to the east; her relations with Arcadia to the north were at best strained, and at worst developed into a series of clashes. About Spartan activity on all three fronts copious information is contained in the ancient sources; the difficulty is that no single source puts the events of the

The era of Spartan expansion (800-540 B.C.)

seventh century into a proper causal and chronological relationship. Little more can be attempted than to assemble the best-attested facts and to arrange them in an order of probability.

Pausanias reports (2.24.7) that when he travelled from Argos to Tegea he came across the graves of Argive soldiers who had fallen in a battle at Hysiae, just north of Thyreatis, in which Argos had defeated the Spartans. This battle Pausanias places in the fourth year of the twenty-seventh Olympiad (669). The date may, of course, be wildly wrong; but a battle in that very region between Spartans and Argives, and especially a battle in which the Argives were victorious, fits well into a plausible pattern of Spartan-Argive intercourse. There are other slight, but perhaps sufficient, indications that in the early seventh century Argos was extending her power and creating an Argive sphere. Moving eastwards she had subjugated Tiryns and the coastal cities of Nauplia and Asine. It was inevitable that at some point the expanding power of Argos should come into conflict with the expanding power of Sparta; and the most likely area for such a conflict to erupt was Thyreatis, lying to the west of the Argolic Gulf. It was later to be the scene of fighting between Spartans and Argives in the sixth century (p. 113) and again in the fifth century (p. 195). Then we have the report of the historian Theopompus, preserved by Strabo 8.6.11, that the inhabitants of Asine in Argolis had been driven out by the Argives and settled by Sparta in a new Asine on the eastern coast of Messenia. That provocative act, as Argos would regard it, could hardly have been carried out until after Sparta had clinched her victory in the First Messenian War; and, if we allow a reasonable time for Sparta to recover from the effects of the war, we again arrive at a date early in the seventh century.

The Argives, like the Spartans, asserted territorial rights by reference to events supposed to have taken place in former generations. Argos, like Sparta, had been awarded to a Heraclid tribe at the time of the Dorian invasion; and the way was thus left open for a vigorous and self-confident king of Argos to claim everything that had once been bestowed upon the Argives. Such a figure appeared in the person of Phidon: according to some authorities a despot who had seized power, according to others a legitimate king. Regarding himself as a direct descendant of the children of Heracles, Phidon used his ancestry to justify the Argive expansion upon which he embarked. Ephorus said that Phidon made an attack on the cities which had been captured by Heracles, and claimed the right to direct the festivals Heracles had founded, including the Olympic Games; so he invaded Elis and celebrated the games himself (Strabo 8.3.33). Other allusions to Phidon suggest that he flourished in the eighth century. On the other hand he is credited with the institution of the first system of weights and measures, and also of the first coinage, in the Peloponnese; and the evidence of these activities would place him much later, *c*. 600. Yet the principal aims of his policy, involving the attack on other cities in Argolis and his claim to celebrate the Olympic Games, place him firmly at the time of the Second Messenian War. It is then that we hear of the first great clash between Argos and Sparta; then also that Sparta first intervened in the recurrent struggle between Eleans and Pisatans for the control of the Olympian sanctuary, with all the ensuing prestige and perquisites. A powerful motive was thus afforded an Argive king, who already had aggressive designs, for acquiring the hegemony of the Peloponnese and making a thrust to the west.

Pausanias is the only extant author to present a narrative of the Second Messenian War in a detailed form (4.14.8–4.23.10). Unfortunately his two principal sources, Myron and Rhianus, took different views of the war: whereas Myron speaks of a conflict between Sparta and her allies on one side and Messenia and her allies on the other, Rhianus has only a stark confrontation of Sparta and Messenia. Perhaps the latter version better suited Rhianus' poetical purposes; it certainly makes it much easier to concentrate the reader's attention on the great Messenian hero Aristomenes, who becomes the most important single figure in the account of Pausanias. The fact that he is there credited with superhuman strength and cunning does not make it incredible that the Messenians did have an inspiring leader named Aristomenes; nor does the fact that Aristomenes slips disconcertingly from one generation to another (for in some sources he takes part in the First Messenian War); but our task is made the more difficult, in trying to sift the factual from the marvellous.

If we were approximately correct in our dating of the First Messenian War, the second will have broken out very roughly in the middle of the seventh century. Its immediate cause is narrated by Pausanias plausibly enough. The Messenians, ground down by the harsh Spartan rule imposed after the first war, resolved to rise in revolt and sent a request for help to the Argives and the Arcadians. These offered immediate and enthusiastic support. Pausanias next speaks of an indecisive engagement between the two sides; but of this there is no independent confirmation. We may pass by without comment the story of the lone hero Aristomenes, who is said to have visited the Spartan acropolis by night and attached a defiant message to the very wall of Athena's temple. Nor need great respect be paid to the mention of the Delphic oracle or its injunction that the Spartans should procure a deliverer from Athens in the person of Tyrtaeus. That tale all too clearly arose from a belief that Sparta could have produced no true poet from her own soil. At the same

The era of Spartan expansion (800–540 B.C.)

time, there is nothing implausible in the double role claimed for Tyrtaeus.

Pausanias next describes a battle at Stenyclerus in Messenian territory. He calls the actual site by the picturesque name of the 'boar's tomb', and says that here the Spartans were defeated by a coalition of their enemies. The site is unidentifiable, and there can be no certainty that such a battle ever took place; nevertheless Tyrtaeus does address the Spartans as having been in their time both refugees and pursuers (No. 11), and his words would be quite consistent with a major Spartan defeat in the early years of the war.

Another battle took place 'at the great trench' (Pausanias 4.17.2). Pausanias does not identify the site more precisely, and his account of the battle itself is unsatisfactory. In the event, he says, the battle was fought solely between the Messenians and the Spartans, the latter having bribed the Arcadian king to withdraw his forces at a critical juncture. This act of treachery led to an overwhelming Spartan victory. The Argives are not mentioned at all. Untrustworthy though Pausanias' details are, there is a slight piece of evidence to suggest that Tyrtaeus (in a poem now lost) alluded to this very battle; and in consequence the battle itself must be regarded as historical. When Aristotle says that soldiers should be brave by nature and not by compulsion (*Nicomachean ethics* 3.8.5), he uses the phrase '(generals) who draw them up in front of trenches and the like'. This phrase was seen by an ancient commentator as a direct reference to the Second Messenian War, described by Tyrtaeus. A recently published fragment of a poem by Tyrtaeus speaks of military tactics; the word 'trench' is perhaps to be read there, but is not certain; practically assured is the word for 'wall', and absolutely sure is the word for 'water'. Whether Tyrtaeus actually mentions a 'trench' or not, it is obvious that a 'trench' could be only one part of a series of defensive works built by one side or the other, incorporating a wall and a trench containing water. The same fragment refers to Argives, and probably refers to Arcadians as well; so that if it is describing Pausanias' 'battle at the great trench' it sees the conflict as (what it most probably was) one between the Spartans on their side and an alliance of Messenians, Argives, and Arcadians on the other.

Following Rhianus, Pausanias recounts that after their final defeat 'at the trench' the few remaining Messenians were led by Aristomenes to the mountainous stronghold of Eira in central Messenia (4.17.10). Thereafter the Messenians did not again engage the Spartans in a pitched battle, but (if Pausanias is to be trusted in this) they were able to inflict severe damage on them in other ways. Using Eira as their all but impregnable base, they sent out bands of guerrillas to harry Laconia and the occupied parts of Messenia. We cannot tell whether these raids had the serious consequences mentioned by Pausanias, who speaks of a famine at Sparta, leading to political unrest; but it is possible that Tyrtaeus composed his poem *Eunomia* (p. 71) in an attempt to settle political differences.

The Spartans were said by Rhianus to have besieged Eira for eleven years. A sceptic might see in this report a suspiciously close resemblance to the siege of the heights of Ithome in the First Messenian War. No doubt some degree of literary manipulation has taken place, but the very bitterness of the Messenian defence has left too many traces in the record for the likelihood of a long siege to be rejected altogether; we have to bear in mind also the fact that Messenian hostility flared up again later, in hopeless circumstances (p. 178). A further witness to the ferocity with which the Second Messenian War was waged may be seen in the treatment meted out to Messenia at the close of the war. The Spartans were not content with captives or hostages, but they extinguished entirely the political identity of Messenia, which thenceforth became for three centuries a part of the Spartan state. Part of the Messenian population was enslaved, part retained a measure of personal freedom, while having to make over to the Spartan overlords a fixed proportion of their produce. Some Messenians were able to escape. These either joined Greek colonies in the west or made their way to Arcadia: even in Arcadia they were pursued by Spartan vengeance (p. 112).

Tyrtaeus is the earliest poet to make explicit references to a new method of warfare which began to be adopted in Greek cities early in the seventh century. The revolution in tactics is well attested on vase-paintings of this date, especially at Corinth. From now on hand-to-hand fighting tended to predominate among the Greeks. A close-knit rank ('phalanx') of soldiers would advance to meet its opponents, each warrior or 'hoplite' protecting his left side with a small round shield; he wore helmet, corslet, and greaves, and was equipped with a sword and a thrusting spear. The phalanx was sometimes supported by light-armed warriors fighting at longer range: archers, slingers, and throwers of stones or javelins. Some Greek states which had a terrain suitable for the deployment of cavalry were adept in that type of warfare: the Spartans employed it reluctantly and to a limited extent (p. 195).

What provoked the crucial change in Greek battle-tactics is unknown. It would probably be wrong to suppose that the change was accomplished in a short time: some of the warrior-scenes on vases depict a style of fighting which contains elements both of hoplite-warfare and of earlier tactics, and in this respect they may reflect actual contemporary practice. To make effective use of such tactics must have demanded long training,

The era of Spartan expansion (800–540 B.C.)

reliable armour and weapons, and above all firm discipline once battle had started. Sparta came to master hoplite-tactics more thoroughly than did the other Greek cities, with profound consequences for her own military and political development and for the history of Greece as a whole. (The employment of hoplite-tactics is well illustrated by the battle of Mantinea, p. 201.) The question arises, when did the Spartans first display their mastery of the new technique. It might be argued that it was at the 'battle of the trench', which proved to be the turning-point of the Second Messenian War. The available evidence indicates that before this engagement the Messenians were at least able to hold their own against the Spartans, and on occasion they defeated them; so did the Argives, if the battle at Hysiae is rightly placed just before the outbreak of the Second Messenian War. After Sparta's victory at the trench she had no further cause to fear a defeat at the hands of Messenians or of Argives.

Tyrtaeus in his poetry refers to tactics which make sense only in the context of hoplite-fighting. But he does not, and does not profess to, describe the course of an actual battle. His words are not those of a manual of warfare, and just like Homer he combines totally incompatible and anachronistic elements. For example at 11.23–24 he describes a shield which stretches from thighs to shoulders: such a shield had long since gone out of use, but it did appear in the *Iliad*, and so perhaps was introduced by Tyrtaeus as a feature of supposedly 'epic' or 'heroic' battle-scenes. But other allusions, if taken together, do provide a fairly consistent picture of the new methods of fighting. The young warriors are exhorted to stand close together in the front line (10.15, 19.12–13); there is no longer room for individual acts of valour, but each man must consider himself part of a unit. The hoplite must be on the alert for missiles thrown by the enemy and must ward them off with his shield (11.28, 19.19). For a good general impression of a hoplite-engagement we may cite 11.29–37:

> Let each man get to close grips with long spear and with sword; let him wound and capture an enemy; placing foot by foot and pressing shield to shield, crest to crest, helmet to helmet, chest to chest, let him come near and fight his man, grasping his sword-hilt or his long spear. As for you, light-armed warriors, here and there crouch beneath the shield, hurl great stones at them and attack them with smooth spears.

The art of Laconian vase-painting was not sufficiently advanced in the age of Tyrtaeus to permit the rendering of battle-scenes; but a generation or two later lead figurines from the Orthia sanctuary depict individual hoplites, carrying their thrusting spear and characteristic round shield (pl. 37, third row from the top).

After recovering from her decisive struggle with Messenia in the seventh century, Sparta attained her finest cultural flowering, as described in the last two chapters. The songs of Alcman were composed, in all likelihood, in the time of comparative peace before the Spartans resumed their career of expansion. The great Spartan achievement in the visual arts belongs, as we have seen, mainly to the sixth century, with a brief after-glow at the beginning of the fifth. It was undoubtedly in the sixth century that Sparta threw off, for a time, much of her provincialism and came into close contact with major Greek cities outside the Peloponnese. The products of her workshops were carried over a wide area, extending westwards to Etruria, southwards to the African coast, and eastwards to Samos and Rhodes. Whether these products were exchanged for others in the course of trade or more complex situations obtained we do not know. (It seems probable, at least, that Spartan merchandise was carried for the most part in the ships of sea-faring states such as Corinth or Samos.) Precisely what Sparta gained as a result of the trade, if trade there was, likewise remains obscure; ivory is certainly one commodity she imported, and that in considerable amounts. In a system of straightforward exchange this precious material would have been procured only at great expense; but, as Sparta began to concern herself with other Greek states and with states outside the Greek world, she may have received, and have bestowed, materials and artefacts as gifts, out of political or diplomatic motives: that this is what sometimes happened, at least on important occasions, is indicated by Herodotus 1.69.4.

At the time that she was pursuing these wider and more civilized interests, Sparta persisted in strife with her neighbours. Messenia being now subdued, and quiescent for a while, Arcadia and Argos were the major obstacles in the way of Spartan expansion. The Spartans' actions against these enemies in turn fall within Herodotus' purview, and he provides by far the most important source for Sparta's external relations in the sixth century.

By way of prelude to his account of the Persian War, Herodotus narrates the rise and fall of Croesus, who ruled the kingdom of Lydia, in western Asia, from about 560 to about 546. Croesus annexed most of the Greek cities on the west coast of Asia and exacted tribute from them. Like many later conquerors, he became enthralled by Hellenic civilization, and seems to have regarded himself as a kind of honorary Greek: at any rate he sent costly gifts to Delphi on making enquiries of the oracle there and set himself to seek an alliance with the leading cities of mainland Greece. The two most important were Athens and Sparta, and this fact enables Herodotus to insert short sketches of events in those

The era of Spartan expansion (800–540 B.C.)

cities at the time of Croesus: divisions at Athens between the despotic and the anti-despotic party, and political developments at Sparta, together with her progress in campaigns against her neighbours.

Herodotus the inimitable story-teller weaves a marvellous tale about Spartan involvement in Arcadia which contains several elements of folk-lore and ancient legend. But, reduced to its essentials, it amounts to a wholly credible narrative of events. The Spartans, says Herodotus, 'had been successful in their other wars' (1.65.1); but only with great difficulty and after a long time did they get the better of Tegea, the first major city of Arcadia which one would reach on travelling north from Laconia. What 'their other wars' might have been we should much like to know: perhaps these were waged against the Pisatans, who had laid claim to the sanctuary at Olympia in despite of Sparta's allies the Eleans; perhaps against the Argives – for, although matters were to come to a head between Sparta and Argos later in Croesus' reign, it is probable that other conflicts preceded that settlement of accounts. In one battle against the Tegeans, the Spartan army was defeated and taken captive. On asking the oracle how they should get the better of Tegea, the Spartans were told that Agamemnon's son and avenger Orestes was buried in Tegean territory; if they brought back his bones and kept them at Sparta, they would conquer the Tegeans. This they contrived to do, and indeed got the better of the Tegeans; whether they accomplished this in a pitched battle or by a process of infiltration Herodotus does not say. The story about the removal of Orestes' bones is by no means to be regarded as a complete fiction; it is only the connexion between that removal and the Spartan victory which is suspect. Bones which were superstitiously regarded as those of an ancestral hero could well serve the cause of propaganda, if produced at an appropriate moment: thus the bones of Theseus were brought to Athens, and those of Orestes' son Tisamenus to Sparta.

Whether she had acquired a maturer wisdom or had gained great respect for the rugged independence of the Arcadians, Sparta did not impose upon them the harsh conditions with which she had visited the Messenians. Sparta treated Tegea not as a subject but as the inferior partner in an alliance. It is reported by Plutarch that when the Spartans and Tegeans had become reconciled they jointly set up an inscription by the River Alpheus, to the effect (among other provisions) that the Messenians must be expelled from the country (*Moralia* 292b). Although in theory this inscription could belong to the time of the later Messenian rising in the fifth century (p. 178), it is more likely to refer to conditions at the end of the Spartan-Arcadian war of the sixth century. The Arcadians, it will be remembered, were allies of the Messenians in the Second

Messenian War, and we have Pausanias' statement that they gave some Messenians sanctuary after the fall of Eira (4.22.2). The Spartans succeeded in imposing at least one condition on their new ally in Arcadia, and saw to it that the Messenians should no longer find a refuge there. No record exists of the part played in the war by the other two Arcadian cities, Mantinea and Orchomenus. There is an obscure tradition that the Spartans were defeated at Orchomenus; this is not easy to fit into the narrative of Herodotus, but his narrative is after all a highly selective one. We have to presume that all the Arcadian cities entered into an alliance with Sparta at about the same time, since our sources give no hint that Sparta treated with Tegea on different terms from the others.

Anachronistic elements have intruded upon Herodotus' account of the overture made by Croesus to the Spartans. The address of the Lydian ambassadors to the Spartans as the 'pre-eminent people of Greece' need not, in itself, be taken too seriously: it might be put down to diplomatic flattery of a common, if unsubtle, type. But when Herodotus reports that Croesus had discovered the two leading states of Greece to be Sparta and Athens, he is surely thinking of a time later than Croesus' reign. For at the time of Croesus' embassy Sparta had not yet acquired even the undisputed hegemony of the Peloponnese; besides, there were powerful political entities in the Isthmus of Corinth, in Boeotia, and in Thessaly, none of which is mentioned by Herodotus in connexion with the embassy from Croesus. The leading part in organizing Greek resistance to the Persians early in the fifth century was of course taken by Athens and Sparta; and Herodotus seems to have shaped his narrative of the Lydian relationship in the light of the later situation.

Herodotus relates further that Croesus was so misguided as to turn eastwards and provoke a conflict with the Persians, who were just then becoming a great power under the leadership of their king Cyrus. Things turned out very badly for the Lydians, whom Cyrus besieged in Sardis, their capital city. Croesus called upon the Spartans to honour the treaty they had made with him and come to his assistance; but they were too late to do so, and Sardis fell to Cyrus. The Aeolic and Ionic Greeks of Asia Minor, alarmed at the extinction of the Lydian power, which had acted as a buffer between them and Persia, sent for aid to Sparta. The Spartans did not accede to their request, but contented themselves with despatching a herald to Sardis: he enjoined Cyrus 'not to destroy any city in Greek territory, for the Spartans would not allow it' (Herodotus 1.152.3). Cyrus had to ask the bystanders who these Spartans might be; on being told, he warned that they would have their own sufferings to speak of, never mind those of the Ionians.

It is fortunate that Herodotus relates a vital episode in the progress of

The era of Spartan expansion (800–540 B.C.)

Spartan expansion (1.82). When Croesus' urgent request reached the Spartans, they were engaged in another phase of their prolonged struggle with Argos. Again the territory of Thyreatis was in dispute. Herodotus states that this had been taken by the Spartans; on the other hand, the Argives were in possession of the Argolic Gulf as far as Cape Malea, and also the island of Cythera. The two armies left the field, after agreeing that the issue should be decided by a combat between three hundred champions from either side. So much is plausible, but what follows in Herodotus' account is harder to believe. He says that all the champions were killed, save for two on the Argive side and one on the Spartan. The Argives returned to their city, thinking they had won the victory; the solitary Spartan took spoils from the enemy dead and carried them back to the army as tokens of *his* victory. Thus the issue was still in doubt, and it had after all to be resolved by a general engagement. This led to a great Spartan victory, which was thereafter celebrated in the *Gymnopaidiai* (p. 60) by the carrying of wreaths known as 'Thyreatic'.

With the conclusion of the Arcadian alliance and the victory over Argos, the way lay open for the establishment of Spartan leadership in the Peloponnese, the rise of the Spartan confederation, and the direct intervention by Sparta in the affairs of states outside the Peloponnese. Before these matters are considered, we ought to discuss the institutions of the Spartan state and the way of life of its citizens.

Bibliography

Archaic Sparta: G.L. Huxley, *Early Sparta* (London, 1962); F. Kiechle, *Lakonien und Sparta* (Munich, 1963); C. Mossé, *PP* 28 (1973), 7–20; L.H. Jeffery, *Archaic Greece* (London, 1976), 111–32.

Sources for relations with Messenia: T. Lenschau, *Philologus* 91 (1936), 289–307; J. Kroymann, *Sparta und Messenien* (Berlin, 1937); E. Schwartz, *Philologus* 92 (1937), 19–46; L.R. Shero, *TAPA* 69 (1938), 500–31; F. Jacoby, *Die Fragmente der griechischen Historiker* IIIa (Leiden, 1943), 109–81; W. den Boer, *Historia* 5 (1956), 162–77; F. Kiechle, *Messenische Studien* (Kallmünz, 1959); L. Pearson, *Historia* 11 (1962), 397–426; H.T. Wade-Gery, *ASI* 289–302.

Sources for relations with Argos: T. Lenschau, *Philologus* 91 (1936), 385–95; A. Andrewes, *CQ* 45 (1951), 39–45; R.A. Tomlinson, *Argos and the Argolid* (London, 1972), 67–86; T. Kelly, *A history of Argos to 500 B.C.* (Minneapolis, 1977), 72–129. Phidon: O. Viedebantt, *Philologus* 81 (1926), 208–32; T. Lenschau, *Philologus* 91 (1936), 385–96; D.W. Bradeen, *TAPA* 78 (1947), 223–41; A. Andrewes, *CQ* 43 (1949), 74–7; G.L. Huxley, *BCH* 82 (1958), 588–601.

Taras: P. Wuilleumier, *Tarente des origines à la conquête romaine* (Paris, 1939); T.J. Dunbabin, *The western Greeks* (Oxford, 1948); J. Bérard, *La colonisation grecque de l'Italie n.éridionale et de la Sicile dans l'antiquité* (Paris, 1957²), 162–75; *Taranto nella civiltà della Magna Grecia* (Atti del Decimo Convegno di Studi sulla Magna Grecia) (Naples, 1971). Temple: R. Koldewey and O. Puchstein, *Die griechischen Tempel in Unteritalien und Sicilien* (Berlin, 1899), 55. Cults: G. Giannelli, *Culti e miti della Magna Grecia* (Florence, 1963²), 15–59, 241–6. Funerary monuments: H. Klumbach, *Tarentiner Grabkunst* (Reutlingen, 1937); E. Kirsten, *Ant* 14 (1938), 159–66. Terracottas: A.J. Evans, *JHS* 7 (1886), 1–50; H. Herdejürgen, *Die tarentinischen Terrakotten des 6. bis 4. Jhts. v.Chr. im Antikenmuseum Basel* (Basel, 1971). Seated goddess: H. Herdejürgen, *Die thronende Göttin aus Tarent in Berlin* (Waldsassen, 1968). Coins: B.V. Head, *Historia nummorum* (Oxford, 1911), 53–69; C.M. Kraay, *Archaic and classical Greek coins* (London, 1976), 174–6.

The introduction of the hoplite-phalanx: H.L. Lorimer, *ABSA* 42 (1947), 76–138; M.P. Nilsson, *Opuscula selecta* II (Lund, 1952), 897–907; A.M. Snodgrass, *JHS* 85 (1965), 110–22; M. Detienne in *Problèmes de la guerre en Grèce ancienne* (ed. J.-P. Vernant) (Paris/The Hague, 1968), 119–42; P.A. Cartledge, *JHS* 97 (1977), 11–27; J. Salmon, *JHS* 97 (1977), 84–101.

Relations with Arcadia: C. Callmer, *Studien zur Geschichte Arkadiens* (Lund, 1943), 60–77; L. Moretti, *RFC* 74 (1946), 87–103. The Spartan-Tegean inscription: F. Jacoby, *Abhandlungen zur griechischen Geschichtschreibung* (Leiden, 1956), 342–43. The bones of Tisamenus: D.M. Leahy, *Historia* 4 (1955), 26–38. The alleged defeat of the Spartans at Orchomenus: D.M. Leahy, *Phoenix* 12 (1958), 141–65. The battle of the champions in Thyreatis: L. Moretti, *RFC* 76 (1948), 204–13.

7

The Spartan state

The Spartan state comprised Laconia and those parts of Messenia which had come into Sparta's possession by the end of the Second Messenian War. Much of the best land in both Laconia and Messenia was possessed by Spartan citizens (Spartiates). In the remainder dwelt the outlanders (*perioikoi*), free men who were allowed to live and work in the Spartan state but who had no rights of citizenship. In a state so rigorously organized, the activities of Spartiates and outlanders were clearly defined and distinguished from each other. The Spartan kings were assigned choice plots in the outland as their own precincts; with this exception Spartiates did not own any of the outland, nor of course did outlanders own any Spartiate land. Sparta settled garrisons in the outland, appointed magistrates to posts of authority in outland cities, and in every respect treated the outland as her own territory. As in internal affairs, so in external relationships: the outlanders never concluded a treaty with anybody – Sparta made treaties on their behalf and acted in general as their representative. The outlanders were in the Spartan state, but were not of it: they enjoyed its protection but took no part in its political life, having access to Sparta only for commercial purposes and lacking the right to live there. The Spartans did, however, employ outlanders extensively in their army and navy, sometimes as officers, from the late fifth century onwards.

Spartiate territory contained only one city, Sparta itself, and Sparta was hardly a city as that term would have been understood in the rest of Greece; rather it formed an agglomeration of four unwalled villages (*komai*). Other Spartiate towns were of insignificant size and importance, being known also as *komai*. Like the citizens of other Greek states, the Spartiates were divided into groups having a tribal or local basis. From an unambiguous statement of Tyrtaeus (No. 19.8) we know that the Spartiates observed the Dorian tripartition into tribes. Cutting across these tribal divisions are the *phylai*, of which the names of five are preserved. Since four of these names are identical with the names of the four *komai* of the city of Sparta, the *phylai* are almost certain to be purely local divisions. A further term, *oba*, is not attested outside the Spartan state. Its exact meaning has given rise to much dispute. Is it simply a later (and purely Laconian) term for what had previously been called a *phyla*? Or might it have been a sub-division of the *phyla*? Again, it has been suggested that *obai* were not local divisions at all but the constituent parts of the old Dorian tribes. No final decision seems possible, but evidence from other Greek states would certainly suggest that tribal divisions, and tribal loyalties, had not been lost sight of – above all among the Spartans, who showed themselves profoundly aware of their Dorian inheritance. The only sub-division at Sparta positively known to rest upon a tribal basis is the 'clan' *(phratria)*: Athenaeus 4.141f mentions that the Spartans were divided into nine *phratriai* when they took part in the *Karneia;* hence we infer that each of the Dorian tribes consisted of three *phratriai*, which were of significance mainly in the context of cult.

Passing to matters which are better understood, we may examine the political status and function of the Spartiate. The Spartan citizenship was at once more and less exclusive than in other Greek states: less exclusive, in that legitimate birth from two free parents was not an essential requirement; more exclusive, in that a man was ineligible for the citizenship unless he fulfilled two conditions, namely that he had been brought up in the state-regulated system of education *(agoge)* and that he made contributions to the communal messes from the produce of his own estate *(klaros)*. The *agoge* will be discussed in the next chapter; but the Spartiate's estate, or *klaros*, is of such fundamental importance for the understanding of the Spartan state that more must be said about it here.

It seems that all productive land in Spartiate territory was divided into *klaroi:* some forming the precincts of gods and kings, the rest being the estates of the citizens. The estates, once allotted, were indivisible and were not available to members of another state. One Spartan citizen could own more than one estate; but upon each estate no more than one citizen was found. Since Spartiates were completely excluded from trade of any kind, they could not buy or sell estates. There were only two methods by which one could acquire an estate: by being given it and by inheriting it from a natural or adoptive father. The connexion between the citizenry and the soil of their country was thus an indissoluble one. From this fact flow some important political consequences.

In the first place (with the proviso that harvests might fail or other natural disasters befall), each citizen had economic independence. This independence, allied to the aloofness from commerce, precluded the incidence of oppressive debts and extortionate creditors such as Solon set himself to remedy at Athens early in the sixth century. Likewise there was no danger of the rise of an urban class of shiftless citizens, to be the prey of demagogues and agitators. Since the minimum requirement for the citizenship was the possession of an estate, all the citizens (at least in theory) were upon a level of equality: for this reason they received the appellation 'peers' (*homoioi*). We do not know when the Spartan citizens were first called *homoioi*, or when the concept of equality first arose at Sparta. But the introduction of hoplite-warfare (p. 108) may be a relevant consideration. The fundamental change in fighting-methods must have had effects far beyond the battlefield, since now the citizen-body was actively engaged in the thick of the fighting, and engaged in such a way as to promote interdependence and fellow-feeling. If (as seems likely) this attitude spread to the political sphere as well, then the acquisition of political rights by the citizenry ought to be placed in the seventh century.

The institution of a soil-bound citizenry was held to confer one over-riding benefit on the Spartan state: the guarantee of political stability. But the indivisibility of the citizen's estate, the difficulties placed in the way of alienating it, and the prohibition on its being occupied by more than one citizen must have produced serious problems. In an 'ideal' situation the estate would descend from father to son in perpetuity, but the reality was far more complex. For example, a citizen might have no sons, or he might die before begetting children, or he might beget several sons, only one of whom could inherit his estate. Childlessness and lack of sons were provided for, in the sense that a citizen could beget upon a mistress an heir to the estate, or he could adopt an heir; if he had a daughter but no son, she might inherit the estate and, although she was not able to become a citizen herself (women being excluded from the *agoge* and from the communal messes), she could retain possession of the estate until it was again occupied by a male heir. But there was no adequate provision in the case of a citizen who had more than one son. And this is strange, since the state penalized bachelors and encouraged the procreation of sons by alleviating the burden of taxation on citizens who had more than a certain number of sons. Younger brothers must have been persons of indeterminate status: certainly not citizens, but capable of becoming citizens if they gained possession of an estate. The Greek authors do not make it clear what part such 'incomplete' citizens played in the state. At *Hellenica* 3.3.5 Xenophon says of Cinadon (p. 213) that he is 'not one of the peers', and a little later he mentions a class of people called *hypomeiones*, 'inferiors'. Xenophon, as his habit is, simply uses the term without defining it. It cannot, however, mean 'citizens of inferior rank'; such persons were unknown in the Spartan state, where a man was either a full citizen or not a citizen at all. But the *hypomeiones* were possibly citizens' sons who had passed through the *agoge* but who possessed no estate of their own: these would have been potential citizens, awaiting only the opportunity of acquiring an estate.

As in any organized state, the Spartan citizenry had certain well-defined rights and duties; or, to put it more precisely, they had one right and many duties. They were obliged to contribute to the messes and to pay tribute to the state from what their estate produced, to hold themselves available for military service, to provide their own weapons and equipment as hoplites, and to bring up their sons and daughters (but especially their sons) according to the strict educational system prescribed by the state. The one right which balanced all these duties was that of participating in the citizens' assembly. More will be said later about the functions of this assembly; for the time being we may mention two fields in which the assembly had competence, namely that it elected the magistrates and had the final say in most matters affecting the citizenship. Although a man normally became a citizen by entering upon possession of an estate, the state reserved to itself the right of conferring the citizenship upon any Spartan it chose; it was capable also of suspending the civic rights of a Spartiate, or of rescinding them altogether for specified offences, of which the most flagrant was that of cowardice in the face of the enemy.

When a citizen took possession of his estate he naturally acquired everything upon it, including beasts and slaves. The latter were known as 'helots'. It is not certain whether these were in origin dishonoured ex-citizens, prisoners of war, or relics of the non-Dorian population. Nor is it easy to determine their legal status; but at least something can be said about their relationship to the state and to the owner of the estate in question. Although a helot was associated with a specific estate and with no other, he owed a duty directly to the owner of the estate. Most often this duty was fulfilled by work on the land, but we have several references to helots acting as domestic servants. This fact indicates that helots were available as personal attendants of the master. A vivid illustration of the personal relationship which subsisted between helot and master is seen in connexion with military and naval service. Early in the fifth century the helot would accompany his master in the capacity of batman; but by the time of the war against Athens contingents of light-armed helots were sometimes sent out in support of the hoplites. The helots had a similar role at sea. In a passage about a forthcoming naval expedition, Xenophon states that the captains, and perhaps also the marines, will be Spartiates but that the ordinary sailors will be helots or mercenaries (*Hellenica* 7.1.12).

Despite the helot's bondage to an estate and to the owner of the estate for the time being, he was not the property of the owner. Pausanias

The Spartan state

3.20.6 calls helots 'the slaves of the Spartan commonwealth'; and that helots belonged ultimately to the state, not to an individual, is shown above all by the manner in which freedom was conferred on them. The conferment of freedom was not a private business but an act of the state, and the state shared with the master the right of inflicting punishment on helots. The attitude of the state towards helots in general was a highly ambiguous one, and in this ambiguity lay a cause of serious weakness in the whole Spartan system. On the one hand, the institution of helotage was absolutely necessary to the efficient working of the system. In many ways, but not in all, helots were regarded as mere chattels at the disposal of the state, acting through the owners of estates. The very possibility of their enfranchisement shows that they sometimes played a higher role than that. Further, a son born to a Spartiate father and a helot mother was not only recognized but given a special name *(mothax)*: the very bestowal of such a name indicates that unions of this kind were consummated with some frequency. Athenaeus 6.271e–f quotes an earlier authority to the effect that the *mothakes* were free men but not citizens and that they participated fully in the *agoge*. They thus fulfilled one essential condition of citizenship, and would become Spartiates on acquiring an estate or having the citizenship conferred on them, as happened with Lysander in 405 (p. 208). A further non-citizen class, about whom little is known, were the *neodamodeis*.

At the head of the Spartan state stood two hereditary and co-equal kings, who held office for life. One of them belonged to the Agiad house, the other to the Eurypontid; both traced their lineage back to the tribal hero Heracles. Sparta was unique in her retention of the kingship as a living force; unique also in the institution of a double kingship. If the principal functions of the old Greek kings were those of war-leader, chief representative of the people before the gods, and magistrate, we shall see that the Spartan kings fulfilled all three functions, but especially that of war-leader.

The most extensive description of the rights and duties of the Spartan kings is given by Herodotus 6.56–59. He says that each king is a priest of Zeus, to whom he offers sacrifice on leading an army beyond the borders of Laconia, further that the kings may lead the army against whatever people they wish; any Spartan who interferes with the exercise of this right is thought to be accursed. When on campaign the kings are attended by a bodyguard of one hundred picked men. (It is not known why Herodotus gives this number; we know from many allusions that the royal bodyguard was composed of three hundred *hippeis* – originally mounted soldiers, but hoplites in the wars of the fifth and fourth centuries.) The kings have special privileges at public sacrifices and at the games, are given provisions from the common store, and guard the oracles uttered at Delphi. Few of their judicial powers remain, and those apply to the perpetuation of the family: thus they arrange a marriage for an heiress if her father has not done so, and they preside at occasions on which a Spartiate adopts a son. They sit with twenty-eight elders, so forming the Council (*gerousia*). Extraordinary lamentation is made on the death of a king, with representatives of Spartiates, outlanders, and helots all taking part.

It is an observable fact that, although (as Herodotus says) the kings do lead the Spartan armies in the field, they do not usually declare war, muster an army, or take the decision to go on campaign. Those are matters which fall within the competence of the magistrates acting in concert with the assembly. The anomaly should perhaps be explained along the following lines. Herodotus' description of the Spartan kings is not constructed in a very logical manner; and, if we allow that he is more likely to have based it on jottings made during visits to Sparta than on a collation of the events narrated in his own History, we can easily imagine that he is reproducing the theory of kingship current at Sparta in his time. A people with the conservative instincts of the Spartans might be expected to adhere to old constitutional forms, even when these no longer conformed to practice. It is conceivable that by a polite fiction the kings were said still to be responsible for taking decisions, which in fact were now taken elsewhere. Two further remarks may be made in this connexion. The first is that the Spartan constitution was an admirably flexible one: it did not impose an over-rigid procedure on the conduct of business or assign political rights exclusively to this or that organ of the state. (In so far as the Spartans failed in their highest ambitions, the fault did not lie in the defects of their political system but in the narrowness of vision they brought to their dealings with other states.) This constitutional flexibility allowed considerable scope for the exercise of personal initiative on the part of strong-willed individuals; and a determined king like Cleomenes did sometimes act very much in the way that Herodotus describes (pp. 148–157). The kings, after all, held office for life (not, like the magistrates, for a year at a time) and they still possessed a great residue of hereditary influence, which they could bring to bear even in matters where their actual power was insufficient. In the second place, there are a few indications that the two kings acting together had more extensive powers than were possessed by each king on his own. A king by himself was little more than an honoured member of the Council who acted as general in time of war. He could be required to take his place in the communal mess, called to account for his actions, fined, exiled, or

The Spartan state

deposed. So far as we can tell, none of these sanctions applied to the two kings together. What, then, might have been the origin of the double kingship? Since the two kings acting in concert seem to amount to a single legal person, and that person a very powerful one, is it not justifiable to think that at one time there was only one king? If a particular king, or line of kings, disposed of their absolute authority in an intolerable fashion, a number of possible remedies were available to the Spartans. The one they adopted was perhaps precisely this, that they introduced a colleague into the kingship, so as to moderate individual ambition.

The twenty-eight citizens who, together with the kings, made up the Council represented a survival from the days of real monarchic power. They formed a body of distinguished noblemen, maintained for form's sake and actually consulted by the kings in cases of perplexity. It may be presumed that the choice of Councillors and the right of summoning their meetings had once lain with the kings. In the historical period the latter right seems not to have disappeared completely, although in practice the meetings were usually convoked by the ephors. Councillors were, however, no longer appointed by the kings. They were chosen by the citizen-body according to the following system: selected members of the assembly were shut in a room where they could not see the candidate for office but only hear the acclamation accorded each candidate as he presented himself before the citizens; the one who received the loudest shouts was declared a member of the Council for life. Only citizens of sixty years or more were eligible for election. There can be no doubt that members of the Council enjoyed a position of great influence and dignity, but their actual role in the political system is hard to assess. Aristotle states that the Councillors, including the kings, could by unanimous decision refer a matter to the assembly (*Politics* 2.8.3); how often the Council wished to make such a reference, and how often it was unanimous, we do not know. The Councillors had the important function of acting as judges in capital cases; but they cannot have had sole jurisdiction in such cases, which were sometimes tried by other magistrates. Councillors had a status and a role very similar to those of the kings: they were invested with sufficient prestige and power to enable them to represent the ancient legitimacy, and they still sometimes affected the actual conduct of state-affairs. Examples are hard to come by; but the advice they gave (together with the ephors) was once decisive in a matter of the royal marriage and succession (Herodotus 5.40), and in a debate whether to go to war with Athens in 475 a member of the Council swayed both his colleagues and the assembly (Diodorus 11.50.5–7).

The chief magistrates of the Spartan state were the five ephors, elected annually in the autumn by the citizens' assembly. The ephors were of later origin than the Council; but in time they became a kind of second council, co-existing (and sometimes co-operating) with the Council of Thirty, but exercising far greater power. They messed together during their term of office, and so met daily; by contrast, the Council was convened only at set times. So far as our sources inform us, the chief functions of the ephors were three in number: judicial, probouleutic, and executive.

When the ephors acted as judges, they arbitrated in civil disputes (especially those arising from contracts) and also determined criminal cases. As an important authority makes plain, their criminal jurisdiction comprised both magisterial powers and what we would now regard as the province of the police: 'The ephors are empowered to fine anyone they choose and to exact payment on the spot. They have authority to deprive magistrates of their office and bring them to trial on a capital charge . . . If they notice anyone breaking the law, they proceed to immediate punishment.' (Xenophon *Constitution of the Spartans* 8.4.) If the ephors had such sanctions against Spartiates, it is not surprising that their powers in respect of non-citizens were even more extensive: foreigners they banished from the state on their own authority, at the instance of a king (Herodotus 3.148.2), and outlanders at Sparta they could condemn to death without trial (Isocrates *Panathenaicus* 181). According to Thucydides the ephors could even arrest and imprison one of the kings (1.131.2).

The probouleutic function of the ephors arose rather from the nature of the case than from any arrangements peculiar to Sparta. If the citizens' assembly was large and met comparatively rarely, while the board of competent magistrates was small and in virtually constant session, it became important that the magistrates should thoroughly discuss each matter among themselves and then present an agreed motion to the assembly, which was invited to accept or reject it. The proposal was known at Athens as a *probouleuma;* whence the procedure (no doubt a standard feature of all the democratic states of Greece) may be called 'probouleutic'. The need for this procedure was all the greater at Sparta, because of the infrequent meetings of the assembly and the consequent press of business.

At Sparta the executive functions of the ephors were even more important than the probouleutic. The practice was that the assembly decided on a particular course and then left it to the ephors to carry it out. They had a very wide discretion in bringing to effect the assembly's decisions; so much so that they constituted in fact the day-to-day

The Spartan state

government of the state. Our earliest example comes in Herodotus. Presumably the ephors had been given some general direction to act as they thought best in the crisis brought about by the Persian invasion; at any rate they entered into consultation with the citizen of another state, took his advice, and without further reference to the assembly appointed a commander and sent out the army (9.9–10). Again, Xenophon relates an episode early in the fourth century in which the ephors give effect to a decision already reached together with the assembly:

> Angry for all these reasons, the ephors and assembly decided to make them see sense. So they sent envoys to Elis and said that it seemed right to the Spartan authorities that they should leave the outlying cities autonomous. When the Eleans replied that they would not do so because they held the cities as prizes of war, the ephors declared war and mobilized a levy (*Hellenica* 3.2.23).

It is thus certain that the ephors received and despatched envoys in the name of the Spartan state and made detailed arrangements for prosecuting a war, once a decree in general terms had been approved by the assembly. Given the subject-matter of the historians who recount the events of the fifth and fourth centuries, we hear only of the ephors' actions in war-time or under the threat of war. Whether quite so much was left to their discretion in time of peace must remain in doubt.

At a time not possible to determine exactly, the ephors began to exercise powers beyond the boundaries of the state. As we have seen, it was the ancestral office of the kings to lead armies in the field: that is to say, after the assembly had decided on war and the ephors had made the detailed arrangements. In the early fifth century one of the kings still held the chief command, although he was accompanied by two ephors (Herodotus 9.76.3). No reason for their presence is given by Herodotus, and so we may assume that it was already customary. It was no great step from the ephors' mere presence at headquarters to their interference in military operations; the first recorded instance comes in Thucydides 8.11.3, and Xenophon's *Hellenica* attests a number of directions from the ephors to the army. It is easy to see in the ephors' practice of attaching two of their number to a king on campaign a deliberate encroachment upon the prerogatives of the kings. Aristotle goes so far as to say that a king was accompanied by two of his 'enemies' when he went on a mission abroad (*Politics* 2.6.20). By his use of the word 'enemies' to describe the ephors, Aristotle implies that the ephorate had been introduced into the Spartan constitution to act as a counter-weight to the power of the kings, or at least that the ephorate had come so to act; and in his earlier discussion in the same treatise (2.6.14) he says that the authority of the ephors has become too great and is now tantamount to despotism. Our sources confirm that there was a gradual increase of the ephors' powers, always at the expense of those of the kings. And it is noteworthy that when the extension of Spartan influence abroad called for the creation of new officials, for instance the admiral *(nauarchos)* and the resident magistrate *(harmostas)*, these were appointed not by the kings but by the assembly together with the ephors. When operations at sea became of greater significance than a land-campaign, the admiral exercised what was virtually a second kingship *(Politics* 2.6.22).

The last of the major organs of the Spartan state was formed by the assembly of Spartiates, of which every full citizen over the age of thirty had the right of membership. The ephors convoked the meetings of the assembly, and one of their number presided. The citizens in assembly made important decisions affecting public policy, elected the magistrates (including the ephors), appointed generals and admirals when necessary, conferred and rescinded the citizenship and passed the laws. All of these things are mentioned in our authorities as being within the assembly's sphere of activity, but we are poorly informed about the actual methods by which it conducted its business. It is difficult, in particular, to find a clear answer to the question, what rights of debate were possessed by the assembly. Was it simply a body which (when required to do so) listened to various opinions and endorsed one of them? Or could it, even to a limited extent, discuss the proposals put before it? The historians who allude to its meetings (Thucydides, Xenophon, and Diodorus) frequently mention the classes of persons allowed to address it: the kings, the Counciliors, the ephors, and envoys from other Greek states. Most often these writers give, or purport to give, the speeches made to the assembly by the ambassadors or the Spartan magistrates, as the case might be; and from reading such speeches we could well draw the conclusion that the speeches were everything and that when the citizens had listened to them they were merely required to register their yes or no. But two matters suggest that the truth may not have been so simple. To begin with, the maturity attained by Spartan political institutions by the fifth century makes it difficult to believe that the citizen-body, when formally assembled, had no greater voice than had been possessed by the 'host' in the *Iliad*, which shouted its approval or disapproval when appealed to by the kings. Again, the actual manner in which Thucydides constructed his History (and in which his successors constructed theirs) strongly favours the rendering of speeches at considerable length, so as to display the motives of the leading statesmen and of the leading states. To such a school of historiography there is little of interest and little to be

The Spartan state

gained from the recitation of the opinions of ordinary members of an assembly, even supposing that those opinions had anywhere been recorded. Yet on one crucial occasion Thucydides does describe the procedure of the Spartan assembly; and, as his choice of words shows, he at any rate thought that an actual debate had taken place. It fell to the assembly in 432 to decide whether to go to war with Athens. First envoys from Megara and other cities addressed them, then the Corinthians, then an Athenian delegation. Thucydides now says (1.79): 'When the Spartans had heard the accusations made by their allies against the Athenians, and the Athenians' reply, they excluded all [non-citizens] and deliberated among themselves about the present situation. The majority were of one opinion, namely that the Athenians were already in the wrong and that war should be declared immediately.' Two of Thucydides' expressions here lead the reader to think that some kind of debate, however perfunctory, took place among the citizens; for who 'deliberated among themselves' or 'were of one opinion', if not members of the assembly? It does not seem credible that ephors, kings, and Councillors discussed the matter in the citizens' presence, while the citizens remained silent. The likelihood of such a proceeding seems to be excluded, in any case, by the remainder of Thucydides' narrative. After mentioning the majority view, he records the speech of king Archidamus (against a declaration of war) and that of the ephor Sthenelaidas (in favour of war). After he has made his address, Sthenelaidas assumes his character of presiding magistrate and puts the question, directing the citizens to divide, instead of following their usual practice of voting by acclamation (1.87.1–2). It would undoubtedly have made for a fairer debate if the citizens had been allowed to have their say after, instead of before, the ephor's speech; but Thucydides explains this too, saying that Sthenelaidas was so eager for war that he wanted an unequivocal demonstration in support of his policy; it is, therefore, not hard to understand why Sthenelaidas exploited his privileged position and put the question without permitting further debate.

It is regrettable that we have to place so much reliance on this one passage for information about the Spartan assembly; but, for reasons already given, the Greek historians do not elsewhere provide such a clear instance. Unique though it is, Thucydides' narrative must be taken together with the rest of the evidence when we consider Aristotle's definition of the Spartan constitution:

> Some assert that it partakes of oligarchy and of monarchy and of democracy, saying that the kingship is monarchy, the authority of the Councillors oligarchy, but that the authority of the ephors amounts to democracy, since the ephors are of the people. Others hold the

ephorate to be a despotism, while finding democratic features in the communal messes and other features of daily life . . . The authority of the ephors, then, holds the state together, since the people are quiet because they have a share in the chief magistracy . . . so that the ephorate is beneficial to the conduct of public business, for if a constitution is going to be preserved, the various parts of the city must wish it to exist and to continue on the same footing (*Politics* 2.3.10, 2.6.15).

When Aristotle speaks of Sparta, his remarks fall short of the requisite impartiality, since throughout the discussion he reveals the deep repugnance which Spartan institutions in general arouse in him; and, when he does have something good to say about the Spartan system, his compliment is so heavily qualified as to be robbed of much of its effect. Above all he grossly underestimates the part played by the assembly. He seems to think that the entire political power of the Spartiates was exhausted in the election of the ephors but that, as these were chosen from the whole citizen-body, the citizens' ambition was thereby satisfied. But that is to assume what is manifestly not true: that the sole duty of the assembly lay in the election of magistrates and that the magistrates never appeared before it to gain approval for what they had done or authority for what they proposed to do. When we take into account the powers actually exercised by the assembly, we cannot doubt that, at least as early as the beginning of the fifth century, it was the source of authority in the state, since it provided the initial justification for the performance of public acts. Hence the Spartan state may rightly be called a democracy, in the Greek sense. (The messes and so forth mentioned by Aristotle of course conduced to equality of status, but that does not necessarily amount to democracy.) As Aristotle says, it could be argued that the ephorate constituted an oligarchic element in the state. But the oligarchy exercised by the ephors was only a potential one, being limited in two respects: temporally, in that the ephors were elected year by year; temperamentally, because the ephorate could wield far-reaching powers as a body only if its members were unanimous. The ephorate was, in fact, hardly an oligarchy at all, as that term was used by the Greeks: an oligarchic constitution was commonly one in which effective power lay in the hands of a noble family, or of a few noble families, who exercised it by hereditary right, not by election. But to proceed farther with our discussion involves mention of a man and his reputed achievements: Lycurgus the lawgiver and his settlement of the Spartan state.

A weakly attested tradition attributed the Spartan constitution to Eurysthenes and Procles (Strabo 8.5.5). With this insignificant exception, the

The Spartan state

Greeks in general held that it was Lycurgus who established the Spartan *kosmos* in a definitive manner: *kosmos* here meaning not merely constitution in a political sense but the entire way of life which became typical of the Spartiates. The earliest passage relating to Lycurgus' reforms is of such fundamental importance that it should be quoted in full:

> Before the time of Croesus, the Spartans had the worst laws of practically all the Greeks, holding aloof from one another and from foreigners. It was in the following manner that they changed their ways and became a well-governed state. Lycurgus, a famous man among the Spartiates, went to the oracle at Delphi, and as soon as he had entered the inner chamber the Pythia uttered these words: 'You are come to my richly-endowed shrine, Lycurgus, dear to Zeus and to all who live in the dwellings of Olympus. I am at a loss whether to call you god or man; but I incline to think you a god, Lycurgus.' Some say that in addition to this the Pythia expounded to him the whole manner of life which is now established among the Spartiates; but the Spartans themselves allege that Lycurgus introduced these changes from Crete, when he was guardian of his nephew Leobotas the Spartan king. As soon as he entered upon the guardianship he changed all the usages of Sparta and took care that the new laws should not be broken. Later Lycurgus established the warlike institutions (sworn bands and troops of thirty and communal messes) and also the ephors and Councillors. So it was that the Spartans changed their laws for the better, and after Lycurgus' death they erected a shrine to him. (Herodotus 1.65–66.1.)

Herodotus dates the reforms of Lycurgus to the mid-sixth century. As so often he cites, side by side, a more and a less rational explanation of an event. The similarity of Spartan and Cretan institutions was well recognized by the Greeks; and the down-to-earth version accordingly held that the great reformer had copied some features of the Cretan system. On the other hand, if the oracle did no more than confess an inability to be sure whether Lycurgus was god or man, that was not a very valuable response to take home with him; and there must have been a temptation to ascribe to an oracle the revelation of the new *kosmos* as well, whereby the latter would receive divine sanction. According to Herodotus, the Spartans compromised by venerating Lycurgus after his death.

The oracle's perplexity was shared by many Greek writers. In modern times too there have been found those who think Lycurgus had originally been revered as a god, others who believe that he was indeed a great reformer (much as he appears in Herodotus' account), others again who deny his existence altogether and ascribe the 'Lycurgan' reforms to other causes. The epoch at which Lycurgus, if he existed, brought about his reforms has likewise been the subject of controversy. Thucydides placed the introduction of the Lycurgan *kosmos* at about 804, but he gave no reason for preferring this date (1.18.1). These fluctuating opinions make it harder, but not impossible, to believe in an actual reformer called Lycurgus. But, if there was a Lycurgus, he did not promote all the reforms with which he was credited by Herodotus. Whatever the origin of the Council and of the ephorate, those two institutions cannot have arisen at the same time, partly because both of them (at least in theory) serve much the same purpose, partly because the Council, but not the ephorate, bears all the marks of having once been a body of royal advisers in the days of absolute monarchy. Then there is the lack of useful biographical information about Lycurgus. Herodotus, our earliest authority, is also the most sparing of detail; and it may well be asked how reliable were the sources upon which later authors drew. Finally we have to reckon with the inveterate Greek habit of tracing back to a first inventor whatever was noteworthy or marvellous. And the Spartan *kosmos* was a great marvel which demanded that it be ascribed to the innovative powers of an outstanding genius. If Athens had a Solon, Sparta must have a Lycurgus. The fact remains that the Athenians preserved a great deal about the man Solon, together with much of his work; whereas the Spartans preserved little about the man Lycurgus beyond what is questionable or even incredible.

Among later works Plutarch's *Life of Lycurgus* contains a particularly full account of the life, reforms, and death of the lawgiver who was by that time a legendary figure. Plutarch acknowledges that several irreconcilable dates have been proposed for Lycurgus' achievements. He himself considers it probable that Lycurgus was eleventh in line of descent from Heracles; or in other words that his regency fell at about the middle of the ninth century. Plutarch combines the two versions related by Herodotus, and says that Lycurgus both received the Delphic oracle to the effect that he was god rather than man and adopted some elements of the Cretan constitution. Lycurgus' specific political innovations at Sparta chiefly consisted (according to Plutarch) in defining the respective functions of kings, Council, and assembly. The important passage runs from 5.6 to 6.5 of the *Life of Lycurgus*. Plutarch attributes to Lycurgus the establishment of the Council, which kept the state stable; it avoided the despotic extreme by curbing the power of the kings and the democratic extreme by keeping a check on the people.

In support of his statement about Lycurgus' constitutional reform, Plutarch quotes a *rhetra* which Lycurgus obtained from the Delphic oracle. This has become known as the Great Rhetra. No other passage of Greek literature, of so short a length, has provoked so much discussion. Some of its difficulties were appreciated by Plutarch himself, who gives an explanation of some of the more obscure terms; for us an additional

16 Laconian cup of unknown provenience (Rider Painter). Rider. Diam. 7 in.

17 Laconian cup from Sicyon (Rider Painter). Comasts. Diam. 7 in.

18 Laconian hydria *from Rhodes (Hunt Painter). Battle-scene. Ht. 17 in.*

19 *The same. Comasts.*

20 *Relief-amphora from a Spartan grave. Hunting-scene, battle-scene. Ht. 26 in.*

21 *Laconian (?) bronze crater from Vix. Gorgon-handle, part of procession of warriors and horses. Ht. of crater: 66½ in.*

22 The same. Part of statuette on lid. Ht. of statuette: 7½ in.

23 Bronze statuette from Orthia sanctuary. Ht. 2¾ in.

24 *Bronze statuette from Menelaion. Ht. 5 in.*

25 *Clay head from Spartan acropolis. Ht. 2 in.*

26 Clay ('Dedalic') head from Orthia sanctuary. Ht. 2 in.

27 Bronze mirror and statuette from Taygetus. Total ht. 9½ in.

28 Bronze statuette from Olympia. Zeus? Ht. 4 in.

29 Bronze bull from Spartan acropolis. Ht. 2 in. Length: 3½ in.

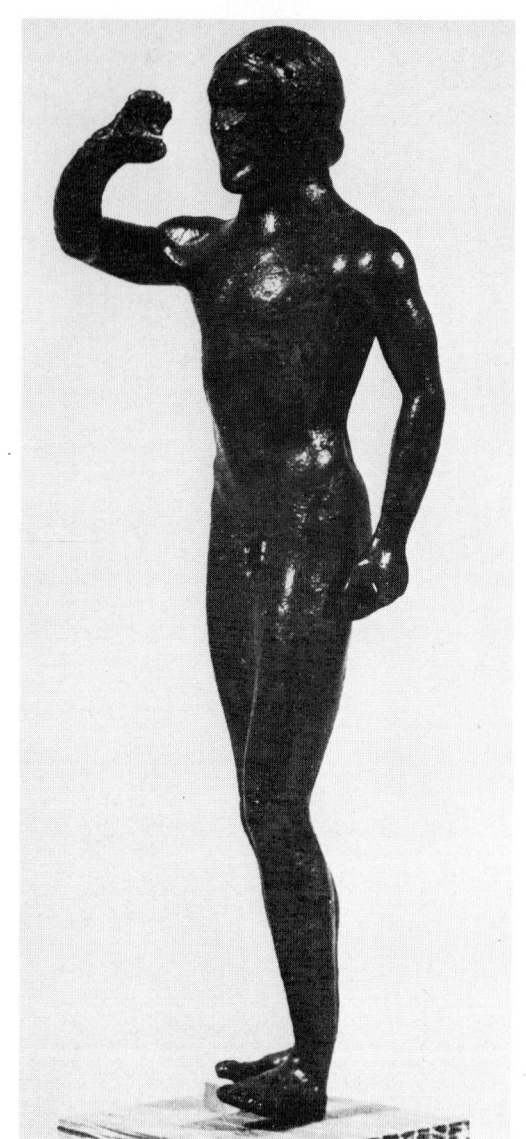

30 *Bronze statuette from Spartan acropolis. Ht. 5 in.*

31 *Bronze statuette from Amyklaion. Ht. 5 in.*

The Spartan state

problem arises from a serious corruption in Plutarch's text, which at one point has produced a succession of completely meaningless letters and which must be emended in the manner which seems most plausible. The word *rhetra* means, properly, a compact or a decree; and it is probable that the *rhetra* quoted by Plutarch was in origin a Spartan decree, later interpreted as an oracular response. At any rate, the authenticity of the Great Rhetra is here accepted, to the extent that it represents a genuine law promulgated by the Spartan state. Its date and purport will be considered later.

Plutarch's version of the Great Rhetra may be translated along these lines:

> [The oracle said that Lycurgus] was to found a shrine of Zeus *Syllanios* and Athena *Syllania*, organize the people in *phylai* and *obai*, establish a Council of thirty including the *archagetai*, and from time to time *apellazein* between Babyka and Knakion; the Council might introduce proposals or refuse to do so, but the final decision lay with the people.

Plutarch goes on to explain the terms *phylai* and *obai*, says that the *archagetai* are the kings, gives the meaning of *apellazein* as 'hold an assembly', and identifies Babyka and Knakion as two rivers near Sparta. He continues:

> When the assembly was in session, Lycurgus allowed none of its members to introduce a proposal; but the assembly was competent to decide upon a proposal put to it by the Council and the kings. Later, however, by the deletion or the addition of items, the assembly twisted and violently perverted proposals laid before it, and so the kings Polydorus and Theopompus added to the Rhetra the following rider: 'But if the assembly makes a crooked proposal, the Council and the kings are not to accept it'; that is, they are not to ratify it but must utterly refuse to do so, and they are to dismiss the assembly, on the ground that it is perverting and changing the proposal contrary to the common good. And they succeeded in persuading the city that the additional provisions had originated with the god, as Tyrtaeus recalls in these words: 'Having hearkened to Phoebus they brought home from Pytho the oracles of the god and his prophecy that was bound to be fulfilled: that pre-eminent in council should be the god-honoured kings, who have charge of the lovely city of Sparta, and the elders; after them the men of the people, responding to the proposals and keeping them straight.' (Tyrtaeus No. 4.)

Thus Plutarch is far from believing that the assembly lacked the power of amendment; on the contrary, some of its amendments proved so troublesome to the 'government' that the latter was obliged to claim divine sanction in asserting its authority. Obscure though it may be in many respects the Great Rhetra marks a stage, and an important stage, in the evolution of the state. Already the Spartans had left far behind a primitive order in which the kings gave instructions and the citizens obeyed them. The time had arrived for the institution of a system of checks and balances; and, if the kings and Councillors saw to it that the system favoured their own interests, still they recognized the part played by the assembly in the legislative process. The reference to a two-fold division of Spartiates into *phylai* and *obai* is also important. If the Great Rhetra was formulated at about the time of Tyrtaeus, the division into *phylai* would already have been ancient; hence it seems that a new scheme, organization by *obai*, was to be superimposed on the old. Only one plausible motive for such a statement suggests itself: while the tribal division was to be retained for civil life and for participation in the cults, membership of local *obai* was to serve in future as the basis of the army. This remained the basis down to, and including, the time of the Persian Wars; but by about the middle of the fifth century the Spartan army was no longer organized in *obai* but in six *morai*: divisions which had nothing to do with locality. The change was probably dictated by two considerations. First came the need to make the army completely flexible, so that if the line were broken the hoplites could re-form with the men who were to hand; they would not be looking about for neighbours or relatives. Secondly, the falling Spartiate population made it imperative to dilute the citizen-army with recruits from the outland, who of course had no connexion with any of the Spartan *obai*.

Plutarch perceives (as, apparently, Herodotus did not) that the ephorate must have had a later origin than the apportionment of power among kings, Council, and assembly. In his *Lycurgus* 7.1, Plutarch states that the first ephors were appointed 130 years after the time of the lawgiver, and they were instituted (according to him) as the result of a far-sighted decision of king Theopompus, who deliberately curtailed the oligarchic element in the state by introducing a check in the form of a board of powerful magistrates. A cynic might retort that, if the ephorate was indeed instituted by the kings, an equally likely motive was the hope of increasing the royal power, if ephorate and Council cancelled out each other's political influence. But all this is surmise. The origin of the ephorate constitutes a problem which cannot yet be solved in a convincing manner. At all events, it began at a later time than that suggested by the tradition (mid-eighth century). If the Great Rhetra is rightly dated to the era of Tyrtaeus (mid-seventh century), the ephorate must have begun between his time and the first mention of the activity of ephors in the historical record, about one hundred years later.

The Spartan state
Bibliography

The Spartan state: U. Kahrstedt, *Griechisches Staatsrecht* I (Göttingen 1922), 1–344; G. Busolt and H. Swoboda, *Griechische Staatskunde* II (Munich, 1926), 633–737. The development of the state: T. Lenschau, *Klio* 30 (1937), 269–89; G. Bockisch in *Beiträge zur Entstehung des Staates* (ed. J. Herrmann and I. Sellnow) (Berlin, 1974), 123–33. Political machinery: A. Andrewes, *Probouleusis* (Oxford, 1954), *ASI* 1–20; W.G. Forrest, *Phoenix* 21 (1967), 11–19; R. Sealey, *CSCA* 2 (1969), 247–69. Comparison of Spartan and Athenian institutions: F. Paenhuysen, *BAGB* (1964), 342–55. Possible Phoenician elements in the Spartan constitution: R. Drews, *AJP* 100 (1979), 45–58.

The outlanders: F. Hampl, *Hermes* 72 (1937), 1–49.

The Spartiates and their estates: U. Kahrstedt, *Hermes* 54 (1919), 279–94; V. Ehrenberg, *Hermes* 59 (1924), 23–72; D. Asheri, *Historia* 12 (1963), 1–21; D. Lotze, *JWG* (1971/2), 63–76. The 'law of Epitadeus', which permitted Spartiates to devise their estates out of the family: D. Asheri, *Athenaeum* 49 (1961), 45–68. *Obai* and *phylai*: L. Pareti, *RAL* 19 (1910), 455–73; A.J. Beattie, *CQ* 45 (1951), 46–58; M.A. Levi, *Quattro studi spartani* (Milan, 1967), 28–42.

Helots: D. Lotze, *Metaxu eleutheron kai doulon* (Berlin, 1959) 26–47; J. Ducat, *AS* 9 (1978), 5–46. Helots on duty with the army: K.-W. Welwei, *Unfreie im antiken Kriegsdienst* I (Wiesbaden, 1974), 108–61. *Mothakes*: D. Lotze, *Historia* 11 (1962), 427–35. *Neodamodeis*: R.F. Willetts, *CP* 49 (1954), 27–32; T. Alfieri Tonini, *RIL* 109 (1975), 305–16.

Functions of the kings: P. Cloché, *LEC* 17 (1949), 113–38, 343–81; D.J. Mosley, *Athenaeum* 49 (1971), 433–5; C.G. Thomas, *Historia* 23 (1974), 257–70. The double kingship: A.D. Momigliano, *AeR* 13 (1932), 3–11; G. Giarrizzo, *PP* 5 (1950), 192–201. The two royal houses: T. Lenschau, *RhM* 88 (1939), 123–46.

Origin and functions of the ephorate: G. Dum, *Entstehung und Entwicklung des spartanischen Ephorats* (Innsbruck, 1878); E. Meyer, *Forschungen zur alten Geschichte* I (Halle, 1892), 244–61; E. von Stern, *Zur Entstehung und ursprüngliche Bedeutung des Ephorats in Sparta* (Berlin, 1894); S. Witkowski, *Eos* 35 (1934), 73–86; W. Norvin, *CM* 3 (1940), 86–118; W. den Boer, *LS* 197–212.

The legend of Lycurgus: S. Wide, *SA* 1 (1892), 90–130; A. Szegedy-Maszak, *GRBS* 19 (1978), 199–209. Lycurgus as lawgiver: V. Ehrenberg, *Neugründer des Staates* (Munich, 1925), 5–54, *Epitymbion H. Swoboda* (Reichenberg, 1927) 19–28.

Text of the Great Rhetra: M. Treu, *Hermes* 76 (1941), 22–42; A. von Blumenthal, *Hermes* 77 (1942), 212–15; F.R. Adrados, *Emerita* 22 (1954), 271–7; C. Pavese, *RFC* 95 (1967), 129–33; A.G. Tsopanakis, *La rhètre de Lycurgue* (Salonika, 1954), and in *Europa: Festschrift E. Grumach* (Berlin, 1967), 303–19.

Interpretation and consequences of the Great Rhetra: K.J. Neumann, *HZ* 60 (1906), 1–80; H. Rudolph in *Festschrift B. Snell* (Munich, 1956), 61–76; H.T. Wade-Gery, *Essays in Greek history* (Oxford, 1968), 37–85; D. Butler, *Historia* 11 (1962), 385–96; W.G. Forrest, *Phoenix* 17 (1963), 157–79; A.H.M. Jones, *ASI*, 165–75; P. Oliva, *ZA* 16 (1966), 123–34; N.G.L. Hammond, *Studies in Greek history* (Oxford, 1973), 47–103; K. Bringmann, *Historia* 24 (1975), 513–38.

8

Life in the Spartan state

Lycurgus was supposed to have instituted not merely a new political system, but a whole way of life. And it is true that in the best-known and best-understood period, comprising the fifth and fourth centuries, the Spartans' outlook and preoccupations differed fundamentally from those of other Greek cities and from those of their own ancestors. We have no means of telling whether the change was a sudden one; whether there was, in fact, a movement postulated by some modern writers, who refer to 'the Spartan revolution'. But it would be correct to say that the social changes did not take place at the same time as any of the important political innovations already noticed. Evidence presented earlier enables us to date the social changes, or at least the beginning of them, to about 500.

For almost two hundred years before that (as far back in time as reliable evidence will take us), Sparta was a Greek state much like any other, always excepting the extraordinary institutions of the double kingship and the ephorate. In the seventh century she had been a famous centre of musical activity, attracting a succession of gifted men and nurturing one of the major lyric poets of Greece. Then, during the sixth century, she entered fully the mainstream of Greek cultural life; her craftsmen, especially her ivory-workers, reached a standard which few other cities could equal, while the very wide distribution of Laconian works of art is sufficient proof of Spartan involvement in oversea commerce. The great age of Laconian vase-painting and ivory-carving was over by the end of the sixth century; but Sparta was not unique in losing her individual voice in these fields, for the arts of Athens now eclipsed those of all other Greek cities. Nevertheless we would gather from the historians (even if there were not at our disposal specialized treatises on Spartan life) that by the beginning of the fifth century a profound change had come over the Spartans. To describe this change involves us in a curious paradox; for it was at the very time that the Spartans began to interfere more than ever in the internal affairs of other states that they deliberately cut themselves off from the cultural life of Greece. Their political intervention was accompanied by personal aloofness; or, to express it another way, intercourse between Sparta and other states was a diplomatic matter, and had little to do with private initiative. We have already noticed that citizens from abroad had no right of domicile at Sparta, but were allowed to live there merely on sufferance. It is most unlikely that such a prohibition was enforced, or even thought of, in the age of Terpander or in that of Bathycles: It was a product of Sparta in the fifth century; and its natural corollary was that Spartan citizens, for their part, were forbidden to travel outside the boundaries of the state, except on official business prescribed by the magistrates.

When we speak of life in the Spartan state, we mean in effect the life of the Spartiates. About the other members of the state, in their civil capacity, little can be said for certain. It would be interesting to know how many Spartiates there were at a given time. A rough estimate can be attempted on the basis of statements in Greek authors. Plutarch states that Lycurgus sought to place the Spartiates on a footing of complete equality by dividing the Spartiate land into nine thousand estates (*Lycurgus* 8.3). The only way of assessing the accuracy of this number is to observe how many hoplites were actually mustered for war. When Herodotus says that five thousand Spartiates marched against the Persians in 479 (9.10.1), we must assume that those were Spartiates in the prime of life (between thirty and fifty-five), and further that at such a crisis the main strength of Spartan manhood would have been mobilized. If these assumptions are correct, and if about three thousand are added for the reserve and for citizens past miliary age, we might consider the total number of Spartiates at that time to have been roughly eight thousand: a figure which agrees fairly well with Plutarch's statement, if the holding of estates in plurality is taken into account.

It emerges from a comparison of our sources (even though no single source states it as a fact) that for the most part the Spartiates did not actually live on their estates. These were scattered throughout some of the most fertile parts of the country; and, while a citizen might well enter into occupation of an estate within easy reach of Sparta, he would not do so if it were situated at some distance. This conclusion is strongly suggested by two facts, one negative and one positive: first we may refer again to the total absence of towns in Spartiate territory; second there is the manner in which the citizens actually spent their time, according to Plutarch and Xenophon.

If the Spartiates lived each on his own estate, it is inconceivable that they did not build strong places for their protection against the perpetual menace of a helot rising. Merely from the absence of such places in the Spartiate lands we might infer that the citizens tended to live at Sparta itself: there they were protected not, indeed, by fortifications but by their own numerical superiority.

The accounts of the authors mentioned put the matter beyond reasonable doubt. When they speak of the Spartiates' way of life in peace-time, they never envisage its being carried on anywhere but at Sparta. And Sparta was often likened by the Greeks to a camp: a well-organized military establishment where the controlling principles were those of comradeship, austerity, and discipline. As we examine each of these principles in turn, we can see that it could have operated only if the great majority of citizens were resident at Sparta.

Comradeship was expressed above all by daily participation in the communal messes. As has been shown, every citizen was required to make a regular contribution to these messes from the produce of his own estate. Plutarch says that contributions took the form of meal, wine, cheese, and figs, together with a little money for the purchase of meat and fish (*Lycurgus* 12.1–2). In the same passage he says that each mess consisted of about fifteen citizens, that the members of a mess had to be congenial comrades, and that they possessed the power of black-balling unacceptable applicants. Xenophon mentions a further important effect of the messes, namely that they brought together in close contact citizens of various ages: a fact which both produced an illusion of equality and enabled the young to learn from the older men (*Constitution* 5.5).

The messes encouraged austerity by providing very simple fare, precluding private indulgence, and bringing the conduct of each citizen under the scrutiny of his fellows. The institution of communal messes was not peculiar to Sparta, but the Spartiates embraced the institution in a more thorough-going manner than did the citizens of other states. In other respects too the Spartiates went to extraordinary lengths to preserve the simplicity and austerity of life enjoined by the 'laws of Lycurgus'. The great legislator was said to have forbidden altogether the use of gold and silver, either for making objects of adornment or for minting money. However that may be, it is recorded as a fact that an iron currency was the only one tolerated at Sparta, which in that respect was quite out of step with the rest of Greece. By the fifth century the Spartiates did not practise any kind of handiwork, although it is by no means certain that they had never done so, and the possibility should be allowed that some of them had participated in the production of artefacts during the previous century. Spartan citizens engaged in no professional activity or business transactions of any kind; they did not buy or sell within the boundaries of the Spartan state, nor did they enter into commerce with the citizens of other states. Manual crafts and commercial transactions were undertaken by the outlanders (presumably with

Life in the Spartan state

the assistance of helots); it is known that Gytheum, the principal port of Laconia, lay in the outland, and by way of that city imports and exports chiefly flowed. We can well believe Plutarch when he says that no teacher of rhetoric, no seer who prophesied for money, no keeper of prostitutes, and no gold-smith or silver-smith came into Laconia; but he is open to the charge of exaggeration in denying that imports by sea were completely unknown (*Lycurgus* 9.3). To complete the picture of the austerity which prevailed in the Spartan state, we may mention the small extent to which reading and writing were practised. Plutarch naturally attributes this to a deliberate restriction on the part of the lawgiver (*Lycurgus* 13.1–2); we may see it, rather, as a further mark of a society which had turned its back on the higher arts of civilization, except in so far as these directly promoted political cohesion and military prowess.

The discipline for which Spartan soldiers were famous, and which brought them for a time to the hegemony of Greece, was inculcated in the camp-like conditions of their city. Everything tended to the habit of obedience and conformity, from the institution of the messes (at which the young men would be expected to remain silent and respectful in the presence of their elders) to the citizens' practice of watching and criticizing the Spartiate youth at exercise. At any rate we have this report by an eye-witness who had himself lived at Sparta in the fourth century:

> We all know that obedience to the magistrates and to the laws is observed at Sparta to the highest degree. But I think that Lycurgus did not even try to introduce this discipline until he had secured the assent of the leading men in the city. I draw this conclusion for the following reasons. In other cities the more powerful men are not seen readily to go in fear of the magistrates, but consider that to do so is the mark of a slave. But at Sparta the leading citizens display the greatest deference to the magistrates, and actually take pride in their humility towards them: running instead of walking in obedience to their summons, in the belief that if they take the lead the others will follow; and that is what has actually happened. (Xenophon *Constitution* 8.1–2.)

How did the Spartiate pass his day? That part of it not taken up with attendance at the mess he devoted to his other public duties. He kept his body fit for military service by hunting and gymnastic exercises, participated in the divine cults, and engaged in improving conversation. Men in their prime were encouraged to compete with one another in healthy rivalry. The abundance of leisure which, according to Plutarch, was bestowed by Lycurgus of set purpose upon the Spartiates and also their practice of watching boys at exercise led to the formation of homosexual relationships. Boys of the age of twelve and above sometimes had 'lovers' (*erastai*) among the citizenry. Both Plutarch and Xenophon are quite explicit on that point; of course they hasten to add that such liaisons are spiritual only and that those arising merely from physical attraction are frowned upon. Our authorities do not, however, make it clear in so many words how widespread the practice was, whether it was considered a mark of prestige or something slightly shameful for a boy to have a lover, and to what extent the lover thought of the relationship as a permanent one. But a revealing comment is made by Plutarch to the effect that young men under the age of thirty (and therefore not yet able to exercise their full civic rights) never made their way to the market-place but had their domestic needs seen to by relatives and lovers (*Lycurgus* 25.1). There is a clear implication that at least in some cases (we do not know in how many) a boy kept his lover until he was far into young manhood and also that the lover would be so closely attached to him as to behave towards him like a member of his own family.

The fact that a lover could be regarded as a relative is not to be wondered at in a state like the Spartan, which contained many elements of a primitive kind of communism. As Plutarch puts it: 'Nobody was allowed to live as he wished; in the city, as in a camp, the Spartans had a fixed way of life and an occupation directed to the public welfare, thinking that they belonged wholly to the fatherland and not to themselves.' (*Lycurgus* 24.1.) In consequence, duties to the state were exalted far above duties to one's family; or perhaps it would be better to say that no well-defined duty to the family existed at all, save to the extent that the family enabled a citizen to fulfil his responsibilities towards the state. Two practices attested at Sparta well exemplify this attitude: one concerned with the begetting of children, the other with rearing them.

Plutarch ascribes to Lycurgus the wish to rid the state of the debilitating vice of jealousy. Accordingly he proclaimed that it was perfectly honourable for a Spartiate to share the begetting of children with worthy fellow-citizens. Thus if an elderly man had a young wife, he might introduce her to a younger man of whom he approved and adopt any offspring of their union. Again, a citizen might admire another man's spouse for the splendid children she bore her husband and for her own wifely virtues; then, if he gained the husband's consent, he could beget children upon her (*Lycurgus* 15.6–7). Plutarch does not imply that such relationships constituted the norm in the Spartan state. He mentions them as illustrating certain general principles which obtained at Sparta: namely that sons did not belong to their fathers but were considered the common property of the state, and further that selective breeding was thought at least as important for citizens as for domestic animals, in contrast to the random methods practised elsewhere. These principles are fully in accord with those enunciated by Xenophon in the first chapter of his *Constitution of the Spartans*.

A father had no right to decide whether to rear his newly-born son or not. He was obliged to take the baby to the elders of his tribe for inspection. If they were satisfied that it was strong and healthy, they gave it back to its father to be brought up; if not, they ordered it to be exposed (Plutarch *Life of Lycurgus* 16.1). A Spartiate's son was nurtured by his parents only until he was seven years old. At that age he was removed from his family and, from his eighth to his twenty-first year, he was educated by the state according to a rigorous discipline of quasi-military type. This state-controlled education, or *agoge*, occupied a central place in the Spartan system; in the normal course of events (as already noticed), it was essential for a would-be citizen to have passed through the *agoge*. The Greek authors use a number of technical terms to identify the age-classes of the *agoge*, and some of the terms recur in inscriptions of Roman date found in the Orthia sanctuary. That such terms were in use is a matter of interest: they show the *agoge* to have been so highly organized that the boys of each year were given a name of their own. It is, however, very difficult to reconcile the usage of the various sources, which contradict one another in some particulars. Fortunately the main outlines of the *agoge* can be reconstructed from two principal sources, Xenophon's *Constitution* 2–3 and Plutarch's *Lycurgus* 16–18, without having recourse to the disputed terminology.

An important magistrate, the Warden of the Boys, was appointed to take charge of the *agoge*. His authority over the boys resembled that of a general over an army. He was assisted in the enforcement of discipline by a number of citizens called Whip-bearers, and we may assume that this title was no empty one: in a society which regarded children as the property of the state, a boy could be reproved or punished by any citizen. Immediately on his beginning the *agoge*, the seven-year old boy was enrolled in one of the 'troops' (*agelai*, the same term that was used in Crete). Each troop was captained by one of the boys, whose orders the rest had to obey. Only the rudiments of reading and writing were taught; instruction consisted for the most part in inculcating habits of obedience, bodily fitness, and courage to conquer in battle. At the age of twelve a boy's regimen became even more severe. He was no longer allowed to wear a tunic but was issued with only one cloak a year. Boys slept by troops upon rush-beds, and their activity by day partook more and more of a military character. Youths in the senior age-class of the *agoge* behaved like officers, organizing war-games for the boys and in the evening presiding in the mess. Boys were encouraged to go out and steal food for their mess, but if caught stealing they were whipped. Athletic contests formed a large part of training in the *agoge*; and these were sometimes (perhaps always) given a religious connotation. Boys sometimes attended the communal messes of the Spartiates, ostensibly to learn from their elders' example but also (it may be) to check any excesses of the citizens by their presence.

The daughters of Spartiates too had to undergo physical training, but they probably still lived at home, and in any case their activities were not regulated so minutely as were those of the boys in the *agoge*. Nevertheless girls and young women regularly went out in public, instead of following the usual Greek custom of remaining indoors. Like the boys, they were expected to be simply and scantily dressed.

The picture painted by Xenophon and Plutarch is very clear in its main outlines. It seems also to be a true picture, although rather an idealized one. Spartiates did indeed win victories at Olympia in the fifth century, and at the chariot-race, an event which called for the expenditure of greater resources than any other. But these are rare flashes, which do not seriously detract from the accuracy of the statements about Spartan austerity. It is obvious that the theoretical proportion of one citizen to one estate remained theoretical: some Spartiates contrived to own many estates; aristocratic lineage still counted for something; and perhaps the rich and influential managed to increase their wealth by engaging in foreign transactions, despite the embargo on such activities. Nevertheless the traditional view of the Spartan state is not seriously at fault; at least during the fifth century it *was* isolationist, agricultural, militaristic, neither having nor wanting the amenities of life taken for granted in the commercial states of Greece, and above all ensuring a continuance of these attitudes by the strict regimen of the *agoge*. It seems that we have to reject the notion (seductive to the ancient Greeks and remaining influential in very recent times) that the profound change which affected Sparta was caused by a series of legislative acts. For reasons advanced above, it is not easy to believe in Lycurgus as a historical figure; not, at any rate, a figure of such potency that he was able to carry out all the political reforms with which he was credited. But, even if the great legislator did prescribe laws much in the way he was said to have done, it strains credulity to be told that he also wrought a change in the character of a whole people. When Solon and Cleisthenes changed the laws of Athens, they did not change the Athenians; although, naturally, the new arrangements they made may have had some effect on the Athenian character over a period. But, in the case of the Spartans, the change was so far-reaching and the new way of life was embraced with such dedicated zeal that other causes for the change must be pondered. To begin with, it

Life in the Spartan state

must be said that Spartan isolationism was self-imposed; it was not brought about by the operation of economic factors over which Sparta had no control. The rich lands of Laconia and Messenia were available to her in the fifth century, as they had been in the sixth; her harbours were rarely threatened with blockade and, if they were, she did not depend on them for the necessities of life. By her rise to the leadership of the Peloponnese, Sparta had obtained a much louder voice in the affairs of Greece, and consequently the opportunity of acquiring a larger share in Greek commerce – if she wanted it.

The Spartans must have had a compelling reason for foregoing the material benefits which would have accrued to them had they maintained their long-standing intercourse with other states. To turn their back on their former trading-partners, to practise self-sufficiency to the ultimate degree, and to make military proficiency the be-all and end-all of their life: all this presupposes the existence of some real or imagined enemy, against whom it was necessary to guard by keeping a perpetual state of readiness. But at the end of the sixth century there was no external enemy to awaken such a violent reaction on the Spartans' part. By mastering the south-western Peloponnese, by cowing the Argives, and by entering into a series of alliances with the Arcadian cities, they had made their state impregnable, at least for the foreseeable future. If no external enemy threatened, it becomes necessary to ask whether the Spartiates adopted their military regime in response to danger from within the state. To ask the question is, in effect, to answer it, for there is only one conceivable quarter from which such a threat could come: the helot-class.

Whether or not there was ever a formal and deliberate apportionment of Spartiate land, as the tradition alleges, there must have been a time at which the Spartan citizenship was first made dependent upon ownership of an estate. We may surely presume that at the outset the Spartiates lived on their own estates and even, perhaps, took some part in cultivating them. By leaving, in time, that task to the helots, they certainly acquired the leisure for taking part in the chase and other outdoor pursuits; but disadvantages too could arise from the arrangement. One might be that the citizens were too widely dispersed to have much contact (still less to make common cause) with each other. A second problem was presented by the great preponderance of the helot-population over the citizenry in any given region. Hence we can point to at least two strong motives which might have impelled the Spartiates to leave their estates and seek mutual support and protection within their city. Once established there, they made it their over-riding concern to safeguard themselves. This they did not by the purely defensive expedient of building walls but by making their army so powerful as to intimidate the helots. The remorseless search for military efficiency produced the type of state which has been described; much that was humane and civilized was lost in the process, but the price was one worth paying from the Spartiates' point of view. The military machine, which we may suppose to have been brought to perfection for the main purpose of keeping the helots in subjection, in fact proved during the fifth century a matchless instrument for furthering Spartan designs abroad.

We find in two important passages evidence of the attitude towards, and the treatment of, the helots by the Spartan state. Whatever the qualities of individual helots, and whatever the personal bond between a citizen and his helots, the state regarded the helot-class as a whole as its enemy and was capable of taking the most drastic measures against them. Thucydides mentions an episode in the war against Athens, in which the Spartans attached a party of helots to a force commanded by Brasidas:

> The Spartans were glad to have a pretext for sending out some of the helots, in case they exploited the present situation (with Pylos occupied by the enemy) and rose in rebellion. Indeed the Spartans had once acted in the following manner, out of fear for the spirit and numerical strength of the helots (the majority of their decisions always being taken with the object of protecting themselves against the helots); they declared that the helots who claimed to have fought most bravely on the Spartans' behalf should be set apart, with the excuse that they were going to be freed; but in reality the Spartans were putting them to the test, thinking that those who claimed the right to be freed before the others would be the most likely to make an attack on themselves. About two thousand of the helots were segregated. They put on garlands and visited the temples, as if they had already been freed; but not long afterwards the Spartans made away with them, and no one knew how each man had met his end. (4.80.3–4.)

Secondly Plutarch must be quoted when he describes the notorious *krypteia:*

> At intervals the magistrates would send the most sensible of the young Spartiates into various parts of the country. They carried daggers and as much food as was necessary, but nothing else. By day they scattered into obscure places, where they hid themselves and kept quiet; but at night they descended upon the highways and slaughtered any helots they caught. Often too they made their way across the fields and killed the strongest and best of the helots . . . I believe that cruel acts of this sort were first practised by the Spartiates in later days, especially after the serious earthquake when the helots, in concert with the

Messenians, rebelled against them, devastated their territory, and threatened the city with considerable danger. (*Lycurgus* 28.2–3.)

Plutarch may be right in his surmise that the *krypteia* was instituted after the helot revolt of 464 (p. 178). But if the helots were able to launch such a dangerous attack upon the Spartan state (admittedly by taking advantage of the effects of an earthquake) at a time when the Spartans enjoyed by far the most formidable reputation of all the Greeks, it is not hard to imagine how serious a threat the helots had long posed to the Spartans. The *krypteia* is sometimes regarded nowadays as being in effect a 'rite of passage': a ceremony by which a Spartiate youth proved his fitness for later admission to the citizenship. Such a view of the *krypteia* is quite plausible in itself, but it does entail a rejection of Plutarch's idea that cruelty of the kind perpetrated in the *krypteia* was not introduced until after the helot rising of the fifth century; since, if the *krypteia* really was a 'rite of passage', it would have been incorporated long before that date as an essential part of the *agoge*.

The relentless pursuit by the Spartans of the single aim of military efficiency undoubtedly achieved that aim, at least in the short term; but the price paid in the lack of social cohesion was so great that when an attack was made upon Sparta by a determined enemy the state was not able to withstand it. The rise and fall of Spartan military power will be examined in subsequent chapters; for the present it may be sufficient to consider some possible reasons for the eventual decline of Sparta, in so far as that was connected with her internal constitution and with the way of life which her citizens had imposed on themselves.

The first stage in the process of decline was placed by Plutarch in the latter part of the fifth century, with the advent of gold and silver as spoils of war, contrary to the 'laws of Lycurgus' (*Lycurgus* 30.1). Writing in the early fourth century, Xenophon gives similar reasons for the manifest degeneration of Sparta from the ideal state he has been sketching in the earlier part of his treatise:

> If anyone were to ask me whether I think the laws of Lycurgus remain unchanged, I certainly could not bring myself to assert that they do. I am aware that in former days the Spartans chose to live at home together on modest means and not to become harmosts in other states, where they would be flattered and corrupted. I am aware also of their going in fear, at one time, of being found in possession of gold; but now there are some who actually boast of having it. I understand that previously there were regulations providing for the expulsion of foreigners and also that citizens were not permitted to live abroad, in case they acquired degenerate habits from foreigners; whereas now I

conceive that the men who have the highest repute at Sparta set their hearts on becoming perpetual harmosts in foreign territory. (*Constitution* 14.1–4.)

Although the influx of wealth and the ambition of some Spartiates to act as magistrates abroad do represent some derogation from the Lycurgan norms of behaviour, these can hardly be regarded as adequate causes of Spartan decline. The problem is subjected to a more profound analysis by Aristotle in his *Politics*. He identifies three prime defects in the Spartan system: the constant danger of a helot rising (2.6.2–4), the status of women (2.6.5–9), and the disposition of estates (2.6.10, 5.6.7). The fear of helots is rightly put at the beginning of this list. Aristotle is correct again in stating that it was not simply the harsh treatment accorded the helots that made them seize opportunities for revolt; account had to be taken, in addition, of the fact that in any rising the helots could expect support from the half-pacified enemies and disgruntled tributaries by whom Sparta was surrounded. It is less easy to assess the relevance of Aristotle's second point, the place of women in the Spartan state. He obviously felt affronted by the great freedom enjoyed by women at Sparta, in contrast to their subjection in other cities. When he says that Spartan women were not trained to a hardihood commensurate with their freedom and that in consequence they became licentious and dissolute, he seems to be in conflict with other authorities, who speak of the obligation imposed on women to participate in gymnastic exercises. But it is true that they were not subjected to a regimen as rigorous as that of the *agoge*, and so Aristotle may be justified in alluding to their comparative lack of discipline as contributory to the Spartan decline.

Aristotle's third reason for the decline seems by far the most significant, and it must be given serious consideration at this point. He contrasts the theory underlying the 'Lycurgan' distribution of equal estates with the actual practice of the early fourth century:

> It has come about that some of the Spartiates possess an excessive amount of property and others far too little; hence the available land has come into the hands of a few. This matter too has been badly regulated by the laws. In making it discreditable to buy or sell an existing estate Lycurgus acted rightly, but he allowed anyone who wished to give or bequeath land. The result was certain to have been the same in the one case and in the other. Again, almost two-fifths of the whole Spartiate land is in the possession of women, because of the large number of heiresses and the habit of granting large dowries; it would have been better if these had been forbidden altogether or restricted to a small or moderate amount. As things are, however, it is open to a citizen to bestow an heiress on whatever husband he

Life in the Spartan state

chooses ... Thus, although the country could support fifteen hundred cavalry and thirty thousand hoplites, they do not even number one thousand. The defects of Spartan arrangements in this respect have been clearly displayed by their own experiences; for the city was not able to withstand a single stroke but perished on account of its small population. It is said that in the time of previous kings they shared the citizenship (with foreigners), so that in those days there was usually no shortage of population even though they spent much time on campaign; the number of Spartiates is stated to have been as high as ten thousand. Whether this is true or not, it is better for a city to keep up its male population by seeing that property is owned on a basis of equality. The law relating to parentage also militates against the provision of a remedy for this fault. With the intention of making the Spartiates as numerous as possible, the lawgiver induced the citizens to have as many children as possible; for there is a law at Sparta exempting a father of three sons from military service and a father of four from payment of all taxes. (*Politics* 2.6.10–13.)

The 'single stroke' to which Aristotle refers is the Theban attack which led to the defeat of the Spartan army at Leuctra (p. 227). If Aristotle's figures are correct, there had certainly been a fatal drop in the number of Spartan citizens during the century separating the battle of Plataea from the battle of Leuctra. That the decline was a gradual one is indicated by Thucydides' computation of the number of Spartans who fought at the battle of Mantinea (p. 201). Although making the reservation that details were hard to come by because of the secrecy which prevailed at Sparta, he deduces that 3,584 'Lacedaemonians' took part. It has been shown that Thucydides probably made a mistake in his assessment and that his figure should be doubled. In either case, the drop to one thousand by 371 fully justifies Aristotle in mentioning dearth of man-power as a major element in the Spartan decline. Aristotle does not, however, make it clear whether the small number of Spartiates was a *cause* or a *symptom* of decline. If (as seems likely) Sparta's fall is attributable largely to her loss of man-power, that loss itself probably arose from the exploitation by the rich of the one great defect of the system. That defect is correctly identified by Aristotle as the freedom to devise an estate out of the family. The concentration of more and more estates into the hands of fewer and fewer citizens made a mockery of the designation of the Spartiates as 'equals'. This process could have been arrested by placing a limit on the number of estates which could be held by any one citizen, but it could hardly have been reversed without a profound change of heart, for the situation described by Aristotle was a product of the disesteem in which the family was held; and the disesteem was itself bound up with the Spartans' dedication to war.

Bibliography

The messes and the *agoge*: M.P. Nilsson, *Opuscula selecta* II (Lund, 1952), 826–69. The *agoge*: W. den Boer, *LS* 233–98; A. Brelich, *Paides e parthenoi* I (Rome, 1969), 112–207.

Austerity: H.W. Stubbs, *CQ* 44 (1950), 32–7; A.J. Holladay, *CQ* 71 (1977), 111–26. Iron money: B. Laum, *Das Eisengeld der Spartaner* (Braunsberg, 1925).

Manual work in the Spartan state: R.T. Ridley, *Mnemosyne* 27 (1974), 281–92; G. Berthaume, *Mnemosyne* 29 (1976) 360–4; P.A. Cartledge, *LCM* 1 (1976), 115–19.

Literacy in the Spartan state: P.A. Cartledge, *JHS* 98 (1978), 25–37; T.A. Boring, *Literacy in ancient Sparta* (Leiden, 1979).

Homosexual relationships: E. Bethe, *RhM* 62 (1907), 438–75; A. Semenov, *Philologus* 70 (1911), 146–50; K.J. Dover, *Greek homosexuality* (London, 1978), 179–88.

Age-classes in the *agoge*: A. Diller, *AJP* 62 (1941), 499–501; H.-I. Marrou, *REA* 48 (1946), 216–30; A. Billheimer, *TAPA* 78 (1947), 99–104; R. Meister, *SOAW* 241/5 (1963).

The *krypteia*: H. Jeanmaire, *REG* 26 (1913), 121–50.

Population: E. Cavaignac, *Klio* 12 (1912), 261–80; L. Ziehen *Hermes* 68 (1933), 218–37.

Social problems: P. Oliva, *Sparta and her social problems* (Amsterdam/Prague, 1971).

9

The era of Spartan intervention (540–491 B.C.)

With the conclusion of the Arcadian alliance and the victory over Argos, the way lay open to the establishment of Spartan hegemony in the Peloponnese, the rise of a Spartan confederation, and the direct intervention by Sparta in the affairs of other states. It was in the sixth century that Sparta contrived to win the anti-despotic reputation she later held among the Greeks. The rise of despots (*tyrannoi*) in a number of Greek cities during the seventh and sixth centuries represented a development absolutely contrary to that of the Spartan state. The Spartans, for their part, retained a strong monarchical element in their constitution and, at least in theory, they placed a check on excessive oligarchical power by the institution of the ephorate. Whatever the virtues or defects of the political system which evolved at Sparta, at least there *was* a system, in the sense that a balance had been struck between the opposing forces in the state. This balance, which Sparta achieved before 600, seems to have eluded the majority of Greek cities for many years. In most of them the monarchy had declined to the point of political impotence by about 700; the royal power came, quite naturally, into the hands of the hereditary nobility. The misery arising from struggles between rival aristocrats and the jealousy with which the aristocratic class as a whole guarded its privileges led, in some states, to revolution and the seizure of power by a despot.

It is no accident that the states most prone to despotic rule were those with strong commercial interests: those, in other words, where the new middle class had ·advanced to prosperity by sea-faring, trade, and artisanship, yet found itself excluded from participation in the process of government. Such states were Corinth, Sicyon, Athens, and Samos. The despot who usurped power might himself be one of the new mercantile class or a disgruntled aristocrat who had managed to gain a following among the merchants. Once he had seized power the despot sometimes founded long-lived dynasties, as with the Cypselids at Corinth, the Orthagorids at Sicyon, and the Pisistratids at Athens. No general statement can be made about the character of the absolute rule exercised by the Greek despots. Some of them were considered mild and just, others were execrated for their cruelty and arbitrary government. Cypselus, the founder of the Corinthian despotism, was given a good name by Ephorus and a bad one by Herodotus: a fact which suggests that the reputation of a despot depended as much on prejudice as on the facts of the case. Whatever their character as individuals, the despots often promoted vigorous cultural development by their munificent patronage, and the period of despotism was an exceptionally brilliant one at each of the four cities just named.

It would be simple-minded to suppose that the Spartans tried to put down despotism out of sheer hatred of absolute rule. Although their motives may have varied slightly from case to case, their principal aim was that of fomenting unrest in other cities: this they turned to their own advantage, and so extended their influence. Such an aim appears most clearly in Spartan operations against Samos and Athens late in the sixth century. Their action in these quarters is well documented, but we are left in little doubt that they had intervened earlier in some other states. In fact, we might infer from a statement of Thucydides that the Spartans had been responsible in general for bringing despotism to an end in the sixth century; but at this point his words are unfortunately as vague as his style is disjointed: 'The Athenian despots and those in the rest of Greece (which had been under despotic rule long before Athens had) – most of them, that is, and the latest (except those in Sicily) were deposed by the Spartans (1.18.1).' Plutarch, in his turn, specifies the despots who were deposed by Sparta: '[The Spartans] expelled the Cypselids from Corinth and Ambracia, Lygdamis from Naxos, Pisistratus' sons from Athens, Aeschines from Sicyon, Symmachus from Thasos, Aulis from Phocis, and Aristogenes from Miletus, and put an end to the despotism in Thessaly when king Leotychidas deposed Aristodemus and Agelaus. These matters are described in greater detail in other writers (*Moralia* 859c–d).' In this list, the only despots positively known to have been deposed by the Spartans are those at Sicyon and Athens. The last of the Cypselid despots was deposed at Corinth *c.* 580, according to the traditional date. It is possible that the Spartans were responsible; whether they were or not, they seem to have benefited from the change of regime from despotism to oligarchy, since nearly sixty years later Spartans and Corinthians made common cause in the attack on Samos.

A thin and ambiguous ray of light is shed on the Spartan action at Sicyon by a papyrus-fragment (Rylands no. 18). After what may be an allusion to someone's 'going across to Epirus' (that is, the Corinthian colony of Ambracia in Epirus), we have the sentence: 'And Chilon the Spartan being ephor and commander of the army, together with Anaxandridas, put down the despotic regimes in Greece: those of Aeschines at

The era of Spartan intervention (540–491 B.C.)

Sicyon, of Hippias [the son] of Pisistratus [at Athens] . . .' Chilon bore a very celebrated name. He was regarded, along with Thales, Solon, and Periander, as one of the great sages: men who combined wisdom with practical ability. It is not really known upon what grounds Chilon was included in this company. The traditional date of his ephorate is 556/555, whereas Anaxandridas was a Spartan king from about that time until c. 520. Thus there is nothing untoward in the notion of their embarking on a joint enterprise, but it is disconcerting to find an ephor named before a king: does this mean that our fragment is part of a biography of the sages and so would naturally mention the sage first, or is it part of a history implying that Chilon took the initiative in promoting Sparta's anti-despotic policy? The date indicated by the papyrus for the deposition of Aeschines (roughly mid-sixth century) is in accord with Aristotle's chronology, whereby the Orthagorid despotism lasted for a hundred years (*Politics* 5.9.21). But, if Chilon and Anaxandridas deposed Aeschines at Sicyon, they could not have brought about the fall of Hippias at Athens: that happened later, in the reign of Anaxandridas' son Cleomenes. Chilon had perhaps acquired the reputation of 'despot-destroyer' *par excellence:* in consequence, he was given credit for all the major operations undertaken by Sparta against despots.

The despotism of Polycrates at Samos lasted for sixteen years from about the year 532. It was a time of lavish expenditure on public works, hospitality to poets and artists, and the establishment of the most considerable naval power in the eastern Aegean. The story of Spartan intervention in the island as told by Herodotus (3.39–60) does not bring out with requisite clarity all the motives which actuated the Spartans. They themselves, according to Herodotus, said that they bore Polycrates a grudge for having seized Spartan gifts while in transit; and it was for this reason that they were willing to give a favourable hearing at Sparta to a number of Samians expelled by Polycrates. But Herodotus himself gives a hint that larger matters of policy were in question than resentment over the bowl and the corslet alleged to have been taken by one of Polycrates' ships. It was at this time that the Persians, having conquered the Lydian empire, were thrusting still farther westwards; and Cambyses, the son of Cyrus the Great, contemplated an attack on Egypt. Polycrates had previously been on terms of friendship with the Egyptian king, but he now expressed his willingness to assist Cambyses by sending a fleet in support of his attack. The crews of the ships sent by Polycrates, says Herodotus, were composed of Samians whose loyalty to the despot was suspect. And we can well believe that by this one act Polycrates contrived both to rid himself of potential rivals and to display his support for the new world-power which was emerging in the east.

As Polycrates was able to achieve two aims at a single stroke, so were the Spartans. By lending aid to Polycrates' political enemies, they might install at Samos a government friendly to themselves; but they would also place a check on the expansion of Persia. It is not likely that the Spartans yet comprehended the true extent of the Persian menace, but they had observed the fall of Croesus, and could surely draw the appropriate conclusions from that event.

The Corinthians, like the Spartans, bore an old grudge against Polycrates, and accordingly they participated in the Spartan expedition to Samos. This was, as Herodotus emphasizes, the first time that Dorian Greeks had taken their arms so close to the continent of Asia (3.56.2). They came in great force and attacked Polycrates' city from both the seaward and the landward side; but, despite individual acts of valour, they were beaten off. They then resorted to siege, but this too came to nothing, and after forty days they sailed back to Greece.

So the enterprise ended in fiasco; in order to understand why, we would need to know much more in detail about the course of the campaign. It is remarkable that Herodotus does not identify the leader of the expedition. Perhaps its total failure was due to lack of unified command, which was vitally necessary in view of the participation of Corinthians and Samian exiles as well as Spartans. Not long after he had repelled the invaders from Greece, Polycrates met a shabby end in Asia at the hands of a Persian satrap: neither the reason for his death nor the manner of it is clear. The nonentity Maeandrius next became despot in Samos, but held power for only a short time before the island was annexed by the Persians (c. 517). By this time Darius had inherited the Persian empire from his father Cambyses, while at Sparta the kingship in the Agiad line had descended from Anaxandridas to Cleomenes. The latter took a decisive part in shaping Spartan policy at home and abroad for much of his reign, which seems to have lasted for about twenty-five years. Herodotus has Maeandrius going to Sparta and making a display of his costly possessions; Cleomenes was afraid that Maeandrius would bribe the Spartans into helping him regain power, and ordered the ephors to expel him. Despite his lack of success in persuading or corrupting the Spartans, Maeandrius must have had some good reason for applying to them, even after their failure against Polycrates; and he must have had a reason for applying to Cleomenes and not to the ephors. Maeandrius perhaps calculated that, if any state were to furnish help, that state was likely to be Sparta, now (to all appearance) under the direction of its young and vigorous king Cleomenes. The later events of his reign show that Cleomenes did sometimes engage in rash adventures

The era of Spartan intervention (540–491 B.C.)

beyond the Peloponnese, but they show also his notable reluctance to be drawn into direct confrontation with Persia.

It is a notorious fact that Herodotus blackens the character of Cleomenes whenever an opportunity presents itself; and, if there is no opportunity, then one is invented. Herodotus seems to be following a Spartan source hostile to Cleomenes' memory. That such a source existed comes as no surprise, in view of the feuds between Cleomenes and his colleague and the consequent emergence of rival versions of past events. Herodotus produces no evidence (at least from the earlier part of Cleomenes' reign) for calling the king 'utterly insane', and his actions, as narrated by Herodotus himself, are not those of a madman. It is upon his actions that we must concentrate, leaving aside the frequently dubious motives suggested by Herodotus. His story of the career of Cleomenes' half-brother Dorieus (which may be assigned roughly to the years 514–510) shows that Dorieus was wholly in the wrong, and Cleomenes blameless (5.39–48). Dorieus, says Herodotus, could not endure being a subject of Cleomenes and gathered a number of Spartiates, whom he took to Libya in the hope of founding a colony there. He was greatly at fault in not seeking the advice and consent of the Delphic oracle, which were essential to prospective colonists. His plans came to nothing, and after only two years he was driven out of Africa. Returning to Sparta, he decided to found a colony in Sicily. On this occasion he did consult the oracle, and received an encouraging response. But, instead of persevering in his original intention, he allowed himself to be drawn into a conflict between Greek cities in Italy. In the fighting he and the majority of his followers perished.

We now come to a series of events, occupying five years or so after 510, which reveal some important truths about the Spartans' anti-despotic reputation and which involve the earliest deliberations of the Spartan Alliance. These events are recounted by Herodotus, and comprise four separate occasions on which the Spartans invaded Attica with the intention of deposing Pisistratus' son Hippias from power at Athens. Like Polycrates at Samos, the Pisistratids at Athens had expelled a number of their political rivals, including the Alcmaeonids. Those powerful aristocrats used part of their wealth to ingratiate themselves at Delphi by paying for the construction of a temple. They also bribed the priestess to give a certain reply to any Spartan who visited Delphi seeking an oracle: she was to work into the response an injunction that the Spartans should set Athens free. On receiving this injunction, the Spartans decided to send an army under the command of the Spartiate Anchimolius 'to expel the Pisistratids from Athens, even though these were their friends; for they cherished the divine command above human relationships' (Herodutus 5.63.2). So the Spartans had no deep-seated aversion from despots as such; but friendship with them was outweighed by the need to support a strong oligarchic faction or to remain in good standing at Delphi. This first Spartan invasion of Attica ended in disaster. The Pisistratids enlisted the aid of some Thessalian cavalry, who rode down the Spartans, killing many of them (including Anchimolius) and driving the remainder back to their ships.

The second invading force was led by Cleomenes, who chose an overland route. The Spartans this time succeeded in shutting up the Pisistratids on the Athenian acropolis; the despots' children were captured, and restored only on condition that the Pisistratids left the country.

With the expulsion of the despots there ensued a struggle for power at Athens between Isagoras, a supporter of the Pisistratids, and the Alcmaeonid Cleisthenes, who later framed a democratic constitution for the Athenian state. Isagoras accused Cleisthenes of seizing power with popular support and invited Cleomenes to come again and expel him. Cleisthenes thought it prudent to retire from the country. Cleomenes came none the less and banished seven hundred households denounced by Isagoras, but was not able to browbeat the Council into submission. Thereupon Cleomenes, Isagoras, and their followers seized the acropolis. But the tables were turned on them, and the acropolis was besieged and taken. Of those found inside, the Athenians were sentenced to death, while the Spartans were allowed to leave under truce. This grotesque humiliation of Cleomenes is attributed by Herodotus to his disregard of the words addressed to him by a priestess as he was making his way up to the acropolis: 'Back, Spartan stranger, do not enter the temple; it is unlawful for Dorians to pass in here'. He said, 'I am not a Dorian, lady, but an Achaean'. (5.72.3.) The tendency of Herodotus to find a supernatural explanation for remarkable events is well known; and the exchange between Cleomenes and the priestess would not call for special notice were it not for Cleomenes' reply; for, it might be asked, who *was* a Dorian, if not a Spartan king? Here we seem to have a distinction sometimes, but by no means always, made between the sons of Heracles (who were of course Achaeans) and the Dorians who came with them into the Peloponnese (p. 41). At such a moment it was natural for Cleomenes, endowed with the gift of repartee noticed by Plutarch, to dwell on his 'Achaean' lineage from the Heraclids and to overlook the Dorian component in his ancestry. The whole episode of the third invasion is described by Aristotle (*Constitution of the Athenians* 20) along lines very similar to those followed by Herodotus; but he makes no allusion to Cleomenes' encounter with the priestess, which may well be apocryphal.

The era of Spartan intervention (540–491 B.C.)

While he was advancing into Attica or withdrawing from it, Cleomenes was approached by the inhabitants of Plataea, a small town on the road between Athens and Thebes. The Plataeans felt themselves squeezed between their two powerful neighbours, and requested protection from Sparta. This Cleomenes refused to give, suggesting that the Plataeans would do better to make their request at Athens. Herodotus rightly observes that this advice was given not so much out of good will towards the Plataeans as from a desire to antagonize the Thebans against Athens (6.108.2–3).

The fourth and last invasion of Attica likewise ended in ignominy for Cleomenes. Without divulging his intention, he raised a large army from various parts of the Peloponnese: with this he forced his way into Attica as far as Eleusis, twelve miles north-west of Athens. Meanwhile Boeotians and Chalcidians, acting in concert with Cleomenes, threatened the other borders of Attica and ravaged the countryside. Surrounded by enemies, the Athenians would have been in a desperate situation if Cleomenes' force had not broken up and scattered before battle was joined. First the Corinthian contingent departed, on the ground that they were acting wrongly in invading Attic soil. Although Herodotus says no more than this, we are to infer that Cleomenes did not make plain his real purpose (that of establishing Isagoras at Athens) until the army had reached Eleusis. But, what was potentially still more dangerous, the other Spartan king Demaratus also refused to go on with the expedition, and left for home. This is the first hint of a rift between the two kings, which was later to have grave consequences. As a direct result of the dispute at Eleusis (reports Herodotus) the Spartans passed a law to the effect that thenceforth one king only was to go on campaign at any one time. It is unclear how the enactment of this law arose directly from the disagreement between Cleomenes and Demaratus, unless it was intended to save face before Sparta's enemies and allies by enforcing unity of command in the field. Cleomenes throughout seems to have behaved in an unconstitutional manner, since it is expressly stated that he (and not the Spartan assembly nor the ephors) decided on war, raised an army, and led it off to an undisclosed destination. The episode undoubtedly demonstrates what an energetic and self-willed Spartan king could achieve, but it shows too how great were the limitations in practice upon the exercise of his powers.

After the disintegration of Cleomenes' army and his own return to Sparta, the Spartans proposed to restore Hippias as despot of Athens. (We would imagine that Cleomenes was the instigator of this proposal, whether openly or not, but his part in the affair is not stated by Herodotus.) The *volte face* in Spartan policy is only apparent. We have already seen that the Spartans had originally been on friendly terms with the Pisistratids and had moved against them only because they hoped to gain greater advantages from the establishment of an oligarchy. Herodotus gives two reasons for the different course now followed by the Spartans (5.90–91). In the first place they had learnt of the Alcmaeonids' trick in bribing the Pythian priestess. But, in the second place, their own eyes showed them how powerful Athens was becoming under a democracy; only a despotism, they thought, could keep in check the popular elements in the state.

At this point in his narrative (5.91), Herodotus makes casual mention of a momentous development in Spartan history. The Spartans summoned an assembly of their allies, at which they acknowledged their mistake in expelling Hippias and proposed that they should now restore him. The Corinthian delegate made a long speech in which he exemplified the dangers and horrors of despotism by reference to the history of the Cypselids in his own city; for this reason, he said, the Corinthians at least could not support the proposal. Hippias in person made a brief reply, but all the other allies of Sparta now joined Corinth in opposing his restoration. The Spartan plan therefore came to nothing. It is far from certain that the Spartans had any long-term object in view when they called the assembly. Their principal aim was probably that of avoiding a repetition of the incident at Eleusis, by ensuring that Sparta would never again embark on any foreign adventure without having first secured the sworn allegiance of her allies. Better (they may have reasoned) to lose an argument in assembly than to be deserted on the battlefield and so exposed to danger and ridicule.

The assembly is important in that it marks the earliest occasion recorded by Herodotus on which the Spartans formally convoked a meeting of the allies and requested a decision on a matter of high policy. It is especially to be noted that the Spartans had the right of calling the assembly, but also that their opinion could not outweigh the unanimous voice of the allies. In these two elements there reside the germs of what was to become the Spartan Alliance; or, as it is sometimes known (contrary to ancient usage), the Peloponnesian League or Confederation. Leagues based on cult-precincts (*amphiktyoniai*) had long been known among the Greeks; but the Spartan Alliance was different in nature from these, since it arose purely from the political self-interest of its members and had no necessary connexion with a particular centre: the allies sent their delegates to Sparta as a matter of practical convenience, not because any special sanctity inhered in that city. The Alliance was in no sense an exclusive organization. Once the Spartan system of contracting treaties with other states became well established, it was easy for any number of

The era of Spartan intervention (540–491 B.C.)

other states to be admitted to the Alliance. This ability to accommodate new members without restriction, and without the imposition of tribute, was one of Sparta's great strengths as she advanced to political, as well as military, pre-eminence in Greece.

Among modern writers, two schools of thought have emerged as to the character of the Spartan Alliance: one holding that from its very inception it had a formal structure and constitution of its own, the other that it was only a fairly loose confederation of like-minded states who combined for the promotion of their common interests under the general leadership of Sparta. Whatever the truth of this matter, we may say that in the account of the assembly called to discuss Hippias' restoration there is not yet a clear sign of the third important element in the Spartan Alliance: namely that if the assembly decided for war the allies bound themselves 'to follow the Spartans wherever they led, by land or by sea' (Xenophon *Hellenica* 2.2.20). This principle does not seem to have been acted upon until the Spartans and their allies set out for the battle of Plataea (p. 169); while the defection of the Corinthians from Cleomenes in the fourth invasion of Attica proves that there was not yet any obligation on the allies to follow the Spartans wherever they led.

Meanwhile the vast designs of the Persians were taking clearer shape with the entry of Darius into Thrace. But the Asiatic Greeks thought they saw an opportunity of slipping off the Persian yoke, and their disaffection led to the complex series of events now known as the Ionian Revolt. The seat of the rebellion was Miletus, and its moving spirit the Milesian regent Aristagoras. Like the envoy sent by the Aeolians and Ionians in the time of Cyrus (p. 112), Aristagoras in his turn came to Sparta, urging Cleomenes to intervene in Asia. The probable date of Aristagoras' visit is 499. What passed between him and Cleomenes is given by Herodotus, with much romantic embellishment. Reduced to its essentials, Aristagoras' plea was couched in such a way as to appeal first to the sentiment and then to the cupidity of the king. That the Ionians should be enslaved to the barbarian brought shame on all Greeks (he said), but especially on the Spartans, who held the premier place in Hellas. To defeat the Persians in war would be easy: their bows and short spears were no match for the hoplite-phalanx. Besides, untold wealth was there for the taking in Darius' dominions and above all in Susa his capital. In revealing that Susa lay a three months' march from the sea Aristagoras made a false step and Cleomenes broke off the interview, remarking that he could never persuade the Spartans to conduct a campaign in such distant regions. Rebuffed by Cleomenes, Aristagoras went before the assembly at Athens with his request. The Athenians agreed to send twenty ships to help the Ionians. This force was hopelessly insufficient to turn the scales decisively against Darius, but it had the effect of irritating him intolerably. He was able to crush the revolt, mainly because the Ionians and their allies lacked a coherent policy and a decisive leader. When things became critical Aristagoras thought only of flight, leaving behind the confusion he himself had precipitated. The Athenians, assisted by a small contingent from Eretria, did have what may have seemed at the time a spectacular success. They made their way to Sardis, Croesus' old capital and now the seat of a Persian satrapy, and lit a fire which destroyed the greater part of the city. But that was a pinprick to Darius, not a serious setback, and it merely made him determined to punish the Athenians when the time was ripe. It would be going too far to credit Cleomenes with an accurate foreknowledge of these events; but he might very well have reached a number of correct conclusions even on the facts known to him, for instance that intervention would have to be made in great force if it was to be effective and that (despite the fatuous or deceitful optimism displayed by Aristagoras) the Persian empire was at that time too vast and too powerful to be broken up by a military force sent from Greece.

It next fell to Cleomenes to settle accounts with Argos, at least for that generation. The Argive war involving Cleomenes should probably be dated to about the year 494. In that year Miletus was taken by Darius, so bringing the Ionian Revolt to an end. In his account of the oracle foretelling the doom of Argos, Herodotus mentions that it was one which the Pythia gave in common to the Argives and to the Milesians (6.77.2), implying that the fall of Argos and that of Miletus were separated from each other by no long interval. Cleomenes set off from Sparta in high hopes, encouraged by an oracle which prophesied that he would 'take Argos'; but he was unable to obtain favourable omens for the land-crossing into Argive territory. Putting his troops on board ship, he landed them on the Argive coast in the region of Nauplia. The Argive army offered battle to the Spartans, but had much the worst of it. Many of them were killed, and more still took refuge in a grove sacred to Argos, the eponymous god of the place. Cleomenes lured them out one by one and treacherously slew them; the remainder perished when he ordered his helots to fire the precinct. So, Cleomenes reasoned, he had 'taken Argos' and fulfilled the prophecy. Sending back to Sparta the bulk of his army, he retained a thousand troops and went to offer sacrifice in the temple of Hera four miles from the city of Argos. On his return home Cleomenes was brought by his enemies before the ephors, on the charge that he had been bribed not to take Argos, when it was in his power to do

The era of Spartan intervention (540–491 B.C.)

so. But he told them that he thought the oracle had been fulfilled by his taking the shrine of Argos; Cleomenes then claimed to have seen a portent while sacrificing in the temple, and this confirmed him in his belief that he would not capture the city. The Spartans, says Herodotus, were satisfied with this explanation; but two puzzles remain, and Herodotus does nothing to elucidate them. The first, and the easier to solve, concerns the identity of the 'enemies' who laid the accusation against Cleomenes. Knowing so little of the political background of this epoch of Spartan history, we can only surmise that an anti-Cleomenes faction had been formed round the other king Demaratus, whose disagreement with Cleomenes had led to the abandonment of the fourth invasion of Attica. Upon the other problem no light can be thrown: it remains incomprehensible that Cleomenes should spare the city of the inveterate enemy, when it lay open before him; unless indeed he was guilty of the charge of bribery and turned it aside by yet another of his glib stories. According to an Argive tradition (preserved by Plutarch *Moralia* 245c–e and Pausanias 2.20.8–9 but not mentioned by Herodotus), Cleomenes did move against the city after his defeat of the Argive army, but was repulsed by a makeshift force of women, slaves, and elderly inhabitants under the leadership of the poetess Telesilla. This version is no more, and no less, credible than that offered by Cleomenes himself.

The Argive affair caused a great stir at Sparta, but it was soon overshadowed by a far more serious event: the attempt by Darius to extend Persian power into the waters of the western Aegean and the Greek homeland. At the outset his intervention took a diplomatic form. He sent heralds to each of the Greek states demanding a gift of earth and water in acknowledgment of his overlordship. At Athens and Sparta the persons of his heralds were outraged, in contempt of international usage, but many of the less powerful states thought it prudent to submit. Among these states was Aegina, an island of great commercial importance lying some twelve miles from the Piraeus. Athens considered Aegina to be within her sphere of influence, and was afraid (or affected to be afraid) of an attack launched against herself by the Persians, using Aegina as a convenient base for their operations. On learning of the Aeginetans' submission to Darius, the Athenians reacted in a way which tells us much about their relations with Sparta and also about the standing of Sparta in the Greek world. The involvement with Aegina also precipitated a major political crisis at Sparta, which in turn led to the downfall of king Demaratus.

In 491 the Greeks were close to outright conflict with Persia; there had been so many warnings of this (Darius' demand for earth and water being only one of a series) that far-sighted statesmen in Greece must have been aware of what impended. But even at such a crisis the various cities did not cease to consult their own self-interest. We read in Herodotus:

> Among the islanders who gave earth and water to Darius were the Aeginetans. By so doing they immediately incurred the antagonism of the Athenians, who thought that the Aeginetans had made the gift out of hostility towards themselves, with the intention of joining the Persians in an attack on them. The Athenians were glad to seize this pretext and going to Sparta they accused the people of Aegina of having betrayed Greece by their action. Upon hearing this accusation, Cleomenes . . . crossed to Aegina in order to arrest the men chiefly responsible. But when he attempted to arrest them, they stood their ground, the most prominent of them being Crius the son of Polycritus. He said that Cleomenes would regret it if he took away the Aeginetans, for he was acting without the backing of the Spartiates and had been bribed by the Athenians; otherwise he would have come in company with the other Spartan king to carry out the arrest. He said this acting on instructions contained in a letter from Demaratus. (6.49.1–6.50.3.)

Cleomenes withdrew from Aegina, and by so doing he implicitly acknowledged the force of Crius' argument.

Not everything in Herodotus' account is cogently expressed, but no real doubt can be entertained about the central features: the Athenians' resort to Sparta, as to a kind of pan-Hellenic tribunal, instead of themselves proceeding to take action against Aegina; and the willingness of the Spartans, or at least the willingness of Cleomenes, to intervene in such a cause. Herodotus goes on to say that during Cleomenes' absence in Aegina malicious reports were spread about him at Sparta by Demaratus. On his return home Cleomenes determined to rid himself finally of this troublesome colleague in the kingship, and he was not scrupulous about the methods he used. He revealed a doubt about the legitimacy of Demaratus' birth and came to an agreement with Leotychidas (like Demaratus a member of the Eurypontid family) that, if he secured Leotychidas' accession to the kingship, Leotychidas would accompany him to Aegina and help him settle matters there. Leotychidas accordingly denounced Demaratus, but the Spartans could not decide who was in the right and turned to Delphi for guidance. Cleomenes had tampered with the oracle, which then gave judgment against Demaratus. He was deposed from the kingship, and after being publicly insulted by Leotychidas (who had now been installed as king of the Eurypontid line) he left Sparta and eventually made his way to Persia: there he had a courteous reception at the court of Darius, and later also at the court of

The era of Spartan intervention (540–491 B.C.)

Darius' son Xerxes. Accompanied by his new colleague Leotychidas, Cleomenes returned to Aegina. Seeing that both Spartan kings had now descended upon them, the leading Aeginetans offered no further resistance and allowed themselves to be seized and taken to Athens as hostages. With this act, the career of Cleomenes as an effective force in Spartan and Greek affairs virtually comes to a close. His attempt to stir up trouble for his own country and his death, and also the subsequent fate of Aegina, belong to a new chapter.

Bibliography

Greek despotism: M.E. White, *Phoenix* 9 (1955), 1–18; A. Andrewes, *The Greek tyrants* (London, 1956); H. Berve, *Die Tyrannis bei den Griechen* (Munich, 1967); C. Mossé, *La tyrannie dans la Grèce antique* (Paris, 1969). Chilon and the Rylands papyrus: D.M. Leahy, *BJRL* 38 (1956), 406–35. The alleged Spartan embassy to Lygdamis: D.M. Leahy, *JHS* 77 (1957), 272–5.

Cleomenes: T. Lenschau, *Klio* 31 (1938), 412–29. Dorieus: A. Schenk von Stauffenberg, *Historia* 9 (1960), 181–215.

The Spartan Alliance: G. Busolt, *Die Lakedaimonier und ihre Bundesgenossen* I (Leipzig, 1878); G. Niccolini, *RIL* 38 (1905), 538–57; J.A.O. Larsen, *CP* 27 (1932), 136–50, 28 (1933), 257–76, 29 (1934), 1–19; D.M. Leahy, *CP* 49 (1954), 232–43 (Aegina); E. Will, *Korinthiaka* (Paris, 1955), 607–63 (Corinth); K. Wickert, *Der peloponnesische Bund von seiner Entstehung bis zum Ende des archidamischen Krieges* (Königsberg, 1961).

Aristagoras: G. De Sanctis, *RFC* 59 (1931), 48–72; J.A.S. Evans, *AJP* 84 (1963), 113–28.

10

The Persian Wars and their aftermath (490–432 B.C.)

In 490 Darius appointed two generals to raise an army and a fleet of sufficient size to visit the king's vengeance on Eretria and Athens, the cities which had insulted him when their army set fire to Sardis (p. 154). Herodotus reports that the Pisistratids kept pouring into his ears slanders against the Athenians and that Darius used this as a pretext for conquering the nations which had refused to give him earth and water (6.94.1); but the truth of this observation is not exactly borne out by the succeeding narrative, for the Persian generals show no intention of attacking Sparta, but regard Athens as their goal and the restoration of Hippias as the end of their mission. Datis, one of the generals, led his forces against Eretria, which he captured and burnt. After a few days he landed on the Attic coast, in the neighbourhood of Marathon. When they learnt of the enemy's landing, the Athenians too decided to send an army to Marathon; at the same time they sent the incomparable runner Philippides to ask for aid at Sparta. The Spartans acceded to the request, but said they could not set out until the moon was full.

So it was that the Spartans did not stand beside the Athenians when they won their victory at Marathon: a victory which did not so much remove the threat of a Persian conquest (for that, it seems, was not yet in contemplation) as avoid the resumption of despotism at Athens. But why did the Spartans not march to the Athenians' aid? We cannot believe that Philippides' message gave the Spartans their first intimation of the coming of the Persians: it simply told them that the barbarian had actually reached Attica, and the Athenians must have hoped that the understanding which had prevailed at Aegina would be effective now. The Spartan intervention in Aegina, though a very forceful one, was undertaken on the personal initiative of Cleomenes. Whether his policy was supported wholeheartedly by the ephors we are not told. It is conceivable that some interests at Sparta by no means applauded the Aeginetan adventure; if so, they would not have regarded with enthusiasm the commitment of a Spartan force to the defence of Attica, when their own state was in no danger at all. All this is a matter of surmise, since Herodotus does not name Cleomenes (or anyone else) as the instigator of Spartan policy at the

The Persian Wars and their aftermath (490–432 B.C.)

time of Marathon. The reason furnished by the Spartans in answer to Philippides was, in fact, a religious one. They meant that they could not undertake a military expedition at the time of the *Karneia* (p. 59). If it is thought that the Spartans pursued a pro-Athenian course in the early part of the fifth century, or at least that Sparta and Athens found that they had many interests in common, then the reason given by the Spartans for not going immediately to Marathon will be seen as perfectly genuine. Support for that view is found in a later passage in Herodotus, where he says that after the full moon (which marked the end of the *Karneia*) two thousand Spartan troops left for Attica and arrived after only two days; they had missed the battle, but they wished to see the place where it had been fought, and gave the Athenians unstinted praise for their great exploit (6.120).

The Spartans' attitude towards the Athenian request and their eventual compliance with it are adequately explained by Herodotus; and no more would need to be said if it were not for an allusion in Plato's *Laws*, which puts the matter in a different light: 'The Athenians sent messengers into all parts of Greece, but no one was willing to come to their aid except the Spartans; and these were hindered by a war they were waging at the time against the Messenians and by other difficulties about which we have no knowledge. And so they arrived late by one day for the battle of Marathon (3.698d–e).' This account contains no hint of the religious scruple which Herodotus adduces as the sole reason for the delay; conversely, Herodotus does not mention a war with the Messenians. The two versions are not irreconcilable: Herodotus could be reporting what the Spartans *said*, because they were reluctant to reveal their embroilment with the Messenians. There are, in any case, one or two indications that Plato's account must not be written off as a complete fiction. Strabo 8.4.10 speaks of four wars against Messenia; and this number can be made up only if it is assumed that the third war took place at some time between the second (p. 106) and the well-attested rising of 464 (p. 178). Again, Pausanias says that Messenians helped Anaxilas the despot of Rhegium in the seizure of Zancle in Sicily, for which help Zancle was renamed Messene (4.23.9). This event is associated by Pausanias with the Second Messenian War, but wrongly so, for Anaxilas ruled at Rhegium in the first quarter of the fifth century. Hence the Messenian migration of which he speaks could very well have followed an unsuccessful rising against Sparta in 490. Pausanias' mention of a Spartan offering at Olympia is also to the point. He describes it as a very tall statue of Zeus, dedicated by the Spartans at the beginning of the Second Messenian War and inscribed with a couplet praying that the god will be gracious to the Spartan cause (5.24.3). The inscription is preserved, and the form of the letters shows that it certainly cannot be as early as the Second Messenian War and that it is unlikely to be so late as the rising of 464; it would, however, fit a Messenian revolt in 490.

A factor which complicates the history of this period is the activity of Cleomenes. Herodotus gives an impressive account of the insanity which overtook him towards the end of his life, when he was still nevertheless a formidable figure (6.74–75). The treacherous methods which Cleomenes had employed in the deposition of Demaratus were divulged at Sparta. In fear of being put on trial once more, Cleomenes made his way to Thessaly. Later he was in Arcadia, where he initiated a revolt and organized the Arcadians against Sparta, binding them with awful oaths. The Spartans were alarmed when they heard what was happening in Arcadia, and brought back Cleomenes to reign again at Sparta; but he fell into a delirium, and committed suicide while confined in the stocks. He was succeeded in the Agiad line by his brother Leonidas. No reason is given for Cleomenes' journey to Thessaly. It will be remembered that the Thessalians gave Athens good service at the time of the first Spartan invasion of Attica (p. 150); it may be, then, that Cleomenes hoped to incite the Thessalians to further anti-Spartan acts. That is certainly what he did in Arcadia, according to Herodotus. Arcadia did not yet constitute a political entity; and two of the Arcadian cities, Tegea and Mantinea, were often at odds with each other. Yet the issue of coins early in the fifth century with the legend ARKADIKON does suggest that there was a loose confederation of Arcadian cities: Cleomenes might have formed such a league, or might have worked upon it to his own advantage, once it had been formed. In either case, the apprehension aroused at Sparta is easy to understand. Herodotus does not say whether Cleomenes left Sparta before or after the battle of Marathon; for all we know, he was still at home, and exercising a strong influence on Spartan policy, when the message arrived from Athens. On the other hand, if he was already stirring up trouble in Arcadia, his activity might amount to one of the 'other difficulties' mentioned by Plato.

At some unspecified time after the battle of Marathon, the Aeginetans brought a complaint against Leotychidas in respect of their hostages who were still held by the Athenians. Leotychidas was arraigned before a Spartan court, which held that he had wronged the Aeginetans. He was condemned to be given up and taken to Aegina, in exchange for those of her citizens still in Athenian hands. This changed attitude at Sparta to the Aeginetan question suggests that some influential citizens had all along opposed the interventionist policy of Leotychidas (or rather of Cleomenes); it is possible too that Leotychidas had incurred personal opprobrium by his deviousness and corruptibility. In the event he was

The Persian Wars and their aftermath (490–432 B.C.)

spared the punishment prescribed by his countrymen; instead he went to Athens with the Aeginetan envoys to request the restoration of the hostages. The Athenians refused the request, and so began a protracted period of conflict with Aegina, in which the respective fleets of the two states played a large part: in fact it was their war with Aegina which led the Athenians greatly to strengthen their naval arm. The war was not brought to an end until the need for common action against Persia supervened (p. 163).

Some four years after his severe check at Marathon, Darius died and was succeeded by Xerxes. Ambition and desire for revenge led the new king to make even more grandiose plans than those of his predecessors. Within two years of his accession he had put down a revolt in Egypt and had begun preparations for the actual conquest of the Greek homeland, with the intention of making it a province of his empire. Perceiving some defects in the arrangements for Darius' expedition, the Persians realized that half-measures were useless. Adequate forces had to be assembled. Elaborate measures had to be undertaken; these included the digging of a canal across the promontory of Athos in Chalcidice, so that the fleet would not have to sail round the dangerous headland, and the bridging of the Hellespont for the army to march across. Above all, close co-operation had to be maintained between army and fleet. Although the Persians appreciated many of the problems attendant on a conquest of Greece, they did not appreciate all of them. The supreme moral advantage enjoyed by the Greeks is often emphasized by Herodotus: they were free citizens of autonomous states, defending their own country against a horde of slaves. Of course they often threw away this advantage because of mutual suspicion and inter-state rivalries; but Xerxes, on his side, did not dispose of a united force. His army must have been enormous; but, apart from the courageous and well-trained Persian bodyguard (the ten thousand 'immortals'), the host was drawn from a bewildering medley of subject nations. The degree of discipline attained by Greek hoplites, and above all by the Spartans, with their unbroken chain of command and unquestioning obedience to orders, was beyond the reach of Xerxes' promiscuous army. And the hoplite-phalanx itself far outmatched any formation that the Persians could bring against it. The Persians often employed tactics which had been more or less obsolete in Greece for two centuries; and the one arm in which they were superior, namely cavalry, would be of no use to them if the defenders chose (as they did) narrow passes in which to offer battle. The fleet of Xerxes, though very large, lacked the cohesion and skill in seamanship which marked the Athenian navy; it was, moreover, manned entirely by non-Persian sailors from the subject provinces, who were unlikely to fight with bitter fanaticism in the Persian cause.

Herodotus puts his finger unerringly on the main reason for the eventual success of the Greeks. The Persian plan of keeping army and navy close together for mutual support was excellent in theory; but the Persians adhered to it long after it had ceased to be useful, and because of their reluctance to separate one arm from the other they never struck a decisive blow. The Greeks on the other hand chose the Athenian way, the aggressive deployment of naval forces in narrow sea-passages, and not the Peloponnesian way, which amounted merely to the defence of a well-fortified position on the Isthmus of Corinth. That the latter policy would have been fatal as well as selfish is shown by Herodotus in a series of compelling arguments:

> If the Athenians, out of dread of the impending danger, had abandoned their country or, even if they had not abandoned it but stayed and yielded to Xerxes, no nation would have tried to withstand the king by sea. If nobody had withstood Xerxes by sea, the following result would have come about on land: even though many lines of walls were drawn across the Isthmus by the Peloponnesians, the Spartans would have been betrayed by their allies – not from free will but out of compulsion, once their cities had been captured one after the other by the barbarian fleet. Then the Spartans would have been alone, and in this plight they would have performed great deeds and perished honourably. (7.139.2–3.)

Herodotus here looks at the war from the Greek view-point; but the logic is no less impeccable when he puts a speech in the mouth of Demaratus. The ex-king of Sparta has come to Greece in the retinue of Xerxes (p. 157), and he advises the king to send a strong fleet to the island of Cythera, a base from which he will be able to harry the Spartans' own country, instead of being held up indefinitely at the Isthmus (7.235). Whether such advice was ever tendered to Xerxes we do not know; if so, he did not take it, and lost an opportunity which was not likely to be repeated.

The scale and nature of the Persian preparations apprised the Greeks that a great invasion was imminent, and that its course would lie through Thrace, Macedonia, and Thessaly. At about the time that Xerxes carried out a review of his army at Sardis (spring 481), those Greek states which were determined to resist the Persians sent delegates to a congress at the Isthmus of Corinth. This congress must have met repeatedly to give directions for the prosecution of the war; perhaps, once convened, it was in more or less continuous session, communicating by messengers with the respective states. Athens and Sparta, the two most powerful anti-

The Persian Wars and their aftermath (490–432 B.C.)

Persian cities, took the initiative in making proposals to the congress. At their earliest recorded meeting the members of the congress made three decisions. The first was negative, to the effect that all conflicts between Greek cities (for instance the Athenian-Aeginetan war) should be brought to an end forthwith. On the positive side, it was resolved to send spies to Sardis, to find out what they could about the Persian forces and their intentions, and also to dispatch envoys to four prominent Greek states, inviting them to join the resistance against Persia. Although hostilities did cease between Athens and Aegina, the various missions were all fruitless. The spies were discovered at Sardis, and contemptuously sent back to Greece, with the object of intimidating the delegates when they heard the scale of the Persian preparations. Nor was support forthcoming from any of the Greek states canvassed: Argos, Corcyra, Crete, and Syracuse.

The Greek delegates at the Isthmus now received a message from Thessaly, urging them to send a strong force to secure the pass of Tempe, between the peaks of Ossa and Olympus. The Thessalians undertook to co-operate with such a force; but they said that if none were sent they would be unable to hold the pass by themselves and would have to ask mercy from the Persians. The request was granted. About one thousand hoplites took ship and encamped in the pass: they were commanded by a Spartan general and by the Athenian statesman Themistocles, who had taken the major part in persuading his countrymen to look to their naval defences. The Greeks at Tempe were warned by Alexander, the Macedonian king, not to stay where they were, in case they were overwhelmed by the Persian forces. Perhaps that would have been their fate; but it is not obvious why they thought that this friend of Persia was actuated by good will towards themselves. None the less they heeded his warning and retired to the Isthmus, leaving Thessaly undefended; the Thessalians then carried out their threat, and went over to the Persians.

Having made the decision to abandon the northern part of Greece, the delegates at the Isthmus resolved to hold the pass of Thermopylae, a narrow coastal strip in Locris squeezed between mountains and the Malian Gulf. An army entering Greece from the north would probably, but not certainly, come that way; the pass was narrower than that of Tempe and much closer to home. The military force holding Thermopylae was to collaborate with a fleet standing off Artemisium, in the north of Euboea. While the Greeks made their dispositions, Xerxes was marching through Thrace and Macedonia and into Thessaly. The news of his arrival in Pieria, the region to the north of Tempe, provoked the immediate dispatch of the Greek forces to their respective stations. Moving southwards, Xerxes bivouacked in Malian country west of

Thermopylae, and the Greek army took up its position in the pass. According to Herodotus the latter consisted of 300 Spartiates, 2,800 hoplites from other parts of the Peloponnese, 1,100 from two Boeotian cities (700 from Thespiae and 400 from Thebes), an unspecified number of Locrians, and 1,000 Phocians. The commander-in-chief was the Spartan king Leonidas. He was responsible for incorporating the Theban contingent in his army; they joined him, but all the time they were contemplating desertion to Xerxes. The small size of the Spartan contribution is explained by Herodotus in the following way. The three hundred Spartiates formed the king's personal bodyguard, or *hippeis* (p. 119). The rest of the Spartan army was expected to come up as soon as the *Karneia* had come to an end. Likewise the rest of the allied troops at Thermopylae represented only a token force, to be brought up to strength when the Olympian festival had been celebrated. Matters at Thermopylae were not expected to move to a crisis so swiftly. But when Xerxes moved to the mouth of the pass, hoping to frighten the Greek army away by a display of his strength, Leonidas requested reinforcements from the various allied states. Meanwhile he prepared to meet the Persian onslaught, detaching the Phocians to guard the path over the mountains; for if the Persians seized this they could descend upon the Greek rear. Before the Greek cities had time to send fresh forces to Leonidas' support, he came under Persian attack on three successive days (late August 480), but he was able to beat these off, owing largely to the valour and skill of his own *hippeis*. There is no telling how long Leonidas would have held out, had not the traitor Ephialtes guided the Persians over the mountains by way of the path where the Phocians were posted. These were put to flight by the enemy archers, and the Persians descended the mountain, preparing to cut off the Greeks. When the Greek forces became aware of their approaching encirclement, they all made off, except only the Spartans, the Thespians, and the Thebans: the men of Thespiae staying out of their own free will, those of Thebes under compulsion by Leonidas, who kept them with the army as hostages. Herodotus gives two different reasons for the departure of the allies. According to one version, Leonidas sent them away so that they could make good their escape; whereas it would have been dishonourable for the king and his guard to desert the position they had come to defend. But Herodotus himself inclines to believe another version, whereby Leonidas devoted himself to certain death, because of a Delphic oracle delivered to Sparta at the beginning of the war; this prophesied that Sparta would either fall to the Persians or lose one of her kings in battle. In the event Leonidas and his tiny force were overwhelmed, though they fought with reckless bravery to the end and inflicted serious losses on the

The Persian Wars and their aftermath (490–432 B.C.)

enemy. The Thebans made their way to the Persian side, where their only reward was to be branded. Herodotus mentions three epitaphs that were later set up on the battlefield: one recording the feat of four thousand Peloponnesians in withstanding three millions of the enemy, one saying that the Spartans lie there obedient to their city's command, and one honouring the seer Megistias.

Thus by Herodotus' time the exploit of Leonidas and the Spartiates had already passed into legend. But how much is legend, and how much is truth? The tradition which Herodotus follows is sometimes assailed on the ground that he has been so misled by Spartiate propaganda as to swallow the story of the hopeless defence by the three hundred Spartiates, whereas there were in fact one thousand Spartans present at Thermopylae. This criticism is based on two pieces of evidence: first the words of the epitaph, which speaks of four thousand Peloponnesians, although the figures given by Herodotus amount to only 3,100; second it is stated by Diodorus that there were one thousand Spartans, including three hundred Spartiates. But these references do not necessarily bring us to a complete knowledge of the size of the Spartan contingent. It is possible that Herodotus failed to record the full numbers from all the Peloponnesian states: the 'missing' nine hundred may not have come from Sparta itself.

Other questions provoked by Herodotus' narrative of Thermopylae are more serious. Our questions concern principally the composition of Leonidas' army and the exact motives for the departure of the allied forces. It is easy to credit the dissensions mentioned by Herodotus as frequently arising among the Greeks; and, however clear and cogent a plan Leonidas may have had, he was perhaps unable to impose it on the Peloponnesian allies – still less on the men of Locris. There are two curious features about the constitution of the army: the total absence of Athenians and the presence of the four hundred Thebans. The lack of an Athenian component is not alluded to by Herodotus. We know that the Athenians had participated in the force sent earlier to Tempe, and their failure to join Leonidas is inexplicable. Nor can we easily believe in the presence of the Theban contingent. If the Thebans' loyalty was so suspect, why did Leonidas saddle himself with them at all? A still graver problem is posed by Leonidas' decision to dismiss everyone except the Thespians and Thebans and fight on, in the certain knowledge that there was now no means of escape. We can disregard the oracle, which foretold that Sparta would survive only if she lost one of her kings: that is plainly something invented afterwards, to provide a motive for Leonidas' decision to remain, which had no obvious military justification, however heroic it may have been, For we can hardly accept the suggestion that it was for purely military reasons that Leonidas sent away the allies and stayed behind to cover their withdrawal. If the withdrawal of the whole army seemed the correct solution (as no doubt it was, in view of Leonidas' inadequate resources), there was no compelling reason for the Spartiates not to form the rearguard of the retreating army; their extreme skill in defence, amply attested in the fighting at Thermopylae, would probably have sufficed to ward off the Persians. Not enough facts are now at our disposal to explain either Leonidas' retention of the Thebans or his dismissal of the allies. It remains likely that both Leonidas and the Greeks at the Isthmus made a serious miscalculation: Leonidas in not deploying his army to the best advantage; the Greek command in not acting more promptly and purposefully to hold the pass, once they had reached the decision to fight at Thermopylae. These shortcomings were transformed by Spartiate tradition, or Spartiate propaganda, into the story of a small band of heroes giving their lives for the salvation of Greece.

The strength of the Greek fleet which mustered at Artemisium is assessed at 271 warships with three banks of oars (triremes), together with a few ships propelled by fifty oarsmen (penteconters). The Athenians contributed by far the largest number from any single city. The Spartans' naval arm was not yet well developed, and they sent only ten triremes; nevertheless the Spartan admiral Eurybiadas was put in command, either because Spartan prestige stood so high or (as Herodotus alleges) the allies refused to serve under an Athenian. Themistocles commanded the Athenian ships; despite his formal subordination to Eurybiadas, he had a powerful influence on the course of the naval operations, by reason of the Athenians' strength at sea and of his own forceful character. When the Greek ships arrived at Artemisium, the Persian ships had already taken up a position across the strait to the north. An important component in the Persian plan of campaign was an attempt to catch the Greek fleet in the rear; for this purpose they told off two hundred ships, with orders to sail right round the eastern coast of Euboea and then sail up the Euripus from the south. But these ships had a disastrous passage. They managed to round the headland of Geraestus, but were then driven by a storm into the 'Hollows' and wrecked on the numerous promontories. Meanwhile the fighting off Artemisium, like that at Thermopylae, is said to have lasted for three days. On the first two, Greek ships attacked the Persian fleet and inflicted some losses; the third day saw a major engagement, in which the Greeks came off slightly the better, although many ships on either side were destroyed. It is possible that if Leonidas' army had been able to hold the pass the Greeks

The Persian Wars and their aftermath (490–432 B.C.)

would have won a decisive victory at sea. As it was, on hearing the news of Thermopylae, they sailed southwards round Cape Sunium and put in at Salamis.

After forcing the pass of Thermopylae, Xerxes brought his army through Phocis and Boeotia into Attica. By this time Attica had been evacuated by many of its inhabitants, who took their possessions to Salamis, Aegina, or Troezen. Xerxes was now devastating Attica, and had occupied the Athenian acropolis. A great conflict was obviously in the offing: once the Persian army had wrought its vengeance on Attica, it would presumably make immediate plans for the invasion of the Peloponnese; and the fleet was sailing through the Euripus to its support. To meet the threat on the landward side, a large Greek army met at the Isthmus under the command of Leonidas' brother Cleombrotus and began the construction of a wall. If the Persian fleet were to make its way unimpeded to Cenchreae on the eastern side of the Isthmus, it could give powerful aid to Xerxes' army and enable him to break into the Peloponnese. But the presence of a very strong concentration of Greek ships at Salamis presented so serious a challenge to any Persian attempt to sail through the Saronic Gulf towards Cenchreae that it had to be dealt with before conclusions were tried at the Isthmus.

The Persian fleet seems to have lain in the great harbour of Phalerum, just east of the Piraeus, for about a fortnight; no doubt in the hope that the Greek ships would either come out and do battle in the open sea or sail to the Isthmus. But the Greeks stayed where they were, and the Persians at last made a move towards the end of September 480. Between the eastern promontory of Salamis and the Attic coast there is a narrow strait, and lying aslant this strait is an islet, called in antiquity Psyttaleia. In great secrecy and under cover of darkness the Persians carried out two daring operations: they first landed men on Psyttaleia, to rescue any shipwrecked members of their crews in the forthcoming battle and to do the Greeks what harm they could; then they sent a number of their ships to take up a position (roughly in a west-east line) along the coast of the mainland. Thus they were now facing the line of Greek ships beached on the promontory of Salamis. The Greeks remained unaware of the Persian intrusion into the strait until late at night. At dawn the Greeks stood off from the shore; the Persian vessels which had made their way into the strait attacked them, while the remainder of the Persian fleet blocked off the southern entrance of the strait. The west wing of the Persian fleet was held by a Phoenician squadron, lying opposite the Athenians, the east wing by Ionians, who confronted the Spartans. The battle lasted all day, but its course cannot be followed with exactness. Herodotus unfolds a rapid succession of brilliant pictures, but does not write a coherent narrative. The essential features of the action, however, appear to be these. The Persian fleet could not get the better of the Greeks who, fighting desperately and helped by the greater weight of their ships, were able to bear down on the enemy in the confined space and inflict crippling losses. Xerxes was bitterly angry with the Phoenicians, whom he blamed in particular for the defeat; on the Greek side it was naturally the Athenians who were responsible for the outcome. The Persian defeat became a rout, those ships which escaped making for the haven of Phalerum, where the land-forces stood ready to assist them; but on their way the Persians had to run the gauntlet of an Aeginetan squadron, which mauled them badly. Finally an Athenian force landed at Psyttaleia and killed all the Persians they caught there.

In one day's fighting the Greeks had destroyed the fighting capability of Xerxes' fleet and so had removed from his army the naval support which had been an essential part of the grand Persian strategy. Xerxes was instantly aware of the magnitude of the Greek victory, but the Greeks themselves came only slowly to a full realization of it. The relics of the Persian fleet now made for home, being pursued by the Greeks only as far as Andros. Xerxes withdrew his troops to Thessaly, where his general, Mardonius, selected the flower of the army to spend the winter with him; the remainder accompanied the king back to the Hellespont. Themistocles paid a visit to Sparta. The citizens bestowed upon him and upon Eurybiadas an olive crown in recognition of their triumph; they moreover gave Themistocles a magnificent chariot and had him escorted to the borders of Laconia by three hundred *hippeis*. In what light should we regard this visit? Were it not for Herodotus' explicit statement, and Themistocles' known character, we might be inclined to see it as cementing the close alliance between Athens and Sparta which had so notably advanced the Greek cause at Salamis. But Herodotus (who throughout maintains an anti-Themistoclean bias) depicts Themistocles as a man who had not received the credit he thought due to him and so went to Sparta, where he was heaped with extraordinary honours. If that is the correct explanation, the Spartans took some advantage of political divisions at Athens.

When the campaigning season began in the spring of 479, what was left of the Persian fleet mustered at Samos; but this time in a purely defensive role, for they now had the task of looking out for signs of incipient rebellion among the Ionian subjects. The Greek ships gathered at Aegina, under the command of Leotychidas. For the time being, the Greek fleet showed no greater disposition to move into eastern waters than the Persians did to sail westwards. It was only reluctantly that the

The Persian Wars and their aftermath (490–432 B.C.)

Greeks allowed themselves to be persuaded to take their ships as far as Delos, in (wholly inadequate) response to the Chians' request for help in enabling them to rise against Persian rule.

The first move by Mardonius was not military but diplomatic. He sent as envoy to Athens the Macedonian king, Alexander, who offered the Athenians a treaty of friendship if only they would cease hostilities towards Xerxes. Spartan delegates, in their turn, urged the Athenians to have nothing to do with such tainted overtures. The Athenians reproachfully told them that they had no intention of doing so.

Mardonius' attempt to break up the Greek alliance having failed, he moved his army south through the friendly territory of Boeotia and occupied Attica in midsummer. Herodotus reveals some of the tensions which had arisen between Athens and Sparta in regard to the prosecution of the war. The Athenians were content to stay in their city so long as there seemed any hope that a Peloponnesian army would march to their support and help them hold Attica against the invaders. When this hope was not fulfilled, they evacuated Attica and again took refuge at Salamis. The Spartans claimed that they could not move until after the celebration of the *Hyakinthia* (p. 60); besides, they were awaiting completion of the wall across the Isthmus. Since these were the people who had so powerfully enjoined the Athenians not to make a separate peace with Persia, and since the Isthmian wall had in fact been built during the previous year, the Spartan pretexts do not ring entirely true. Herodotus has it that the ephors kept putting off their answer to the Athenian envoys from day to day until finally a man from Tegea opened their eyes to the fact that the war concerned Sparta no less than Athens. In this dramatic fashion, Herodotus is perhaps drawing attention to a serious difference of opinion at Sparta: one side considering the Peloponnese a self-contained unit which could be sealed off from the rest of Greece (especially now that the enemy was weak at sea), the other side favouring joint action with Athens to rid Greece of the barbarian once and for all.

So perhaps the Tegean's argument is meant to symbolize the victory at Sparta of the latter opinion. It must be admitted that, once the Spartans had decided to intervene on the Athenian side, they took swift and decisive action. A force of five thousand Spartiates (which must have formed the bulk of the citizen-army) was dispatched to the Isthmus under the command of Pausanias, the nephew of Leonidas, who held the regency for Leonidas' son Pleistarchus. On the following day the Spartans sent five thousand outlanders to augment their army. When they arrived at the Isthmus the Spartans were joined by their Peloponnesian allies, and marched forward with them to Eleusis. The Argives informed Mardonius of the departure of the Spartan army. He withdrew his forces to Tanagra in Boeotia; from there he moved in a westerly direction along more or less level ground between Mount Cithaeron and the Asopus, eventually camping by the latter river in a strongly fortified position. Meanwhile the Peloponnesians had been joined by an Athenian contingent at Eleusis; the whole army then crossed into Boeotia and took up position on the slopes of Cithaeron, facing the Persians. Since the Greeks chose not to descend to the plain, Mardonius was forced to attack them with cavalry where they stood. The Persian attacks were concentrated upon the Megarians; for a while they were hard pressed, but on being reinforced by some Athenians they struck back with such effect that they killed the general in command of the cavalry. The Persians attempted to retrieve the corpse, but the main body of the Greek army came up and drove them off.

This limited success was a source of great encouragement to the Greek side. Pausanias next led his army westwards to Plataea and drew them up, partly on level ground and partly on low hills, between Asopus and the Cithaeron range. We cannot elicit from the pages of Herodotus all the reasons for this movement or even the precise location of the Greek forces once they had made it. Herodotus mentions that the ground towards Plataea was more suitable for a camp, especially as it had a better water-supply; but we may doubt whether that consideration alone would have induced Pausanias to leave a position in which he was able to hold his own against the enemy cavalry. The Greek army in its second position must have lain south of the river Asopus, its line extending from the plain due north of Plataea to the ridge which runs north-east of the town. The right wing was held by the Spartans, the left by the Athenians. Learning that the Greek army had marched towards Plataea and had occupied a line south of the Asopus, Mardonius led his own forces to the west and drew them up north of the river. There followed a lull of ten days, broken only by some Persian cavalry-attacks and by a Persian operation designed to stop supplies getting to the Greeks from a pass over the Cithaeron.

On the following day, says Herodotus, the Persian general Artabazus urged a retreat to the stronghold at Thebes and the disbursement of immense wealth in an attempt to bribe the Greek states into taking the Persian side; but the temper of Mardonius favoured an immediate action, especially as the Greeks were constantly receiving reinforcements while his own supplies ran low. The Persians accordingly launched a cavalry-attack along the whole front: this did not amount to a charge, but took the form of mounted men riding up to the Greek line, just outside spear-range, and discharging their arrows. The Greeks were greatly distressed by these attacks, and Pausanias decided to withdraw them by night to a ridge nearer Cithaeron where they would be less vulnerable

The Persian Wars and their aftermath (490–432 B.C.)

and, moreover, in a better position to defend the supply-route over the pass. Amompharetus, the commander of the Pitanate company from Sparta, refused to move, saying that it was dishonourable for a Spartan soldier to retire in the face of the barbarian. Exasperated by his stubbornness, Pausanias led the Spartans to their new position, confident that Amompharetus would not stay behind when all his countrymen had marched off; and so it proved. Quite apart from this unexpected breach of the Spartiate discipline, the Greek withdrawal was carried out in a most disorderly manner. The Greek centre (that is, the entire army except Spartans, Tegeans, and Athenians) made its way to Plataea instead of to the ridge prescribed by Pausanias. When on the following day news was brought to Mardonius of what had occurred, he drew the conclusion that the Greeks were in full flight. Although he was wrong in making this assumption, he was right to think that the most favourable moment for a Persian attack had arrived, with the Spartan and Athenian contingents separated both from each other and from the rest of the Greeks. He therefore sent the Persian cavalry across the Asopus, which fell upon the Spartans and Tegeans as they were marching to their new position. Seeing the Persians move off to the attack, other components of Mardonius' army also prepared to attack the Spartan force; their efforts were accompanied by much noise and little discipline. Pausanias requested the Athenians to come to his aid, but they were unable to do so, being by this time hard pressed by Greeks who were fighting in Mardonius' army.

According to Herodotus the ensuing 'battle of Plataea' was fought exclusively by the Spartans and Tegeans and then by the Athenians, and what had previously been the Greek centre took no part. As for the fight in the Spartan-Tegean sector, this in Herodotus' narrative turns imperceptibly from a cavalry-attack on a marching column into a pitched battle between forces of infantry; it further appears that Mardonius has come up to encourage his troops. How are we to explain this radical change in the character of the engagement? Either Herodotus has left out a number of details so as to concentrate on the main action or the Spartans and Tegeans were all the time making their way to higher ground at the foot of Cithaeron so as to force the issue on terrain unsuitable for horsemen. In the engagement, the Tegeans and secondly the Spartans made a counter-attack. The Persians, as their habit was, erected round themselves a fence of wicker-work shields; this the Greeks managed to break down, and then their superb fighting skill, together with the Persians' lack of armour, gradually turned the issue in their favour, and their success was sealed when Mardonius and his bodyguard were killed.

The victory won by Pausanias near Plataea is termed by Herodotus 'the most splendid of all those known to us' (9.64.1). The compliment is justified on at least three grounds: first, Pausanias' grasp of over-all strategy and his refusal to be drawn to the Asopus, then the steadfastness of the phalanx and the bravery of individual soldiers in attacking the Persian élite, finally the decisive nature of the battle which marked the end of direct military intervention by Persia in the affairs of Greece; thereafter the Persians had to effect their purposes by means of diplomacy or bribery. The troops who had been routed by Pausanias fled to their camp or to the stockade they had built in Theban territory, while Artabazus took a large force with him to Phocis, preparing to lead them back to the Hellespont. As for the Athenian contingent, they were attacked by Greeks in Mardonius' army, but of these only the Boeotians showed much stomach for the fight; eventually they were driven off with heavy losses.

The Spartans pursued the remnants of the Persian army to the stockade, but could not force an entrance. The Athenians, when they came up, scaled the wall and made an opening through which they and their allies rushed, putting to the sword those inside and seizing the treasure left by the Persians. Having divided the spoil, the allies saw to the burial of the fallen. Each state, says Herodotus, buried its dead in a separate grave; and cenotaphs were erected by those cities which ought to have sent soldiers to the battle – but did not! We encounter a difficulty in Herodotus' account of the Spartan burials. The Spartans, he says, made three tombs: one for 'priests', among whom were valiant officers (including Amompharetus); one for the other Spartiates; and one for the helots (9.85.1–2). Since the word 'priests', given by the manuscripts, makes no perceptible sense, the emendation to 'eirens' is often adopted. But this change, while solving one problem, creates another, since we could hardly suppose that a high officer of the Spartan army was still an eiren (a man under thirty, not yet having full civic rights). What we need is a word meaning 'citizens of exceptional distinction' (so accounting for the burial of these men apart from the other Spartiates); and it may be that behind the transmitted word there lurks a specific Laconian term for such men, which has been corrupted into the more familiar expression.

The presence in Boeotia of a large and victorious army afforded the allies an opportunity of settling accounts with the Thebans for their betrayal of the Greek cause and active support of the enemy. By besieging the city and ravaging Theban territory, the army compelled the surrender of the pro-Persian leaders; one of these escaped, but the rest were taken back to Corinth, where Pausanias had them put to death.

Herodotus asserts that on the very day of the battle of Plataea the

The Persian Wars and their aftermath (490–432 B.C.)

Persians suffered a defeat at Mycale. The coincidence is suspicious; perhaps it arises from Herodotus' desire to draw together the two threads of his story, one concerned with the army under Pausanias, the other with Leotychidas' fleet. It will be remembered that Leotychidas had taken the fleet to Delos in the spring (p. 169). While he was at Delos, the king received some refugees who had made their way from Samos without the knowledge of the Samian despot. They urged upon Leotychidas the necessity of striking an immediate blow against the Persian fleet; if the action were successful, they claimed, it would provoke an anti-Persian rising among the Ionian states. For some reason, Leotychidas was much more favourably impressed by the Samians' arguments than he had been by those of the Chians. He shortly afterwards took the fleet to Samos, where it anchored close to the temple of Hera. The Greeks could not bring the Persians to battle at sea; the latter, realizing that they were no match for the Greek fleet, withdrew to Mycale and beached their ships under the protection of Persian troops. A stockade of stones and tree-trunks was erected round the ships, and the enemy waited to see what Leotychidas would do. At the king's order, a herald shouted to the Ionians serving with the Persian army to remember liberty first of all, and then the watchword 'Hera'. The Persians were apprehensive at the approach of the Greek ships and the herald's proclamation; they disarmed the Samian contingent and sent away the Milesians – allegedly to guard the passes. The Athenians attacked the Persian barricade from the beach, while the Spartans marched round to the rear and made their onset from that side. The shields of the Persians were broken down, and they were driven within the fortification. This too the Greeks stormed, and killed many Persians. Fugitives making their way over the passes were set upon by the Milesians; the few Persians who survived eventually came to Sardis.

The Greeks with Leotychidas divided the booty they had taken on storming the Persian camp; they then burnt the camp and all the enemy ships. But they were unable to take on the large Persian army in the vicinity; still less could they hope to wrest the Asiatic seaboard from Persian hands. Nevertheless the virtual destruction of Xerxes' naval power meant that the Greek islands close to Asia were restored to Hellas; and to that extent Herodotus is justified in stating that 'Ionia successfully revolted from the Persians for the second time' (9.104). This very question of the Greek settlements in the east engaged the attention of the Greek commanders once their fleet had crossed from Mycale back to Samos. It was suggested that all Hellenes should be evacuated from Asia and resettled in the Greek motherland. At this point a dispute arose between Spartans and Athenians. The Peloponnesians said that room should be found for those displaced by expelling from Greece the inhabitants of cities which had taken the Persian side; but the Athenians were alarmed at the prospect of Peloponnesians (in effect, Spartans) gaining control of affairs in the very centre of Greece, especially since Athens claimed to be the mother-city of the Ionian colonies. The proposal for evacuation and resettlement on such a large scale was dropped on the objection of the Athenians; instead the Greeks admitted to their alliance the men of Samos, Chios, and Lesbos, and other islanders who had fought on their side.

The Greek fleet now sailed to the Hellespont, with the intention of breaking down the Persian bridges; but on their arrival they found the bridges already broken. Leotychidas and the Peloponnesians saw little point in engaging the Persians in that region, and they returned home. The Athenians decided to stay and lay siege to the fortified city of Sestus in the Chersonese. This they did under the command of Xanthippus (the father of Pericles), who captured the place during the winter. These Athenians were no longer implementing a pan-Hellenic policy, or a policy laid down by the Spartan king: it was solely to Athens that they looked for their instructions.

So the fragile Greek alliance, which had been formed for the specific purpose of opposing the Persians, did not long survive their expulsion. Far from being crushed by her travail in the war, Athens emerged from the conflict in exalted, self-confident mood. Without a struggle (indeed their sigh of relief is almost audible in the pages of Thucydides), the Spartans resigned to Athens the leadership of the Hellenic league. They themselves, while of course retaining the primacy of their own alliance, became increasingly isolationist and took comparatively little part in activities beyond the Peloponnese. As for the Athenians, they assumed with enthusiasm the leadership which the Spartans had allowed to drop from their grasp. The breath-taking advances in art and poetry which now took place at Athens, her intellectual development, and the rapid maturation of her democratic institutions had no parallel in any other Greek state. The boundless energy which made these achievements possible drove the Athenians (unlike Sparta) to adopt a policy of expansion. When the Hellenic league disintegrated, Athens formed an alliance of her own; since her political power was founded to a large extent on her naval supremacy, she concluded treaties principally with the maritime states of the Aegean and cities on the coasts of Asia Minor, the Propontis, Chalcidice, and Thrace. Unlike Sparta again, Athens acknowledged the fact that her alliance was based on inequality between herself and the other members. From the time of the formation of the

The Persian Wars and their aftermath (490–432 B.C.)

Athenian alliance in 477, tribute was levied on many of its members. For a number of years the treasury of the alliance was kept in the precinct at Delos, so conveying the impression that the proceeds of the tribute were devoted to the common purposes of the alliance; but even this pretence was dropped in 454, with the transference of the treasury to Athens. By that year, if not earlier, the Athenian alliance had effectively become an empire. Towards states which seceded from the alliance, such as Naxos and Thasos, the Athenians showed themselves imperious and vindictive. They led the forces of their allies on far-flung expeditions: to Eion in Thrace and to the Eurymedon in southern Anatolia, in both of which places Cimon was successful against Persian forces. The island of Scyros was captured and turned into an Athenian colony. Carystus, a town in southern Euboea, was forced to capitulate. Some of the more ambitious enterprises, however, met with failure. The Athenians could not force their way into Thessaly; and, after a struggle lasting for six years, they had to give up their attempt to detach Egypt from the Persian empire. Undeterred by the latter reverse, the Athenians sent another fleet under Cimon's leadership into eastern waters (c. 450); it was successful in Cyprus in actions both by land and by sea. If Diodorus of Sicily is right in assigning the Peace of Callias to the years immediately following the Athenian victories just mentioned, Athens did no less than make terms with the Persian king Artaxerxes on behalf of all the Greeks. According to the treaty concluded between Artaxerxes and Callias the Athenian ambassador, the Greek and the Persian areas of influence were formally delimited. Although the Persians retained control of Cyprus and Egypt, they bound themselves neither to sail into the Aegean Sea nor to advance nearer the coast of Asia than a three days' journey (Diodorus 12.4.5). Finally, in illustration of the widespread character of Athenian interests, there may be mentioned the foundation of colonies at Amphipolis in Thrace and at Thurii in southern Italy.

Since the Athenians pursued their adventures in so many parts of the Mediterranean, they were bound to come into conflict with one or other of Sparta's allies. The war which eventually broke out between Sparta and Athens was caused partly by Athenian provocations, partly by the sullen suspicion which Sparta entertained of her more enterprising and more brilliant rival, and partly because Corinth (a powerful ally of Sparta and, like Athens, a great commercial city) crossed the path of the Athenians more frequently and more dangerously than the latter were prepared to tolerate. To explore these causes we must go back to the year following the expulsion of the Persians.

In 478 the Athenians took back the household goods they had removed for safe keeping at the time of Mardonius' invasion and set about the reconstruction of the walls and buildings of their city which the Persians had destroyed. The zeal and single-mindedness they brought to the task, under the guidance of Themistocles, caused alarm at Sparta. The Spartans suggested that, so far from erecting new walls, the Athenians should join themselves in throwing down all fortifications outside the Peloponnese, so as to deny any future invader the use of Greek citadels; and the Greeks should regard the Peloponnese as their secure refuge and base of operations. The Athenians, remembering the attitude of Sparta in the previous year, were hardly likely to be swayed by arguments such as these, whose insincerity was patent. The building was pressed on with renewed vigour, and a start was made on a great naval base at the Piraeus. These works the Athenian ambassadors justified at Sparta, on the ground that they would enable their city to speak in the councils of the alliance from a position of strength. The Spartans could do nothing about it, and bit back their resentment.

Despite this difference of opinion between Athens and Sparta, the two states did co-operate in one last expedition, under Pausanias' command. The combined fleet made first for Cyprus, large parts of which they took from Persian control. The Greek ships next sailed to the Hellespont, laid siege to the stronghold of Byzantium (then held by the Persians), and captured it. With Byzantium and Sestus in their possession, the Greeks became masters of the trade-route into the Black Sea.

A political consequence of great importance flowed from the action at Byzantium: a consequence which marks a shift of gravity away from the Peloponnese towards Athens and the maritime states. Once Pausanias was master of Byzantium, he threw off the habits of courtesy and frugality for which Herodotus praises him. He became aloof and arrogant, and started to ape the Persian dress and way of life. The allies, and in particular the Greeks of Asia, could not tolerate his conduct, and requested Athens to assume the leadership of the league. The Athenians complied, and formed their own alliance of non-Peloponnesian states; the Peloponnesians still adhered to the Spartan Alliance. This disillusionment with Sparta cannot have arisen merely from the behaviour of Pausanias; if it had, Sparta would have been asked to provide a new commander, not to relinquish the leadership altogether. With the accession of the Ionians, the Hellenic league had taken on a distinctly pro-Athenian complexion; and the situation was radically different from that of the Persian War, in which the majority declined to accept Athens as leader, even in naval operations (p. 166).

Pausanias was not content to play the despot; while at Byzantium he corresponded with Xerxes, and undertook to bring the whole of Greece

The Persian Wars and their aftermath (490–432 B.C.)

under Persian domination. The Spartans thereupon recalled Pausanias and accused him of treason and of misconduct towards individuals; the court acquitted him on the principal charge but found against him on the lesser, for which it exacted a fine. In the next two or three years Pausanias behaved rather as a privateer than as the guardian and regent of a Spartan king. After his trial at Sparta, he seized a ship and sailed back to Byzantium without the ephors' authority. Expelled from there by the Athenians, he made his way to Asia Minor. The ephors heard rumours that he was again negotiating with Persia, and ordered him to return. After spending some time in prison at Sparta, he contrived to escape; and all the time the ephors were casting about for a specific charge they could bring home to him. Slow as they often were to act against a Spartiate, unless they had irrefutable proof, they were still slower on account of Pausanias' membership of one of the royal houses. Even after some helots turned informer and revealed Pausanias' plan to foment a rebellion with helot support, the ephors could not bring themselves to move against him; nor could they when a messenger actually showed them a letter written by Pausanias to Xerxes. Only when they heard Pausanias convict himself out of his own mouth did they resolve on action; nevertheless he had time to take refuge in a building attached to the temple of Athena. The ephors walled him up and starved him almost to the point of death. He died just after being brought out; in obedience to an oracle, his body was buried at the entrance of the temple.

The strange end of Pausanias is eloquent testimony to the demoralizing effects which the wealth and luxury of Persia could exercise; and exercise more effectively in the case of one bred up in the rigours of the 'Lycurgan' system. (By a curious parallel, Themistocles aroused the hatred and suspicion of *his* countrymen: during the period of his ostracism he stayed at Argos, promoting the anti-Spartan policy of that city; when summoned back to Athens to answer charges of conspiring with the Persians, he fled to the east and became a Persian satrap.) Thucydides' description of the final years of Pausanias has a Herodotean ring. For all its copious detail, it does not indicate the length of time Pausanias spent in Byzantium before his expulsion, and gives no hint of the means by which the Athenians expelled him. It is a still graver defect that Thucydides does not realize how much Pausanias' actions leave to be explained. It was a law of the Spartan state that citizens might not go abroad except on public business and with authority from the magistrates (p. 133). The violation of this law by Pausanias and his long sojourn abroad are not seen as difficulties by Thucydides. But we do not need to penetrate very deeply beneath the surface of Thucydides' narrative to become aware that even among the ephorate some good will was felt towards Pausanias; and how could there not be, in view of the incomparable services he had rendered so short a while before? In default of further information, the ephors' tardiness in invoking the law and their reluctance to bring Pausanias to trial a second time may be attributed to this residue of gratitude.

Some ten years after Pausanias' death we again hear of happenings at Sparta. In 464, as the result of a closely-connected sequence of events, the fabric of the Spartan state was threatened, and a further deterioration took place in Spartan-Athenian relations. A serious earthquake struck the city of Sparta and, as usually occurred when the Spartiates were in a difficulty, the helots rose in revolt. Taking with them some disaffected outlanders from two Messenian towns, they barricaded themselves on Mount Ithome and defied Spartan attempts to dislodge them. Thucydides says that the trouble at Ithome was advanced by the Spartans as a reason for their failure to go to the help of the Thasians who had been beaten by the Athenians and were now besieged on their island (1.101). If there were no more to it than that, the Spartans' reply to the people of Thasos would have to be regarded as a mere pretext for doing nothing. But since Sparta next called in the help of Athenians, under the command of Cimon, she must have been hard pressed indeed. Some details adduced by Diodorus, though they may not be entirely accurate, do something to explain the great distress under which the Spartans laboured. He says that many citizens were wiped out by the earthquake and that only the prompt action of Archidamus, the Eurypontid king, saved the state. He hastily led out the remaining Spartiates, who formed a phalanx and repelled from the city a force of helots which was advancing against it. Frustrated in their main purpose, the helots retired to Ithome and used it as a base for guerrilla-raids into the Spartiate domains (Diodorus 11.63–64).

The Spartans resented the presence of the Athenians, and suspected their motives. They were afraid that the Athenian army, actually present within the Spartan state, would be induced to go over to the side of the rebels and make common cause with them against Sparta. So the Spartans sent away Cimon's force, without vouchsafing any reason, although they retained for the work other allies. The news of this rebuff was received with such resentment at Athens that the Spartan alliance was repudiated forthwith. The Athenians allied themselves instead with Argos, so giving the clearest possible indication of their displeasure. With this open and serious breach between Athens and Sparta, we have come to the second turning-point in their relationship; and yet there is no

The Persian Wars and their aftermath (490–432 B.C.)

evidence that the Spartans were troubled by, or were even aware of, the rapid exhaustion of good will on the Athenian side.

Thucydides reports that the rebels who made their base on Ithome held out there for nine years before surrendering to the Spartans; but that figure cannot be right, since it would involve an intolerable telescoping of dates between 464 and 455. The problem is usually solved by emending Thucydides' text so as to make the fall of Ithome occur in 459 or thereabouts; but there are several factors to be taken into account, and the mere substitution of a different numeral does not do justice to them (see Bibliography). Whenever it was that their resistance ended, the helots at Ithome were allowed to go free on condition that they left the Peloponnese; if one were again caught on Peloponnesian soil, he was to become the personal slave of his captor. (This condition implies that helotage represented an appreciably higher status than did chattel-slavery.) The Athenians demonstrated their hostility to Sparta by receiving the rebels and settling them at Naupactus.

The city of Megara, which occupied a strategically important position between Attica and Corinthia, left the Spartan Alliance, in consequence of a boundary dispute with Corinth, and joined the Athenians. Thus Athens gained the use of a base on either side of the Isthmus, and she further tightened her grip on the Isthmus by building a wall between Megara and Nisaea; but in doing so she laid up a great store of hatred at Corinth, which was to poison relations between the states for many years to come.

It was not long before open warfare erupted between Athens and members of the Spartan Alliance, among whom Corinth played the principal part. An Athenian fleet attacked Halieis on the Argolic Gulf, but was driven off by Corinthians and Epidaurians; since Halieis is close to Argive territory, it may be presumed that the attack was made by Athens in furtherance of the designs of her recently-enrolled ally Argos. Against Aegina, Athens was much more successful; she captured an Aeginetan fleet, and besieged the city. The Corinthians gave help to the enemies of Athens by sending hoplites across to Aegina; their soldiers also made a sally into Megarian territory. Athens was forced to fight on three fronts: in Megaris, in Egypt, and at Aegina. But the Athenians (as they often did) rose to the emergency. They refused to withdraw troops from either Egypt or Aegina, but mustered a scratch force of reserves; these marched into Megaris and compelled the Corinthians to retire. At about this time the Athenians strengthened communications with their harbours by building long walls, one to the Piraeus and one to Phalerum.

It is not recorded that Sparta took any part in these skirmishes. She was no doubt still recovering from the effects of the earthquake and the rebellion; besides, she would have gained little from involving herself in such indeterminate fighting as had taken place so far. But in 457 (by which year we must suppose that they had made some recovery) the Spartans were offered an opportunity and a challenge which they could not fail to take up. The Phocians made an attack upon Doris, the small area revered as their motherland by all Greeks of the Dorian name. The Spartans mobilized a considerable army and sent it northwards under the command of Nicomedes, the regent for king Pleistoanax. With such a force, Nicomedes was easily able to get satisfaction from the Phocians; but the question of his departure back to the Peloponnese involved him in a certain difficulty. If he took his army over the Corinthian Gulf, there was a danger that Athenian ships might cut off his withdrawal; on the other hand, now that Athens was allied to Megara, she could block the land-route across the Isthmus. The Peloponnesian army decided to wait in Boeotia. It appears that there was an anti-democratic party at Athens which wanted them to intervene, establish an oligarchy, and destroy the chief bulwark of the democracy, the walls to Phalerum and the Piraeus. But the days of Cleomenes, who had been able to strike directly at Athens and force her to accept a new constitution, were past. The Athenians, in spite of their commitments in Egypt and Aegina, dispatched to Boeotia their entire available force of hoplites: this, together with Argive and other contingents, numbered 14,000 men. The clash between them and the Peloponnesian army took place at Tanagra in the summer of 457. Both sides suffered heavy losses, and there was no clear-cut result. The Spartan Alliance claimed the victory, but it was not a decisive one; Nicomedes made no move towards Athens, but forced his way back to the Peloponnese by way of the Isthmus. The initiative remained with the Athenians; and in the following year they sent another army to Boeotia, which won a victory over the inhabitants and established a short-lived Athenian supremacy in central Greece. Another success for Athens came with the capitulation of Aegina, which now joined her alliance as a tributary member. The final exploits of this brief period of Athenian ascendancy took the form of highly provocative actions against Peloponnesian states. An Athenian fleet sailed round the Peloponnese: landing on Laconian territory they burnt the Spartan dock-yard at Gytheum; they then captured Chalcis, a Corinthian settlement on the north coast of the Gulf, after which they made a descent on the south side and defeated a Sicyonian force. Not even the utter failure of their arms in Egypt and Thessaly quenched their ardour for adventures in the Peloponnese. Pericles now makes his first recorded appearance as an Athenian general. Taking command of a thousand troops he sailed from Megaris to

Sicyonian country, where he disembarked and defeated an army which had come out against him.

The two great powers realized the danger inherent in this situation. Hence, in 452 or 451, a five-year treaty was concluded between Athens and the Spartan Alliance; at about the same time, and perhaps arising from the same desire for a breathing-space, Sparta and Argos agreed upon a treaty to run for thirty years. These moves ought to have stabilized the political situation; but Peloponnesians and Athenians continued to behave in a bellicose fashion, only they were careful to avoid direct conflict while the treaty was in force. An example of the way in which the two sides kept nibbling at each other's interests and prestige is provided by the Sacred War, when the Spartans went to Delphi, removed the sanctuary from Phocian control, and gave it to the Delphians; but after their departure an Athenian force arrived and restored the holy place to the Phocians.

To the mid-fifth century belongs the attempt by Pericles to widen the treaty into a pan-Hellenic peace. According to Plutarch, he proposed in the Athenian assembly that envoys should be sent to the Greek states, inviting them to send delegates to a general congress at Athens; 'but the proposal came to nothing, nor did the congress of states take place, because of Spartan opposition – so it is said'. (*Life of Pericles* 17.3.)

Shortly after the expiry of the five-year treaty, the Athenians again found themselves in open conflict with the Spartan Alliance. Athens was losing her grip on central Greece. In 447 the Boeotians successfully rose in revolt. A year later came rebellion in Euboea; Pericles had just gone over to subdue it when he heard that the western border of Attica was threatened. Megara had seceded, and had enlisted Peloponnesian aid in the massacre of an Athenian garrison. Pericles marched westwards; at the same time a Peloponnesian army, commanded by king Pleistoanax (who had now attained his majority), went into Attica as far as Eleusis. Pleistoanax contented himself with ravaging the country, and turned back without offering battle. On his return to Sparta he was accused of taking a bribe, and was banished from the city: he lived in exile in Arcadia for the next twenty-one years. There is more than a faint suspicion that Pericles applied some of the secret funds, of which he refused to give an account, to the bribery of highly-placed Spartans: his object being to postpone the war (which he now saw was inevitable) until a time when Athens should be in complete readiness.

Pleistoanax' withdrawal removed the military pressure on the Athenians, who promptly sent back their army to Euboea. They were not content with re-conquering the island, but imposed a political settlement along democratic lines. Thucydides places immediately after the Euboean settlement a most important political event, the conclusion in 445 of a thirty-year treaty between Athens and Sparta. We do not know the motives of the two sides in reaching this agreement. In a speech written early in the fourth century the Athenian orator Andocides (himself a delegate to Sparta in 392) mentions that his grandfather was one of the embassy of ten sent to Sparta to negotiate the treaty (*On the peace* 6). Andocides' feeble grasp of historical events is well known, but he ought perhaps to be acquainted with the doings of his own grandfather; if he is right in this, the initiative was taken by Athens. Did the sending of the embassy represent a victory for the Periclean policy of buying time, or was it the work of opponents of Pericles who genuinely sought a lasting peace? Clearly attested provisions of the treaty are these: Athens relinquished Troezen, Nisaea and Pegae in Megaris, and Achaea in the northern Peloponnese; both sides bound themselves to make only defensive alliances with other states; a city which did not belong to any alliance might join either the Athenians or the Spartans (Argos was mentioned specifically as not belonging to either side); the parties undertook to refer disputes to arbitration; and Aegina was guaranteed autonomous status within the Athenian empire. There was also some stipulation as to freedom of trade, but Thucydides does not precisely formulate this clause: an omission which poses a problem for us, since the clause was later adduced by the Megarians as the basis of their complaint against Athens. On the whole, more seems to have been conceded by Athens than by the other side; but in return the existence and extent of the Athenian empire were given formal recognition by the treaty. In effect, the greater part of the Greek world (except the western colonies) was carved up and distributed between the two contracting parties.

For the next ten years we hear of no conflict, and no good ground for conflict, between Athens and the Spartan Alliance. But in 435 the scene rapidly darkened, and the leaders on both sides (whether bellicose by temperament or not) were caught up in an accelerating movement towards war: a movement which in the end they proved powerless or unwilling to check. Sparta herself had no specific cause of quarrel with Athens: it was Corinth who clashed with Athenian interests in two widely-separated regions. These incidents inflamed Corinthian hatred for Athens, and drove Corinth to bring pressure upon Sparta for a declaration of war.

In the first incident, a long-standing dispute between Corinth and her colony Corcyra erupted in actual conflict. A Corinthian fleet was defeated by the Corcyraeans in a sea-battle in the summer of 435. That a great

The Persian Wars and their aftermath (490–432 B.C.)

maritime power like Corinth should be so humiliated was a bitter blow to her citizens, who began building an armada, and recruiting crews to man it. The inhabitants of Corcyra became alarmed at the extent of Corinthian preparations; they belonged to neither of the two power-blocs, but now they sought the help and alliance of Athens against Corinth. The Athenians, not without considering the advantages which might accrue to them from the friendship of such as state as Corcyra, made a defensive alliance with her, as was allowed under the terms of the thirty-year treaty. The Corcyraean fleet went out to do battle with the Corinthians in the late summer of 433. The Corinthians won a distinct advantage, but were prevented from pressing it home by the presence of ten Athenian ships: these were careful not to attack the Corinthians, but they successfully hampered their pursuit of the Corcyraean fleet. A further small force arrived from Athens in time to prevent the Corinthians from renewing their attack; they therefore returned home, discomfited for a second time and still more incensed against Athens.

Later in the same year, Athens took action in another part of her empire which involved her in an even more serious collision with Corinth. The Athenians had deep-seated interests in Chalcidice and Thrace. They had, some time before, planted a colony at Amphipolis; and the city of Potidaea, though in origin a Corinthian colony, was a tributary member of the Athenian Alliance. The situation was complicated by the activity of Perdiccas the Macedonian king, who was trying to stir up trouble between Athens and Corinth. The Athenians delivered an ultimatum to Potidaea, stating that the city was to break off relations with Corinth, pull down her walls, and give hostages to guarantee compliance with these conditions. The winter of 433–432 was passed in diplomatic negotiations. The Potidaeans sent envoys to Athens, requesting mitigation of the harsh terms which had been imposed on them, and to Sparta to see what help she was prepared to offer. They were rebuffed at Athens, but were assured by Sparta that she would invade Attica if the Athenians moved against Potidaea. That city consequently felt herself in a strong position, and revolted from the Athenian Alliance in the spring of 432. A fleet of Athenian ships, sent originally to carry on war against Perdiccas, arrived off Thrace in early summer; but when they found Potidaea and other cities in open rebellion they sailed on to Macedonia, summoning reinforcements from Athens. Corinth did not remain inactive in the face of the Athenian threats to her colony. She raised a force of volunteers from the Peloponnese and sent them to Thrace. The Athenians responded by dispatching a strong force of hoplites together with forty ships. These joined the contingent which had been sent against Perdiccas. A treaty was hastily concluded with him, and the augmented

Athenian force marched south to Potidaea. They won a victory against the joint Potidaean-Corinthian army, and proceeded to invest the city.

At this point Corinth felt sure that she could no longer direct the entire Peloponnesian effort against Athens, and urged Sparta to commit the Alliance to a formal declaration of war.

Bibliography

Evidence for a Messenian War c. 490: W.P. Wallace, *JHS* 74 (1954), 32–5. The date of the inscription on the Spartan offering at Olympia: L.H. Jeffery, *JHS* 69 (1949), 26–30. Spartan relations with Arcadia in the early fifth century: A. Andrewes, *Phoenix* 6 (1952), 1–5. Spartan relations with Athens: J. Wolski, *Meander* 18 (1963), 187–200.

The war with Xerxes: G.B. Grundy, *The great Persian War and its preliminaries* (London, 1901); G. Giannelli, *La spedizione di Serse da Terma a Salamine* (Milan, 1924); C. Hignett, *Xerxes' invasion of Greece* (Oxford, 1963). Xerxes' policy towards Sparta and Athens: F. Schachermeyr, *HZ* 172 (1951), 1–35. The league of Greek states against Persia: P.A. Brunt, *Historia* 2 (1953–1954), 135–63. The battle of Thermopylae and the problem of Leonidas' decision to remain: F. Miltner, *Klio* 28 (1935), 228–41; H.M. Last, *CR* 57 (1943), 63–6; J.R. Grant, *Phoenix* 15 (1961), 14–27; A. Dascalakis, *Problèmes historiques autour de la bataille de Thermopyles* (Paris, 1962); J.A.S. Evans, *GRBS* 5 (1964), 231–7; G.P. Phillip, *Gymnasium* 75 (1968), 1–45; R. Hope Simpson, *Phoenix* 26 (1972), 1–11. The battles at Thermopylae and Artemisium: W.K. Prentice, *TAPA* 51 (1920), 5–18; J.A.S. Evans, *Historia* 18 (1969), 389–406.

The Athenian alliance and empire: H. Nesselhauf, *Klio* Beiheft 30 (1933); G.E.M. de Ste. Croix, *Historia* 3 (1954–1955), 1–41; D.W. Bradeen, *Historia* 9 (1960), 257–69; R. Meiggs, *The Athenian empire* (Oxford, 1972).

The career of Pausanias: J. Wolski, *Eos* 47 (1954), 75–94; M.E. White, *JHS* 84 (1964), 140–52; A. Lippold, *RhM* 108 (1965), 320–41; C.W. Fornara, *Historia* 15 (1966), 257–71; A.E. Parshikov, *VDI* 103 (1968), 126–38. Pausanias and Themistocles: P.J. Rhodes, *Historia* 19 (1970), 387–400. The later career of Themistocles and his connexion with Argos: W.G. Forrest, *CQ* 54 (1960), 221–41.

The earthquake at Sparta: R. Sealey, *Historia* 6 (1957), 368–71. Cimon's expedition(s) to help the Spartans at Ithome: G.A. Papantoniou, *AJP* 72 (1951), 176–81. The date of the fall of Ithome: G. Klaffenbach, *Historia* 1 (1950), 231–5; S. Accame, *RFC* 80 (1952), 113–19; D.M. Lewis, *Historia* 2 (1953–1954), 412–18; J. Scharf, *Historia* 3 (1954–1955), 153–62; D.W. Reece, *JHS* 82 (1962), 111–20; M.L. Lang, *GRBS* 8 (1967), 267–73.

The secession of Megara from the Spartan Alliance: R.P. Legon, *Phoenix* 22 (1968), 211–21.

The battle of Tanagra: D.W. Reece, *JHS* 70 (1950), 75–6.

The Spartan expedition to Delphi and its background: G. Zeilhofer, *Sparta, Delphoi und die Amphiktyonen im 5. Jht. v. Chr.* (Erlangen, 1959), 43–50.

11

The war against Athens (432–404 B.C.)

At the Corinthians' request, Sparta summoned a meeting of her allies in the summer of 432. The anti-Athenian case was brought by Corinth, who accused Athens of having broken the thirty-year treaty by her action at Potidaea and called upon Sparta to throw off her lethargy and lead the Alliance into a war against Athens. Further complaints were made of Athens by two other delegates: the Aeginetan, to the effect that Athens had denied autonomy to his state, contrary to the treaty, and the Megarian, that his country was excluded from trade throughout all territories under Athenian control. When these arguments had been presented, the non-Spartans were asked to withdraw, and the matter was discussed in the Spartiate assembly. The constitutional implications of the ensuing debate were examined earlier (p. 125). Here we may notice that Thucydides ascribes to king Archidamus arguments for putting off actual hostilities and to the ephor Sthenelaidas a speech advocating an immediate declaration of war, as requested by the Corinthian delegation. Although Sthenelaidas' speech carried the day, it is important to consider the differences between his attitude and that of Archidamus.

Even after Sparta had declared war, she did not wage it with conspicuous vigour. Several times in Thucydides' narrative we find allusions to the existence of two factions at Sparta: one aggressive and impatient of Archidamus' delaying tactics; the other not really alive to the reality of the situation and, amidst the general turmoil of the Greek world, trying to preserve the aloofness which had previously marked Spartan policy. At least the realities had been made plain to the citizens by Archidamus, who had reflected deeply on the possible consequences of the assembly's decision. He pointed out that, though the military strength of Sparta and her allies was very great, it would not in itself avail to bring Athens to her knees; a Peloponnesian army could indeed invade Attica annually as the grain was ripening and deprive the Athenians of that year's crop, but it could not attack Athens herself nor cut off her imports. The reason lay in the control which Athens exercised over the Aegean Sea. This posed a great threat to Sparta: it enabled Athens to provision herself uninterruptedly and to collect the tribute from her allies. Athens, unlike Sparta, was assured of a regular income for warlike purposes, above all for the payment of her ships' crews; unlike Sparta, again, she possessed a large fund in reserve upon which to draw in emergencies. In view of all these undisputed facts, Archidamus' policy was the only prudent one: namely that the Spartans should exert diplomatic pressure on Athens, and meanwhile see what supplies they could gain and what alliances they could conclude among Greek and non-Greek peoples.

The Spartan assembly rejected Archidamus' advice and voted for war. Delegates from all the allied states took part in a conference at Sparta later in the summer of 432. Once more the Corinthians insisted on an immediate declaration of war, and once more they carried with them the majority of the allies. But upon what precise grounds was the Spartan Alliance to declare war on Athens? Previously the Corinthians and others had adduced specific infringements of the thirty-year treaty, and above all the Athenian intervention in Potidaea, as the grounds of war. At the general congress of the Alliance, the Corinthians seem to have felt that more justification was needed for their implacably hostile attitude to Athens than such matters as the Potidaean conflict, which were of no consequence to any members of the Alliance except themselves: they therefore introduced a new theme, which was subsequently presented to the Greek world as the great motive for Sparta's embarking upon war. This was the theme of 'Sparta the liberator'. The city which had once won renown by removing despots in individual cities was now going to fight against the despotism which Athens had imposed on other states. There is no evidence that at the beginning of 432 the Spartans regarded themselves as the liberators of Hellas; they were first invited by Corinth to assume that proud role, but they later played it with increasing conviction. Thucydides gives it as his belief that the 'truest cause' of the war was not the one publicly alleged on either side, but arose from Spartan alarm at the aggrandizement of Athens (1.23.6). This is clearly a well-considered judgment by Thucydides, and as such it must be treated with respect. At the same time, it receives no obvious confirmation from Thucydides' own narrative, according to which the Spartans neither sought an occasion for war with Athens nor prosecuted it wholeheartedly. But it is misleading to speak simply of the 'Spartans' in this context, as if Sparta was a monolithic state remorselessly pursuing a policy once laid down. There were various shades of opinion at Sparta just as there were at Athens; and, although we do not possess nearly as much information about Spartan politics and politicians as about their Athenian counterparts, we do become aware of the deep divisions between the Spartan leaders, for instance over Archidamus' conduct of his campaigns or over the dispatch of Brasidas to the north.

The war against Athens (432–404 B.C.)

The Spartan Alliance, having decided on war in August 432, thought that too little of the campaigning season remained that year for the initiation of any offensive measures. The succeeding autumn and winter were spent in a series of diplomatic exchanges between Sparta and Athens. First the Spartans raked up long-past events, whereby they alleged that Athens had incurred ritual pollution; in so doing they tried to pose as the guardians of the purity of Hellenic religion and also to throw some discredit on Pericles. Were the Spartans really trying to achieve their end by peaceful means, as Archidamus suggested they should, and so were undermining the prestige of the warmonger Pericles; or did they feel themselves wholly committed to war, and for that reason attacked their most resolute enemy? In either case, they failed, and were in turn accused by the Athenians of living under a curse. Coming to grips with reality, Sparta sent further ambassadors to press the demands made by her own allies: Athenian withdrawal from Potidaea, conferment of freedom on Aegina, and the repeal of the Megarian decree. No answer to these demands was forthcoming, and the Spartans then presented an ultimatum, in which for the first time they borrowed from the Corinthians the slogan 'liberators of Hellas': 'the Spartans desire peace', they said, 'and there will be peace if you grant the Greeks their autonomy' (Thucydides 1.139.3). Pericles now proposes in the Athenian assembly the response to be made to this ultimatum. He has already shown that he is not going to yield on any point. The answers given by the Athenians at his suggestion are not, therefore, to be taken seriously: the Megarians will be granted access to the harbours of the Athenian empire if the Spartans do not enforce against Athens and her allies their long-established policy of expelling foreigners (p. 122); the Athenian allies will be given their autonomy if Sparta's allies are allowed to act in conformity with their own interests, not with those of Sparta (a notable piece of gobbledygook, as if Sparta, and not Corinth or Megara, had presented to the Alliance reasons for going to war); the Athenians are willing to submit to arbitration; they will not begin the war, but will resist aggressive acts committed against them. The last statement is consistent with Pericles' oft-repeated advice to his countrymen; well aware that Athens could not provide an army to match the Peloponnesian hoplites, he advocated a strictly defensive war on land, together with concentration on the naval arm. He further warned the Athenians against extending their dominions in time of war. These principles were obviously sound, and they served Athens well, so long as she adhered to them.

The conflict between Athens and Sparta, usually known as the Peloponnesian War, lasted from 431 to 404. It fell into two distinct parts: the Archidamian War (431–421) and the Decelean War (413–404).

When the season for military operations began in 431, the Greek world stood on the brink of war, without knowing what form it would take. The Spartan Alliance comprehended all the states of the Peloponnese (except Argos and Achaea), the people of Megaris, those of Boeotia, Locris, and Phocis in central Greece, and also Ambracia, Leucas, and Anactorium in the north-west. Ranged against these were the Athenian allies: in central Greece only Plataea and Naupactus; in the north-west, the islands of Corcyra and Zacynthus, and much of Acarnanian territory; the Aegean islands (except the Dorian settlements in Melos and Thera), and the coastal regions of Asia Minor, Thrace, and the Hellespont.

The outbreak of hostilities in the spring of the year was not directly due to the act of either great power, but arose from a tiny episode which, in normal times, would have had no far-reaching consequences. A little more than three hundred Thebans made their way by night into Plataea, under the mistaken impression that the majority of the inhabitants wished the city to become a dependency of Thebes; when their presence was discovered, they were hunted down wherever they could be found. The Thebans belonged to the Spartan Alliance, the Plataeans to the Athenian; and when the latter complained at Athens of the Theban action it was clear that the thirty-year treaty had been broken, and both sides made urgent preparations for war. Requests for help were sent to quarters which assumed great importance in the later stages of the war, namely Persia and the Greek colonies in Italy and Sicily. So far as military operations were concerned, king Archidamus mustered a Peloponnesian army at the Isthmus of Corinth and led it into Attica in a leisurely manner and by a roundabout route. Not until the end of May, when the grain was ripening, did he launch a serious invasion of Attica. His delay aroused bitter criticism at Sparta; but in fact his strategy was perfectly sound. He hoped that when the Athenians saw the enemy occupying their territory and robbing them of the harvest they would leave the protection of their walls and offer battle. That is exactly what many of them were preparing to do, when Pericles restrained them. But, although Archidamus was justified in seeking a pitched battle with the Athenians in the first year of the war, it is an indication of the poverty-stricken character of Spartan policy that four more invasions of Attica were carried out during the Archidamian War. If the Peloponnesians could have waged an all-out war of attrition, their actions would be more easily comprehensible; since, even though Athens could get her supplies from abroad, the constant devastation of her arable land would have worn down her morale in the end. But this crude strategy, unsupported by more

The war against Athens (432–404 B.C.)

inventive measures, contained a serious flaw: while the Peloponnesian army was on Attic soil, there was nothing to prevent the Athenians from going on expeditions of their own.

In 430 the Athenians, crowded behind their walls, lost a substantial part of their population as the result of a devastating plague, which did not affect the Peloponnese. This serious setback caused them to send delegates to Sparta with an offer of peace; and the death of Pericles, which occurred in the following year, removed the most powerful of the anti-Spartan voices at Athens. But the Spartans showed no positive reaction to the Athenian proposals, which were consequently dropped. Despite their afflictions and the rebuff they had sustained at Sparta, the Athenians waged war with immense panache, and for the first five years they made all the running. They carried out attacks on Megaris, expelled the Aeginetans from their island and settled it with their own citizens, sent out a large marauding fleet which did considerable damage in the east of the Peloponnese, caused great embarrassment to the Spartans by arresting their ambassadors on the way to Persia and Persian envoys on the way to Sparta, and carried out a brilliant naval operation in the Gulf of Corinth against a numerically superior Peloponnesian fleet.

By contrast Sparta and her allies were slow to move and, when they did move, they acted so indecisively or so timidly as to lose many opportunities that were presented to them. For example their military and naval enterprises in north-west Greece were defective both in planning and in execution. The Spartan general, Cnemus, made his way into Acarnania, but he incorporated some non-Greek contingents in his army, and when battle was joined their lack of discipline earned them heavy losses and forced Cnemus to withdraw. As part of what should have been a concerted plan, a hundred triremes were sent to Zacynthus, but even a fleet of that size was unable to detach the island from Athens. At this time, and for long afterwards, Brasidas was the only Spartan general with the resource and daring to carry out the kind of operation which the Athenians were devising constantly; but he was not yet entrusted with the sole command, and his plans were frustrated by the pusillanimity of others. An instance is furnished by the small Peloponnesian operation of 429. The Megarians urged that a surprise attack should be mounted from their territory upon the Piraeus. The Athenians, confident in their naval supremacy, at this time set only a negligent guard on their principal port, and they would have lost a number of ships and much prestige if such an attack had been pressed home. It was the kind of expedition to appeal to Brasidas; and, in accordance with the plan, he, Cnemus, and other leaders set out with forty ships from Nisaea. But apprehension of the risks they were running arose in the command, and it was decided to make for Salamis instead. The Peloponnesian force landed there and inflicted much damage on the Athenian installations. The city of Athens was thrown into a panic by alarm-beacons, the citizens thinking that hostile ships had actually entered the Piraeus; when they learnt the truth they launched their own triremes, in some disorder, but were too late to catch the fleet before it returned to Megaris.

Of all the chances lost by the Peloponnesians, the least comprehensible was their failure, in the years 428 and 427, to exploit the secession of Lesbos from the Athenian empire. The war between the two great powers provoked political dissension, and even outright civil war, in Lesbos as it did in a number of other Greek states: the democratic parties looking to Athens to support, the oligarchic to Sparta. In Lesbos the oligarchs of Mytilene, the principal city, were bent on forming a union with other towns on the island (naturally with themselves at the head of the confederation), and these were the instigators of the revolt against Athens; only Methymna, which had a democratic constitution, remained loyal. Mytilene had wanted to join the Spartan Alliance before the outbreak of war, but the Spartans would not admit her.

The Mytilenaeans established a strong position for themselves, but realized that they could not hold out for long against a strong Athenian fleet; they therefore sent a deputation to Olympia, where the delegates of the Spartan Alliance were attending the Games (August 428). Lesbos, with the exception of Methymna, was received into the Alliance, and it prepared to withstand Athenian attacks. Athens was not yet able to bring a sufficiently large force to bear upon Mytilene, but began a siege of the city during the summer. In February 427 a Spartan envoy named Salaethus took ship for Lesbos, slipped into Mytilene despite the blockade, and put heart into the rebels by promising that the Peloponnesians would undertake a two-pronged action in the coming summer. They proposed to make an even more determined raid than usual on Attica and, at the same time, to send a fleet to Lesbos. The invasion of Attica was carried out, under the leadership of the Spartan regent Cleomenes; it caused the Athenians great harm, but did not in itself force them to slacken their grip on Mytilene. This could have been broken by the forty ships which set out from the Peloponnese with the Spartan admiral Alcidas in command. But this fleet took so long to get clear of Peloponnesian waters and made such poor time on its eastward voyage that the Mytilenaeans could no longer hold out and had to request terms from the Athenians. Alcidas' fleet arrived in the eastern Aegean a week after the capitulation of Mytilene, and it then anchored off the headland of Asia just across the strait from Chios. There Alcidas was urged at least

The war against Athens (432–404 B.C.)

to make an attempt to recapture Mytilene, in the hope that it was not irrevocably under Athenian control. The admiral declined; nor did he accede to another suggestion made to him, that he should seize an Ionian city, make it his base, and try to deprive Athens of the substantial revenues she received from the Asiatic tributaries. Alcidas gave orders for some Greek captives he had taken to be killed, and sailed to Ephesus. Putting in there, he was visited by Samian exiles, who complained that if the Spartan policy of 'liberating Hellas' involved the execution of Greeks who were the unwilling subjects of Athens, then that policy was more likely to attract hostility than good will in the Greek world in general. This remonstrance did persuade Alcidas to free other prisoners, but he now washed his hands altogether of the affairs of Asia and set sail for home.

The exceedingly sorry picture cut by Alcidas in Thucydides' narrative is perhaps to be modified a little in the light of an inscription found to the south of Sparta. The text gives a list of contributions 'for the war' from a number of sources, both private and public. Among the states named are Ephesus and Melos. This inscription possibly belongs to the year 427; if it does, it both gives an insight into the Spartans' methods of getting money to carry on the war (since they had no financial reserves and did not yet exact tribute from their allies) and provides some small justification for Alcidas' dilatory progress. His late arrival was perhaps due to a stop at Melos, and his making for Ephesus would be explained by the funds that had been promised from that quarter.

If Alcidas did combine the office of revenue-collector with that of admiral, it is to be hoped that he was more successful in the former capacity than in the latter. He brought his squadron home in poor shape; on making port at Cyllene in Elis, he was joined by thirteen allied ships. It was the Spartan plan to send on the fleet to Corcyra, where a civil war had broken out. The Spartans hoped that if their ships arrived at Corcyra with little delay they would intervene decisively on the oligarchic side before the Athenians brought in a strong enough force to stop them. Alcidas was clearly not the man to execute such a plan as that. Nevertheless he must have had powerful friends at Sparta, for he was continued in his command, with Brasidas attached to his staff as adviser. On their arrival at Corcyra, the Peloponnesian ships fought a successful action against a modest number of Athenian and Corcyraean vessels; but, despite the entreaties of Brasidas, Alcidas refused to follow up his victory by an attack on the city of Corcyra, and left for the Peloponnese as soon as a fresh Athenian squadron approached.

The one Spartan success in 427 was that Plataea was forced to surrender; but, since Archidamus had begun the siege of the city two years previously, the success cannot be called a brilliant one. Five magistrates were brought from Sparta to assign punishment to the Plataeans; they simply asked each of the survivors whether he had been of service to Sparta or her allies in the war. The Plataeans called to mind the loyalty which their fathers had displayed to the Greek cause fifty-two years before (p. 170); but the Spartan magistrates were persuaded by a Theban delegation not to tolerate the anomaly of a neutral city which was yet a member of the Athenian Alliance; they repeated their question, to which the Plataeans could only answer 'no', whereupon they were led off to execution. The women of Plataea were sold into slavery, and a year later the city itself was levelled with the ground.

An attempt by the Peloponnesians to invade Attica in the following summer was frustrated by an unusual number of earthquakes; but the Spartans displayed initiative in a fresh direction, by planting a colony at Heraclea in Trachis: this they hoped would be strategically useful to them, affording a base in the very heart of Greece for possible attacks on Euboea and for expeditions to Thrace. In the event, the colony fulfilled only some of the hopes reposed in it; after a few years it fell into a decline because of maladministration.

Two squadrons of ships were sent out by Athens in the summer of 426, each under the command of a leading general. Nicias sailed to Melos, a neutral state, with the aim of bringing it within the empire; when the Melians refused to yield, he ravaged their island. Demosthenes took thirty ships round the Peloponnese and, after some skirmishes on the way, he made his base at Naupactus. The Spartans were prevailed on to send a force of allied hoplites against that city: this they did in late September. One thousand Acarnanian hoplites were brought in by Demosthenes, and the accession of this force enabled him to defy the Peloponnesian army. The Peloponnesians withdrew into Aetolia and waited there until the Corinthian colonists in Ambracia were ready to join forces with them. A general engagement followed during the winter, in which Demosthenes inflicted a major defeat on the combined Peloponnesian and Ambraciot forces.

Each of the two succeeding summers witnessed an alarming Athenian coup, which brought the war very close to Sparta herself. In 425, while Archidamus' son Agis was leading his army into Attica, a squadron of forty ships on its way to Sicily was placed at Demosthenes' disposal for a marauding expedition round the Peloponnese. There was nothing novel in that, but on this occasion Demosthenes was determined on something more than a mere raid. He chose Pylos, on the west coast of Messenia, where he landed, established a base, and fortified it. The bold stroke succeeded beyond expectation. The Spartans were painfully slow in

32 Terracotta mask from Orthia sanctuary. Ht. 9 in.

33 Terracotta mask from Orthia sanctuary. Ht. 4½ in.

34 Terracotta roof-tile from the modern town. Diam. 12½ in.

35 Clay head from Orthia sanctuary. Ht. 8 in.

36-7 *Selection of lead figurines from Orthia sanctuary. Ht. between ¾ and 2½ in.*

39 *Marble relief from Chrysapha. Heroized dead. Ht. 34 in.*

38 *Limestone relief from Orthia sanctuary. Horse.* 5 × 4 *in.*

40 *Marble relief from the modern town. Dioscuri. Ht. 21 in.*

41 *Ivory plaque from Orthia sanctuary. Goddess with animals.*
2 × 1½ in.

42 *Ivory comb from Orthia sanctuary. Judgment of Paris. Breadth (when complete): 3 in.*

43 *Ivory plaque from Orthia sanctuary. Lapith and Centaur. Ht. 3 in.*

44 *Ivory group from Orthia sanctuary. Lioness, calf, man. Length of base: 2½ in.*

45 Ivory plaque from Orthia sanctuary. Warship. Length: 9½ in.

46 Remains of the marble statue of a warrior (Leonidas ?) (crest of helmet restored). Ht. to top of helmet, excluding crest: 30 in.

The war against Athens (432–404 B.C.)

making a move against Demosthenes, and in fact they did nothing effective until after the return of Agis' army, which had been hurriedly recalled from Attica. This dilatoriness gave the Athenians the opportunity of converting Pylos into a secure place. But the Spartans, when they did at last arrive in any strength, made light of their task. They thought that, if only they could deny a base to any Athenian reinforcements coming in by sea, they could overpower at their leisure the Athenians' hastily-constructed defences. Four hundred and twenty Spartan hoplites, with their attendant helots, were accordingly conveyed to the small island of Sphacteria, which blocks off part of the bay. A simultaneous attack by land and sea was made on the Athenian position, but the enemy stood firm, and two days later they counter-attacked, bringing havoc to the Spartan ships and making themselves masters of the sea in that region. Their mastery meant that the Spartans who had gone over to Sphacteria were now cut off, since the Athenian ships could sail round the islet at will and prevent anyone from leaving or arriving.

The consternation caused at Sparta by these events would be incredible, were it not for the fact that there were many well-connected Spartiates among the hoplites cut off on Sphacteria. A truce was concluded (according to which the Spartans had to give up their entire fleet of sixty warships), pending the outcome of political negotiations at Athens. The Spartan delegates who then went to Athens thought that their opponents would be very ready to agree to a general treaty, since the Athenians had themselves previously made overtures (p. 189). The Spartans misjudged both the hour and the temper of the Athenian assembly. The Athenians had opened negotiations in 430 when they were suffering from the plague, and seriously wondered whether they could carry on the war against their formidable adversaries. Five years later they were in the ascendant: they seemed to have nothing to lose by continuing the war, and the Spartans everything. Furthermore the Athenian assembly had fallen under the sway of Cleon, a crude demagogue possessed of great military skill, who continued Pericles' anti-Spartan policy without comprehending the need to stay on the defensive. He suggested that a treaty should be discussed, but on very stringent terms. The hoplites on Sphacteria must surrender, and be brought to Athens; they were to be released only after the ratification of the treaty, and among the terms of the treaty was to be the cession to Athens of Achaea and Troezen, as well as Nisaea and Pegae in Megaris. The Spartan envoys replied that they could not discuss such terms in public (of course not, since they would be bargaining about the rights of their allies, not about their own). But Cleon would not hear of private discussions, and negotiations were accordingly broken off.

With the return home of the Spartan delegates, the truce at Pylos came to an end. The Athenians refused to give back the Spartan ships, alleging violations of the truce, and hostilities were resumed more bitterly than before. The Spartans managed to get supplies across to Sphacteria, and it was the Athenians who now began to feel the pinch. Cleon taunted his enemy Nicias with his failure to sail to the relief of his countrymen, and he himself set out for Pylos in command of a small force, with the intention of collaborating with Demosthenes in an assault on Sphacteria. A surprise landing was effected, an outpost overwhelmed, and the main body of hoplites attacked. What troubled the Spartan defenders most was that the enemy did not employ the usual hoplite-tactics, of which the Spartans had a complete mastery, but assailed the phalanx from a distance with stones and arrows. Retreating to a fortified position, the Spartans held out for long, dusty hours until they were trapped by an attack in the rear. The unremitting onslaught wore down the diminishing number of survivors, until they astonished the Greek world by surrendering to the Athenians. They were taken to Athens, and kept in prison as hostages. The Athenians installed a garrison at Pylos, and a number of Messenians used it for making raids upon Laconian territory. Distressing as these were to the Spartans, much more so was their fear of a revolt by the helots; but, although they sent a number of deputations to Athens in an effort to secure the release of the hostages, they could not induce the Athenians to give them up.

While the war was being waged at Pylos, the Peloponnesian cause suffered a reverse on another front. Nicias organized a strong force and made a damaging invasion of Corinthia by land and sea. The same general struck a serious blow at Sparta in May 424. Carrying out at last a policy advocated in the Persian War (p. 162), he took a squadron of ships, two thousand hoplites, and a small detachment of cavalry, and landed at Cythera. The Athenians defeated the Spartan outlanders who came out to do battle with them, and established a strong position on the island. From this base they made a number of raids on coastal towns such as Asine and Helos. In a powerful chapter (4.55), Thucydides gives reasons for the Spartan failure to expel the enemy from Cythera. They had been plunged into despair by the unexpected defeat at Sphacteria; two fortified places in the Spartan state were in the occupation of the Athenians; above all the Spartans had to be on their guard against any rising which might lead to constitutional changes. Even in military matters the Spartan shortcomings had become manifest at Sphacteria. An exclusive commitment to hoplite-warfare was all very well, so long as the enemy were content to fight their battles on the same terms; if they did not, they could prove, at the very least, a serious nuisance to the

The war against Athens (432–404 B.C.)

Spartan hoplites. In consequence the training of cavalry and archers was put in hand at Sparta, but only on a small scale. Meanwhile the Athenians used their base at Cythera to inflict further damage on Sparta by sailing to Thyreatis, where the Aeginetan refugees had been settled (p. 189). The Spartan troops on garrison-duty were not able to save their protégés, and the Athenians took home with them both Spartan and Aeginetan captives; the former were put in prison along with the hoplites from Sphacteria, the latter were executed.

Only one man at Sparta could rescue the military reputation of his countrymen, and that man was Brasidas. He saw that their one hope lay in taking the offensive; and in the summer which had seen the enemy occupation of Cythera he summoned an allied army to the Isthmus for an operation against the cities in Thrace and Chalcidice which formed part of the Athenian empire. While at the Isthmus, he received word of a revolt in Megara. The leaders of the democratic faction had requested help from Athens for the overthrow of the oligarchs; the Athenians, responding with alacrity, occupied the walls between Megara and Nisaea and captured the Peloponnesian garrison at Nisaea. Brasidas brought up his army, which was then joined by a Boeotian detachment, and saved Megara itself from Athenian occupation. Strong hoplite forces were present on either side; but the Athenians were outnumbered and did not care to offer battle, while Brasidas was happy to have won a victory without fighting. An Athenian plan to exploit a democratic rising in Boeotia ended in disastrous failure, with a major Athenian defeat at Delium early in November.

In the meantime Brasidas was leading his army to its original destination. He passed rapidly through Thessaly and into Macedonia. There king Perdiccas undertook to supply half the provisions of the Peloponnesian army in return for assistance against his neighbour Arrhabaeus. He meant military assistance, and was affronted when Brasidas offered himself as arbitrator. Perdiccas thereupon reduced the amount of supplies he was willing to give; Brasidas marched on, and early in September he came to Acte. He made it his first task to seduce the people of Acanthus from Athens. His speech to the Acanthians, though it contained some threats, was on the whole couched in conciliatory terms; and the claim to be the 'liberator of Greece' was more consistent with the fair dealing of a Brasidas than with the casual brutality of an Alcidas. By his mere words Brasidas won Acanthus from the Athenian empire and enrolled it among the autonomous allies of Sparta. Stagirus, a few miles to the north of Acanthus, also joined the Spartan Alliance.

Late in the year, when there were some falls of snow, Brasidas made a rapid march inland to the Athenian colony of Amphipolis. Part of its population was already prepared to welcome him; and he won over the remainder by a moderate proclamation in which he gave leave to those who wished to depart within five days. The proclamation pleased all parties in Amphipolis, and they opened the gates of their city to Brasidas. It was now the Athenians' turn to feel alarm, as they heard of these bloodless triumphs, which might well cause other Athenian allies to secede. But the petty-mindedness and short-sightedness of a powerful faction at Sparta denied Brasidas any reinforcements from home. The principal motive was jealousy, but concern was felt also for the Spartan prisoners at Athens; moreover the Spartans in general had conceived a desire to end the war. Despite the lack of support, Brasidas engaged in further campaigning during the winter, his most striking exploit being the capture of Torone.

The character of the war had undergone a change, partly from the Athenians' ill success in Boeotia, partly from the energy and political moderation displayed by Brasidas. By the summer of 423 both Sparta and Athens were bent on peace, and they concluded an armistice, to last for one year. The Athenians' hope that the conclusion of the armistice would prevent further defections from their empire at once proved baseless; for two more Chalcidic cities, Scione and Mende, went over to Brasidas. He was accorded extraordinary honours at Scione, being crowned as the liberator of Greece and treated as a victor in the games: these honours were given to Brasidas personally, not as a representative of Sparta. Brasidas claimed that Scione had defected before the ratification of the armistice, but the Athenians held (rightly) that its defection had come about two days afterwards. Incensed at the treachery of Scione, the Athenians resolved (on Cleon's motion) to take vengeance upon it as soon as they could.

At this moment, when Brasidas most needed to stay close to Scione to ward off the impending Athenian attack, Perdiccas requested his help in another campaign against Arrhabaeus. Brasidas had no choice but to comply. Joining forces with Perdiccas, he won a decisive victory. But a powerful Illyrian army came up in Arrhabaeus' support and caused Perdiccas and Brasidas to retreat. Their withdrawal was not, however, properly concerted. The Macedonian forces with Perdiccas fled headlong, leaving Brasidas to face the Illyrians alone. This he did by forming his hoplites into a square and instructing small detachments of young men to rush out and deal with individual attacks as they were made. His tactics blunted the edge of the assault, and he was able to extricate his army in good order. Brasidas' soldiers considered that they had been deserted by Perdiccas; while the king regarded Brasidas as an enemy, and took steps to reach an accommodation with Athens.

The war against Athens (432–404 B.C.)

On his return to Torone, Brasidas found that an Athenian fleet with Nicias in command had arrived and that Mende had fallen; Nicias proceeded to lay siege to Scione. Perdiccas entered into a formal agreement with the Athenians, from which the latter derived an immediate benefit. A move had at last been made at Sparta to send reinforcements to Brasidas, and the Spartan general Ischagoras had set out with an army on his way to Thrace. Perdiccas prevailed on the Thessalians not to let this army pass through their territory; instead Ischagoras came to Brasidas with the two governors whom the Spartans had appointed for their new allies: Clearidas for Amphipolis and Pasitelidas for Torone.

In the last year of the Archidamian War, Thrace continued to be the main theatre of operations. As spring was approaching in 422, Brasidas made an ineffectual attempt to break into Potidaea by night. This was so easily thwarted by the Athenian garrison that we may suspect the presence of some factor which goes unnoticed by Thucydides; the most probable is Brasidas' (mistaken) belief that a party inside the city was likely to rise in his support. In the event he could do no more than lead his army back to quarters.

In high summer Cleon appeared off Scione with thirty ships, twelve hundred Athenian hoplites, three hundred cavalry, and some allied troops: small numbers, considering that they were certain to encounter Brasidas. It seems that the Athenians were willing to afford him moderate support in his aim of dislodging Brasidas from Thrace, but did not throw behind him the whole resources of the state. Cleon on this expedition received half-hearted backing from Athens, just as Brasidas did from Sparta. For some obscure reason Brasidas was absent from his main base at Torone. The Spartan governor was too slow-moving and too weak in resources to save the city from Cleon's attack. Brasidas was on the way, but on hearing that Torone had fallen he took his army back to the north. Cleon left a garrison at Torone, sailed round Acte, and made his base at Eion, intending to make an attempt on Amphipolis. Brasidas posted his troops on high ground on the opposite side of the Strymon and observed what the enemy did. When the Athenians moved against Amphipolis, he led his forces into the city. But he did not move out the army to confront Cleon directly; instead, he planned a manoeuvre worthy of what was to be his last battle. Thinking that Cleon had not seen his entry into Amphipolis, Brasidas proposed to make a sudden sally with 150 Spartiates; then, when Cleon moved up to annihilate this tiny force, Clearidas with the rest of the army was to emerge and fall on the Athenians unexpectedly. But Cleon had seen, and having no wish to meet Brasidas' whole army before reinforcements arrived from Athens he ordered a withdrawal. As his right wing moved round, they left their right side unprotected; at this precise moment Brasidas rushed out with his few hoplites, routed the centre, and cut off the left flank. Clearidas, according to orders, led the rest of the army against the Athenians; their left wing fled, but the right held out for some time, although leaderless, for Cleon was killed as he was trying to make his escape. When the right too were dislodged, the entire Athenian army were in rout, and made their way back to Eion as best they could. Brasidas had received a fatal wound in the fighting, and died shortly after hearing the news of his great victory. His body was given public burial at Amphipolis, and the people of the city adopted Brasidas as their founder instead of the Athenian Hagnon, and instituted a cult in his honour. Clearidas began the peace-time administration of the city, and the Athenian fleet sailed home from Eion.

The peace-party both at Athens and at Sparta now came into the ascendant. The two chief obstacles to peace, Cleon and Brasidas respectively, had been removed in the battle of Amphipolis; Nicias at Athens and at Sparta king Pleistoanax, who had recently returned from exile (p. 181), took the initiative towards the conclusion of a treaty. The motives which impelled the two sides to peace are lucidly expounded by Thucydides (5.14-15). The Spartan disasters at Pylos and Cythera had been counterbalanced, if not outweighed, by the failure of Athenian arms in Boeotia and in Thrace; at Sparta there was the additional reason that the thirty-year treaty with Argos (p. 181) was on the point of expiring, and the Spartans shrank from the prospect of waging war with Athens while they had a belligerent opponent on their very doorstep. Negotiations continued throughout the winter, and a treaty was ratified in March 421. It was to last for fifty years. Matters were regulated between the two sides in Thrace, on the terms that Athens held what Cleon had captured and that Amphipolis was restored to her. In return the Athenians undertook to evacuate Pylos and Cythera and to give back all prisoners held anywhere on their territory. Sparta and Athens, as individual cities, took a further step: they concluded a defensive alliance, also to run for fifty years. The danger of a helot revolt was never far from the Spartan consciousness. A clause in the pact setting up the alliance stated that in the event of a rising of slaves the Athenians would do their utmost to help Sparta; it was not thought necessary to make reciprocal provision for a rebellion of Athenian slaves.

Neither the treaty nor the alliance brought with it any guarantee of lasting peace. In the first place the Spartans were not able to perform what they had promised. When they ordered Clearidas to surrender Amphipolis, he said he could not do so against the will of the inhabitants.

So for the time being Amphipolis remained under Spartan control, while on their side the Athenians refused to give back Pylos. Secondly, by reaching the accommodation with Athens, Sparta alienated some of her own allies and brought about a realignment of political and military forces in the Peloponnese. The Boeotians, Corinthians, Eleans, and Megarians opposed the cessation of hostilities, and with good reason. Sparta alone derived any benefit from the agreement, and she had achieved none of the aims for which her allies had originally urged her to war. As Corinth had been decisive in bringing pressure to bear on Sparta for a declaration of war, so now she took the initiative in proposing a new system of alliances. She suggested to the Argives that they should put themselves at the head of an alliance and so fulfil their ancient dream of acquiring the hegemony of the Peloponnese. Argos eagerly embraced the opportunity. Mantinea, with her subject towns, and then Elis joined the Argive alliance; but Tegea and Boeotia refused to renounce the Spartan connexion. The greatest fear at Sparta was that Corinth would formally join Argos, and a Spartan embassy to Corinth tried to forestall this; but the Corinthians did not immediately commit themselves.

Spartan affairs were again at a low ebb. It was thought advisable for Pleistoanax to make a display of force in the central Peloponnese by freeing a small area from Mantinean control. At about the same time two groups of Spartan soldiers returned home. The helots who had fought bravely with Brasidas were emancipated and settled on a tract of land on the border of Laconia and Elis. But the prisoners taken at Sphacteria, on whose behalf Sparta had humiliated herself, were deprived of their citizenship.

The summer of 421 was spent in diplomatic exchanges between Athens and Sparta, in which the Athenians complained that Amphipolis had still not been given up and that some important allies of Sparta had not acceded to the treaty. November saw the election of a new ephorate, which contained at least two members strongly opposed to the treaty, and contemplated the formation of an anti-Athenian alliance comprising Sparta, Boeotia, Corinth, and Argos. The Boeotians as usual were very slow to act, but a Spartan deputation went to Thebes and cemented a bipartite alliance. This caused great offence at Athens, because of her hatred of Thebes, and provided a favourable climate in which an anti-Spartan movement could flourish. For, just as the new ephors at Sparta canvassed anti-Athenian views, so at Athens suspicions of Sparta were being kept alive. In the following year the most prominent Athenian to speak out against Sparta was Alcibiades, who was to exert a powerful influence on the course of Greek history for several years to come. He advocated an Athenian alliance with Argos; and this was presently concluded against the advice of Nicias, who still thought that an alliance with Sparta offered the best hope of security. Two other Peloponnesian peoples, the Mantineans and the Eleans, joined the Athenian-Argive alliance, but the Corinthians did not. The Athenian-Spartan alliance had become a dead letter, but it was not formally renounced.

In 419 Alcibiades, who had been elected an Athenian general, led a minor expedition to the northern Peloponnese in concert with the Argives. Further aggressive intentions were manifested by Argos in that summer. She sent a raiding force into the territory of Epidaurus, a faithful ally of Sparta; and Epidaurus was strengthened by a garrison of Spartan troops. These apparently insignificant events formed the prelude to a major military effort by Sparta in the summer of 418. King Agis took the field against Argos with a large force, including Tegean, Boeotian, and Corinthian contingents. Sparta felt it necessary not only to give assistance to Epidaurus but also to assert her authority before the whole of the Peloponnese slipped out of her control. The Argives, who had with them allies from Mantinea and Elis, drew up their line opposite that of Agis. Argive leaders unofficially suggested to Agis that the two sides should conclude a four-month truce; and Agis, just as unofficially, accepted the suggestion. This incident demonstrates the large reserves of power possessed by a Spartan king when on campaign; even though the allies showed great resentment at Agis' refusal to fight, they did not question his authority, but dispersed grumbling to their several cities. Reinforcements accompanied by Alcibiades now reached Argos from Athens; under Alcibiades' energetic persuasion the allies of Argos (but not Argos herself) resumed the war and moved against Orchomenus, the Arcadian city which was allied to Sparta. Orchomenus capitulated, whereupon the Argive allies proposed to make an attempt on Tegea. The pro-Spartan faction in that city addressed an urgent request for help to the ephors at Sparta, and the request arrived at a time when bitter recriminations were being made against Agis. It was bad enough (said the Spartans) that the king had thrown away the opportunity of winning a victory over Argos; worse still that his feeble policy had opened the way for the enemy into Arcadia and enabled them to capture an allied city without striking a blow. It was proposed to impose an enormous fine on Agis and to pull down his house. The enforcement of these measures was temporarily suspended on Agis' assurance that he would perform a great deed on behalf of the city; nevertheless ten Spartiate 'advisers' were sent with him to the war.

Agis' chance to do his great deed was provided by the Tegean message; and with unusual dispatch a Spartan army set out for Tegea, the king

The war against Athens (432–404 B.C.)

summoning allied troops from Corinth, Boeotia, and Phocis. Tegea was saved by this prompt action by Agis, and he then led the army into Mantinean country. Here they were caught unawares by the appearance of the enemy. Falling hurriedly into line, Agis' army fought a classic hoplite-battle, which was marked by Spartan indiscipline as well as by Spartan valour. Agis, who was in the centre of the line, saw that his left wing was edging to the right and was liable to be encircled by the Mantineans who held the enemy right. He accordingly ordered two companies to move across from the right wing; but their commanding officers did not obey the order, and in consequence the king's fears were realized: his left wing was surrounded and routed, but the centre pressed home the attack, broke the enemy line, and retrieved the situation. The Argive and Athenian detachments made their escape, but the Mantineans suffered heavy losses. King Pleistoanax, who had set out from Sparta with another army, was still on the march when he heard of Agis' victory, so he turned back; and messengers were sent to the Spartan allies to tell them that their services were not now required. Agis refrained from pursuing the defeated enemy, and led the army home for the celebration of the *Karneia*.

Agis' exploit at Mantinea redeemed his own reputation and that of the city; the victory was a purely Spartan one, and much more impressive (in the eyes of the Peloponnesian states) than the remoter feats of Brasidas had been. Sparta obtained the first fruits of her firm action in the autumn, when Argos repudiated her alliance with Mantinea, Elis, and Athens and concluded a treaty with Sparta. In the following year a democratic faction seized power at Argos and, with Athenian help, built long walls to the sea. The Spartans did not this time react very swiftly, and it was only in winter-time that Agis took an army and demolished the walls.

The restoration of Spartan prestige might have enabled the Greek world to achieve a degree of equilibrium and even to live at peace, had it not been for a grandiose scheme of conquest which Athens set on foot in the summer of 415. During the Archidamian War, the Athenians had intervened several times in the affairs of Sicily; now they fitted out a magnificent armada, with the ostensible purpose of bringing aid to their allies in Egesta against the neighbouring Selinuntians, who were allied to Syracuse (the most powerful of the Greek cities in Sicily). It was, however, no secret that the real design of Athens was the conquest and annexation of the whole of Sicily; and the pursuit of this design eventually led to a renewal of the war between Athens and Sparta. Alcibiades, the principal advocate of the Sicilian expedition, was appointed a general, along with Nicias and Lamachus. As the armada was about to set sail from the Piraeus, Alcibiades was accused of having committed scandalous acts of sacrilege, but he was nevertheless allowed to go to Sicily with the fleet.

Almost from the first, the Sicilian expedition suffered from indecision and differences within the high command. Instead of making straight for Syracuse and attacking in force, the Athenians spent the whole summer in reconnaissance and attempts to win support. It was not until October that they landed near Syracuse. Then, it is true, they won a victory, but not a crushing one; and after the action they sailed off to winter-quarters. Meanwhile steps had been taken to involve Sparta and her allies in the Sicilian conflict. Alcibiades was recalled to face charges preferred against him at Athens; but he slipped away from the escorting ship and made his way to Sparta, where he vigorously promoted an anti-Athenian policy. The Syracusans, for their part, sent envoys to the Peloponnese asking for help against the attack by Athens. The envoys were enthusiastically welcomed at Corinth, always ready to strike a blow at Athenian imperialism; and the Corinthians sent envoys of their own to commend the Syracusan cause at Sparta. The Spartans had been contemplating some action against Athens but, as their custom was, they had been slow to commit themselves to a definite plan. Now, hearing the reports of the Syracusan ambassadors and a speech by Alcibiades, they appointed a very able and energetic Spartiate, Gylippus, as commander-in-chief at Syracuse, with orders to make arrangements in conjunction with the Corinthians and Syracusans and to sail for Sicily as soon as practicable.

Certain incidents in the summer of 414 showed direct conflict between Sparta and Athens to be very near. Sparta sent an allied army into Argos, and an Athenian fleet of thirty ships came to the help of the democratic party there; these ships were not content with taking defensive measures, but ravaged some of the coastal regions of Laconia. This act by the Athenians constituted a clear breach of the treaty between themselves and Sparta. At the same time Gylippus arrived at Syracuse, having acquired some additional forces on the way. The Athenians had begun building walls with which they hoped to invest the city, and in a skirmish they had lost their general Lamachus, so that Nicias was left in sole command. The arrival of Gylippus put new heart into the Syracusans, and by erecting a counter-wall they removed the danger of complete encirclement. Nicias felt the defenders' resistance stiffening ominously, and found the army at his disposal inadequate to contain it. He wrote a letter to Athens, couched in very gloomy terms, asking for reinforcements. These were voted by the Athenian assembly in December 414, and at the same time Demosthenes and Eurymedon were appointed colleagues of Nicias.

The war against Athens (432–404 B.C.)

In the following spring Agis led an army into Attica. The Spartans were in confident mood, because of the Athenian involvement in Sicily; besides, they could now justifiably accuse Athens of aggression, whereas in the Archidamian War they had themselves been the aggressors. The practice of invading Attica annually and destroying the crops (a practice which had provoked irksome, but far from fatal, to the Athenians) was abandoned. Agis advanced to Decelea, a place about eleven miles north of Athens, which he fortified, with the intention of occupying it all the year round and maintaining a hostile presence near the enemy capital. The fort at Decelea not only deprived the Athenians of the produce of their own soil but threatened the supply-route from Euboea.

At Syracuse, Gylippus kept up a constant pressure on the besieging forces. He attacked and captured Athenian forts which had been built on the coast south of the great harbour. When Demosthenes, the most resourceful of the Athenian generals, made an assault on Syracusan positions to the west of the city, he was repulsed with serious losses. Morale among the Athenians was running very low; they made no progress, but on the contrary their own resources were being slowly eaten away. Nicias' colleagues advocated withdrawal, but in the end they accepted his advice to stay. The Syracusans became aware of the plight of their enemies and conceived the hope not merely of driving them off but of winning a decisive victory. A limited Syracusan attack by sea was successful, and caused despondency among the Athenians, as they reflected that even their navy was now proving inferior. But this defeat was only the foretaste of a full-scale battle in the great harbour, which involved all the triremes available. The Syracusans won a great victory, depriving Athens of the splendid fleet which had set out with such high hopes and leaving the Athenian army at Syracuse without naval support. It was plain that the army would have to withdraw by land to some friendly Sicilian city. Such a withdrawal the Syracusans were anxious to prevent, fearing that the army would be re-equipped and sent against them a second time. Gylippus sent out parties to make road-blocks and to harass the retreat as much as possible. Nicias' part of the army and that commanded by Demosthenes became separated; and each, after suffering an intolerable number of casualties, was forced to surrender. The prisoners (some seven thousand of them) were harshly treated and, despite the protest of Gylippus, the Syracusans insisted on executing both Nicias and Demosthenes.

The resilence of the Athenian people was never displayed to better effect than in the months following the Sicilian catastrophe. They did not panic and did not sue for peace, but took thought for the organization of their alliance and for the fortification of Sunium, so as to protect the shipping-lane by which supplies were brought to Athens. For the time being their dispositions had to be made from a defensive point of view, but it was not long before they again sent out small fleets, to the considerable embarrassment of the Peloponnesians.

Nevertheless the initiative now plainly lay with Sparta; it was up to her to exploit a situation in which the allies of Athens were very restive and even the neutral states were inclined to embrace the Spartan cause. At the same time, the purity of that cause seems to have become tarnished. We no longer hear of Sparta's mission to liberate Greece; rather, says Thucydides, the Spartans 'determined to engage in the war with all their heart, thinking that . . . if they destroyed the Athenians they would forthwith acquire the secure hegemony of the whole of Greece' (8.2.4). What detailed plans the Spartans had for the further prosecution of the war (if they had any) we do not know. But at least they grasped the necessity of pressing hard in the two areas where they were able to do most harm to the Athenians: the aggressive use of the Decelean fort and the breaking-up of the Athenian system of alliances. In pursuance of these policies, Agis went to Decelea late in the year. He first gave effect to a Spartan resolution that the allies should be required to provide a fleet, without which it was impossible to undertake offensive operations against the eastern possessions of Athens. Then, at Decelea, Agis received deputations from Euboea and Lesbos, expressing the desire of their respective states to secede from Athens and join the Spartans. He appointed a 'harmost' for Lesbos: the first time, to our knowledge, that this term had been applied to a resident magistrate sent by Sparta to govern one of her allies. Meanwhile an embassy from the island of Chios had arrived at Sparta, intimating that the Chians too wished to come over to the Spartan side.

The years 412 and 411 brought an almost unbroken series of reverses to Athens. Several constituent states of the Athenian empire said they were eager to secede; and yet Sparta, left to herself, would hardly have stirred sufficiently to apply even the slight nudge necessary to detach these states. But she was not left to herself. Alcibiades once more provided the driving force which Sparta lacked; at his instigation a Peloponnesian fleet under Spartan command sailed for the east, fomented revolt in Chios, induced the Ionian cities of Miletus and Cnidus to come over, and brought Rhodes out of the Athenian orbit. The reception of Rhodes into the Spartan Alliance was marked by a significant change in policy. Tribute was imposed on an ally for the first time: an act which marks the transition of the Alliance into an empire of Athenian type. If Alcibiades urged on the Spartans by the force of his personality, the Persians did so with money. Two Persian satraps offered to be

The war against Athens (432–404 B.C.)

paymasters of the Peloponnesians if they would intervene against Athens in their respective parts of Asia: Tissaphernes in Ionia and Pharnabazus at the Hellespont. Tissaphernes, with whom Sparta treated first, was a devious and unreliable ally. The payments he made fell short of what he had promised, and the strong fleet he had undertaken to bring from Phoenicia never materialized. Still, the Spartans concluded three treaties with Tissaphernes, acting as plenipotentiary for the Persian king. In the first, Persia promised to wage war on the Spartan side against Athens, and in return for this undertaking Sparta recognized Persian suzerainty of the Greek cities of Asia. In the second, the Persian king bound himself specifically to maintain allied forces which were on Asian soil at his invitation. In the third, the offer of maintenance is hedged about with conditions, which reflect Tissaphernes' fear of unbridled Spartan power and his determination to prolong the war between Sparta and Athens, by keeping them on a level footing. In this policy he was following the advice of Alcibiades, who in late 412 had joined his court, having realized the suspicion in which he was held by the Spartans. Alcibiades as usual pursued the course which suited himself; and, since he was planning to return to political life at Athens, he wished to be able to claim that he had advanced Athenian interests with the satrap.

The following year was marked by political upheaval at Athens: the democratic constitution was in abeyance for a few months, and power was concentrated in the hands of four hundred oligarchs who made overtures to Agis at Decelea and to the ephors at Sparta, but received no encouraging response. The Hellespont replaced Ionia as the main theatre of operations in the east. An army under Spartan command marched from Miletus up to Abydus, which was induced to revolt and join the Spartan side. An Athenian fleet went at great speed to the Hellespont, but found Abydus impossible to recapture; whereupon it made Sestus its base. The Spartan cause was making little headway in Ionia. Tissaphernes continued to play his double game, while the Spartan admiral Astyochus showed himself inert and stupid. Astyochus was removed from his command and superseded by Mindarus, who sailed to the Hellespont with seventy-three ships, in the hope of faring better at the hands of Pharnabazus.

Torn by faction and deprived of many of their eastern possessions, the Athenians suffered a further and more serious blow. In response to an invitation from Euboea, a Peloponnesian fleet with the Spartiate Agesandridas in command set out from Epidaurus and put in at Oropus, ravaging Aegina on the way. An improvised Athenian fleet was rushed to Eretria, opposite Oropus, but this was put to flight by Agesandridas, and the whole of Euboea then seceded from Athens. Thucydides gives a penetrating analysis of what happened, and of what might have happened, at this juncture (8.96). The Athenians were deep in despair: their army in Samos was in revolt, they had no ships and no crews in reserve, there was sedition in their own city, they had lost a fleet and now Euboea as well; they were afraid of an imminent Peloponnesian attack on the Piraeus, which they could do nothing to prevent. And if, says Thucydides, the Peloponnesians *had* made for the Piraeus and besieged it they would have compelled the Athenian ships in eastern waters to come home, so leaving undefended their entire maritime empire; but 'on this occasion, as on many others, the Spartans proved the most complaisant of enemies for the Athenians'.

The Spartans made no plans for gripping Athens in a pincer-movement, with Agis coming down from Decelea and Agesandridas putting into the Piraeus with his victorious fleet. The people of Athens breathed a sigh of relief, as they had done after the Sicilian affair, and tried to retrieve what they could. The Four Hundred were deposed, and an assembly set up, consisting of those citizens who had the means to take the field as hoplites, with their own equipment. At the same time a decision was taken to pardon and recall Alcibiades, whose energy and ability were much needed by the city. So Athens, who seemed to take as much heart from her defeats as did the Spartans from their victories, determined to reassert herself in the region of the Hellespont. Not only prestige but economic necessity dictated this strategy, for with the loss of Attica and Euboea Athens was heavily dependent on grain-ships which had to sail past Byzantium and out through the Hellespont.

The Athenians ordered their fleet to sail from Samos to the Hellespont, where it met the Peloponnesian ships, defeated them in a battle, and forced them back to Abydus. From their base at Sestus the Athenian fleet went into the Propontis and brought back into their empire the city of Cyzicus, which had revolted.

These actions, in the high summer of 411, initiated a period of four years during which Athens recovered much of the ground she had lost. In 410 Mindarus took his fleet to make an attempt on Cyzicus, and Pharnabazus brought up an army. Alcibiades arrived with a superior fleet and forced the Peloponnesians on shore. Mindarus disembarked and offered battle on land. He was killed in the fighting, which turned out disastrously for the Peloponnesian side. The Athenians captured or destroyed their entire fleet, and Alcibiades was free to sail across the Propontis and set up a customs-post at the Bosporus. Hippocrates, Mindarus' second-in-command, addressed a despairing letter to the Spartan magistrates, and this was intercepted, and read at Athens: 'Our ships are destroyed, Mindarus is dead, the crews are starving, we are at a

The war against Athens (432-404 B.C.)

loss what to do.' But Pharnabazus consoled the Spartans for the loss of their ships, pointing out that these could easily be replaced out of the limitless resources of the Persian empire. Pharnabazus' words provide a key to the understanding of this stage of the war. However many victories the Athenians won, they could do little to loosen the grip which Sparta was able to exert on their economy; and, if the Athenians were once to lose their fleet, they would have lost the war, since they could not build another. In fact, the Athenians continued to hold their own at sea, and in 408 they had two successes at the Bosporus which were of vital importance to their import-trade. In the first they landed near Chalcedon and defeated a joint army commanded by Pharnabazus and the Spartan harmost Hippocrates. They then laid siege to Byzantium, and the gates of that city were thrown open to them by a pro-Athenian faction.

Alcibiades had again been instrumental in gaining these successes, and in recognition of his services he was appointed a general and allowed to return to Athens; he soon left once more and made for his base at Samos (407). The same year saw two important changes on the side of Sparta and her allies. Darius, the Persian king, appointed his younger son Cyrus to co-ordinate the war-effort with Sparta; at the same time Lysander was sent as Spartan admiral to Rhodes, and so began his long career as a director and executant of Spartan policy. Going to Cyrus at Sardis, he received a lavish amount of money, and negotiated arrears of pay for his crews. Later he fought a naval battle off Notium, north of Ephesus on the Ionian coast, in which he had distinctly the better of Alcibiades' fleet. Because of this reverse Alcibiades lost favour at Athens, and was superseded by Conon. Lysander finished his year of command, and in 406 Callicratidas went out as Spartan admiral. As Lysander had done, he went to Cyrus to get pay for his men, but was kept kicking his heels in Sardis. He indignantly left for Miletus, without having seen Cyrus, and resolved to wage war, if necessary without the aid of barbarian gold. Raising a sum locally from private contributors, he began operations at Lesbos by storming Methymna and trapping Conon's ships in the harbour of Mytilene. But the main Athenian fleet was assembling at Samos, and soon afterwards it sailed up to take station in the islands called Arginusae, lying between Lesbos and Asia. Callicratidas left Eteonicus at Mytilene with fifty ships, and at dawn on the following day he made a most rash onslaught on the entire Athenian fleet, which had been drawn up in such a way that its line could not be broken – not, at least, by the forces at Callicratidas' disposal. Callicratidas was lost overboard, the Athenian right wing defeated the Spartan contingent and so started a rout of the rest. The Athenians lost twenty-five ships, the

Peloponnesians about seventy. When Eteonicus heard of the defeat, he sent his ships to Chios and led back the army to Methymna.

During the winter, the troops of Sparta's allies made their way to Chios. Disaffection arose in the army, and Eteonicus quelled it by distributing money he had obtained from the Chians. Chians and other Spartan allies met at Ephesus and requested the re-appointment of Lysander as admiral. Since this was contrary to Spartan law, a compromise was reached, whereby Aracus became titular admiral and Lysander held the effective command.

On his arrival at Ephesus in the summer of 405, Lysander set himself finally to break the sea-power of Athens. He ordered Eteonicus to bring from Chios the army under his command, arranged for the repair of ships which had seen service, and had new ones built. Lysander was diplomat as well as military leader. He knew how to do business with the Persians, and succeeded in getting funds from Cyrus. With his augmented fleet he entered the Ceramic Gulf, opposite Cos, and stormed a town allied to Athens. From there he sailed to Rhodes; but his reasons for doing so are unknown. He soon set out for the Hellespont, and the Athenians too sent their fleet into that quarter. Making his base at Abydus, Lysander went to Lampsacus (a city of the Athenian empire) and stormed it, with the vigorous support of a land-force under Spartan command. Meanwhile the Athenian fleet had made for Sestus. Having taken on supplies they sailed to Aegospotami, just across the Hellespont from Lampsacus. Here the Athenians drew up their ships in line of battle but, Lysander making no response, they sailed back to Aegospotami. Exactly the same thing happened on the next three days. But on the succeeding day, when the Athenians had as usual taken their ships back to shore, Lysander sent scouts to report what the Athenians did after coming into harbour. As soon as he heard that they were scattered a long way from their ships, Lysander ordered his own crews to make for shore at full speed and pounce on the enemy ships. Only nine Athenian triremes (including Conon's) made their escape; the rest were not fully manned, or not manned at all, and they and their crews fell without a struggle into Lysander's hands.

In one brilliant coup Lysander had destroyed the Athenian fleet. He continued his victorious career by bringing back Byzantium and Chalcedon into the Spartan Alliance and appointing a harmost over them. He then sailed to Lesbos, and established Spartan control over the whole island. The few remaining Athenian allies, with the sole exception of Samos, now prepared to secede; and Eteonicus went to Thrace, which he brought over to the side of Sparta. Lysander himself sailed to Athens with two hundred ships; meanwhile king Pausanias led a Peloponnesian army into Attica and pitched camp in the suburbs of Athens. Lysander cleared Athenians from Melos and Aegina and recalled the original inhabitants, ravaged Salamis, and finally anchored in the Piraeus, which he closed against the entry of merchant-ships.

With both Spartan kings on Attic soil and Lysander's fleet at the Piraeus, there was nothing left for the Athenians to do except sue for peace, in the hope that they would at least be allowed to keep their long walls intact. Their ambassadors were rebuffed by Agis, who referred them to the ephors at Sparta; but the ephors did not even permit them to enter Laconia until they came with acceptable proposals, including an undertaking to break down the long walls. So the Athenians sent plenipotentiaries to Sparta, to conclude a treaty on terms laid down by the conqueror. A congress of the allies was convened at Sparta, at which a number of cities (most notably Corinth and Thebes) insisted that Athens should be destroyed completely. But the character of the Alliance was different from what it had been in 432. Then Sparta had allowed herself to be persuaded to go to war by the clamour of her allies; now she over-rode their opinion and refused to enslave a city which in other days had exhibited such valour in the pan-Hellenic cause. The terms she dictated to the Athenians were, however, harsh ones. They were to pull down their long walls and the walls of the Piraeus, recall political exiles, surrender all their warships save twelve, have friends and enemies in common with Sparta, and follow the Spartans by land and sea wherever they led. (The last two clauses were regularly inserted in treaties between Sparta and her allies.) The Athenian assembly accepted these terms, and the destruction of the long walls was begun. The war was brought to a formal conclusion in 404, with Agis' withdrawal from Decelea and an expedition to Samos by Lysander, who restored the island to its previous inhabitants and appointed a 'decarchy' of ten governors to rule it. Lysander then sailed to Sparta with the immense booty he had acquired and a large sum of money left over from Cyrus' last donative.

Bibliography

The causes and immediate antecedents of the war: H. Nissen, *HZ* 27 (1889), 385–427; G. Dickins, *CQ* 5 (1911), 238–48; G.B. Grundy, *CQ* 7 (1913), 59–62; A. Andrewes, *CQ* 53 (1959), 223–39; D. Kagan, *The outbreak of the Peloponnesian War* (Ithaca/London, 1969); G. E. M. de Ste. Croix. *The origins of the Peloponnesian War* (London, 1972); R. Sealey, *CP* 70 (1975), 89–109; E. Bar-Hen, *AS* 8 (1977), 21–31. Meetings of the Spartan and Athenian assemblies just before the outbreak of war: A.H.M. Jones, *PCPS* 182 (1952–1953), 43–6. Diplomatic activity just before the outbreak of war: G. Pasquali, *SIFC* 5 (1927), 299–315; H. Nesselhauf, *Hermes* 69 (1934), 286–99.

Background of the war: G.B. Grundy, *Thucydides and the history of his age* (Oxford, 1948).

The Archidamian War. General study: D. Kagan, *The Archidamian War* (Ithaca/London, 1974). Spartan strategy: P.A. Brunt, *Phoenix* 19 (1965), 255–80; I. Moxon, *RSA* 8 (1978), 7–26. The Megarian decree: P.A. Brunt, *AJP* 72 (1951), 269–82. The role of Megara: T.E. Wick, *Historia* 28 (1979), 1–14. Political parties in Lesbos: T.J. Quinn, *Historia* 20 (1971), 405–17. The Spartans and Lesbos: G. Bockisch, *Klio* 43–5 (1965), 67–73. The Spartan inscription relating to contributions 'for the war': M. Fränkel, *RhM* 57 (1902), 534–43; F.E. Adcock, *Mélanges G. Glotz* I (Paris, 1932), 1–6. The Pylos campaign: U. von Wilamowitz-Moellendorff, *Kleine Schriften* III (Berlin, 1969), 406–19; J.B. Wilson, *Pylos 425 BC* (Warminster, 1979). The Amphipolis campaign: J. Papastavru, *Klio* Beiheft 37 (1936), 15–23. Thucydides' delineation of Alcidas, Archidamus, Brasidas, and Cnemus: H.D. Westlake, *Individuals in Thucydides* (Cambridge, 1968), 122–65. Thucydides and Brasidas' campaign in Thrace: L. Bodin, *Mélanges O. Navarre* (Toulouse, 1935), 47–55; A.L. Boegehold, *CP* 74 (1979), 148–52. The Spartan-Athenian alliance: U. von Wilamowitz, *op. cit.* 380–405.

Agis' campaigns in 418: W.J. Woodhouse, *King Agis of Sparta and his campaign in Arkadia in 418 B.C.* (Oxford, 1933); D. Kagan, *CP* 57 (1962), 209–18.

The Decelean War. The Spartan occupation of Decelea: E.T. Salmon, *CR* 60 (1946), 13–14. The activity of Lysander: D. Lotze, *Lysander und der peloponnesische Krieg* (Berlin, 1964). The battle of Notium: G. De Sanctis, *RFC* 59 (1931), 222–9.

Spartan sea-power: K.J. Beloch, *RhM* 34 (1879), 117–30. Spartan harmosts: G. Bockisch, *Klio* 46 (1965), 129–239. Spartan involvement with Persia: D.M. Lewis, *Sparta and Persia* (Leiden, 1977).

12

The era of Spartan supremacy (404–370 B.C.)

In the summer of 404 Lysander had become the strongest man in the strongest city. His victory at Aegospotami, achieved with such elegance and economy of means, placed him among the first rank of commanders Sparta had ever produced; after the victory he had gone from city to city in the crumbling Athenian empire, imposing peace and installing Spartan governors ('harmosts') and in some places oligarchic groups of ten ('decarchies'). At the same time tribute was exacted from the cities, just as it had been by the Athenians. Sparta, who had begun the war 'in order to liberate Greece', now helped herself to the revenues which came to her from the maritime states of the Aegean. This was the first, and only the first, false step she took immediately after her victory. The very completeness of that victory caused her serious constitutional problems. Having 'liberated' the Greek cities only to bring them more fully into subjection, the Spartans found that their state possessed no machinery for administering such a widespread empire. Hence Lysander's makeshift expedient of entrusting power to decarchies, whether or not these provided an efficient mode of government in a particular case. The decarchies, in fact, did not survive very long (we do not know how long); but harmosts continued to combine the function of civil administrator and military governor.

Lysander in his own person constituted an acute problem to the Spartans, and one very close to home. Some of our sources say that he kept quasi-royal state at Samos, when he had settled affairs there, and that on returning to Sparta he tried to make the kingship elective, in the hope that it would devolve upon him. These plans, if indeed they were seriously meditated by Lysander, came to nothing; but the victory he had won certainly gave him an extraordinary prestige at Sparta. Even before being re-appointed to office, he exercised authority alongside, and sometimes even in conflict with, the ephors and kings. He is first seen in this role shortly after the capitulation of Athens. The Athenian oligarchs had accomplished another *coup d'état*; and, in order to strengthen their position, they sent envoys to Sparta. The envoys were received by Lysander, who arranged for the dispatch to Athens of a Spartan garrison and a Spartan harmost. Under Spartan protection, the oligarchs conducted a sickening reign of terror. Civil war broke out between them and democratic rebels, and the latter established themselves in the Piraeus. Again the oligarchic regime appealed to Lysander, and again he responded, this time going to Attica in person, while his brother Libys blockaded Piraeus by sea. It seemed that Lysander was setting out on another career of conquest: a prospect which no doubt displeased many in authority at Sparta, but especially the Agiad king Pausanias. He was afraid that Lysander would not only enhance his reputation but acquire Athens as a personal domain. Pausanias accordingly persuaded a majority of the ephorate to send him with an army to take control of the situation. Many of Sparta's allies took the field as well, but the beginning of a serious rift in the Spartan Alliance now appeared. Both Thebes and Corinth refused to provide a contingent. They were becoming apprehensive of Spartan ambitions, and thought that Sparta meant to take over the city of Athens and use it as her own stronghold.

Pausanias stationed his army near the Piraeus, commanding the right wing himself and assigning the left to Lysander. The king first enjoined the rebels to disperse; when they refused, he made an attack upon them; their vigorous counter-attack caused him to withdraw. Re-grouping his army, Pausanias pressed home a second attack. He let it be known, however, that if his opponents sent envoys to him they would be well received. Envoys duly appeared, and Pausanias gained the ephors' support in appointing a commission of fifteen members to reconcile the opposing parties at Athens.

The conciliatory attitude of Pausanias was entirely successful in this case. It might have succeeded in other cases as well, had not a faction at Sparta preferred to resolve differences by the application of brute force; king Agis and his successor Agesilaus were the executants of the more aggressive policy. Thus between 399 and 397 Sparta provoked a dispute with the people of Elis, on the grounds that they had previously allied themselves with Athens, Argos, and Mantinea and had prevented Spartan athletes from competing at Olympia. Of course the Eleans could offer no effective resistance to an army led by Agis; again, Spartan allies who joined his army did not include either Corinthians or Thebans. Agis compelled the people of Elis to accept Spartan demands, but did not deprive them of their right to conduct the Olympic Games.

King Agis died after completing the Elean campaign, and the succession was disputed between his brother Agesilaus and his son Leotychidas. Doubts arose (or were contrived) about the legitimacy of Leotychidas' birth. The influence of Lysander proved decisive at this point. He persuaded 'the city' (a term which presumably comprises

The era of Spartan supremacy (404–370 B.C.)

Council, ephorate, and assembly, as well as the other king) to appoint Agesilaus to the kingship. Although Lysander may honestly have thought that Agesilaus would make the better king, he surely consulted his own interests in promoting Agesilaus' candidature. And in fact Agesilaus turned out to be as much of an imperialist as was Lysander himself; nevertheless, like Pausanias, he was irked by Lysander's pretensions, and more than once he had to remind him who was king, and who commoner.

During the first year of Agesilaus' reign the foundations of the Spartan state were disturbed by a projected revolution. This was the most serious attempt to subvert the constitution that is attested in the classical period (for we cannot be certain to what extent Lysander had translated into action his ambitious dreams). The exact aims of the conspiracy, led by Cinadon, are not made clear by Xenophon (*Hellenica* 3.3.4–11). Xenophon states that Cinadon 'was not one of the peers' (cf. p. 117), and quotes Cinadon's reference to the fact that the Spartiates now formed only a small minority of the free population. Here we have a vivid illustration of the dwindling strength of the Spartiates, identified by Aristotle as contributory to the downfall of the Spartan state (p. 143). But, while we can confidently say that Cinadon wanted to break the monopoly of political power enjoyed by the Spartiates, we do not know what manner of constitution he favoured to replace the 'Lycurgan' arrangement. Cinadon seems to have laid his plans well, except in one respect, that of security. News of the conspiracy came to the ears of the ephors, who took it very seriously and managed to trick Cinadon into revealing the names of his confederates. He did not deny the charge, but answered that 'he wanted to be inferior to nobody at Sparta' (*Hellenica* 3.3.11): his words would make an effective political slogan, but they are too vague to inform us about his intended programme.

Meanwhile Sparta had been drawn once again into the affairs of Asia; and it is hard to see how she could have avoided involvement in that region, in view of the numerous Greek cities there which looked to her as their leader and protector. Cyrus, the Persian prince who had been of great assistance to Sparta in the closing stages of the war against Athens (p. 207), led a revolt against his brother Artaxerxes II in 401. The army of Cyrus contained many Greek mercenaries, and his expedition as far as Babylon marks the first large-scale employment of Greek mercenary troops; thenceforward they took an increasingly large part in the battles of the time – even in battles fought between Greek cities. Sparta gave Cyrus the naval backing he requested, but his adventure ended with his own death and the stranding of a Greek army far from the sea. When the members of this army eventually made their way back to the Bosporus, they formed a body of hardened veterans available for service wherever the pay was adequate.

After putting down the rebellion led by his brother, Artaxerxes sent Tissaphernes into the south-west of Asia Minor, with general powers. He demanded that the Greeks of Ionia should be his subjects; and they, as their ancestors had often done, sent envoys to the leading Greek city for help against the barbarian. Sparta first dispatched Thibron with a considerable force: this seems to have contained very few Spartiates (and, indeed, there were now very few Spartiates to go round), but it was augmented by men who had taken part in Cyrus' campaign. Thibron's success in military operations fell far short of expectation, and he was replaced by a much more capable Spartan commander in Dercylidas. He forced both Tissaphernes and Pharnabazus to the defensive, and at a peace conference called upon Persia to respect the independence of the Greek cities in Asia; the Persians on their side demanded the withdrawal of the Spartan army.

Such was the progress that Dercylidas had made by the summer of 397. In the following year the Spartan authorities received a report that the Persians had been seen mustering an immense fleet in Phoenician waters. A congress of allies was summoned to Sparta, and at this meeting Lysander's extraordinary position was again made manifest. He proposed that an allied expedition should be sent to Asia under the joint command of himself and king Agesilaus. The ostensible aim of the expedition was, of course, the circumvention of the Persian threat; but Xenophon remarks that Lysander hoped also to re-establish the decarchies which had been suppressed by the ephorate (*Hellenica* 3.4.2). It is not surprising that Lysander had excited the enmity of powerful interests at Sparta. Agesilaus, with whom Lysander was appointed to share the command in Asia, regarded him neither as an enemy nor as a friend, but as an extremely able citizen who sometimes had to be taught his place. The king was to prove himself in this campaign, and in many subsequent campaigns, an excellent military commander and an astute strategist. Yet he displayed on occasion a certain *folie des grandeurs* which cannot be concealed even by Xenophon, his great apologist. Agamemnon, in the days of legend, had put in at the Boeotian port of Aulis on his way to Troy. Agesilaus thought it appropriate for him to do the same. He went to Aulis with a single trireme, and was in the act of offering sacrifice when horsemen sent by the leaders of the Boeotian League forcibly prevented him from continuing and threw down the victims from the altar. That a Spartan king should be so insulted on friendly soil clearly indicates the strength of feeling against Sparta in some quarters in Boeotia. It is upon such incidents as these (some of which are trivial, or even ludicrous, in themselves) that we have to base our knowledge of the widening gap between Sparta and her three most powerful allies, Athens, Corinth, and Thebes. The refusal of Thebes and Corinth to send military forces at Sparta's request has been noted twice (p. 212); now we have the insult offered to Agesilaus in Boeotia; and it must have been at about this time that some Athenians privately sent equipment to Conon's fleet, presumably for use on the side of Persia against Sparta (*Hellenica Oxyrhynchia* 6–7). For the moment Agesilaus sailed away from Aulis, full of anger against the Thebans, which he was to vent upon them before many more years had passed.

Agesilaus' first act on taking up his command in Asia was the continuation of the truce concluded between Dercylidas and the Persian satraps. Tissaphernes promptly broke the terms of the truce and brought up a force of cavalry, which mauled Agesilaus' army in Phrygia. Agesilaus plainly had not sufficient forces to deal with this treacherous enemy; he therefore wintered in Ephesus, strengthening his cavalry and turning the entire city into a 'workshop of war' (Xenophon *Hellenica* 3.4.17). The campaigning season of 395 was now approaching; Lysander and his small band of Spartiates had been replaced by others; and Agesilaus led his army in the direction of Sardis. The details of Agesilaus' march are unclear, but at a spot near the river Pactolus he brought a Persian army to battle before it was fully ready. It withstood a Greek cavalry-attack, but broke under the pressure exerted by the hoplite-phalanx. Artaxerxes blamed Tissaphernes personally for the Persian defeat, and sent a new satrap, Tithraustes, to replace him and have him executed. Tithraustes entered into negotiations with Agesilaus, saying that with Tissaphernes out of the way there was no longer any cause of dispute between Sparta and the Persian empire; Agesilaus should therefore take his army home, and the Greek cities in Asia should be autonomous, with the proviso that they paid the traditional tribute to the king of Persia. Agesilaus replied that he was not empowered to make an agreement on those terms and that he would have to refer the matter to the authorities at Sparta. While awaiting a reply from Sparta, he proposed to lead his army into Phrygia (the satrapy of Pharnabazus) and spend the winter there. Before leaving for Phrygia, he appointed Peisander admiral, with orders to fit out a fleet for operations in the coming spring. Agesilaus resumed the initiative on his entry into Phrygia, devastating the country, attempting to seduce provinces from their allegiance to the Persian king, and keeping Pharnabazus on the move like a nomad. But when a conference had been arranged between him and Pharnabazus, Agesilaus was won over by that charming man, and offered to march out of his territory. This he did at the beginning of spring in

394. He now found himself at the head of a powerful army, with nothing very much for it to do. Once more Agesilaus, the competent winner of battles, showed how poor a grasp he had of larger issues. He evolved the plan of augmenting his forces still further and taking them on a grandiose expedition into the interior of the Persian empire, detaching provinces as they went. He was not given the opportunity of putting this plan into effect. During the previous year, the smouldering anti-Spartan sentiments within the Alliance had erupted, and Sparta was suddenly confronted by a coalition of enemies. Agesilaus was ordered to start for home, and did so immediately, leaving a harmost in Asia and leading his army by the route which Xerxes had followed in 480.

It is a pity that the inner motivation of events in Greece during 395 cannot now be grasped. What actually happened can be told in a few words. Thebes, Corinth, and Athens, together with Argos, took up such a hostile attitude towards Sparta that she was compelled to strike a blow against them, in case they forged a potent anti-Spartan confederacy. Xenophon attributes the anti-Spartan outburst to Persian treachery and a Persian bribe. According to his account, Tithraustes had secured the services of Timocrates, a Rhodian. To this man he entrusted a large quantity of gold, desiring him to give it to various influential persons in Greece if they undertook to involve their respective cities in war with Sparta. We need not doubt that Timocrates was sent on such a mission. But Tithraustes could hardly have expected, and we can hardly believe, that the mission was so successful that in the course of a single summer Argos, Athens, Corinth, and Thebes severally decided on war against Sparta; that Thebes took appropriate action for starting a war; and that Athens mobilized support for Thebes. It is impossible that Timocrates achieved all this in so short a time, however much money he distributed. We must think, rather, of a conspiracy maturing over a few years, in reaction against the high-handed attitude of Sparta and her indifference to the claims and the rights of her allies. The part played by Timocrates, and perhaps an important part, lay in finding corruptible politicians who would not give effective support to an anti-Spartan policy unless they were suitably rewarded.

The war which broke out in 395, and which lasted for eight years, is known as the Corinthian War, because many of the military operations were conducted at or near the Isthmus of Corinth; but in fact the first major engagements took place in central Greece. The Thebans provoked hostilities by invading Phocis. The Phocians were too weak to defend their country single-handed, and requested help from Sparta. The ephors acted without delay. They sent Lysander to Phocis, with orders to

The era of Spartan supremacy (404–370 B.C.)

collect an army of Phocians and other allies and then to make his way to Haliartus, a town in Boeotia between Thebes and Orchomenus, where he was to meet Pausanias on a specified day. Lysander carried out his orders and, indeed, did more than he had been asked to do, for on his way to Haliartus he induced Orchomenus to leave the Boeotian League, of which Thebes was the head. Meanwhile Pausanias waited at Tegea, collecting an allied army. The initiative had passed to Sparta, and the Thebans felt that they would not be able to resist the onslaught of a strong Spartan army, unless help were forthcoming from some quarter. So they abandoned the ancient hostility between their city and Athens, and sent envoys to ask for help from the Athenian assembly. A Theban spokesman, according to Xenophon, presented a catalogue of complaints against Sparta: she had taken land from the Eleans, had refused her allies a share in war-booty and in the government of conquered territories, and in short had behaved towards her allies like a master towards his helots. There followed a unanimous vote in the assembly to forgive the Thebans all the hostile acts they had committed in the past and to make common cause with them against Sparta.

Lysander arrived at Haliartus before Pausanias. Instead of waiting for the king's appearance, he went up to the walls of the town and tried to remove it from the League. A Theban force came up, and in the ensuing skirmish Lysander was killed. The Thebans had the worst of the fighting, but their spirits rose when they realized that not only had Lysander fallen but his army was melting away. They were thrown into consternation by the arrival of Pausanias, but recovered when he remained inactive and particularly when they were reinforced by an Athenian army. Pausanias requested permission to take up the bodies of Lysander and others. This the Thebans granted, on condition that the Spartan army was led away forthwith. Pausanias accepted the condition; but on returning to Sparta he was brought to trial on capital charges, accused of negligence in arriving late for the rendezvous with Lysander and of cowardice in that he had failed to fight for the corpses. He was condemned to death, but fled to Tegea, where he spent the remainder of his life; his son Agesipolis now assumed the Agiad kingship. According to Strabo, the downfall of Pausanias was engineered by the other royal house; after going into exile, he is said to have written a treatise on the laws of Lycurgus (8.5.5).

Sparta had gained little and lost much in the first year of the Corinthian War. But in the following summer her military machine again functioned with its usual efficiency, although Spartan success on land was offset to some extent by a defeat at sea. Sparta attacked her enemies from two directions, first by a force mobilized by the ephors and sent north to

Corinthia, second by Agesilaus' excellent army which thrust southwards into Boeotia. The first engagement, fought in the neighbourhood of Corinth, was a typical hoplite-contest in which it was very difficult to get the better of a Spartan army. In this case the allied forces on the left of the Spartan line were defeated, but the Spartans themselves broke through the Athenians who were stationed opposite, wheeled round, and made short work of the Argives, Thebans, and Corinthians. The Spartan victory in this quarter effectively quashed the notion (entertained by some hotheads on the other side) of an invasion of Laconia; all that the Corinthians could now hope to achieve was the fortification of the Isthmus as strongly as possible, in the hope of containing any Spartan thrust into Attica and Boeotia. What the Spartans lacked at this juncture was a fleet, which would have enabled them to turn the walls of the Isthmus and land troops to the north. But the ships which Agesilaus had entrusted to Peisander (p. 215) were lost in a battle off Cnidus. Peisander, with inadequate and unreliable forces at his disposal, tried to break the enemy line, which was commanded jointly by Pharnabazus and Conon. Deserted by many of the allied craft, Peisander was forced to the shore, where he was killed fighting by his ship. This victory was energetically followed up. Pharnabazus and Conon sailed to a number of Aegean islands, from which they expelled Spartan harmosts, so earning an enthusiastic reception everywhere. Pharnabazus disembarked at Ephesus and sent Conon with a small fleet to Sestus, promising that he himself would march overland to the Hellespont. But Dercylidas, the Spartan harmost at Abydus, crossed to Sestus and saw to it that the city remained loyal. He prepared to hold it against all comers, and the enemy could make no headway against it. In any case Pharnabazus had conceived plans for taking the war much closer to Sparta; and these plans he was to bring into effect in the following year.

In the meantime Agesilaus had brought back his army to Greece. The anti-Spartan states drew up a powerful force to meet him in the plain of Coronea, on the road from Thebes to Phocis. In the enemy army were contingents from Boeotia, Euboea, Athens, Argos, Corinth, and other cities. The soldiers of Agesilaus were drawn from a still wider area of the Greek world, and even from some places outside it. The Spartiates serving with the army had now dwindled to a very small proportion; the majority consisted of *neodamodeis*, outlanders, allies, and men from Ionia and the Hellespont. Still, they had fought together in Asia and had followed together the long road back; they were, furthermore, well equipped and well led. As might have been expected under these circumstances, Agesilaus won a major victory. The Spartans and Thebans respectively broke through the enemy line and then came to grips

The era of Spartan supremacy (404–370 B.C.)

with each other; the Thebans were routed, some finding refuge on Mount Helicon, but many being killed as they fled. Agesilaus' victory, though an imposing one, had little political or strategic significance, except that it inhibited the enemy coalition from again seeking a pitched battle with a Spartan general. As with Agis after the battle of Mantinea (p. 201), Agesilaus made no attempt to exploit his victory (for example by proceeding to Thebes), but disbanded his army and sailed home.

In the remaining years of the Corinthian War, Sparta was concerned to break the stalemate at the Isthmus and to reach an accommodation with Persia which would leave her supremacy intact, at least in mainland Greece. On land the anti-Spartan states made Corinth their base, while the Spartan base was at Sicyon. Large forces were no longer deployed; the war became an affair of garrison-duty (which fell most onerously upon Corinth) and of small-scale sorties. Mercenary troops took more and more part in what fighting there was. Spartan interests were threatened by three developments. First, and most damaging in the short term, was the activity of the fleet under Pharnabazus and Conon. These commanders established a base at Melos; from there they conducted raids into Laconian territory and left a garrison at Cythera. Pharnabazus went to the Isthmus and gave money for the prosecution of the war against Sparta; he also sent Conon (at Conon's request) to Athens, with the intention of rebuilding the long walls demolished in 404 (p. 209). When the work was completed, Athens became once again a defensible city, so constituting a second threat to Sparta (if still only a potential one). The third threat arose from the political union of Argos and Corinth. Since this came into being with the sole object of fighting Sparta more effectively, it had no deep roots; but it was most offensive to Sparta, who insisted on its dissolution at the end of the war.

The Spartans seem to have evolved no overall strategic plan for dealing with their predicament. They more than held their own, but they could not bring themselves to strike a decisive blow at the enemy alliance. For instance the wall between Corinth and the sea was breached, and the Spartan commander broke through and won a battle; but nothing was done to exploit this advantage. Agesilaus too had some success in the promontory to the north-west of Corinth; yet this was outweighed by a furious attack on part of his army by javelin-throwers, and he had to lead home his crippled force by night, so as to escape the derision of the inhabitants. Raids were made into Argive territory, as they had been for long past, by both Spartan kings; and Agesilaus led an expedition into Acarnania at the request of the Achaeans.

Sparta realized that she would make little headway against her opponents so long as Pharnabazus was giving such active support to the

Athenians; she therefore sent Antalcidas as envoy to Tiribazus, the pro-Spartan satrap at Sardis, with proposals for a peace treaty between the Spartans and Artaxerxes (392). Antalcidas, in the name of Sparta, renounced any claims on the Greek cities in Asia and proposed that all Greek states should be autonomous. Envoys from Sparta's principal enemies also waited on Tiribazus. They would have none of the Spartan proposals, which would injure their interests in various ways: Athens would have to relinquish the islands of Imbros, Lemnos, and Scyros; Argos and Corinth would have to dissolve their union; and Thebes would lose her control over the other cities of Boeotia. Tiribazus undertook to take back the proposals to Artaxerxes at Susa, but before leaving he imprisoned Conon, the leader of the Athenian delegation, and secretly gave money to Antalcidas to help furnish a new fleet.

In the absence of Tiribazus, Artaxerxes sent a new satrap named Struthas, who worked strongly against Sparta. To counterbalance his influence, the Spartans dispatched Thibron as admiral. He made raids into Persian territory from his base at Ephesus and won over a number of cities, but he was eventually killed in a sudden Persian attack. It now fell to Sparta to replace Thibron in Asia and also to accede to a request for aid from an oligarchic faction in Rhodes. The first fleet sent to Rhodes proved inadequate, and it had to be reinforced by a number of ships under the command of Teleutias, the brother of Agesilaus. Athens was alarmed at the growing sea-power deployed by the Spartans; Thrasybulus was accordingly ordered to lead an expedition to the eastern Aegean. He could do nothing against the Spartan forces off Rhodes, and so sailed to the Hellespont, where he had some success. After Thrasybulus' death in action, Spartan forces went to the Hellespont to try to undo his work in that area, but they were overwhelmed by the Athenian general Iphicrates with his javelin-throwers, and the Spartan harmost was killed.

Iphicrates' action had secured, for the time being, Athenian dependencies in the region of the Hellespont; but on the other hand Athens was losing control of the waters round her own coasts. Teleutias established himself at Aegina, and sailed the sea doing what mischief he could; among other exploits, he made a daring raid on the Piraeus and captured merchant ships off Sunium.

The Corinthian War might have dragged on longer still, but the means of ending it was provided by Artaxerxes in 387. In that year Antalcidas returned with Tiribazus from Susa, bearing the terms of a treaty which the king imposed on the Greek states. Antalcidas was admiral as well as diplomat. Learning that the Athenians had gained the upper hand at the Hellespont, he made ready a large fleet (to which the Syracusan despot

The era of Spartan supremacy (404–370 B.C.)

Dionysius contributed twenty ships), and set out for Abydus. He captured the ships of the enemy, made himself master of the sea, and prevented merchantmen from sailing to Athens. In this situation the Athenians were thankful to accept the King's Peace (also known as the Peace of Antalcidas). They could hardly move from the Attic coast without being harassed by Teleutias' fleet; their supplies from the Black Sea were cut off; and if they continued fighting they might sustain a defeat even more catastrophic than that of 404, when at least they had been allowed to keep their independence. Argos too felt that she would benefit from the King's Peace: Spartan incursions into her territory had lately become more and more troublesome, and she seemed powerless to prevent them. And the Spartans themselves looked forward to an end of the hostilities which drained their resources by requiring them to keep garrisons at the Isthmus and at Orchomenus.

The King's Peace provided that the Persians were to keep the whole of Asia Minor for themselves and that all Greek cities outside Asia should be autonomous; Artaxerxes threatened to wage war upon any of the belligerents who refused to abide by the terms of the Peace. The arrangement prescribed by Artaxerxes was known as a *koine eirene*: a 'common peace', according to which all Greek states became free and equal. Once made, the King's Peace was regarded as the desirable norm; and, when treaties were concluded later in the century, they had the aim of restoring the Greek world to this norm. It was necessary, even though humiliating, for the Greeks to resort to the Persian king for a settlement of their continuing differences. Despite the advanced state of political thought and of political mechanisms in some of the Greek cities, the cities in general had failed to develop an adequate system of 'international law' to keep the peace. Oaths, which were supposed to be binding, did not prevent the constant repudiation of treaties when these came into conflict with self-interest. The Spartan Alliance, which in theory could have formed a sound basis for the building of a pan-Hellenic league, had been abused by Sparta herself; and the only answer, as Artaxerxes realized, lay in the dissolution of all alliances. Agesilaus appointed himself the interpreter and guarantor of the Peace. He insisted that Corinth and Argos should bring their federation to an end and that Thebes should relinquish control over the other Boeotian cities. Sparta thus used the Peace as an instrument for isolating her enemies from one another and for regaining her supremacy.

In the three years following the conclusion of the Corinthian War, Sparta embarked on a course of recrimination, setting herself to punish those of her Peloponnesian allies who had given her less than wholehearted support in the war. Agesilaus was strongly in favour of this policy, and he may even have been the author of it. The Spartans made an example of Mantinea, with a demand that she should demolish her walls. When she refused, king Agesipolis mustered an army and marched into Mantinean territory, laying waste the country. The Mantineans persisted in their refusal; whereupon Agesipolis blocked the river which flowed through the city, and forced them to give way when their buildings were liable to be destroyed by flooding. So the walls of Mantinea were demolished after all; an oligarchic government with strong pro-Spartan leanings was placed in power; and the city was dissolved into its constituent villages.

As with many other cities of the Peloponnese, Phlius contained factions both friendly and unfriendly towards Sparta. A number of pro-Spartan citizens had been expelled, and these came to Sparta with their grievance. The ephors took up their cause, which they referred to the authorities at Phlius; these were afraid that, if they did not comply with the ephors' demand, they would share the fate of the Mantineans, and so they admitted the exiles. The affair did not end there; the exiles thought they had not received their due, and again appealed to Sparta. They now received the support of Agesilaus, who led an army to Phlius and forced it to surrender; he then imposed a Spartan garrison on the city, and appointed commissioners to frame a new constitution.

In 383 the Spartans became deeply involved in the domestic politics of Thebes; and, in their haste to seize a temporary advantage without considering the probable consequences, they set in motion a series of events which was to cost them their supremacy in Greece. The Theban adventure came about quite fortuitously, as the by-product of an expedition to Chalcidice. Delegates had arrived at Sparta from Acanthus and Apollonia, reporting that the power of Olynthus was on the increase and that there was a danger of a joint Olynthian-Theban-Athenian alliance; moreover their own cities were likely to be drawn, though unwillingly, into the Olynthian ambit unless Sparta took action to prevent it. An expedition in these circumstances was easy to justify within the terms of the King's Peace, since Sparta could claim to be preserving the autonomy of Greek cities. An assembly of the Spartan Alliance sanctioned the dispatch of a strong force, and part of this sailed immediately with Eudimas in command. He set up headquarters at Potidaea and awaited the arrival of his brother Phoebidas, who had been ordered to march over land with the bulk of the army. When Phoebidas came into Boeotia with his army, his attention was diverted towards Thebes. At this time Thebes was split into two powerful parties, one supporting Spartan interests, the other bitterly opposed to them. The Theban magistrate Ismenias was the leader of the anti-Spartan faction; while another magistrate, Leontiades, was markedly pro-Spartan. Leontiades approached Phoebidas, saying that it was within his means to lead a small number of Spartan hoplites to the Theban acropolis; once in control of that, Sparta would have the mastery over Thebes. The plot succeeded; Phoebidas established himself on the acropolis, and brought Thebes under direct Spartan control. Ismenias was placed under arrest, and his followers fled to Athens.

Phoebidas' action met with disapproval in the ephorate and in the Spartan assembly: not on moral grounds, in that he had annexed another city in flagrant defiance of the King's Peace, but because the necessary authority of the Spartan state had been lacking. But on the advice of Agesilaus the *fait accompli* was accepted at Sparta, since it was thought to be so much in Spartan interest to have a foot-hold at Thebes that Phoebidas' technical fault should be overlooked. Once embarked on this course, the Spartans (quite logically, from their point of view) put Ismenias on trial. Three judges from Sparta and one judge from each of the allied states went to Thebes and tried Ismenias on the charge that he had co-operated with Persia and had received money from Artaxerxes. The judges found Ismenias guilty (as they were bound to do), and sentenced him to death. The lack of an international tribunal was never so keenly felt as at this time, when Sparta became both prosecutor and judge in her own cause and, moreover, charged Ismenias with the very 'crimes' which she herself had committed.

The Greeks in general acquiesced in the Spartan occupation of Thebes, and nothing positive was done to upset it until 378. In the intervening years Sparta took up the Olynthian question, which the affair at Thebes had interrupted. Teleutias was sent to Chalcidice as harmost, but in his second year of campaigning he was killed and his army defeated. The Spartan assembly voted to send an expedition on a larger scale, with Agesipolis in command. But the king died of a fever on this campaign, and his embalmed body was sent home to Sparta; he was succeeded by his brother Cleombrotus. (His father Pausanias was still living at Tegea; he dedicated a stone at Delphi in honour of his dead son, and the inscribed base of this is extant.) The Spartans did not relax their pressure on Olynthus, and eventually the city capitulated, swearing to be a true ally of Sparta.

In 379, after the conclusion of their Olynthian campaign, the Spartans were to all appearance at the very peak of their power. Thebes had been reduced to subjection; Corinth was completely loyal; the Argives had been humbled, and gave no more trouble; Athens found herself without allies; while those of Sparta's allies who were guilty of unfriendly acts had been punished. So Xenophon sums up the situation, correctly so far as we can tell, except for his statement about Athens; she was, in fact, quietly acquiring allies, although the formation of a formal confederacy did not come about for another two years. Xenophon, like Herodotus and Thucydides before him, is fascinated by the contrast between resplendent good fortune and the fall which succeeds it (*Hellenica* 5.4.1). Xerxes' army had set out in the pride of power, and gone back broken and defeated; so had the armada which the Athenians had sent to Sicily. And the Spartans, who had broken the King's Peace when they arrogantly seized the acropolis of Thebes, were overwhelmed from that very quarter.

The counter-revolution at Thebes was engineered by a man close to the government, in collusion with Theban exiles who had gone to Athens. Leontiades and the pro-Spartan magistrates were assassinated, and the exiles were summoned home. A Spartan harmost still held the acropolis: he sent for help to Plataea and Thespiae, but some Plataeans were intercepted and killed before they could reach the city. The harmost's nerve failed him, and he ordered the evacuation of the acropolis under a truce: for this act of cowardice he was afterwards sentenced to death at Sparta.

Thus the Spartans had lost one opportunity of regaining control of the situation. They lost a second in the ensuing winter, when the ephors mobilized an army and sent it to Thebes under Cleombrotus' command. He seems to have wandered about Boeotia without purpose and without result, eventually disbanding his army at the Isthmus; he had however left at Thespiae a harmost named Sphodrias.

The Thebans had so far come off lightly, but they were aware of the punishment that awaited them, so soon as the Spartans returned with a stronger army and a more competent commander. Instead of going to Athens in a straightforward manner and asking for help, they tried to secure Athenian support by means of a trick. They induced the harmost Sphodrias, a foolish braggart, to invade Attica: this he did early one evening, saying he would be at the Piraeus by dawn. But daybreak found him only a little way inside Attic territory, which he proceeded to ravage. Some Spartans who happened to be staying at Athens were furiously asked the meaning of this outrage, but they replied that Sphodrias was acting on his own initiative, and would assuredly be executed at Sparta for his breach of discipline. The Athenians believed them, but their indignation was redoubled when, although Sphodrias was indeed tried on a capital charge, the influence of Agesilaus secured his acquittal. The Athenians, for obvious historical reasons, cherished no love for Thebes; but they felt that they must now join her in resisting Spartan aggression.

The era of Spartan supremacy (404–370 B.C.)

The building of warships was begun in earnest in Athenian dockyards, while defensive works were set up in Boeotia. These defences caused considerable trouble to Agesilaus, when he arrived from Sparta with an army. He engaged in skirmishes with the Thebans, and nothing more; the harmost he left behind at Thespiae was killed in further fighting.

In the spring of 377 the Athenians placed on a formal basis their alliance with Thebes and other cities. The decree setting up this new Athenian confederacy has been recovered in modern excavations: the alliance, it says, has come into being 'so that the Spartans should permit the Greeks to be free and autonomous and to remain at peace, in quiet possession of their territory, and so that the common peace sworn to by the Greeks and the Persian king should remain valid in perpetuity'. The Athenians did not thereby set up an imperial system, such as they had fashioned in the fifth century, but an association of free states in which the old 'tribute' was replaced by 'contributions'. According to Diodorus, the Spartans responded to the re-emergent power of Athens by organizing their own Alliance in a stricter manner than before, so as to facilitate the levying of military forces for the forthcoming war against Athens and Thebes.

There followed six years of disconnected warfare (377–371), in which the Spartans made a little headway in Boeotia, but had considerably the worst of naval operations against Athens. But the deep distrust in which Thebes was held at Athens prevented the two cities from taking really effective action in common. Agesilaus led one expedition to Boeotia, which caused the Thebans much distress, but illness kept him at home in the following season, and his place was taken by Cleombrotus; but Cleombrotus could not manage even to enter Boeotia. His ineffectual conduct was condemned at a meeting of the Spartan Alliance, which pressed for the construction of a fleet. But the Peloponnesian fleet, when it was ready, offered little opposition to Athenian ships under Timotheus, who had been sent to cruise round the Peloponnese. Timotheus proceeded to Corcyra, and brought that island within the Athenian orbit, without however imposing any political changes. In consequence of a truce between Athens and Sparta, Timotheus was recalled; but then the Zacynthians complained to Sparta about the treatment their people had received at Timotheus' hands. The Spartans alleged that the truce had been broken, and raised another allied fleet. Appointing Mnasippus admiral, they ordered the fleet to look after Spartan interests in the north-west, especially in Corcyra. Mnasippus landed on the island and blockaded the city; the Corcyraeans made a desperate sally against the besiegers and relieved the pressure on themselves by killing Mnasippus and some of his troops. The remainder now evacuated Corcyra, on learning that Iphicrates was at hand with another Athenian fleet. Iphicrates combined all the available ships at Corcyra and sailed to Cephallenia, preparing to make an attack on Laconian territory.

In 374 news reached Sparta of an ominous development in Thessaly. Polydamas of Pharsalus reported the expansionist designs of his neighbour Jason of Pherae. But Sparta could spare no forces with which to check Jason's ambitions; Jason brought Pharsalus within his orbit, he was elected 'overlord' (*tagos*) of Thessaly, and he thereupon became a new and incalculable force in the Greek world, having at his command a fleet and a powerful army. But at this time the attentions of Sparta were occupied by events in Boeotia. The feebleness of Cleombrotus, combined with the ill success of Sparta at sea, enabled Thebes to go over to the offensive, especially since she now had in Epaminondas a general and statesman of genius. After forcing the Boeotian cities into a new confederacy, the Thebans moved against Phocis; and, in response to a Phocian appeal, Cleombrotus was sent to that region, with orders to muster an allied army. From Xenophon's scarcely credible account we gather that he stayed there for three years, doing nothing positive, but (it must be admitted) preventing further Theban incursions into Phocis. The Thebans turned against Plataea and Thespiae; and these attacks finally aroused repugnance at Athens for the entire course of Theban policy. The Athenians determined to make a great effort towards renewing the pan-Hellenic peace, and to that end they sent a delegation to Sparta, led by Callias; they prevailed on Thebes and other states to take part in the peace conference. The Spartan assembly voted for peace, on condition that everywhere harmosts should be withdrawn, fleets and armies disbanded, and cities left autonomous. All the participants agreed to these terms, the so-called Peace of Callias; but on the next day the Thebans purported to replace their name by that of 'Boeotians', so asserting their claim to the hegemony of Boeotia. Agesilaus would not hear of the change, and the Thebans left for home, excluded from the Peace and destitute of allies.

All the contracting parties complied with the terms of the Peace, except Sparta. She pursued her vendetta against Thebes (as, on this occasion, she was formally entitled to do), and ordered Cleombrotus to take his army into Boeotia. The king, entering Boeotian territory by an unexpected route, encamped near Leuctra in Thespian country. Both sides now wished to force the issue. Cleombrotus drew up his troops facing north, with their back to a hill; as was customary, he took command of the right wing. The Thebans had no allies to fight on their side except some soldiers from the Boeotian League. But Epaminondas made two dispositions which were to prove the undoing of the Pelopon-

The era of Spartan supremacy (404–370 B.C.)

nesian army, in spite of its numerical superiority. First he stationed a detachment of his excellent cavalry in front of his left wing, hoping that this would sweep away the Peloponnesian horsemen, who were of mediocre quality. Then the left wing of the Theban hoplites was made immensely deep (fifty men compared with the Spartan twelve); with this Epaminondas intended to drive irresistibly into that part of the opposing phalanx where the king had taken up his position. Between the armies stretched level ground, upon which the Theban horse could be deployed to great advantage. A cavalry engagement began while Cleombrotus was still leading the hoplites into battle. His cavalry were driven back upon the hoplites, and threw them into confusion even before the Theban wedge smashed into them. The Spartan right was broken; the king, several of his high-born companions, and four hundred other Spartiates were killed; and Sparta's allies had no heart for continuing the fight once they saw what had befallen Cleombrotus.

The ephors, on hearing the news from Leuctra, mobilized the rest of the army under Agesilaus' son Archidamus. Before he could reach Boeotia, Jason had arrived there at the head of a powerful army of mercenaries. With the backing of this force, he set himself up as the arbiter of Boeotian affairs, and advised Thebans and Spartans to conclude a truce. Both sides were glad to take his advice. The remnants of the Peloponnesian army made their way to Megaris, where they were met by Archidamus; he made no attempt to advance, but took both armies back to the Isthmus and disbanded them.

The battle of Leuctra showed, with horrifying clarity, the depth to which the Spartan state, and the Spartan army, had now sunk. Up to that time the Spartans had won virtually all the pitched battles they fought on land; but they had done so by relying excessively on their superb hoplite-phalanx. Even in the fighting of the fifth century they had been troubled by cavalry and javelin-throwers; now that a master-tactician integrated cavalry and hoplites into a striking force of formidable power, the Spartans had no answer, and looked for none. But, even if there had arisen a Spartan commander of a temperament to match that of Epaminondas, he could have done little in the end, with the pitifully small number of citizens at his disposal. When we consider that the four hundred Spartiates lost at Leuctra represent more than one-fifth of the citizen-body, we see that it would have been impossible to put off much longer a decisive engagement, and one fatal to Sparta. Even with the help of her allies, she was quite unable to defeat the Thebans; still less contemplate action against a combined force of Thebans and Thessalians.

Jason was assassinated in the following year, and the way was left open for the inauguration of a brief period during which Thebes became the leading state in Greece. Whether or not the Spartans realized that they had finally lost their supremacy at Leuctra, they must have become aware of it when they witnessed operations in the Peloponnese in 370. Mantinea insisted on rebuilding her walls, and the Spartans could not prevent her from doing so. Then Epaminondas brought in a Theban army to guarantee the integrity of a newly-formed Arcadian League. He also oversaw the foundation of a new city, called Megalopolis, which was to be the capital of the League. Epaminondas was not content with robbing Sparta of her long-standing influence in Arcadia. In this, or perhaps in a subsequent year, he deprived her of the entire territory of Messenia, which for three centuries had formed part of the Spartan state, and established a new capital, Messene, on the slopes of Mount Ithome. The Thebans, before going home, completed the humiliation of Sparta. They entered Laconia and made their way along the banks of the Eurotas, burning and plundering. Helots were hastily promised their freedom if they took their place in the ranks, and allies arrived in sufficient force to prevent a Theban incursion into the city of Sparta. The enemy pursued their destructive career southwards; crossing the Eurotas at Amyclae, they went to Helos and carried out a prolonged attack on Gytheum. Sparta now had to appeal to Athens to rescue her from the Theban army. Little affinity though Athens felt with Sparta, she felt less with Thebes, and regarded as intolerable the prospect of a Theban hegemony in Greece. So she sent an army into the Peloponnese; but by the time of its arrival Epaminondas had already left for home.

Sparta never subsequently had a controlling voice in the affairs of Greece. But, although the reality of power had passed, the Spartan 'idea' lived on with enhanced vigour in Greek and European literature and thought. The subject of Sparta cannot be left without a brief glance at this strange phenomenon.

Bibliography

The Spartan supremacy: H.W. Parke, *JHS* 50 (1930), 37–79. Spartan politics at the end of the fifth century: S. Luria, *Klio* 21 (1927), 404–20; R.E. Smith, *CP* 43 (1948), 145–56; C.D. Hamilton, *AJP* 91 (1970), 294–314; W.E. Thompson, *RSA* 3 (1973), 47–58. Harmosts: G. Bockisch, *Klio* 46 (1965), 129–239.

The battle at the Piraeus: S. Accame, *RFC* 66 (1938), 346–56.

The decarchies: E. Cavaignac, *REH* 90 (1924), 285–316; A. Andrewes, *Phoenix* 25 (1971), 206–16.

The era of Spartan supremacy (404–370 B.C.)

The conspiracy of Cinadon: E. David, *Athenaeum* 67 (1979), 239–59.
Agesilaus' campaigns in Asia: C. Dugas, *BCH* 34 (1910), 58–95. The battle of Sardis: F. Cornelius, *Klio* 26 (1933), 29–31; J.K. Anderson, *CSCA* 7 (1974), 27–53.
Pausanias' treatise: E. David, *PP* 34 (1979), 94–116.
The battle near Corinth: E. Cavaignac, *REA* 27 (1925), 273–8; J. Roy, *PP* 26 (1971), 439–41.
Agesilaus' foreign policy: R.E. Smith, *Historia* 2 (1953–1954), 274–88.
The Corinthian War. General studies: P. Treves, *RFC* 65 (1937), 113–40, 278–83, *Athenaeum* 26 (1938), 65–84, 164–93; S. Accame, *Ricerche intorno alla guerra corinzia* (Naples 1951); C.D. Hamilton, *Sparta's bitter victories: politics and diplomacy in the Corinthian War* (Ithaca/London, 1979). Origins and outbreak of the war: T. Lenschau, *PW* 53 (25th Nov. 1933), 1325–8; I.A.F. Bruce, *Emerita* 28 (1960), 75–86; D. Kagan, *PP* 16 (1961), 321–41. Chronology: E. Aucello, *Helikon* 4 (1964), 29–45; G.E. Underhill, *JP* 22 (1894), 129–43. The union of Corinth and Argos: G.T. Griffith, *Historia* 1 (1950), 236–56. Antalcidas' operations at the Hellespont: F. Graefe, *Klio* 28 (1935), 262–70; P. Meloni, *RAL* (8th ser.) 4 (1949), 189–203.
The King's Peace. General studies: U. Wilcken, *Über Entstehung und Zweck des Königsfriedens* (Berlin, 1942); V. Martin, *MH* 6 (1949), 127–39. Origins: E. Aucello, *Helikon* 5 (1965), 340–80. Sources: M.A. Levi, *Acme* 8/2–3 (1955), 105–11. The effect of the Peace on the Greek world: R. Seager, *Athenaeum* 62 (1974), 36–63. The concept of a 'common peace': A.D. Momigliano, *RFC* 62 (1934), 482–514; T.T.B. Ryder, *Koine eirene: general peace and local independence in ancient Greece* (Oxford, 1965).
Spartan relations with Thebes after the King's Peace: E. von Stern, *Geschichte der spartanischen und thebanischen Hegemonie vom Königsfrieden bis zur Schlacht bei Mantinea* (Dorpat, 1884); H.M. Hack, *AJP* 99 (1978), 210–27. Spartan politics 386–379: D.G. Rice, *Historia* 23 (1974), 164–82. The truce of 374: A.G. Roos, *Mnemosyne* (4th ser.) 2 (1949), 265–85.
The second Athenian confederacy: G. Busolt, *Der zweite athenische Bund* (Leipzig, 1875); V. Ehrenberg, *Hermes* 64 (1929), 322–38.
The peace conference of 371: H. Swoboda, *RhM* 49 (1894), 321–52.
The Spartan army at the battle of Leuctra: G. Busolt, *Hermes* 40 (1905), 387–449.
The Arcadian League: J. Roy, *Historia* 20 (1971), 569–99. The foundation of Megalopolis: E. Lanzillotta, *RSA* 5 (1975), 25–46.

13

The idea of Sparta

As we have seen, the idea or legend of 'Lycurgan' Sparta clearly emerged in Xenophon's *Constitution of the Spartans* (p. 141). In that work, Xenophon distinguished the Lycurgan ideal (which had no shortcoming whatever) from the contemporary reality, caused by the intrusion of wealth and the habits and morals of barbarians. The contrast between real and ideal runs like a continuous thread through many of the allusions to Sparta made by the ancient Greek authors. Although, no doubt, elements of the Spartan legend were in existence before the Persian Wars, we can trace its development only as far back as that epoch. And already we are confronted by the two prominent facets of the legend. The ideal is represented by Leonidas, the archetype of the Spartan warrior, who devotes his life to the state and who abhors two things above all: cowardice in battle and disobedience of his country's laws. Pausanias too is deeply versed in the Lycurgan way of life and remains blameless, even heroic, so long as he follows it. But when he turns aside from it, he too becomes an archetype: the simple soldier who once looked with contemptuous incredulity upon the luxury displayed in Mardonius' tent is in the end seduced by that very luxury; and the citizen, who previously merged himself with the state, goes off on a private errand and works against his countrymen. Herodotus heard at Sparta of these men, whose character and career had passed into legend: the noble king who fell at Thermopylae and the flawed regent who met a shameful death in his own city. It is as if a moral tale had been woven about the two figures, to serve as a warning example to future generations of Spartiates; and the tale was spiced with short, pithy sayings, illustrative of Spartan practical wisdom, of the type found in the 'Spartan apophthegms' later collected in Plutarch's *Moralia*.

Thus a suggestion can be made as to the approximate time at which the Spartan legend first became crystallized and as to the manner in which it was enshrined in Hellenic literature: the Spartiates fashioned the legend in the early decades of the fifth century, and Herodotus propagated it in his History. Now there arises a more difficult question: once the legend of the ideal Sparta had come into being, why did it not wither away at the

The idea of Sparta

end of the fifth century, when the Spartans manifestly no longer abode by the Lycurgan *kosmos*? Or, if the power of propaganda managed to keep the legend alive even then, how did it survive the disastrous Spartan defeats of 371 and 362, after which Sparta had little means of influencing the opinions of the other Greeks? In order to answer these questions, we have to bear in mind the predilections and prejudices of the writers who were chiefly responsible for the continuation of the Spartan legend in the fifth and fourth centuries. These authors were all Athenians, or at least men who came to live and work at Athens. What was it they saw in Sparta (the very antithesis of their own great city, as Thucydides convincingly demonstrates) that led them to throw their weight behind the legend? In one word, it was *orderliness*. The major prose-writers of classical Athens were far from being enamoured of extreme democracy; either (like Thucydides) they favoured a moderately democratic constitution, with restricted franchise, or (like Plato) they had no time at all for what they saw as the riotous excesses of the Athenian democrats.

Thucydides makes his partiality plain on a number of occasions. For him, the worst features of the democracy were personified in Cleon. Having once bent the citizens to his will by brutal speeches and violent actions, Cleon used his power to pursue private vendettas. In Thucydides' eyes such a man was no better than a despot. Thucydides finds that the perfect balance is achieved in an assembly containing a select number of citizens. Thus he comes out in support of the assembly of Five Thousand, established after the loss of Euboea in 411 (p. 206): 'during its first phase the Athenians obviously had their best constitution, at least in my life-time; there was a moderate mixture of the few and the many' (8.97.2). But the Athenian assembly of Five Thousand was a short-lived institution: it was at Sparta that the desirable compromise formed a permanent feature of the political system. This opinion Thucydides expresses in speaking of the people of Chios: 'the Chians alone, next to the Spartans among the people I know of, have maintained their self-control after acquiring prosperity; and the more powerful their city became, the stronger they made their government' (8.24.4). In the following passage Thucydides speaks even more directly of the stability of the Spartan polity: 'the Spartan state received good laws at an earlier period than did any other, and it has never come under the rule of a despot; for four hundred years or a little more the Spartans have had the same constitution' (1.18.1). Thucydides places the 'Lycurgan' political settlement at much too early a date; but the important point is that he traces back the stable institutions of Sparta to a remote phase of recorded history. What impresses him most is the immutability of the organs of Spartan government. But his admiration involves him in a paradox, of which he seems scarcely to be aware. Time and time again in his own History Thucydides relates episodes which testify to the strength of the forces tending to undermine the harmonious Spartan state. The most powerful force seems to have been fear of the helots; also operative were tensions between different interests in the state, which alone can explain the frequent incoherence of Spartan policy. The Spartan state *was* politically stable, in the limited sense that the organs of government did retain their outward form unchanged for a very long period; but the ossification which set in was at last fatal to the well-being of the state, since there existed no constitutional channel whereby much-needed reforms could be introduced. Besides, the political stability of Sparta was not always matched by what we might call psychological stability: even apart from their hysterical fear of a helot rising (which their own conduct did so much to precipitate), the Spartiates sometimes failed to display the resignation in the face of adversity which is found at Athens: the loss of a few hundred hoplites caused greater consternation at Sparta than was induced in the Athenians by the collapse of the entire Sicilian expedition. But despite everything Thucydides looks at the 'Lycurgan' state and finds it praiseworthy: its laws, precisely regulating at all points the life of its citizens, have given Sparta a balanced order which leaves no room for despotism on the one hand or for mob-rule on the other. Thucydides allows the theoretical virtues of the Spartan constitution to outweigh the many practical defects; and in so doing he not merely perpetuates the Spartan legend but shows that he has himself fallen under its spell.

A gap of twenty or thirty years separates the work of Thucydides from the composition of the great dialogue of Plato's maturity, the *Republic*. Like Thucydides, Plato both inherited the concept of an ideal Spartan state and became aware of the moral degeneration of Spartan society after the victory over Athens. Socrates in the *Republic* adumbrates an imaginary city which, being founded on virtuous principles, will promote virtue in the individual citizens. The citizens will be grouped in three divisions. The highest class will comprise the 'guardians', who are the effective rulers of the city. Then will come the warriors, who are charged with the city's defence and with the suppression of malefactors. Finally there will be all the rest: producers, traders, financiers, and so forth. Socrates attaches the greatest possible importance to the genetic selection, education, and training of the guardian-class; and we shall see that his proposals resemble in many details the institutions of 'Lycurgan' Sparta. But, even before coming to the details, we apprehend how similar is Socrates' procedure in general to that ascribed to Lycurgus: Socrates undertakes to fashion an entire society according to fixed,

The idea of Sparta

undeviating principles, just as Lycurgus is said to have done; and, however admirable and exactly formulated the principles may be, both the real city of Lycurgus and the imaginary one of Socrates contain within them the seeds of their own decline.

As we watch the gradual unfolding of Socrates' ideal city in the third, fourth, and fifth books of the *Republic*, we keep catching hints of Sparta – even though the name 'Sparta' is hardly ever mentioned. An important part of the guardians' training consists of a flexible kind of gymnastics, which prepares them for war and the endurance of pain and hardship; furthermore their diet must be frugal, and their lives free from sexual irregularities (*Republic* 3.404a–e). The same goes for the Spartiates, of course; and a further resemblance to Sparta is seen in the injunction to the guardians to expose children who are born with defects – whether these are physical, mental, or moral (3.410a). Like the Spartiates, the guardians are to eat in communal messes and live together like soldiers on campaign; in addition, they are to have no truck with gold or silver (the very presence of these metals would contaminate them) (3.417a–b). The guardians may not journey abroad on their own occasions, any more than the citizens of Sparta are allowed to do (4.420a). Just as the citizenship of unworthy Spartiates could be rescinded, so a guardian might be removed into one of the other classes; the guardians should possess wives and property in common; the unity and harmony of the state are paramount, and each individual contributes to its welfare in the manner dictated by his own nature; the state, once established, is to be a highly conservative one, with the guardians taking care to prevent innovations in gymnastics or in music (4.423c–424b). The young must be silent and respectful in the presence of their elders, rising when they enter or leave (4.425b). The women among the guardians (just like the daughters of Spartiates) are to follow the men's example and engage in gymnastic exercises lightly clothed (5.452b). Absolutely typical of the Spartan system is Socrates' provision that the soldier who leaves the ranks or throws away his weapons or commits similar cowardly acts should be demoted from the class of guardians to that of workmen or farmers (5.468a).

In promulgating (through the mouth of Socrates) a society which has so many points of contact with Sparta, Plato did a great deal to perpetuate the Spartan legend. What appealed to him most about Sparta was that the individual had no right to a life of his own: his interests were identified completely with the interests of the state. It was the denial of this healthy principle (in Plato's eyes) that led to extreme democracy, which Plato regarded as tantamount to anarchy. But Plato apprehended with great clarity the process of decline in the Spartan state, which he feared would be reflected in his ideal city. He traces the decline in a passage of great vividness and power. A passionate temper comes to the fore in the city. Strife arises between two factions: one bent on evil new ways, the acquisition of property, of gold, and of silver; the other trying to return to the ancient constitution. This strife is resolved by a compromise, which leads to the retention of some of the healthy features but the acquisition of some less desirable ones. The two sides agree to relinquish their original practice of holding goods in common; they now divide the land into lots for private ownership; they enslave the free population whose protectors they previously were, and make them outlanders or slaves; finally they keep a close watch on their slaves, as they busy themselves with war (*Republic* 8.547b–c). This description of the city's decline is not to be understood as a fragment of the actual history of Sparta: it shows, rather, what is liable to happen when a certain stage is reached in political development. Still, the blameworthy results of the compromise resemble very closely some notorious aspects of Sparta: that is to say 'Lycurgan' Sparta, even before degeneration had set in at the end of the fifth century.

Socrates proceeds with his merciless analysis, as he paints the portrait of a state adhering to the ancient simplicity, partly following a new course of selfishness, avarice, and deceit. The warriors still respect the magistrates; they still abstain from farming, artisanship, and all forms of business; they still eat in their communal messes, and practise athletics and martial exercises. On the other hand, the intellectual vigour of the state is stultified. Clever men are no longer admitted to high office; and the state comes under the sway of simple-minded and passionate leaders, who better understand the waging of war than the promotion of peaceful arts. With such persons in control, there arises a fierce lust for gold; but, since the laws forbid its possession, it and the pleasures it buys have to be enjoyed in secret. And what has brought the once-great city to such a pass? The fact that the citizens have been constrained, not persuaded, to obey the laws; but all along the laws themselves, good though they were so far as they went, wholly neglected a vital element of the human personality. Devotion to war has driven out the higher arts of civilization; gymnastic training usurps the place of philosophy and music (*Republic* 8.545d–548c).

When he took up these questions again in the *Laws*, Plato showed much greater liking for the 'mixed' constitution of Sparta, but held to his belief that the Spartans had taken a wrong turn in directing the entire activity of their state towards the achievement of military victories. At the same time, the new city whose foundation is discussed in the *Laws* bears an unmistakable resemblance to Sparta; and we may say that of all the actual cities which existed in Greece it was Sparta which held for

The idea of Sparta

Plato more promising features than any other – even if these had been imperfectly realized. The discussion in the *Laws* concerns the formulation of a set of laws and principles for the government of an imaginary colony. The participants are an Athenian (who speaks for Plato himself), a Spartan, and a Cretan. Plato now holds that there were in origin two kinds of constitution, monarchy and democracy, but the best consists of a mixture of these two (*Laws* 3.693d–e). The Spartan constitution, in fact, seems to offer an excellent balance. The ephorate is a despotic element; and yet, considered from another point of view, the Spartan state is highly democratic. Again, it is an aristocracy; but a monarchy too, and a very ancient one (4.712d–e).

Both the location and some of the practices of the new colony remind one irresistibly of Sparta – although, remarkably enough, the constitution is framed rather on the Athenian model than on the Spartan. Coined money will be completely absent; the debilitating effects of oversea trade will be offset by establishing the colony at some distance from the sea; self-sufficiency will remove the need for imports. The available land is to be divided into 5,040 estates and, so far as possible, the citizens will own equal amounts of property: at all events, both a minimum and a maximum are to be set for their holdings. The citizens are to eat in communal messes; respect for elders and for those in authority will be enforced; both boys and girls will have to undergo training according to a system prescribed and supervised by the state (*Laws* 5.743d–745c, 6.762c–766b). In the *Laws*, as in the *Republic*, Plato admires the thoroughgoing way in which individual interests at Sparta have been subsumed in the interests of the state; so that, despite the democratic element which is undeniably present in the Spartan constitution, the anarchic tendencies of a pure democracy have been restrained. But Plato's objections to the Spartan system as a whole remain the same: the system is that of a military camp, not that of people living together in towns; the entire aim of the state-controlled education is the training of warriors, and instruction in politics and the arts is left out of account (*Laws* 2.666e–667a).

The views of Sparta held by Aristotle, Plato's greatest successor, have been discussed in an earlier chapter (pp. 142–3). Aristotle was no less critical of Sparta than Plato had been; nevertheless he lent his authority to one important aspect of the Spartan legend, namely the stability and permanence of Spartan institutions. The development of the legend may be traced further by examining two other Athenian writers of the fourth century, Isocrates and Lycurgus. Their intellectual powers were negligible, compared with those of Plato or Aristotle; yet, for that very reason, they may have something to tell us about the influence of the Spartan legend upon Athenians who were involved in fourth century politics. Three works taken from the very long career of Isocrates display the same ambiguity of response to the Spartan legend that has already been noted in Thucydides and Plato. Isocrates differs from Plato in having a deep commitment to the Athenian way of life: a commitment most eloquently expressed in the *Panegyricus*, delivered in 380 or thereabouts. Isocrates deplores Sparta's negotiations which led to the King's Peace and her exploitation of the Peace itself; it is in Athens that the glory of Hellas resides, and Athens must retrieve the self-respect of the Greeks by leading a joint expedition against the Persian empire. The co-leader ought to be Sparta; but a Sparta who has purged herself of her evil propensities and returned to the ancient virtue she showed in the Persian Wars.

In the *Panegyricus* Isocrates spoke with anger and scorn of the selfish policies then being pursued by Sparta: so unlike the glorious stand she had once taken for pan-Hellenic freedom. By 366, to which year Isocrates' *Archidamus* belongs, the Spartan supremacy was over, and Thebes was felt to be the common enemy of Sparta and of Athens. The *Archidamus* is a speech supposed to be made by the Spartan prince of that name, the son of Agesilaus (p. 227), at an allied congress. His theme concerns Epaminondas' grant of freedom to the Messenians and his foundation of Messene (p. 228): the two actions of Thebes which harmed Sparta more than any other. Archidamus argues that Sparta has a claim on Messenia which goes back to a time when the Messenians killed their king Cresphontes, and the king's sons made over their country to Sparta as a reward for her avenging Cresphontes. And as for the Thebans, what are they? A people who have only lately come to prominence: long-standing friends of the barbarian, and themselves recently guilty of aggressive acts against Greek cities. In such terms Isocrates' Archidamus justifies both the past history of Sparta and her present grievances. Does the speech, then, represent a complete denial of the position taken up by Isocrates in the *Panegyricus*? It is rather that events in Greece have hurried on since then: in 380 Sparta was seen by many Athenians (perhaps by most) as a crude and unenlightened bully, who had acquired her pre-eminent place by conspiring with Persia; but fourteen years later, by an unpredictable reverse, Thebes had become the enemy, and it was easy for Isocrates to take a longer view and bring to mind the contributions once made by Sparta to the welfare and security of the Greeks.

In his *Panathenaicus*, written in extreme old age and published in 339, Isocrates reverts to the theme of the *Panegyricus*. Again his praise of

The idea of Sparta

Athens leads him to denigrate Sparta: a city, as he mentions in a telling phrase, 'which most people praise in a modest way, although some speak of Sparta as if a race of heroes carried on the government there' (*Panathenaicus* 41). The vehemence of the succeeding attack on Sparta surpasses that of the *Panegyricus*. Then, by an astonishing literary device, which remains incomprehensible to this day, Isocrates introduces a pupil of his to present the Spartan view-point! The device may indeed be inept, but Isocrates would not have resorted to it at all unless he were to some extent in the grip of the Spartan legend. It was quite natural for a man like Isocrates, born into a prosperous Athenian family, to dilate upon the greatness of his native city; but hardly less natural to admire, however grudgingly, the achievements of Sparta. And those achievements are delineated by the 'pupil' in terms which by now have become thoroughly familiar to us. They comprise first of all the establishment of a society so harmonious that political strife and revolution are completely unknown (by implicit contrast to the instability at Athens), secondly the cultivation of valour beyond that attained by any other Greek state (*Panathenaicus* 255–259). The latter aspect aroused the enthusiastic endorsement of Lycurgus in his speech *Against Leocrates*, delivered in 330. He was concerned not with contemporary Sparta but with the self-confident strength possessed by the Spartans in former days: their uncompromising attitude towards traitors and cowards gave good evidence of this (129–130).

The dominant traits of the Spartan legend had been expressed in such a definitive manner during Isocrates' life-time that they were not afterwards lost sight of. In the second half of the third century, the legend of 'Lycurgan' Sparta was invoked to help redress abuses which had arisen at Sparta itself; and, although in the end the movement towards reform was unsuccessful, the legend was left unimpaired and even more potent than before. Two Spartan kings, the Eurypontid Agis IV (reigned 244–241) and the Agiad Cleomenes III (236–222), initiated the reforms. Their story was told by Phylarchus, an Athenian writer with strong pro-Spartan leanings; he depicted the kings as heroic figures who sought to bring back Sparta to the ways of Lycurgus but who were crushed by selfish enemies. Phylarchus' account forms the basis of the *Lives* of Agis and Cleomenes by Plutarch; and these deeply prejudiced documents form practically our only source of information for the reforming movement. Agis set himself to arrest the decline in population by allotting 4,500 estates to Spartiates and fifteen thousand to outlanders (the number of Spartiates to be made up by enfranchising suitable outlanders and foreigners); at the same time, all debts were to be rescinded. It is interesting to see that (if we believe Phylarchus) Lycurgus' prescriptions remain the standard: Agis appeals to the laws of Lycurgus to justify his reforms, and so does the Agiad king Leonidas II in opposition to them. In the event Leonidas and his party prevailed before Agis' reforms could be fully realized, and Agis himself was done to death.

When Cleomenes III succeeded Leonidas, he saw that only a far-reaching political change would enable the social wrongs to be corrected. The reform he first proposed was nothing else than the abolition of the ephorate. This he accomplished, but by violent means (which he claimed to deprecate). Once again Phylarchus says that the action was justified by reference to Lycurgus. Cleomenes stated that the ephorate was of later growth than the kings and the Council, which together had constituted the government in Lycurgus' time; ephors (continued Cleomenes) were first appointed by the kings when the latter were absent on campaign, so as to attend to the daily business of the city; but in time the ephors became intolerably powerful, forming an obstacle to all reforms, however urgently these were needed (Plutarch *Life of Cleomenes* 10.1–3). With the ephors gone, Cleomenes brought about the changes promised by Agis. The institutions of 'Lycurgan' Sparta were revived, so far as was practicable; the number of citizens was made up to the number of four thousand by the co-optation of outlanders; the *agoge* was restored in its full rigour; and athletic exercises and communal messes resumed their old place in the life of the citizens. The new 'Lycurgan' regime lasted only for five years. Cleomenes' vigorous leadership made the Achaean League fear the resurgence of Spartan military power in the Peloponnese. The Macedonian king Antigonus was called in; he brought an army to Laconia, defeated Cleomenes in battle, and forced him into exile. Antigonus then made his way to Sparta and undid all the reforms carried through by Cleomenes.

It is unnecessary to emphasize the hold which the romantic and idealized version of the Lycurgan legend exercised over the mind of Agis and of Cleomenes. What may be of greater interest is the observation that the actions and words of the reformers, as recorded by Phylarchus, have in their turn influenced the development of the legend. We read in Plutarch's *Life of Lycurgus* that the lawgiver promulgated his reforms in the same violent manner which Cleomenes found it necessary to adopt; there are, in addition, similarities of phrasing between the *Life of Lycurgus* and the *Life of Agis* which suggest that the account of Lycurgus' career has been reshaped so as to conform to that of the young king.

The idea of Sparta

In the time of the Roman Republic, Sparta had an implacable enemy in Polybius. Several times in his History, Polybius seized the opportunity of condemning Spartan actions, especially those perpetrated during the supremacy of the fourth century. For Polybius, as for Xenophon, such actions are blameworthy because they represent a falling-away from the institutions of Lycurgus, and especially from the political system he had founded at Sparta. The Spartan constitution interests Polybius not so much for its own sake but (as we saw earlier, p. 15) because it shares with the Roman a 'mixed' character, incorporating the best features of other systems and avoiding the worst.

The Empire witnesses a development at Sparta which we might find astonishing if we were not already aware of the romantic legend and the extent to which it captivated later generations. Imperial Sparta was, of course, no more free and independent than any other city in Greece; but, out of deference to its distinguished past, it was allowed to use certain titles and to indulge in a way of life that was supposed to recall the city of Lycurgus. The numerous inscriptions at the Orthia sanctuary dating from the Roman period show that at some time the *agoge* was revived, at least to the extent of employing the old names for the age-classes (p. 137). The chief contests in which the boys took part were those of hunting and singing: the victors dedicated inscribed stones in the sanctuary of the goddess (p. 55). In the third century A.D. a theatre was built to accommodate the spectators who witnessed the contests and also the flagellation of the boys. So it was that the people of Sparta, utterly bereft of political power and having long since lost kings and ephors, cherished for hundreds of years a small part of their Lycurgan inheritance. Learned antiquarianism was, no doubt, responsible to some extent; but so was the desire to present a popular attraction to tourists by the banks of the Eurotas. An interesting literary reference to the condition of Sparta under the Empire is found in Philostratus' *Life* of the neo-Pythagorean Apollonius of Tyana. In the course of his travels he comes to Sparta:

> Crossing the Taygetus, he saw Sparta bustling with activity and the ancestral practices of Lycurgus being zealously followed. He thought it would be agreeable to converse with the Spartan authorities on matters they wished to ask him about. So on his arrival they asked him in what manner gods should be revered. 'Like masters,' was his reply. 'And in what manner heroes?' 'Like fathers.' Their third question was: 'and in what manner should men be revered?' 'Your question,' he said, 'is not suitable for Spartans' (*Life of Apollonius* 4.21).

The pregnant, and truly 'Laconic', remarks attributed to Apollonius remind us of the great store of apophthegms preserved by Plutarch.

These, together with Plutarch's 'Spartan institutions' and above all his *Life of Lycurgus*, rounded out and enriched the Spartan legend. Since Plutarch was so widely read at the time of the renaissance, he was to a large extent responsible for the transmission of the legend to the modern world.

Bibliography

The idea of Sparta in antiquity: F. Ollier, *Le mirage spartiate* I–II (Paris, 1933–1943); G. Mathieu, *RP* 72 (1946), 144–52; P.H. Epps in *Studies in honor of Ullman* (St. Louis 1960), 35–47; E.N. Tigerstedt, *The legend of Sparta in classical antiquity* I-III (Stockholm, 1965–1978). Herodotus and Sparta: B. Niese, *Hermes* 42 (1907), 419–68. Plato and Sparta: G.R. Morrow, *Plato's Cretan city* (Princeton, 1960). Plato's *Laws* and the Spartan messes: E. David, *AJP* 99 (1978), 486–95. Aristotle and Sparta: P. Cloché, *LEC* 11 (1942), 289–313. Isocrates and Sparta: P. Cloché, *REA* 35 (1933), 129–45. Phylarchus and Sparta: T.W. Africa, *Phylarchus and the Spartan revolution* (Berkeley/Los Angeles 1961). Polybius and Sparta: F.W. Walbank, *ASI* 303–12.

The idea of Sparta in modern Europe: E. Rawson, *The Spartan tradition in European thought* (Oxford, 1969).

Appendix

Chronological table

B.C.	
c. 1450	Construction of Vaphio tholos
c. 1450–1200	Mycenaean house near the Menelaion
c. 1100	End of Mycenaean period; beginning of Dark Age
c. 900–750	Proto-Geometric pottery
c. 800–700	First phase of the Orthia sanctuary
c. 750–650	Geometric pottery
c. 736–716?	First Messenian War
716	First Spartan victory at Olympia
706	Foundation of Taras
c. 700–570	Second phase of the Orthia sanctuary
675?	Foundation of the *Karneia*
669?	Defeat by Argos at Hysiae
c. 650–480	Archaic pottery
c. 650	Tyrtaeus; Second Messenian War
c. 610	Alcman
c. 570	Third phase of the Orthia sanctuary
c. 560	Alliance with Tegea
c. 555	Chilon ephor
c. 550	Construction of Throne of Apollo at Amyclae; conquest of Thyreatis
546	Fall of Sardis
c. 525	Expedition to Samos
521	Accession of Darius
c. 514–510	Career of Dorieus
c. 510–505	Invasions of Attica; deposition of Pisistratids
c. 505	First congress of the Spartan Alliance
c. 500	Construction of Menelaion
c. 499	Visit of Aristagoras to Sparta
498–494	Ionian revolt
c. 494	Defeat of the Argives by Cleomenes
491	Spartan intervention in Aegina; deposition of Demeratus and installation of Leotychidas
490	Persian invasion of Greece; battle of Marathon, Messenian revolt?; death of Cleomenes?
c. 486	Death of Darius and accession of Xerxes; trial of Leotychidas

480	Second Persian invasion; battles of Thermopylae and Artemisium; battle of Salamis; Themistocles at Sparta
479	Battles of Plataea and Mycale
478	Expeditions to Sestus and Byzantium
477	Formation of Athenian League; recall of Pausanias
476?	Expulsion of Pausanias from Byzantium
464	Earthquake at Sparta; helot rising; Ithome besieged
460?	Fall of Ithome; settlement of Messenians at Naupactus
459?	Secession of Megara from Spartan Alliance
458?	Building of long walls at Athens
457	Battle of Tanagra
454	Treasury of Athenian League transferred to Athens
451	Beginning of five-year truce between Spartan Alliance and Athens
c. 450	Beginning of thirty-year peace between Sparta and Argos; Pericles' proposal of a pan-Hellenic peace
c. 448	Sacred War
446	Return of Megara to Spartan Alliance; Peloponnesian invasion of Attica; exile of Pleistoanax
445	Beginning of thirty-year peace between Spartan Alliance and Athens
435–433	War between Corinth and Corcyra
433	Athenian ultimatum to Potidaea
432	Megarian decree?; secession of Potidaea from Athens; war against Athens voted by Spartan Alliance and Spartan assembly
431	Beginning of Archidamian War; Theban incursion into Plataea; Peloponnesian invasion of Attica; expulsion of Aeginetans
430	Peloponnesian invasion of Attica; plague at Athens; Pericles' expedition to Peloponnese; Peloponnesian expedition to Zacynthus
429	Siege of Plataea; Athenian victories in Corinthian Gulf; fall of Potidaea; Peloponnesian expedition to Acarnania; death of Pericles
428	Peloponnesian invasion of Attica; secession of Mytilene
427	Peloponnesian invasion of Attica; capture of Plataea; failure of Peloponnesian fleet to save Mytilene
426	Peloponnesian invasion of Attica foiled by earthquakes; foundation of Spartan colony at Heraclea; Peloponnesian defeat in Acarnania
425	Peloponnesian invasion of Attica; conflict at Pylos; Athenian attack on Corinthia
424	Capture of Cythera by Nicias; Athenian landing in Thyreatis; Nisaea captured by Athenians; their attack on Megara

Chronological table

	thwarted by Brasidas; a number of cities in Thrace and Chalcidice won over by Brasidas; Athenian defeat at Delium
423	One-year armistice between Sparta and Athens
422	Cleon's expedition to Thrace; his defeat at Amphipolis; death of Cleon and of Brasidas
421	Fifty-year treaty and defensive alliance between Sparta and Athens; end of Archidamian War
420	Athenian alliance with Argos, Elis, and Mantinea
419	Argive attack on Epidaurus
418	Agis' invasion of Argolis; battle of Mantinea
415	Athenian expedition to Sicily
414	Conflict between Spartan and Athenian forces in Peloponnese; arrival of Gylippus at Syracuse
413	Beginning of Decelean War; Peloponnesian invasion of Attica; fortification of Decelea; Athenian reinforcements sent to Sicily; major Athenian defeat at Syracuse; loss of Athenian army
412	Revolt of Athenian allies; treaties between Sparta and Persia
411	Secession of Rhodes, Abydus, and Euboea; Athenian fleet at Hellespont
410	Battle of Cyzicus
408	Capture of Byzantium and Chalcedon by Athenians
407	Cyrus co-ordinator of operations with Sparta
406	Battle of Notium; battle of Arginusae
405	Battle of Aegospotami
404	Surrender of Athens; demolition of long walls; end of Decelean War
403	Spartan garrison at Athens; battle at Piraeus
399	Thibron harmost in Asia; Spartan dispute with Elis
397	Accession of Agesilaus; conspiracy of Cinadon; Dercylidas' treaty with the Persians
395	Expedition of Agesilaus to Asia; battle near Sardis; beginning of Corinthian War; battle of Haliartus; death of Lysander and exile of Pausanias
394	Battle near Corinth; battle of Coronea; battle off Cnidus
393	Rebuilding of long walls at Athens
392	Federation of Argos and Corinth; Antalcidas' mission to Susa
390–388	Thrasybulus and Iphicrates successful at Hellespont; Teleutias master of sea round Attica
387	Artaxerxes' proposals for a general peace; operations of Antalcidas at Hellespont
386	King's Peace (Peace of Antalcidas); end of Corinthian War
385	Dissolution of Mantinea
383	Spartan seizure of Theban acropolis
379	Capture of Olynthus

378	Expulsion of Spartans from Thebes
377	Second Athenian confederacy; war between it and Spartan Alliance
374	Jason elected Thessalian *tagos*; temporary peace between Sparta and Athens
371	Peace of Callias; battle of Leuctra; death of Cleombrotus
371–369	Assassination of Jason; Theban invasion of Laconia; establishment of Arcadian League; reconstitution of Mantinea; foundation of Megalopolis and Messene

Index

Abydus 205, 206, 208, 218, 221
Acanthus, Acanthians 195, 222
Acarnania, Acarnanians 188, 189, 192, 219
Achaea, Achaeans 40, 42, 182, 188, 193, 219
Achaean League 238
Achilles 51
acropolis
  Athenian 150, 167
  Spartan 23, 25, 48–50, 83, 89, 92, 93, 96, 106
  Theban 223, 224
Acte 195, 197
admirals 166, 207, 208, 215, 225
adoption 116, 120
Aegean Sea 175
Aegina, Aeginetans 155–8, 160, 161, 163, 167, 168, 179, 180, 182, 185, 187, 189, 195, 205, 209, 220
Aegospotami 208, 211
Aeolic dialects 44
Aeolis, Aeolians 32, 112, 153
Aeschines 146, 147
Aeschylus 62
Aetolia 192
Agamemnon 27, 28, 66–8, 111, 214
agelai 137
Agelaus 146
Agesandridas 205, 206
Agesilaus (Spartan king) 15, 212–16, 218–26, 236
Agesipolis (Spartan king) 217, 222, 223
Agiad family 119, 148, 160, 212, 217, 237, 238
Agis (Spartan king) 192, 193, 200, 201, 203–6, 209, 212, 219
Agis IV (Spartan king) 49, 237, 238
agoge 116, 117, 137, 138, 141, 142, 238, 239
Ajax 26
akroterion 94
Alaric 16, 21
Alcaeus 76

Alcibiades 199–202, 204–7
Alcidas 190, 191, 195
Alcmaeonids 149, 150, 152
Alcman 16, 25, 74–80, 89, 110
Alexander 163, 169
Alexandra 66, 67
alliance
  Argive 199
  Athenian 174, 175, 179, 180, 182, 183, 185, 187–90, 192, 195, 204, 208, 211
  pan-Hellenic 162–74, 176
  Spartan 145, 149, 152, 153, 174, 176, 179–82, 184–90, 192, 193, 195, 200–2, 204, 208, 209, 212, 214, 216, 221, 222, 225
  between Argos and Athens 199–201
  between Sparta and Athens 198, 200
  between Sparta and Thebes 199
alphabet, Laconian 91
Alpheus 111
altars 51–3, 65
Ambracia, Ambraciots 146, 188, 192
amethyst 35
Amompharetus 171, 172
amphiktyoniai 152
Amphipolis 175, 183, 195–9
amphora
  lidded 95
  Panathenaic 50
  relief 51, 89
Amyclae, Amyklaion 16, 20, 22, 23, 27, 33, 40, 54, 56, 62–9, 76, 83, 93, 94, 99
Anactorium 188
Analipsis 38
Anaxandridas (Spartan king) 146–8
Anaxilas 159
Anchimolius 149, 150
Andocides 182
Andros 168
Antalcidas 220, 221
Antigonus 238
apellazein 129

245

Aphrodite 50, 56, 76, 95
apoikia 102
Apollo 23, 33, 48, 54, 56, 58–65, 72, 103, 104
  Throne of 63–5, 76, 93
Apollonia 222
Apollonius of Rhodes 76
Apollonius of Tyana 239
Aracus 208
arbitration 182, 187
Arcadia, Arcadians 41, 42, 104, 106–8, 111, 112, 145, 160, 181, 200, 228
Arcadian dialect 44
Arcadian League 228
Arcesilas 86–7
Arcesilas Cup 84–8
Arcesilas Painter 86, 87
archagetai 129
archers 164, 195
Archidamian War 188–98, 201, 203
Archidamus (Spartan king) 125, 178, 185–8, 191, 192
Archidamus III (Spartan king) 227, 236
Archilochus 71, 76
Arginusae 207
Argos, Argives, Argolis 29, 31, 42, 43, 73, 83, 104–6, 111, 113, 145, 154, 163, 169, 177, 179–82, 188, 189, 199–202, 212, 216, 218–21, 223
Argos (god) 154, 155
Argos, Gulf of 113, 179
Aristagoras 153, 154
Aristodemus 146
Aristogenes 146
Aristomenes 106, 107
Aristophanes 49
Aristotle 15, 102, 107, 121, 123–6, 142, 143, 147, 150, 213, 235
armistice 196
Arrhabaeus 195, 196
arrows 194
Artabazus 170, 172
Artaxerxes 175
Artaxerxes II 213–15, 220, 221, 223
Artemis 54, 55, 58, 95
Artemis Orthia, sanctuary of 21, 23, 25, 51–5, 58, 83, 84, 92, 94–6, 109, 137, 239
Artemisium 163, 166
Asia Minor 31, 32, 173–6, 188, 190, 191, 205, 207, 213–16, 218, 220, 221
Asine 105, 194
Asopus 170–2

assembly of citizens
  Athenian 153, 181, 187, 193, 202, 209, 217
  Spartan 118, 120–6, 128–130, 151, 185, 186, 213, 223
Astyochus 205
Athena 48–50, 59, 95, 106, 129, 176
Athenaeus 16, 61, 75, 76, 104, 116
Athenagoras 67
Athens, Athenians 25, 47, 54, 82, 96, 110–12, 116, 122, 125, 128, 138, 140, 145, 146, 149–58, 160–3, 165–209, 211, 212, 215–26, 228, 231, 232, 235–7
athletic contests 135–8
Athos 161
Atlas 86
Attica 31, 40, 48, 99, 149–51, 155, 158, 160, 167, 179, 181, 183, 185, 188–90, 192, 193, 203, 206, 209, 212, 218, 221, 224
Aulis 146, 214, 215
austerity 134, 135, 138
Ayia Kyriaki 63, 64
Ayia Paraskevi 66, 67
Ayios Stephanos 38
Ayios Vasilios 33

Babylon 213
bachelors 117
Bathycles 63–5, 133
beacons 190
Beloch, K.J. 43, 44
Black Sea 176, 221
Boeotia, Boeotians 89, 112, 151, 164, 167, 169, 170, 172, 180, 181, 188, 195, 196, 198–201, 214, 215, 217, 218, 220–2, 224–7
Boeotian League 214, 217, 226
bones, animal 34, 52
Bosanquet, R.C. 23
Bosporus 206, 207, 213
boys' contests 55, 239
Brasidas 140, 186, 189, 191, 195–9, 201
bronze 26, 32
Bronze Age 25–33, 58
bronzes 50, 57, 91–4
bulls 36, 93
Byzantium 176, 177, 206–8

Callias, Peace of (5th cent.) 175
Callias, Peace of (4th cent.) 226
Callicratidas 207
Callinus 71

Index

Cambyses 147, 148
Campania 90
capital punishment 122
Carystus 175
Cassandra 66
Catling, H.W. 23
cavalry 108, 150, 161, 170, 171, 194, 195, 197, 215, 227
Cenchreae 167
cenotaphs 172
Centaur 96
Cephallenia 40, 226
Ceramic Gulf 208
Ceramicus 82
Chalcedon 207, 208
Chalcidians 151
Chalcidice 161, 174, 183, 195, 196, 222, 223
Chalcis (in Euboea) 91
Chalcis (on Gulf of Corinth) 180
Chalkioikos, temple of Athena 49, 50, 106, 177
Chalkopylos 49
chamber-tombs 30
chariots 83, 89, 90, 138
Chersonese 174
children, begetting and rearing of 136–8
Chilon (Spartan ephor) 146, 147
Chimaera Painter 87, 88
Chios, Chians 169, 173, 174, 190, 204, 208, 231
chlamys 95
Christos, Chr. A. 24
Cicero 15
Cimon 175, 178
Cinadon 117, 213
Cithaeron 170, 171
citizenship, Spartan 116–19, 124, 199, 233
Clark, W.G. 22
Claudian 16, 21
Clearidas 197, 198
Cleisthenes 138, 150
Clement of Alexandria 67
Cleombrotus (Spartan king) 223–7
Cleombrotus (brother of Leonidas) 167
Cleomenes (Spartan king) 120, 147–51, 153–8, 160, 180
Cleomenes III (Spartan king) 237
Cleomenes (Spartan regent) 190
Cleon 193, 194, 196–8, 231
Clytemnestra 66
Cnemus 189
Cnidus 204, 218

coinage
  Arcadian 160
  Peloponnesian 106
  Tarantine 104
colonization 32, 102–4, 149, 175, 192
Colophon 73
comasts 88
comb, ivory 95, 96
Conon 207, 208, 215, 218–20
Corcyra, Corcyraeans 162, 182, 183, 188, 191, 225, 226
Corinth, Corinthia, Corinthians 83–5, 88, 90–2, 104, 108, 110, 125, 145, 146, 148, 151–3, 172, 175, 179, 180, 182–7, 192, 194, 199–202, 209, 212, 215, 216, 218–21, 223
Corinth, Gulf of 180, 189
Corinth, Isthmus of 42, 112, 162, 163, 166, 167, 169, 179, 180, 188, 195, 216, 218, 219, 221, 224, 227
Corinthian War 216–21
Coronea, battle of 218, 219
Cos 208
Council of elders, Spartan 120, 121, 124, 125, 127–30, 213, 238
craters 86, 88, 90, 91
cremation 32, 44
Cresphontes 236
Crete, Cretans 28–31, 36, 38, 40, 41, 92, 102, 127, 128, 137, 163, 235
Crius 156
Croesus 110–13, 127, 148, 154
crops 185, 188, 203
cults 32, 36–8, 47–69, 104, 198
cups, gold 35, 36
Curtius, E. 21
Cyclades 89
Cyllene 191
Cyprus 31, 175, 176
Cypselids 145, 146, 152
Cyrene 84–7
Cyrus the Great (Persian king) 112, 147, 153
Cyrus (Persian pretender) 207–9, 213, 214
Cythera 73, 113, 162, 194, 195, 198, 219
Cyzicus 206

daemons 38
dagger-blades 35
Damonon inscription 49
damos 50, 75
Darius 148, 153–8, 161
Darius II 207

247

Dark Age 47, 64, 68, 69
Datis 158
Dawkins, R.M. 23
decarchies 209, 211, 214
Decelea 203–6, 209
Decelean War 203–9
Dedalic 92, 93
Delium 195
Delos 169, 173, 175
Delphi 48, 58, 62, 68, 72, 103, 104, 110, 127, 150, 181, 223
Demaratus (Spartan king) 151, 155–7, 162
democracy, democratic parties 125, 126, 152, 174, 180, 182, 190, 195, 201, 202, 205, 212, 231, 233
Demosthenes 192–4, 202, 203
Dercylidas 214, 215, 218
despots, despotism 145–52, 158, 159, 173, 186, 220, 231, 232, 235
Dickins, G. 23
Diodorus of Sicily 15, 121, 124, 165, 175, 178, 225
Dionysius 221
Dionysus 62, 76
Dioscuri 28, 95
dolphin 103, 104
Dorian, Dorians 41–5, 62, 92, 99, 100, 105, 115, 116, 148, 150, 180, 188
Doric dialects 41, 42, 44
Doric style in architecture 65
Dorieus 149
Doris 42, 180

eagle 86, 87
earthquakes 140, 141, 178, 180, 192
Egesta 201
Egypt 84, 85, 147, 161, 175, 179, 180
Egyptian name 86
Eion 175, 197, 198
Eira 107, 108, 112
eirens 172
elegiac poetry 71
Eleusis 151, 152, 169, 170, 181
Elis, Eleans 42, 105, 106, 111, 123, 191, 199, 200, 212, 217
envoys 124, 125, 181–3, 186–90, 193, 194, 199, 202, 209, 211, 212, 217, 220, 222, 226
Epaminondas 226–8, 236
Ephesus 190, 207, 208, 215, 218, 220
Ephialtes 164
ephors, ephorate 49, 121–8, 132, 145, 148, 151, 154, 158, 169, 177, 178, 199, 200, 205, 209, 211–14, 216, 217, 222, 223, 227, 235, 238, 239
Ephorus 15, 102, 105, 146
Epidaurus, Epidaurians 179, 200, 205
Epirus 146
epitaphs 165
erastai 135
Eretria 154, 158, 205
Eros 76
estates, Spartiate 116–19, 133, 138, 142, 143, 237
Eteonicus 207–9
Etruria 85, 86, 110
Euboea, Euboeans 163, 166, 175, 181, 182, 192, 203–6, 218, 231
Eudimas 222
Euripides 49, 61, 76
Euripus 166, 167
Eurotas 13, 14, 20, 27, 39, 48, 51, 52, 89, 228, 239
Eurybiadas 166, 168
Eurymedon (Athenian general) 202
Eurymedon (river) 175
Eurypontid family 119, 156, 178, 237
Eurysthenes 126
Evans, A.J. 40

frescoes 31
Furtwängler, A. 23, 63, 64

Gell, Sir W. 17, 20
Geometric pottery 49, 52, 65, 82–4
Geraestus 166
gerousia 120
girls, training of 138
Goethe 75
gorgons 90, 94
Gortyn 73
Greeks, definition of 47, 48
Grote, G. 42, 43, 45
guardians 232, 233
Gylippus 202, 203
Gymnopaidiai 60, 73, 113
Gytheum 13, 99, 135, 180, 228

Hagnon 198
Haliartus 217
Halieis 179
harmosts 124, 142, 204, 207, 208, 211, 212, 216, 218, 220, 223–5
Helen 26–8, 32, 56–8, 95
Helicon 219
Helladic 28–30, 39
Hellenica Oxyrhynchia 15, 215

Index

Hellespont 161, 168, 172, 174, 176, 188, 205, 206, 208, 218, 220
Helos 13, 27, 99, 194, 228
helots, helotage 118–20, 133, 139–42, 154, 172, 177–9, 194, 198, 199, 217, 228, 232
Hera 53, 59, 68, 79, 95, 154, 173
Heraclea 192
Heracles 42, 49, 85, 105, 119, 128
Heraclids, Return of the 15, 41–3, 72, 105, 150
Hermes 59, 76
Herodotus 14, 41, 42, 47, 56, 57, 101, 104, 110–13, 119–23, 127, 128, 130, 133, 146–56, 158–62, 164–73, 176, 177, 224, 230
heroes, Homeric 68, 72
hero-reliefs 51, 67, 95
Heroum 51, 89
Hesiod 87
hippeis 119, 164, 168
Hippias (of Athens) 147, 149, 151–3, 158
Hippias (of Elis) 101
Hippocrates 206, 207
'Hollows' 166
Homer 26–8, 56, 68, 109
homoioi 117
homosexuality 135, 136
hoplites 72, 88, 108, 118, 119, 130, 133, 153, 161, 163, 164, 179, 180, 183, 187, 192–8, 201, 206, 215, 218, 223, 227, 232
hoplite-tactics 108, 109, 117, 194
horses, skeletons of 34
hostages 183, 194
houses
  Hellenistic 53
  Mycenaean 30, 31, 34, 39–41
Hunt Painter 88, 89
hunting 89, 135, 239
Hyakinthia 60–2, 68, 69, 169
Hyakinthine Way 65
Hyakinthos 60–5, 67, 69, 104
hydria 88–90
Hyllus 42
hypomeiones 117
Hysiae, battle at 60, 105, 109

Iapygians 103, 104
Iliad 26–8, 56, 68, 72, 109, 124
Illyrians 196
Imbros 220
'immortals' 161

Ionia, Ionians 32, 63, 85, 112, 153, 154, 168, 173, 174, 176, 191, 204, 205, 207, 214, 218
Ionian Revolt 153, 154
Ionic dialects 44
Ionic style in architecture 65
Iphicrates 220, 226
iron 32, 43, 44, 134
Iron Age 41, 82, 99
Isagoras 150, 151
Ischagoras 197
Ismenias 222, 223
Isocrates 15, 57, 122, 235–7
Italy, southern 102–4, 175, 188
Ithome 100, 108, 178, 179, 228
ivory, ivories 30, 94–6, 110, 132

Jason 226, 227
javelins 219, 220, 227
jewellery 35

kantharos 95
Karne(i)a 59, 60, 74, 116, 159, 164, 201
kings, Spartan 42, 68, 71, 72, 115, 116, 119–25, 128–30, 151, 156, 200, 211, 238, 239
klaros 116
Knossos 40
koine eirene 221
komai 115
kosmos 127, 128, 231
krypteia 140, 141

Laas 27
Laconia 13, 14, 16, 32, 40, 48, 51, 54, 61, 82–90, 92, 99, 100, 104, 107, 111, 115, 135, 139, 168, 180, 194, 202, 209, 218, 219, 226, 228, 238
Laconia, Gulf of 13
Laconian alphabet 91
Laconian dialect 21, 54, 74, 172
Lakedaimon 14
Lakonike 14
Lamachus 201, 202
Lampsacus 208
Lapith 96
lead figurines 55, 56, 67, 94, 109
Leake, W.M. 17, 20
Lemnos 220
lentoid 36–8
Leobatas (Spartan king) 127
Leonidas (Spartan king) 42, 160, 164–7, 169, 230
'Leonidas, statue of' 96, 97

249

'Leonidas, tomb of' 22
Leonidas II (Spartan king) 238
Leontiades 223, 224
Leotychidas (Spartan king) 146, 156, 157, 160, 161, 168, 173, 174
Leotychidas (Spartan pretender) 212
Lesbos 73, 175, 190, 191, 204, 207, 208
Leto 54
Leucas 188
Leuctra, battle of 143, 226–8
Levant 31, 84
Libya 149
Libys 212
limestone votaries 94
Limnae, Limnaion 21, 53, 54
Linear B script 31, 32
lions 89, 96
literacy 135
Locris, Locrians 42, 163–5, 188
Louvre 85
Lycophron 66
Lycurgus (legendary Spartan lawgiver) 16, 51, 126–30, 132–8, 141, 142, 177, 213, 217, 230–4, 237–9
Lycurgus (Athenian orator) 235, 237
Lydia 110, 111, 147
Lygdamis 146
Lykaios 86
lyric poetry 73, 74
Lysander 207–9, 211–17

Macedonia, Macedonians 162, 163, 169, 183, 195, 196, 238
Maeandrius 148
Magnesia 63
Malea 13, 113
Malian Gulf 163
Mantinea, Mantineans 112, 160, 199–201, 212, 222, 228
Mantinea, battle of 109, 143, 201, 219
Marathon
  Mycenaean tholos at 34
  battle at 158–61
marble 94, 96, 104
Mardonius 168–72, 176, 230
Mars 60
'masks' 94
Megalopolis 228
Megara, Megarians, Megaris 125, 170, 179–82, 185, 187–90, 193, 195, 199, 227
Megarian decree 187
megaron 31
Megistias 165

Melathria 38, 39
Melos 188, 191, 192, 209, 219
Mende 196, 197
Menelaion 21–4, 31, 32, 39–41, 55–7, 92
Menelaus 26–8, 32, 33, 56, 57
mercenaries 213, 219, 227
Messene (Peloponnesian) 42, 43, 100, 228, 236
Messene (Sicilian) 159
Messenia, Messenians 30, 31, 40, 72, 100–2, 104–12, 115, 139, 141, 159, 178, 192, 194, 228, 236
Messenian War
  First 100–2, 105, 106, 108
  Second 100, 106–9, 111, 112, 115, 159, 160
  Third? 159, 160
messes, communal 116–18, 120, 127, 134, 135, 138, 233–5, 238
Methymna 190, 207, 208
Miletus, Milesians 146, 153, 154, 173, 204, 205, 207
Mindarus 205, 206
Minoans 28–31, 36, 38, 40
mirror 93
Mistra 17, 22
Mnasippus 225
morai 130
Morea 13, 17
Moschus 76
mothax 119
Munich 90
Mure, W. 21–3
Mycale 173
Mycenae 21, 28, 31, 41, 44, 66
Mycenaeans 28–41, 43–5, 47, 102
Myron 106
Mytilene 190, 191, 207

nauarchos 124
Naucratis Painter 85–6, 88
Naupactus 179, 188, 192
Nauplia 105, 154
Naxos 146, 175
neodamodeis 119, 218
Nestor 28
Nicias (Athenian artist) 63
Nicias (Athenian general) 192, 194, 196, 198, 200–3
Nicomedes (Spartan regent) 180
Nisaea 179, 182, 189, 193, 195
Notium 207

obai 115, 116, 129, 130

Index

Odysseus 26, 28
Odyssey 26–8, 32, 68
Oetylus 27
oligarchies, oligarchy 125, 126, 130, 145, 150, 152, 180, 190, 191, 195, 205, 211, 212, 220, 221
Olympia
  bronze miniatures from 92, 93
  priesthood at 101
  sanctuary of 111
  Spartan offering at 159
  Temple of Hera at 53
  Temple of Zeus at 48
Olympic Games 48, 101, 105, 106, 138, 164, 190, 212
Olynthus 222, 223
oracle, Delphic 48, 58, 72, 103, 106, 120, 127, 128, 149, 154, 156, 164, 165
Orchomenus (Arcadian) 112, 200, 221
Orchomenus (Boeotian) 217
Orestes 111
Orientalizing Movement 83, 84
Oropus 205
Orthagorids 145, 147
outland, outlanders 115, 120, 122, 130, 135, 169, 178, 194, 218, 234, 237, 238

Pactolus 215
palaces, Mycenaean 30–2
Palaiopyrgos 33, 34
papyrus-fragments 15, 107, 146, 147
Paris 66
Paris, Judgment of 95, 96
Parnon 13, 27
partheneia 77–80
Partheniai 102, 103
Pasitelidas 197
Pausanias (Spartan king) 208, 209, 212, 213, 217, 223
Pausanias (Spartan regent) 49, 169–73, 176–8, 230
Pausanias (traveller and antiquary) 16, 20, 21, 23, 26, 49, 51, 53, 54, 57, 59, 61–6, 74, 76, 101, 105–7, 118, 119, 155, 159
Peace, King's 221–5, 236
pediments 53, 56
Pegae 182, 193
Peisander 215, 218
Peloponnese, Peloponnesians 13, 41, 42, 106, 112, 139, 145, 149–51, 164, 165, 167, 169, 170, 173, 174, 176, 179–85, 187–92, 194, 199–202, 204–8, 221, 222, 225–8, 238
pentaconters 166
Perati 40
Perdiccas 183, 195–7
Periander 147
Pericles 174, 180–2, 187–9, 193
perioikoi 115
Persephone 104
Persia, Persians 112, 113, 133, 147–9, 153, 155, 156, 158, 161–77, 188, 189, 204, 205, 207, 208, 213–16, 219–21, 223, 236
Persian empire 154, 161, 175, 207, 215, 216, 236
Persian Wars 110, 161–74, 176, 194, 230, 236
Phalanthus 103, 104
phalanx 108, 153, 161, 172, 178, 194, 215, 227
Phalerum 167, 168, 179, 180
Pharnabazus 205–7, 214, 215, 218, 219
Pharsalus 226
Pherae 226
Phidon 105, 106
Philippides 158, 159
Philostratus 239
Phlius 222
Phocis, Phocians 42, 146, 164, 167, 172, 180, 181, 188, 201, 216–18, 226
Phoebidas 222, 223
Phoenicia, Phoenicians 167, 168, 205, 214
phratriai 116
Phrygia 215
phylai 115, 116, 129, 130
Phylarchus 237, 238
Pieria 163
Pindar 75, 76, 90
Piraeus 155, 167, 176, 179, 180, 189, 190, 202, 206, 209, 212, 220, 224
Pisatans 106, 111
Pisistratids 145–7, 149, 150, 152, 158
Pitanate 171
plague 189, 193
plaques, ivory 95, 96
Plataea 151, 170, 171, 188, 191, 192, 224, 226
Plataea, battle of 143, 153, 171, 172
Plato 15, 159, 160, 231–6
Pleistarchus (Spartan king) 169
Pleistoanax (Spartan king) 180, 181, 198, 199, 201
Plutarch 15, 16, 49, 50, 73, 111,

251

128–30, 133–8, 140, 141, 146, 150, 155, 181, 230, 237–40
Poliouchos 49
Polybius 15, 49, 50, 56, 62, 63, 239
Polycrates (historian) 61
Polycrates (Samian despot) 147–9
Polydamas 226
Polydorus (Spartan king) 129
population of Spartan state 133, 143, 213, 227
Poseidon 49, 68
Potidaea 183–7, 197, 222
pottery
  Corinthian 84
  Geometric 49, 52, 65, 82–4
  Laconian 51, 84–9
  Minoan 29
  Mycenaean 29–31, 33, 34, 38, 39, 82
  Panathenaic 50
  Protogeometric 49, 64, 82 ·
probouleutic 122
Procles 126
Prometheus 87
Propontis 174, 206
Psyttaleia 167, 168
Pylos
  classical 140, 192–4, 198, 199
  Mycenaean 28, 31, 40, 41
pyxides 83

Randolph, B. 17
repoussé 36
Rhegium 102, 104, 159
Rhetra, Great 128–30
Rhianus 106–8
Rhium 42
Rhodes, Rhodians 31, 41, 57, 85, 88, 92, 110, 204, 207, 208, 216, 220
Rider Painter 88
rings, gold 30, 35–8
Ross, L. 21

Sacred War 181
sacrifices 34
Salaethus 190
Salamis 167–9, 190, 209
Samos, Samians 85, 110, 145–8, 168, 173, 174, 191, 206–9, 211
Sappho 75, 76, 79
Sardis 74, 112, 154, 158, 162, 163, 173, 207, 215, 220
Saronic Gulf 167
satrapies, satraps 154, 177, 204, 215, 220

Schliemann, H. 22, 23
Scione 196, 197
Scoglio del Tonno 83, 102
Scryos 175, 220
seal-stones 35–8
Selinuntians 201
Sestus 174, 176, 205, 206, 208, 218
Shaft Graves 29, 30
shields 30, 108, 109, 171, 173
ships
  allied 166–9, 173, 176
  Athenian 154, 161–3, 174, 179, 180, 183, 186, 187, 189–94, 197, 198, 201–9, 220, 221, 225, 226
  Corcyraean 182, 183, 191
  Corinthian 182, 183
  Peloponnesian 189–91, 204–9, 225
  Persian 166–8, 218, 220, 221
  Spartan 166, 193, 194, 218, 220, 221
  Syracusan 221
  Thessalian 226
Sicily, Sicilians 102, 149, 159, 188, 192, 201–3, 206, 224, 232
sickles, iron 55
Sicyon, Sicyonians 145–7, 180, 181, 219
sieges 190–2
silphium 87
Skias, A.N. 24
Skoura 38
Smyrna 85
Socrates 232–4
Solon 116, 128, 138, 147
Sparte, modern 13, 17, 22
Spartiates 14, 89, 115–20, 122, 124, 126, 127, 130, 133–43, 149, 156, 164–6, 169, 171, 172, 177, 178, 185, 193, 197, 200, 202, 205, 213–15, 218, 227, 230, 232, 233, 237
spears 35, 64, 108, 109
Sphacteria 193–5, 199
sphinx 85
Sphodrias 224
squatters 40
Stagirus 195
staphylodromoi 59
statuettes, bronze 91–4
Stenyclerus 197
Stesichorus 58
Sthenelaidas (Spartan ephor) 125, 185
Strabo 15, 100, 102, 103, 105, 126, 159, 217
Struthas 220
Strymon 197
sub-Mycenaean 41

Index

Sunium 167, 203, 220
Susa 153, 220
swords 30, 35
Symmachus 146
symposium 86
Syracuse, Syracusans 163, 201–3, 220
Syria 38

Taenarum 13, 27
tagos 226
Tanagra 170, 180
Taranto 83–5, 102
Taranto, Gulf of 102–4
Taras 50, 85, 102–4
taxation 117, 118, 143
Taygetus 13, 14, 20, 27, 93, 239
Tegea, Tegeans 38, 105, 111, 112, 160, 169, 171, 199–201, 217, 223
Telemachus 27
Telesilla 155
Teleutias 220, 221, 223
Tempe 163, 165
temples
  at Olympia 48, 53
  at Taras 103
  in Orthia sanctuary 52, 53
  on Spartan acropolis 48–50
Terpander 25, 73, 74, 133
terracottas
  Laconian 92, 93
  Mycenaean 30, 33, 39, 56, 67
Thales 147
Thasos, Thasians 146, 175, 178
theatre
  Hellenistic, at Spartan acropolis 20, 48, 89
  Roman, in Orthia sanctuary 53, 239
Thebes, Thebans 151, 164–6, 170, 172, 188, 192, 209, 212, 215–20, 222–8, 236
Themistocles 163, 166, 168, 176, 177
Theocritus 58, 59
Theopompus (historian) 105
Theopompus (Spartan king) 100, 129, 130
Thera 41, 188
Therapne 21, 56, 57
Thermopylae 42, 163–7, 230
Theseus 111
Thespiae, Thespians 164, 165, 224–6
Thessaly, Thessalians 31, 51, 112, 146, 160, 162, 163, 168, 175, 180, 195, 197, 226, 227
Thibron 214, 220

tholoi 30, 31, 34–8, 40
Thrace, Thracians 153, 162, 163, 174, 175, 183, 188, 192, 195–8, 208
Thrasybulus 220
Thucydides 14, 16, 25, 41, 42, 45, 49, 122–5, 127, 128, 140, 143, 146, 177–9, 182, 185–7, 191, 194, 197, 198, 204–6, 224, 231, 232, 236
Thurii 175
Thyreatis 105, 113, 195
Timocrates 216
Timotheus 225
Tiribazus 220
Tiryns 31, 41, 105
Tisamenus 111
Tissaphernes 205, 214, 215
Titans 87
Tithraustes 215, 216
Tlepolemus 57
Tocra 85
tombs 29–31, 34–40, 50, 51, 57
Torone 196, 197
Trachis 192
trade 116, 134, 135, 138, 182, 185
treaties 111, 152, 174, 175, 181–3, 185, 186, 188, 193, 198, 199, 201, 202, 205, 209, 220, 221
Trebenischte 90
tribute 153, 175, 180, 183, 185, 191, 204, 211, 215, 225
triremes 166, 189, 190, 203, 214
Troezen 167, 182, 193
Trojan War 25, 41, 45, 57
Troy 26–8, 58, 214
truces 193, 194, 200, 214, 215, 225, 227
'trumpeter' 93, 94
Tsountas, Chr. 21, 23, 34, 35, 63
tyrannoi 145
Tyrtaeus 71–5, 100, 101, 106–9, 115, 129, 130

ultimatum 183, 187
union, political, of Argos and Corinth 219–21

Vaphio 21–3, 34–9
victor-lists, Olympic 101
Vix 90, 91
Vulci 85

Wace, A.J.B. 23
walls
  at Argos 201

253

at Athens 176, 179, 180, 188, 189, 209, 219
at Isthmus of Corinth 167, 169, 179, 218, 219
at Mantinea 222, 228
at Megara 195
at Potidaea 183
at Sparta 48
at Syracuse 202
at Taras 103
in Mycenaean Greece 31, 33, 34, 38, 43
Warden of the Boys 137
warship on ivory plaque 96
weights and measures 106

Whip-bearers 137
women, place of, in Spartan system 117, 136, 142

Xanthippus 174
Xenophon 14, 15, 117, 118, 122–24, 133–8, 141, 142, 153, 213–17, 224, 226, 230, 239
Xerxes 157, 161–4, 167–9, 173, 176, 177, 216, 224

Zacynthus, Zacynthians 188, 189, 225
Zancle 159
Zeus 27, 32, 42, 48, 66–8, 72, 86, 93, 129, 159